AUSTRALIAN

Signpost

MATHS

NSW

STAGE 2

3

Alan McSeveny Rachel McSeveny Diane McSeveny-Foster

Pearson Australia
(a division of Pearson Australia Group Pty Ltd)
459–471 Church St, Level 1, Building B, Richmond, Victoria, 3121
PO Box 23360, Melbourne, Victoria 8012
www.pearson.com.au

First published 2024 by Pearson Australia
2028 2027 2026 2025
10 9 8 7 6 5 4 3 2 1

Publishers: Sophie Matta and Kerry Nagle
Project Manager: Michelle Thomas
Production Editor: Laura Rentsch
Development Editor: Rachel Elliott
Designer: Anne Donald
Proofreader: Laura Rentsch
Rights & Permissions Editor: Alice McBroom
Cover Design: Jennifer Johnston
Cover Art: Michael Barter
Illustrator: Michael Barter
Publishing Services: Jit-Pin Chong
Printed in Malaysia (CTP-VVP)

ISBN 978 0 6557 0904 6
Pearson Australia Group Pty Ltd ABN 40 004 245 943

Attributions
We would like to thank the following for permission to reproduce copyright material.

123rf.com: Michal Adamczyk, pp. 116, 139 (boomerang); Amorozov, p. 139 (didgeridoo); Hafiezrazali, p. 142 (Rubik's cube); Homy Design, p. 153 (marbles); Ilterriorm, p. 118 (SUV); Ivanspasic, p. 86 (measuring cup); Kung37, pp. 86, 104 (watering can); Learchitecto, p. 137 (ball); Mastak80, p. 145 (brick wall); Mychadre77, p. 118 (sea star); Realiia, pp. 86, 104 (container); Serezniy, p. 112 (lunchbox); Tap10, pp. 86, 104 (esky); Arina Zaiachin, p. 106 (doormat).

Alamy: Rashmi Singh pp. 116, 139 (shield).

Shutterstock: LaMony Betty, p. 86, 112 (bottle); Chachamp, p. 112 (mug); Coprid, p. 103 (jug and bucket); Ddisq, p.149 (traffic); Fotoksa, p. 142 (hats); Horiyan, p. 103 (glass); Dany Kurniawan, p. 112 (aquarium); Luisa Leal Photography, p. 120 (tent); Leon Rafael, p. 142 (dice); Sevenke, p. 103 (pot); Stickybeak TV, p. 89 (Uluru); TitoOnz, p. 137 (globe); TrotzOlga, p. 112 (baking dish); Peter Vanco, pp. 86, 104 (bin).

Unsplash: Eugene Tkachenko, p. 128 (pyramid).

Acknowledgement of Country
Pearson respects and honours Aboriginal and Torres Strait Islander Elders past, present and future. We acknowledge the stories, traditions and living cultures of the Traditional Custodians of the lands on which our company is located and where we conduct our business. Pearson is committed to honouring Australian Aboriginal and Torres Strait Islander peoples' unique cultural and spiritual relationships to the land, waters and seas and their rich contribution to society.

Aboriginal and Torres Strait Islander peoples are advised that this text may contain images, voices and names of deceased persons.

What is Australian Signpost Maths?

Australian Signpost Maths NSW is a mathematics program providing direction and support for teaching and learning. The series covers the content and skills presented in the NSW Mathematics Syllabus K–6, 2024.

A Student Book and an online Teacher Resource are provided for Kindergarten (Early Stage 1).

For Years 1 to 6, a Student Book, an online Teacher Resource and a Mentals Book are provided for each year level. The online Teacher Resources provide a wealth of support for teachers.

The content has been carefully sequenced within each year level and across the K–6 series to take into account students' expected mathematical development. However, from the rich and varied material provided, teachers can develop individual learning programs to meet the needs of each student.

The Student Books are designed to support explicit teaching methods. Many group activities are provided in Activity, Investigation and Fun spots within the Student Books and the online Teacher Resource.

To maximise the benefits of the program, the Student Book, the online Teacher Resource and the Mentals Book should be used together.

Student Books

Mentals Books

Teacher Resource

Structure of Australian Signpost Maths NSW

In the Year 3 to 6 books, the worksheet pages cover all three elements: Number and algebra, Measurement and space, and Statistics and probability.

These are presented in five chapters:

- Number and algebra
- Operations and algebra
- Measurement
- Space
- Statistics and probability.

This gives teachers flexibility in programming that is more appropriate to Years 3 to 6.

The contents cross-reference allows teachers to quickly find the pages where each concept has been covered.

Within the program, explicit teaching, critical and creative thinking, language development and identification and treatment of weaknesses are given high priority.

Identifying and addressing areas of need

Five progress tests are designed to identify each student's areas of need, and the follow-up program after each of the tests is designed to address these needs. A reference to the relevant worksheet page is given for each test question. A remediation record page is used to track the student's progress.

Parallel progress retests are provided for further testing after remediation has taken place.

These testing resources can be found in the online Teacher Resource.

Special features of Australian Signpost Maths NSW

- **The traffic light icons**
  These are found on the top right of each worksheet page in the Student Books. They allow students to assess their own progress and give feedback to the teacher.
  - **Green:** I found this work easy.
  - **Orange:** I found some work on the page difficult.
  - **Red:** I don't understand the work on this page.

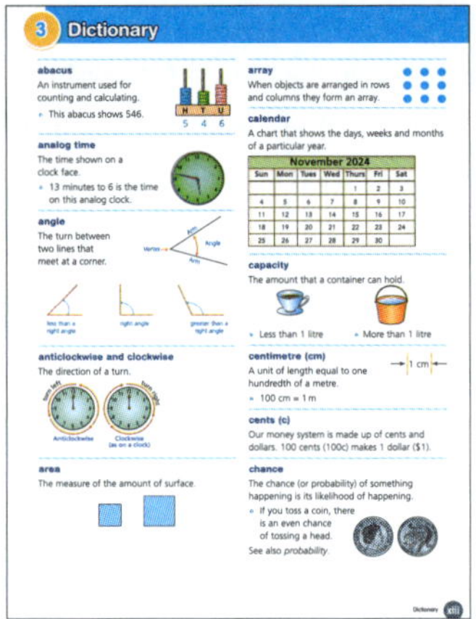

- **Dictionary**
  Terms used in the Student Book and terms that should be understood at this level are recorded here to provide a reference for students and teachers. This is found on pages xiv–xxii of this book.

- **ID cards (Years 1 to 6)**
  These cards review the language of Mathematics by asking students to identify common terms, shapes and symbols. They are designed to be reused and are found in the online Teacher Resource and in the front of the Mentals Books.

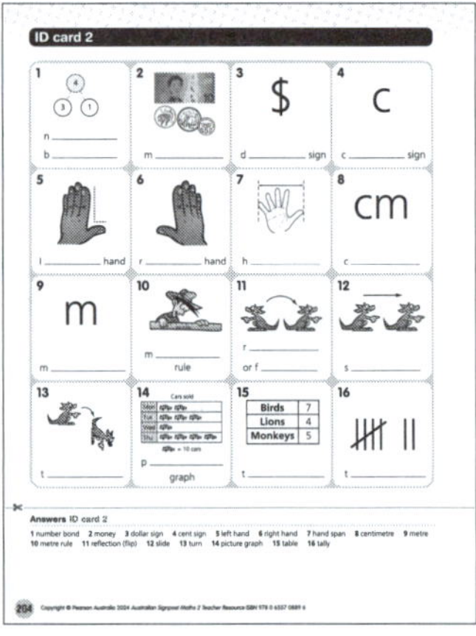

- **Progress tests**
  These allow the teacher to identify each student's strengths and weaknesses. Cross-references for each question direct teachers and students to the pages where that work is introduced. Tables are provided to record the follow-up that takes place and parallel tests are provided for retesting. These tests can be found in the online Teacher Resource.

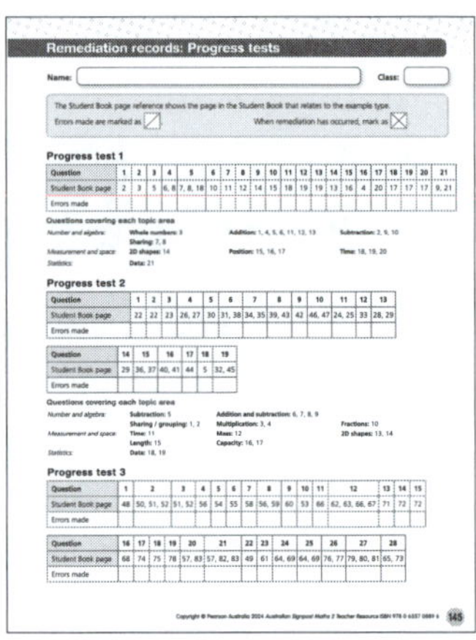

- **Year 3 Consolidation booklet**
  This booklet is found in the online Teacher Resource. It is designed to reinforce work completed in class and provides practice of important skills and addition and subtraction facts. The booklet can be used when there is limited supervision or when a student finishes classwork early.

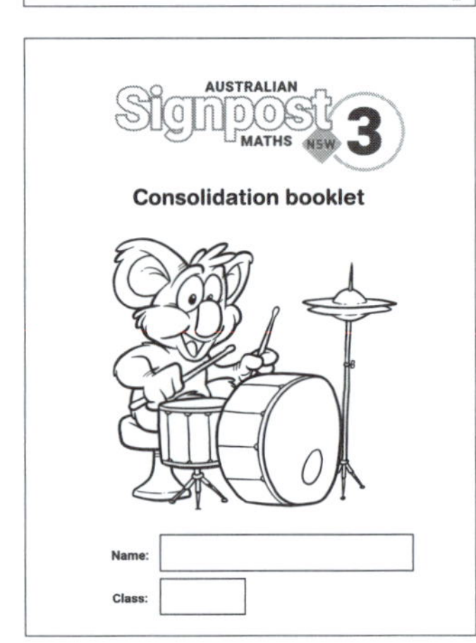

- **Answers**
  These are supplied in the Student Book and the online Teacher Resource.

- **Blackline masters (BLM)**
  References are made to the blackline masters in the online Teacher Resource suggestions provided for each student work page.

- **Differentiation**
  Each Student Book work page has a Teacher Resource page to support it. Cross-references direct the teacher to pages where the concept is introduced and developed. These references may be from the Student Book for the previous year, the current year or the next year.

  The Teacher Resource support pages provide additional learning activities for students who need remediation or extension activities. The blackline masters provide activities to support students of various learning abilities.

- **Cartoons**
  Cartoons are used to motivate and instruct.

- **Extra support pages**
  Addition and subtraction facts are reinforced in Extra Support 1–4.
  The algorithm strategy pages extend the fast worker.
  These are cross-referenced to the Student Book pages.

Australian Signpost Maths NSW icons

Signpost icons are used throughout the book as cues to the essential nature of exercises and activities, and as a guide to ways of engaging with them. These icons often indicate alternative or more concrete approaches to dealing with concepts.

This icon highlights **important rules and concepts** occurring throughout the book. It often appears with worked examples.

Activities provide **applications and enrichment**. These activities usually involve the use of concrete materials and partner or group work.

These enjoyable activities are used to **motivate and involve** students in mathematical pursuits. They usually involve games and puzzles.

Investigations allow students to **explore and discover** maths concepts.

These activities involve the use of computers or other technology.

Structure of the New South Wales Mathematics Syllabus K-6

The NSW Mathematics Syllabus content is presented in three strands:

1 Number and algebra **2** Measurement and space **3** Statistics and probability
Working mathematically pervades each of these strands.

Textbook structure
Within the Year 3 **Contents** (pages vi to xi), we show related pages using these categories:

Chapter 1: Number and algebra
• Counting, number • Place value • Rounding • Fractions • Patterns, algebra

Chapter 2: Operations and algebra
• Addition • Subtraction • Multiplication • Division • Mental strategies • Number patterns
• Money • Problem solving

Chapter 3: Measurement
• Length • Area • Volume • Capacity • Mass • Telling the time • Duration • Problem solving

Chapter 4: Space
• 2D space • Angles, lines • Symmetry, turning • 3D objects • Position, directions

Chapter 5: Statistics and probability
• Collecting data • Surveys • Creating data displays • Analysing data displays
• Chance language • Chance experiments

The **Cross-reference** (pages xii and xiii) give a clear indication of where syllabus content is addressed.
The **Suggested program** is provided in the Contents pages and aligns with the Mentals Book and Progress tests and Retests.
Each Mentals unit reviews the previous 2 weeks' content from the Student Book suggested program.

3 Contents and syllabus overview

Contents cross-reference xii
Dictionary xiv
Chapter 1 Number and algebra 1
Chapter 2 Operations and algebra 30
Chapter 3 Measurement 79
Chapter 4 Space 116
Chapter 5 Statistics and probability 146
Extra support 164
Answers 181

Suggested program: This weekly program aligns with the Mentals Book, e.g. Mentals Book, Unit 9 covers work taught in Weeks 7 and 8 of this book.

Number and algebra			Content						Suggested program	
Page	Unit	Title		Counting, number	Place value	Rounding	Fractions	Patterns, algebra		
1	1:01	Counting		●				●	Week 3	Term 1
2	1:02	Counting		●				●		
3	1:03	Numbers to 1000		●	●					
4	1:04	Numbers to 1000		●	●				Week 4	
5	1:05	Numbers to 1000			●					
6	1:06	Rounding to the nearest 10			●					
7	1:07	Rounding to the nearest 100			●				Week 10	
8	1:08	Numbers to 1000		●	●	●				
9	1:09	Numbers to 1000		●	●			●	Week 11	Term 2
10	1:10	Fractions of a group					●			
11	1:11	Fractions of a whole					●		Week 14	
12	1:12	Numbers to 10 000		●	●					
13	1:13	Numbers to 10 000		●	●				Week 15	
14	1:14	Fractions					●			
15	1:15	Fractions					●			
16	1:16	What's the rule?		●				●	Week 18	
17	1:17	Number patterns		●	●			●		
18	1:18	Numbers to 10 000		●	●				Week 21	Term 3
19	1:19	Place value to 10 000		●	●	●				
20	1:20	Fractions with circles					●		Week 22	
21	1:21	Using fractions					●			
22	1:22	Numbers to 10 000		●	●					
23	1:23	Numbers to 10 000			●				Week 26	
24	1:24	Expanded notation		●	●					
25	1:25	Fractions of a group					●		Week 32	
26	1:26	Fractions of a whole					●			
27	1:27	Numbers to 10 000			●			●		
28	1:28	Numbers over 10 000		●	●				Week 34	
29	1:29	Numbers over 10 000		●	●					

* The teacher will decide when testing occurs. The Progress tests are found in the online Teacher Resource.

* The first two units of the Mentals Book review the previous year and could be completed in Weeks 1 and 2.

Operations and algebra

Page	Unit	Title	Content	Addition	Subtraction	Multiplication	Division	Mental strategies	Number patterns	Money	Problem solving	Suggested program: This weekly program aligns with the Mentals Book, e.g. Mentals Book, Unit 9 covers work taught in Weeks 7 and 8 of this book.	
30	2:01	Arrays				●							Term 1
31	2:02	Square numbers				●						Week 5	
32	2:03	Addition and subtraction		●	●			●					
33	2:04	Number facts, x 2				●							
34	2:05	Number facts, x 5, x 10				●						Week 6	
35	2:06	Multiplication facts				●							
36	2:07	2, 5 and 10 times tables				●			●			Week 7	
37	2:08	Patterns in + and –		●	●			●	●		●		
38	2:09	Relating addition and subtraction		●	●							Week 8	
39	2:10	Money		●						●			
40	2:11	Shopping		●						●		Week 9	
41	2:12	Money		●						●			
42	2:13	Addition to 99		●				●					Term 2
43	2:14	Jump strategy		●	●			●				Week 12	
44	2:15	Jump strategy		●	●			●					
45	2:16	Equalities			●			●				Week 13	
46	2:17	Mental strategies		●				●					
47	2:18	Number facts, × 3 extension				●			●				
48	2:19	× 3 extension				●			●			Week 16	
49	2:20	Multiplication facts				●							
50	2:21	Number facts, × 4				●			●			Week 17	
51	2:22	Times tables				●							
52	2:23	Number facts, multiplication				●			●			Week 19	
53	2:24	Problem solving		●	●	●					●		
54	2:25	Inverse operations, × and ÷				●	●						Term 3
55	2:26	Relating × and ÷				●	●					Week 23	
56	2:27	× and ÷ fact families				●	●						
57	2:28	Relating × and ÷				●	●					Week 24	
58	2:29	Linking × and ÷				●	●						
59	2:30	÷ facts from × facts				●	●						
60	2:31	× and ÷ tables				●	●					Week 25	
61	2:32	Problem solving		●	●	●	●				●		
62	2:33	Addition strategies		●							●	Week 26	
63	2:34	Subtraction strategies			●								
64	2:35	Levelling and constant difference		●							●		
65	2:36	Change from $2		●						●	●	Week 27	
66	2:37	Problem solving		●									
67	2:38	Addition to 99, no trading		●									
68	2:39	Subtraction, no trading		●						●		Week 28	
69	2:40	Addition to 99 with trading		●							●		
70	2:41	Addition with trading			●								
71	2:42	Addition with 2-digit numbers			●							Week 29	
72	2:43	Addition, trading for 100			●								
73	2:44	Addition to 999 with one trade		●	●							Week 30	
74	2:45	Addition, two trades		●				●			●		

Operations and algebra													
Page	Unit	Title	Content	Addition	Subtraction	Multiplication	Division	Mental strategies	Number patterns	Money	Problem solving	Suggested program This weekly program aligns with the Mentals Book, e.g. Mentals Book, Unit 9 covers work taught in Weeks 7 and 8 of this book.	
75	2:46	Subtraction with trading to 99			●			●		●		Week 31	Term 4
76	2:47	Subtraction with trading			●			●			●		
77	2:48	Subtraction with trading		●								Week 32	
78	2:49	Checking subtraction by addition		●	●						●		

* The teacher will decide when testing occurs. The Progress Tests and Retests are found in the online Teacher Resource.

Measurement

Page	Unit	Title	Content	Length	Area	Volume	Capacity	Mass	Telling the time	Duration	Problem solving	Suggested program: This weekly program aligns with the Mentals Book, e.g. Mentals Book, Unit 9 covers work taught in Weeks 7 and 8 of this book.	
79	3:01	Revision of length		●								Week 7	Term 1
80	3:02	Length and width		●									
81	3:03	Measuring with centimetres		●									
82	3:04	Clocks							●	●		Week 8	
83	3:05	Analog time							●				
84	3:06	Analog time							●				
85	3:07	Capacity review				●	●					Week 9	
86	3:08	Estimating the litre					●						
87	3:09	The litre				●	●						
88	3:10	Metres and centimetres		●								Week 11	Term 2
89	3:11	Recording length		●									
90	3:12	Measuring distance		●								Week 12	
91	3:13	Measuring length		●									
92	3:14	Time, minutes past							●			Week 15	
93	3:15	Time, minutes to							●	●			
94	3:16	Time, minutes past and to							●	●			
95	3:17	The kilogram						●				Week 16	
96	3:18	Comparing mass						●					
97	3:19	Using the kilogram						●				Week 21	Term 3
98	3:20	Mass problem solving						●			●		
99	3:21	Area			●							Week 22	
100	3:22	Area using square centimetres			●								
101	3:23	Square centimetres			●							Week 24	
102	3:24	Area			●								
103	3:25	Using litres						●				Week 25	
104	3:26	Capacity problem solving						●			●		
105	3:27	The square metre			●							Week 28	
106	3:28	The square metre			●								
107	3:29	The millimetre		●								Week 31	Term 4
108	3:30	Using the ruler		●									
109	3:31	Length problem solving		●							●		
110	3:32	The cubic centimetre				●					●	Week 33	
111	3:33	The cubic centimetre				●							
112	3:34	Standard metric units		●			●	●				Week 35	
113	3:35	Personal benchmarks		●	●	●	●	●					
114	3:36	The calendar								●		Week 36	
115	3:37	The calendar								●			

* 'Money' can be found in Chapter 2.

* 'Angles' can be found in Chapter 4.

* The teacher will decide when testing occurs. The Progress Tests and Retests are found in the online Teacher Resource.

Space			Content	2D space	Angles, lines	Symmetry, turning	3D objects	Position, directions	Suggested program This weekly program aligns with the Mentals Book, e.g. Mentals Book, Unit 9 covers work taught in Weeks 7 and 8 of this book.	
Page	Unit	Title								
116	4:01	Symmetry				●			Week 3	Term 1
117	4:02	Properties of 2D objects		●					Week 4	
118	4:03	Symmetry around us				●				
119	4:04	Properties of 3D objects					●		Week 5	
120	4:05	Properties of 3D objects					●			
121	4:06	Position and giving directions						●	Week 13	Term 2
122	4:07	Giving directions						●		
123	4:08	Regular and irregular shapes		●					Week 17	
124	4:09	Parallel and perpendicular lines		●						
125	4:10	The rhombus and the kite		●					Week 18	
126	4:11	Shapes revision		●						
127	4:12	Prisms and cylinders					●		Week 19	
128	4:13	Pyramids					●			
129	4:14	Investigating angles			●				Week 20	
130	4:15	Angles			●					
131	4:16	Right angles			●				Week 21	Term 3
132	4:17	Angle turns			●				Week 22	
133	4:18	Describing position						●	Week 23	
134	4:19	Pathway between places						●		
135	4:20	Trapeziums and parallelograms		●					Week 27	
136	4:21	Features of 2D shapes		●						
137	4:22	Spheres					●		Week 34	Term 4
138	4:23	3D objects					●			
139	4:24	Using coordinates						●	Week 35	
140	4:25	Creating maps						●		
141	4:26	3D models					●		Week 36	
142	4:27	The net of a cube					●			
143	4:28	Flip, slide, turn		●					Week 37	
144	4:29	Using flip, slide and turn		●						
145	4:30	Tessellations		●						

* The teacher will decide when testing occurs. The Progress tests are found in the online Teacher Resource.

Statistics and probability			Content	Collecting data	Surveys	Creating data displays	Analysing data displays	Chacnce language	Chance experiments	Suggested program This weekly program aligns with the Mentals Book, e.g. Mentals Book, Unit 9 covers work taught in Weeks 7 and 8 of this book.	
Page	**Unit**	**Title**									
146	5:01	Dot plots				●	●			Week 3	Term 1
147	5:02	Tables		●	●		●				
148	5:03	Tables and graphs		●		●	●			Week 13	
149	5:04	Picture graphs		●		●	●				
150	5:05	Chance						●	●	Week 14	Term 2
151	5:06	Chance outcomes						●	●		
152	5:07	Chance outcomes						●	●		
153	5:08	Making graphs		●	●	●				Week 17	
154	5:09	Reading graphs and tables					●			Week 18	
155	5:10	Dicey graphs		●		●			●	Week 19	
156	5:11	Class investigation		●		●	●			Week 24	Term 3
157	5:12	Predicting outcomes		●		●	●	●	●	Week 29	
158	5:13	Ordering events							●		
159	5:14	Drawing graphs				●	●			Week 33	Term 4
160	5:15	Surveys		●	●		●				
161	5:16	Carry out your own survey		●	●	●	●				
162	5:17	Researching data					●			Week 35	
163	5:18	Repeating an experiment						●	●	Week 36	

* The teacher will decide when testing occurs. The Progress tests are found in the online Teacher Resource.

Extra support pages						
164	1	Addition and subtraction facts	2	Addition facts to 20	3	Subtraction facts to 20
167	4	Know your addition facts	5	Addition problems to 99	6	Addition to 999
170	7	Writing the addition algorithm	8	Addition of money		

Suggested program	Term 1	Term 2	Term 3	Term 4
Number and algebra	1:01 - 1:08	1:09 - 1:17	1:18 - 1:29	-
Operations and algebra	2:01 - 2:12	2:13 - 2:24	2:25 - 2:45	2:46 - 2:49
Measurement	3:01 - 3:09	3:10 - 3:18	3:19 - 3:28	3:29 - 3:37
Space	4:01 - 4:05	4:06 - 4:15	4:16 - 4:21	4:22 - 4:30
Statistics and probability	5:01 - 5:04	5:05 - 5:10	5:11 - 5:13	5:14 - 5:18
Total number of pages:	38	46	47	32

* See the Teacher Resource for a more detailed suggested program.

* The suggested program aligns with the Mentals Book, Progress tests and Retests.

Contents cross-reference

Number and algebra

1	Representing numbers using place value	Pages
	• Reads, represents and orders numbers	1, 2, 3, 4, 5, 12, 13, 19, 22, 24, 27, 29
	- Patterns of numbers	1, 2, 9, 16, 17, 18, 27
	• Applies place value to partition, and regroup	3, 4, 5, 8, 9, 12, 13, 18, 19, 22, 23, 24, 27, 28, 29
	- Use of number lines	1, 2, 6, 7, 9
	- Rounding numbers	6, 7, 8, 19
2	**Additive relations**	**Pages**
	• The principle of equality	6, 32, 37, 38, 40, 41, 42, 43, 44, 45, 46
	- Addition	32, 38, 42, 43, 44, 46, 62, 64, 67, 69, 70, 71, 72, 73, 74, 78, 164, 165, 167, 168, 169, 170, 171, 172, 173
	- Subtraction	32, 38, 43, 44, 63, 64, 68, 75, 76, 77, 78, 164, 166, 174–180
	• The connection between addition and subtraction	32, 37, 38, 54, 78, 166
	• Strategies for addition and subtraction	37, 40, 42, 43, 44, 45, 46, 62, 63, 64, 65, 179
	- Jump strategy	43, 44, 46
	- Problem solving (+ and –)	37, 53, 61, 66, 67, 68, 69, 70, 74, 78, 168, 170, 173, 178
	- Algorithm strategy	42, 67, 68, 69, 70, 71, 72, 73, 74, 75, 76, 77, 78, 168, 169, 170, 171–180
	• Represent money values	39, 40, 41, 65, 67, 68, 69, 70, 73, 75, 171, 172, 173, 180
3	**Multiplicative relations**	**Pages**
	• Patterns: Patterns of multiples	33, 34, 36, 47, 48, 52
	- Even and odd numbers	33, 36, 50
	• Establish multiplication facts using arrays	30, 31, 33, 34, 47, 52, 55, 57
	• Recalls multiplication facts and related division	33, 55, 56, 57, 58, 59, 60
	- × and ÷ fact families	55, 56, 57, 58, 59, 60
	- The commutative property for multiplication	30, 33, 34, 47, 55
	- Multiplication facts	31, 33, 34, 35, 36, 39, 47, 48, 49, 50, 51, 52, 59, 60
	- Division (sharing and grouping)	54, 55, 56, 57, 58, 59, 60
	• Problem solving	53, 61, 66, 115
4	**Partitioned fractions**	**Pages**
	• Create fraction parts of a length	10, 11, 14, 15, 26
	• Model and represent fractions	10, 14, 25, 26
	- Fraction strips and the number line	11, 14, 15, 26
	- Fractions	10, 11, 14, 15, 20, 21, 25, 26

Measurement and space

1	Geometric measure	Pages
	• Position: Interpret movement on a map	121, 122, 133, 134
	• Position: Locate positions on a grid	133, 134, 139, 140
	• Length: Use metres, centimetres and millimetres	79, 80, 81, 88, 89, 90, 91, 107, 108, 109, 112, 113
	- Problem solving with measurement	85, 98, 109
	• Angles: Identify as measures of turn	123, 124, 129, 130, 131, 132
2	**2D Spacial structure**	**Pages**
	• 2D shapes: Features of 2D shapes	116, 117, 118, 123, 124, 125, 126, 135, 136
	• 2D shapes: Reflection, translation, rotation, symmetry, tessellations	116, 118, 143, 144, 145
	• Area: Using square centimetres and square metres	99, 100, 101, 102, 105, 106, 112
3	**3D Spacial structure**	**Pages**
	• 3D objects: Make models	119, 120, 127, 128, 137, 138, 141, 142
	• Volume: Use litres to measure and order containers	85, 86, 87, 103, 104, 110, 111, 112, 113
	• Volume: Using cubic-centimetre blocks	110, 111
4	**Non-spacial structure**	**Pages**
	• Mass: Using the kilogram	95, 96, 97, 98, 112, 113
	• Time: Represent and read analog time	82, 83, 84, 92, 93, 94
	- Using clocks	82, 83, 84, 92, 93, 94
	- Duration and calendars	93, 94, 114, 115

Statistics and probability

1	Data	Pages
	• Collect discrete data	146, 147, 148, 149, 153, 156, 160, 161, 163
	• Organise and display data	146, 149, 153, 156, 159, 161, 163
	• Interpret and compare data	146, 147, 148, 149, 153, 154, 156, 159, 160, 161, 162, 163
2	**Chance**	**Pages**
	• Chance experiments	150, 151, 152, 155
	- Possible outcomes	150, 151, 152, 155, 156, 157
	- The language of chance	150, 151, 152, 155, 157, 158

3 Dictionary

abacus

An instrument used for counting and calculating.

- This abacus shows 546.

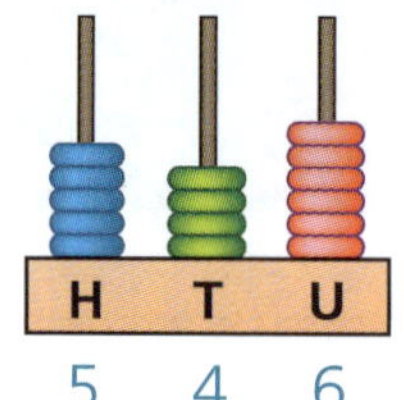

analog time

The time shown on a clock face.

- 13 minutes to 6 is the time on this analog clock.

angle

The turn between two lines that meet at a corner.

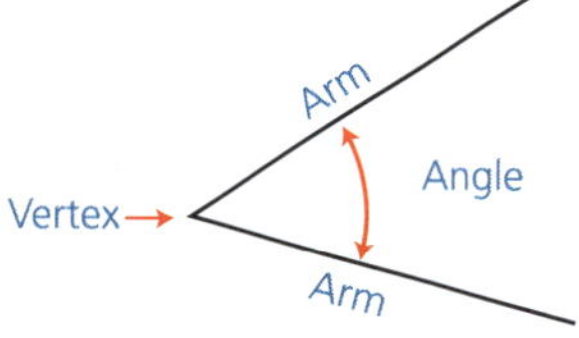

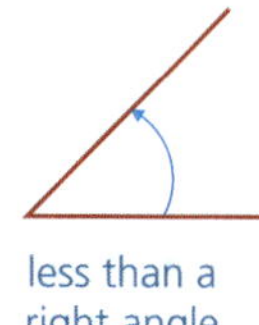
less than a right angle

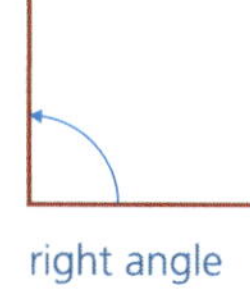
right angle

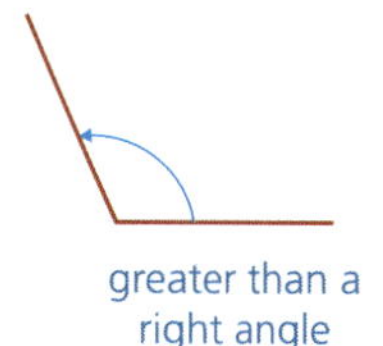
greater than a right angle

anticlockwise and clockwise

The direction of a turn.

Anticlockwise

Clockwise (as on a clock)

area

The measure of the amount of surface.

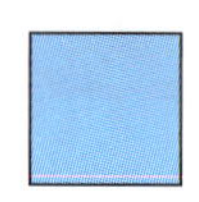

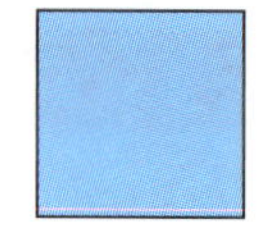

array

When objects are arranged in rows and columns they form an array.

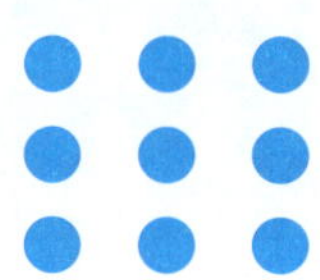

calendar

A chart that shows the days, weeks and months of a particular year.

November 2024						
Sun	**Mon**	**Tues**	**Wed**	**Thurs**	**Fri**	**Sat**
				1	2	3
4	5	6	7	8	9	10
11	12	13	14	15	16	17
18	19	20	21	22	23	24
25	26	27	28	29	30	

capacity

The amount that a container can hold.

- Less than 1 litre
- More than 1 litre

centimetre (cm)

A unit of length equal to one hundredth of a metre.

- 100 cm = 1 m

cents (c)

Our money system is made up of cents and dollars. 100 cents (100c) makes 1 dollar ($1).

chance

The chance (or probability) of something happening is its likelihood of happening.

- If you toss a coin, there is an even chance of tossing a head.

See also *probability*.

clockwise

See *anticlockwise*.

column graph

Groups are compared using the lengths of columns or bars. The graph can be vertical or horizontal.

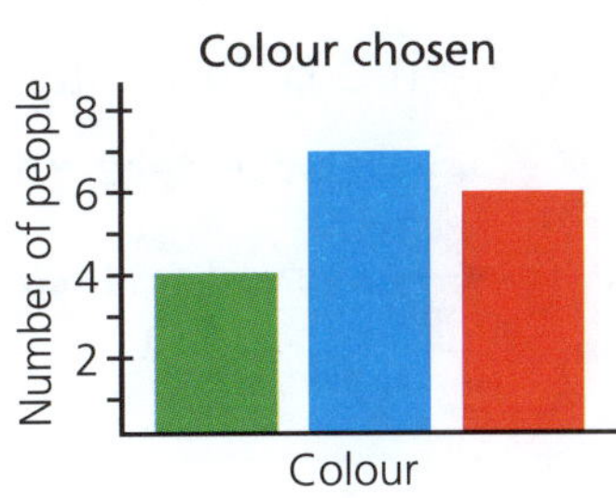

cone

See *3D objects*.

corner (vertex)

A corner is where sides or edges meet at a point.

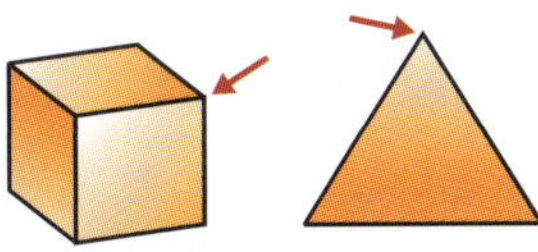

cross-section

The shape formed when an object is cut.

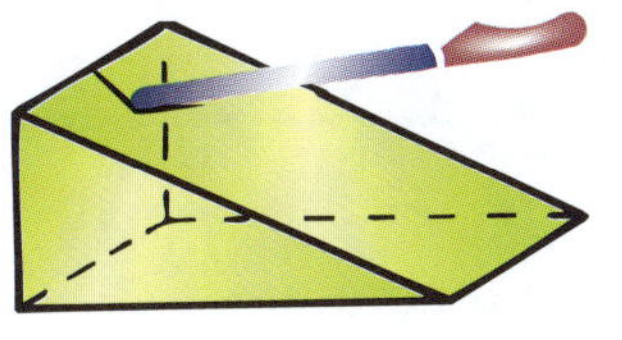

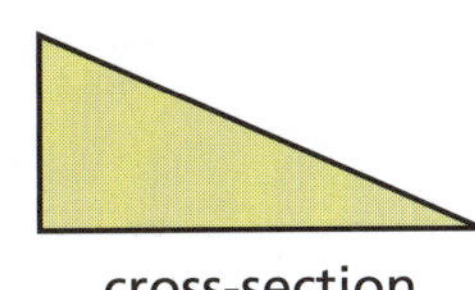

cross-section

cube

See *3D objects*.

curved surface

A curved surface on a 3D object is not flat. It allows an object to roll. A cylinder and cone each have one curved surface.

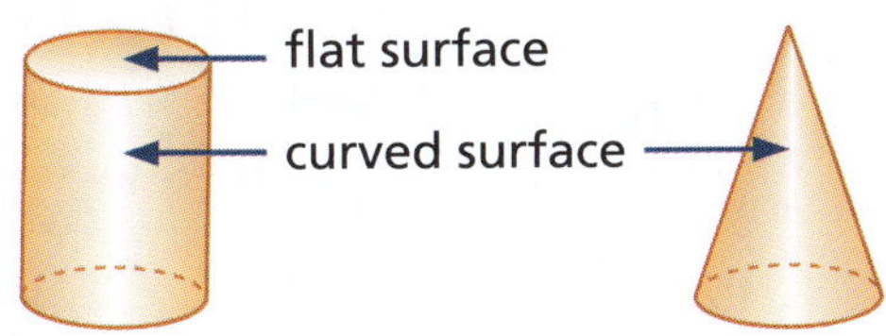

cylinder

See *3D objects*.

cubic centimetre

A unit for measuring volume that is equal to a cube (ones block) with sides of length 1cm.

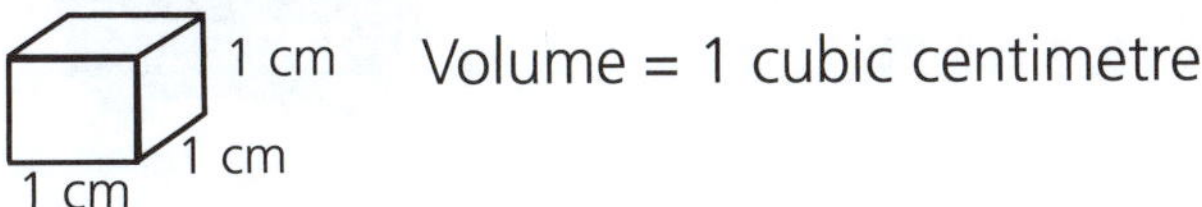

data display

A data display shows categories of objects and allows us to compare them.

Graph:

Table:

Dogs	Cats
4	2

date

The date shows the day, the month and the year. For example, 30.5.23 means the 30th day of the 5th month (May) in the year 2023.

decimal notation

The decimal point separates the whole number from the fraction.

0·7 means 7 tenths.

6·5 means 6 ones and 5 tenths.

7·5

↑

decimal point

difference

How many more?

The difference between 16 and 13 is 3.

For smaller numbers, line up each group in a row to find the difference.

For larger numbers, place the numbers on a number line to find the difference.

digital time

Time expressed using digits.

- This digital clock shows 24 minutes past 10.

digits

Symbols used to write a number.

- 6 Six is a 1-digit number.
- 47 Forty-seven is a 2-digit number.

division (÷)

Breaking up groups into equal parts.

- 6 ÷ 3

  a Sharing 2 each

  b Grouping 2 groups

edge

Two faces of a 3D object meet at an edge.

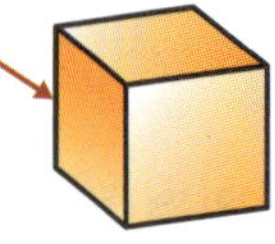

even number

Any number that is a multiple of two and can be grouped in twos. They end in 0, 2, 4, 6 or 8.

- 16, 300, 4394

The other counting numbers are **odd**.

expanded notation

A way of writing numerals to show the place value of each digit.

- $137 = (1 \times 100) + (3 \times 10) + 7$
  $= 100 + 30 + 7$

face

A flat surface of a three-dimensional object.

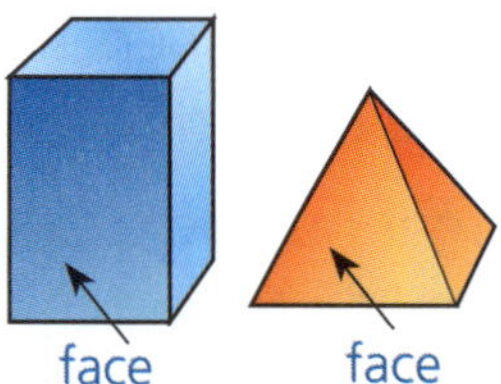

flat surface

A cylinder has 2 flat surfaces, one on both ends, and one curved surface.

A cube has 6 flat surfaces.

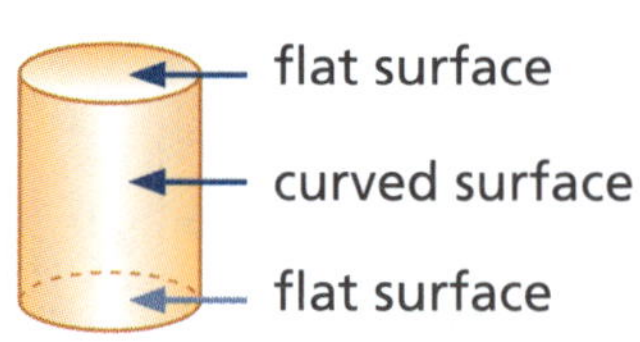

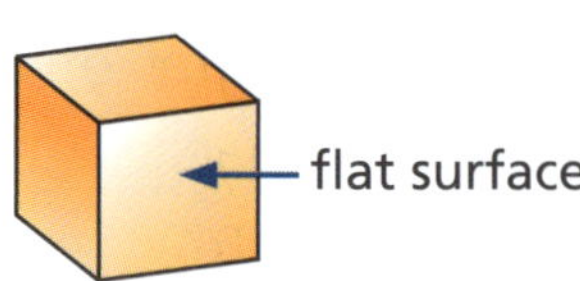

fraction

Any part of a whole, group or object.

- 2 out of 6 shaded

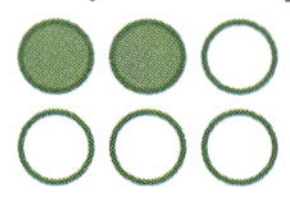

- $\frac{1}{4}$ is shaded

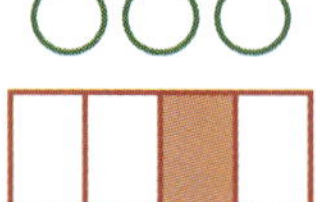

gram (g)

A unit of mass used to measure how heavy something is.

- 1 kilogram = 1000 grams

graph

A diagram or drawing used to record a collection of data.

- Column graph

  Groups are compared using the lengths of columns or bars. The graph can be vertical or horizontal.

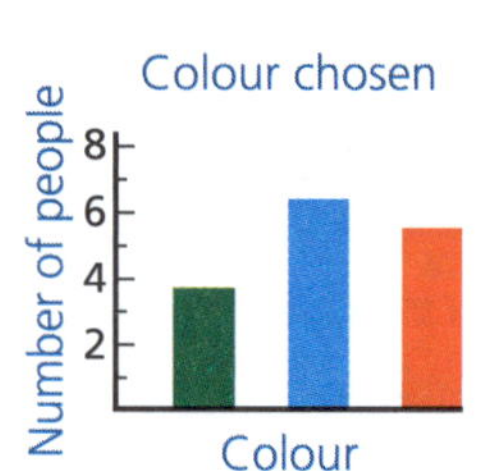

- Picture graph

  A picture is used as a unit to show how many.

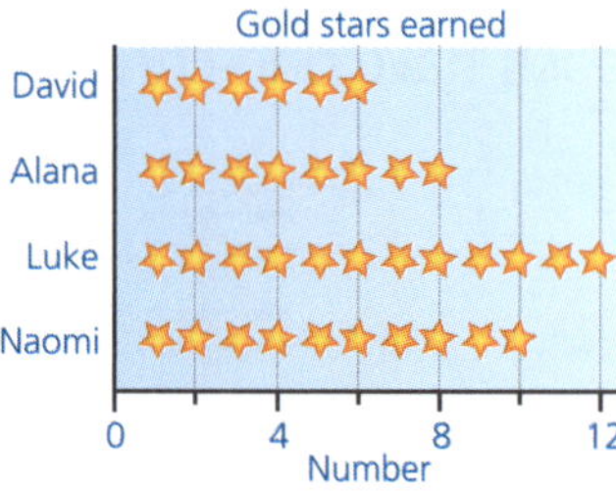

- Dot plot

  A dot is used instead of a picture to show one item.

heft

To compare masses by lifting them with your hands.

hexagon

See *2D shapes*.

inverse operations

Adding 8 is the opposite (the inverse) of subtracting 8.

- 100 + 8 – 8 = 100

Multiplying by 2 is the opposite (the inverse) of dividing by 2.

- 4 × 2 ÷ 2 = 4

jump strategy

Adding or subtracting numbers, jumping by tens or ones.

- 52 – 14 = 38

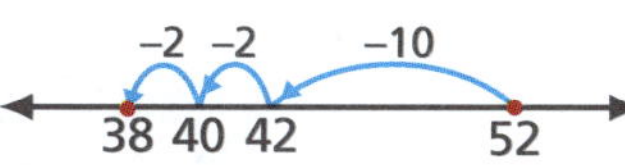

kilogram (kg)

The basic unit of mass, equal to 1000 grams.

- 1 kg = 1000 g

left and **right**

- Left

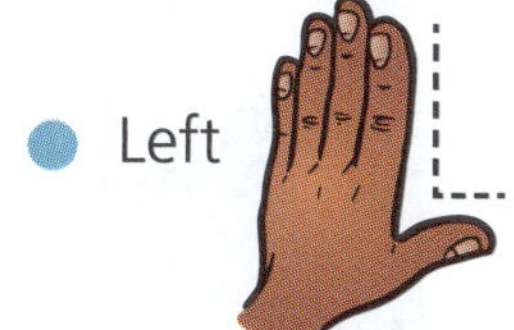

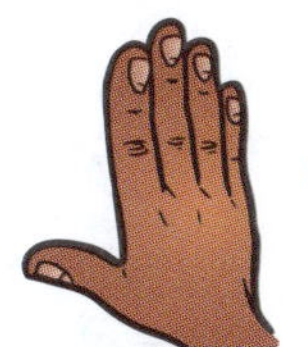

- Right

line

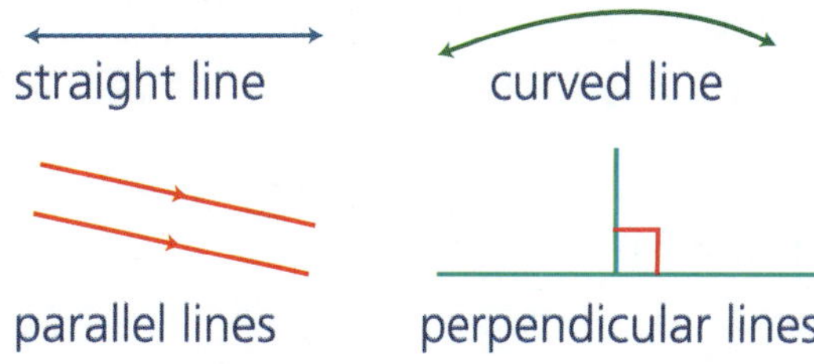

line of symmetry

A line that divides something in half so that each half is a mirror image of the other part.

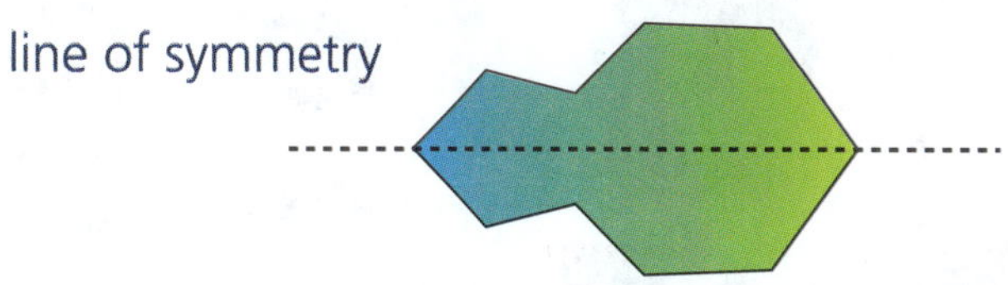

litre (L)

A unit of capacity (or volume) used for the measurement of liquids.

- 1 L = 1000 mL

map or **plan**

A picture of an area viewed from above.

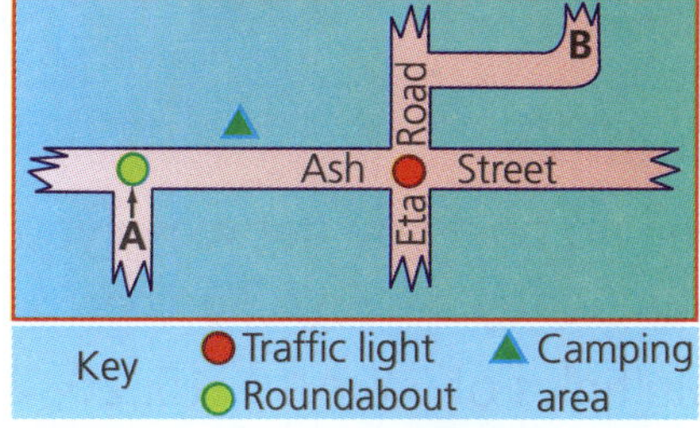

mass

The amount of matter in an object, a measure of how heavy it is.

metre (m)

The basic unit of length, equal to 100 centimetres.

- 1 m = 100 cm

millilitre (mL)

A unit of capacity (or volume) equal to one thousandth of a litre.

- 1000 mL = 1 L

millimetre (mm)

A unit of length equal to one tenth of a centimetre, or one thousandth of a metre.

- 10 mm = 1 cm
- 1000 mm = 1 m

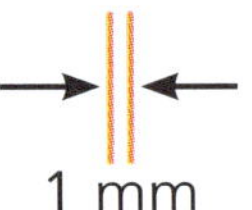

money

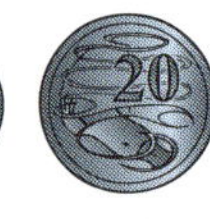

multiple

The number you get when you multiply a certain number by a whole number.

Multiples of 5 are 10, 15, 20, 25, …

multiplication (×)

Combining equal groups.

- $3 \times 5 = 15$

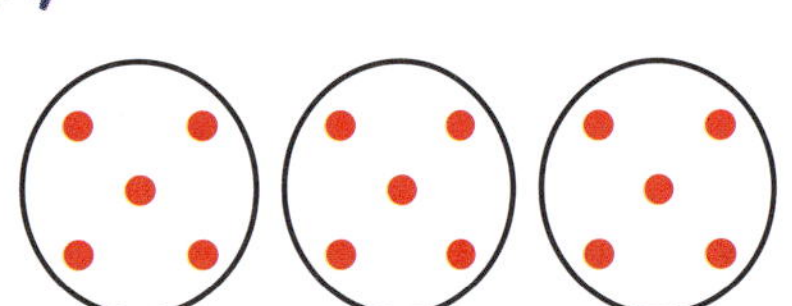

net

A flat shape that can be folded to make a three-dimensional object.

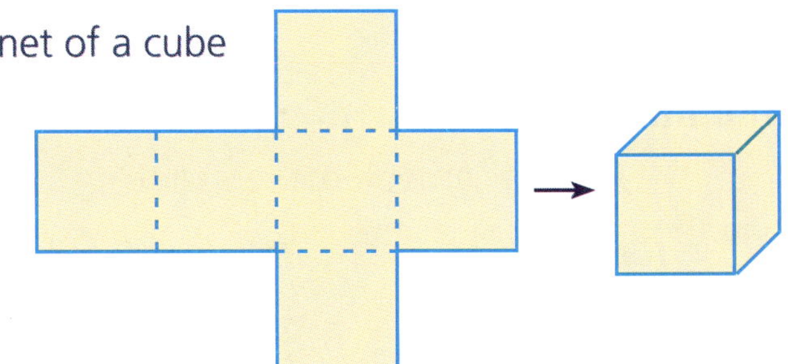

number bonds

These show how a number can be broken up into parts (e.g. the top number, 4, can be broken up into 3 and 1).

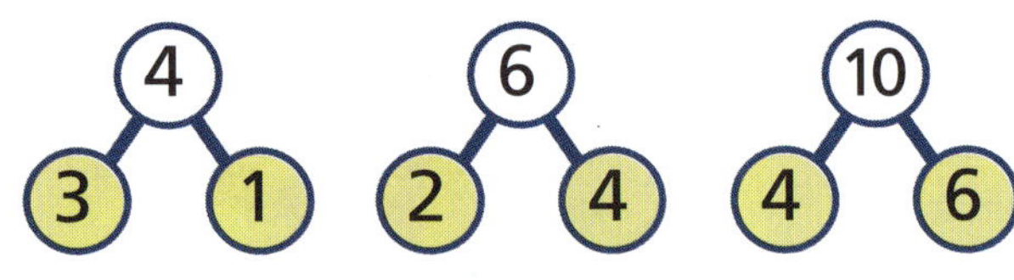

number line

A line on which numbers are marked.

Number lines can be used to show operations.

- $2 + 2 + 2 = 6$

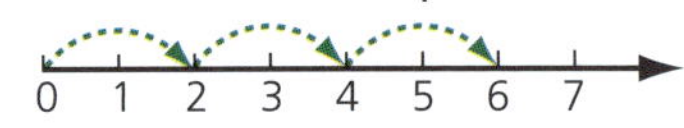

numeral expander

Breaks up a number into hundreds, tens and ones.

- 

  This numeral expander shows 439.

perimeter

The distance around the outside of a shape; the boundary.

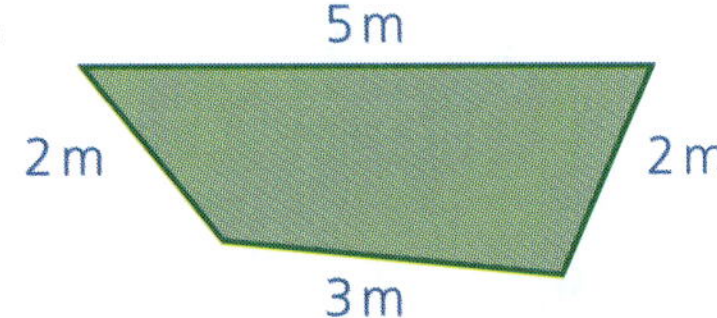

- Perimeter = 2 m + 3 m + 2 m + 5 m
  = 12 m

place-value blocks

These are used to represent numbers.

ones block

tens block

hundreds block

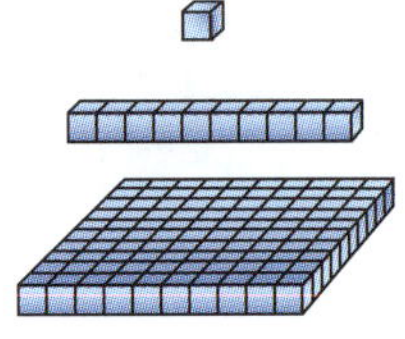

thousands block

42 shown as:

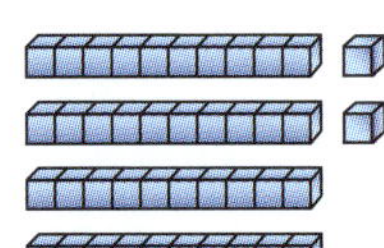

113 shown as:

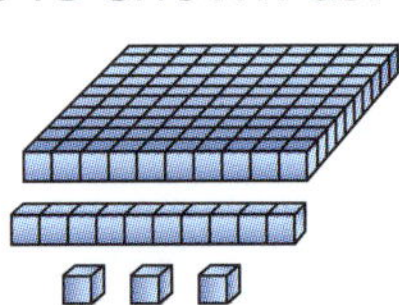

prism

A three-dimensional object with a uniform cross-section. The ends are identical shapes and all other faces are rectangles. Prisms are named by the shape of their ends.

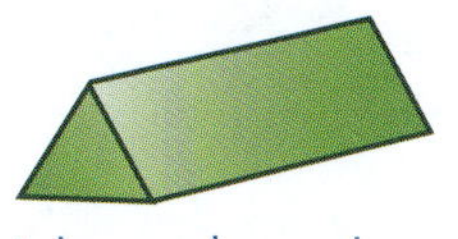
triangular prism

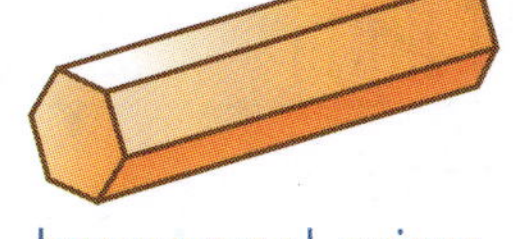
hexagonal prism

probability

The probability (or chance) of something happening is its likelihood of happening.

- **Chance language**

  possible, impossible, certain, more likely, less likely, least likely, outcome, event

pyramid

A three-dimensional object that has a polygon for a base and triangles for all other faces. Pyramids are named by the shape of their base.

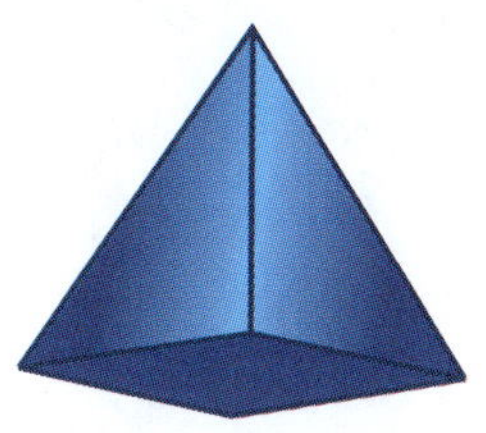
square pyramid

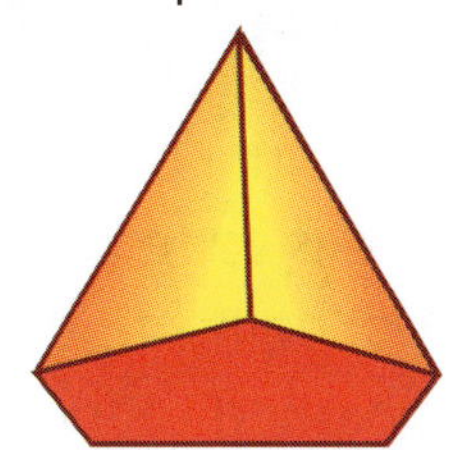
pentagonal pyramid

quadrilateral

A two-dimensional shape with four straight sides.

quarter of a whole or collection

One of four equal parts.

One quarter of the rectangle is coloured.

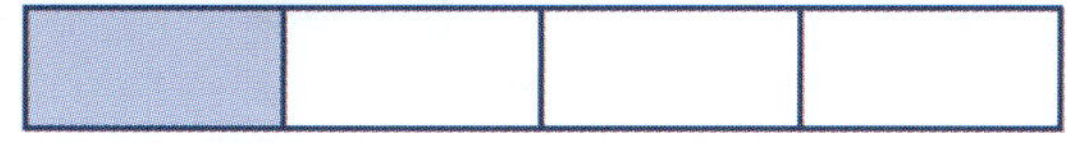

One quarter of the collection is coloured.

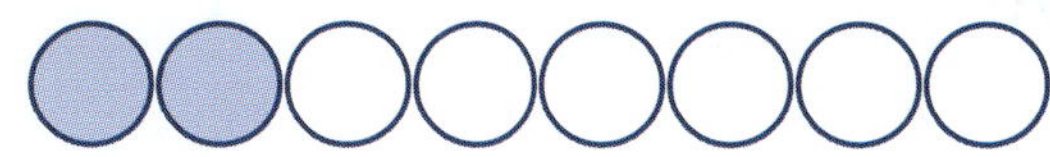

A quarter of 8 is 2. Another way to say this is 8 divided by 4 is 2. That is $8 \div 4 = 2$.

Three quarters of the rectangle is coloured.

Three quarters of the collection is coloured.

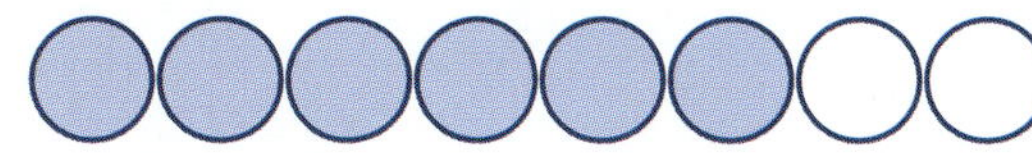

rectangle

See *2D shapes*.

regular and irregular shapes

Regular shapes have all sides and all angles equal. Irregular shapes do not.

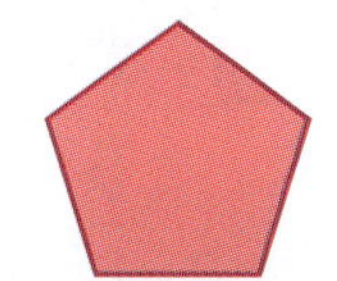
regular shape

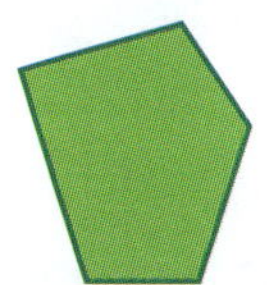
irregular shape

right and left

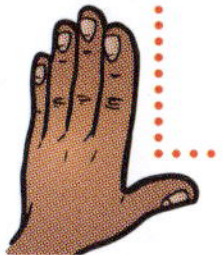

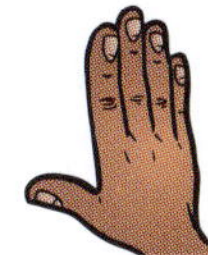

- Right

rounding

We usually round to the nearest 10, 100 or 1000, ...

Money is rounded to the nearest 5 cents.

- 18 rounds to 20

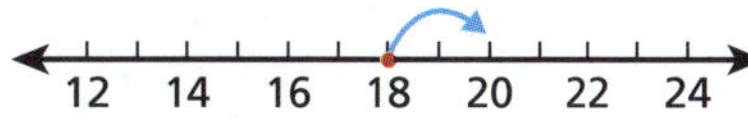

skip counting

Counting on, adding the same number each time.

- 5, 10, 15, 20, 25, ... is skip counting by 5.

sphere

See *3D objects*.

split strategy

Adding numbers by splitting them into their parts.

- 36 + 52 = 30 + 6 + 50 + 2
  = (30 + 50) + (6 + 2)
  = 80 + 8
  = 88

square

See *2D shapes*.

square centimetre

A unit for measuring area that is equal to a square with sides of 1 cm.

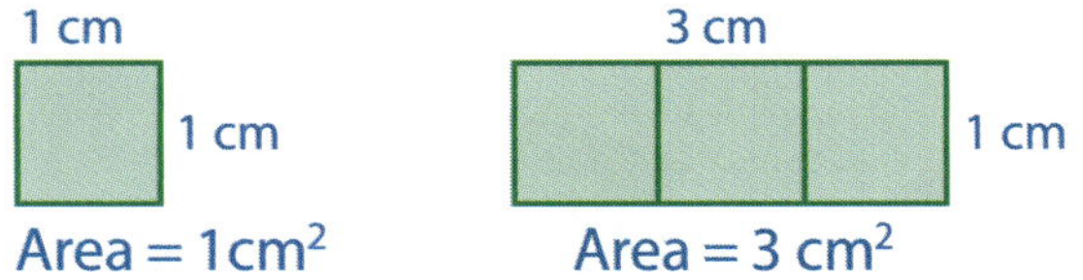

A square metre is a square of length 1 metre.

square number

The number we get when we multiply a whole number by itself.

- 1, 4, 9, 16, 25, …

survey

A list of questions used to discover information.

symmetry

If a figure has a line of symmetry, it can be folded so that the two halves exactly overlap. Each half is a mirror image of the other.

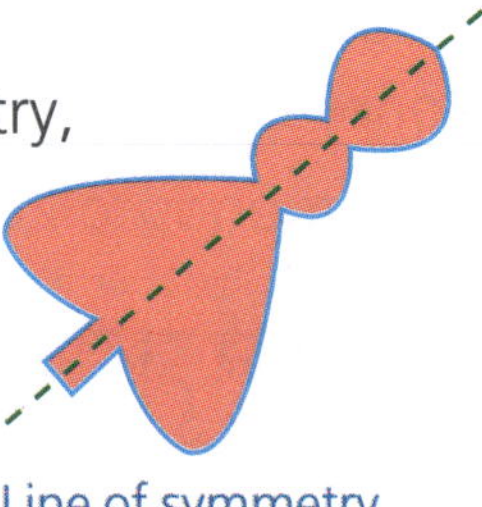

Line of symmetry

table

A simple way to display information in rows and columns.

Birds	12
Lions	2
Monkeys	6

tally

To keep count by making a mark for each item. To make counting easy, the marks are drawn in groups of five, with each fifth mark crossed over the other four marks.

- 卌 卌 卌 ||| = 18

time words

Days			
Sunday	Monday	Tuesday	Wednesday
Thursday	Friday	Saturday	

Months			
January	February	March	April
May	June	July	August
September	October	November	December

Seasons			
Summer	Autumn	Winter	Spring

- clocks

analog clock digital clock

- o'clock

When the minute hand (long hand) is pointing to 12, the time is an 'o'clock' time. The hour hand (short hand) points to the hour (e.g. the hour hand below is pointing to the 3 so it is 3 o'clock).

3 o'clock

- half past

When the minute (long) hand is pointing to the 6, the time is a 'half past'. The hour (short) hand on the clock points halfway between the 3 and the 4 so it is half past 3.

half past 3

- quarter past

When the minute (long) hand is pointing to the 3, then the time is 'quarter past'. The hour (short) hand on the clock is a quarter of the way from 6 to 7, so it is a quarter past 6.

- quarter to

When the minute (long) hand is pointing to the 9, then the time is 'quarter to' the next hour. The hour (short) hand on the clock is a quarter of the way from the next number 7, so it is a quarter to 7.

- The number of days in each month:

How to know the number of days in each month.

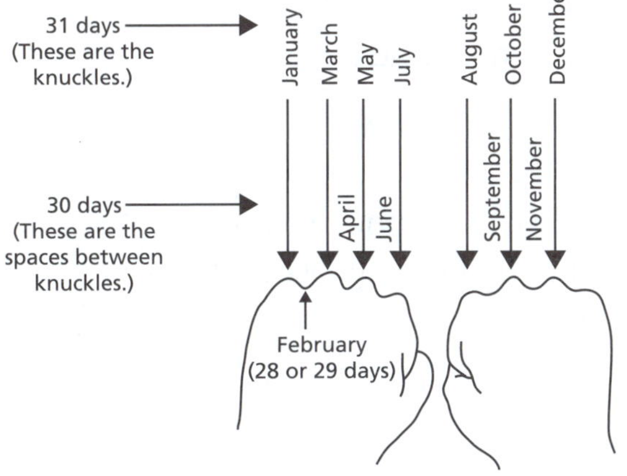

30 days has September, April, June and November. All the rest have 31, except February alone, which has 28 days clear and 29 days each leap year.

timeline

Shows a sequence of events in time.

turn

Moving a shape in a clockwise or anticlockwise direction.

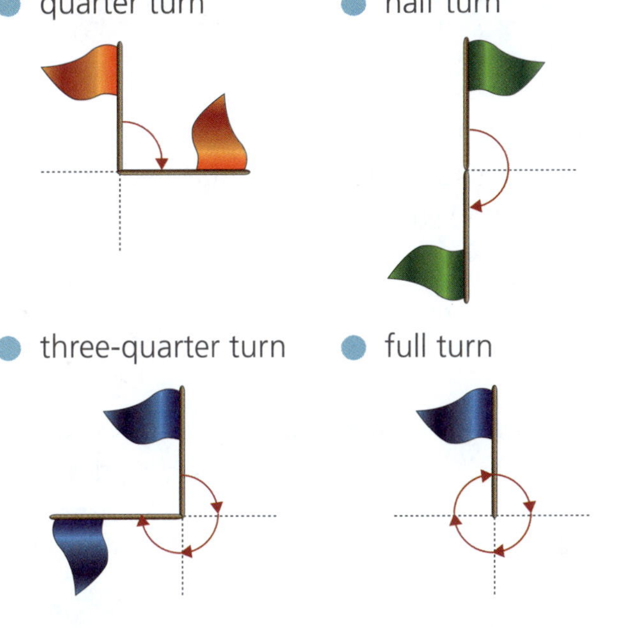

vertex

A point at which two or more lines meet to form a corner on a plane shape or object.

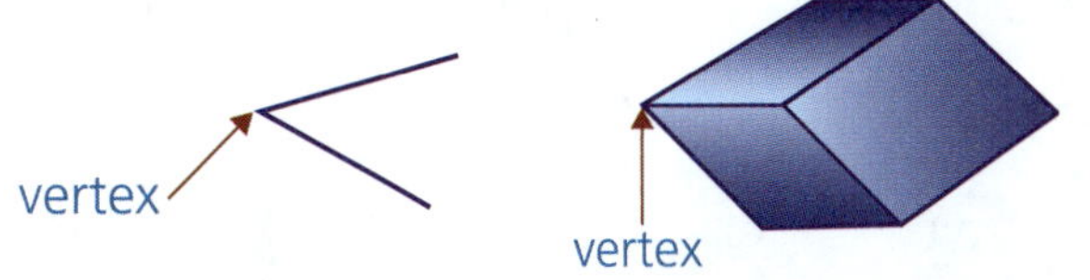

The plural of *vertex* is *vertices*.

volume

The amount of space an object takes up.

year

There are 365 days in a year and 366 days in a leap year (which is every 4th year). There are 12 months in a year.

2D (two-dimensional) shapes

Flat shapes are two-dimensional.
They have length and width.

circle
1 curved side

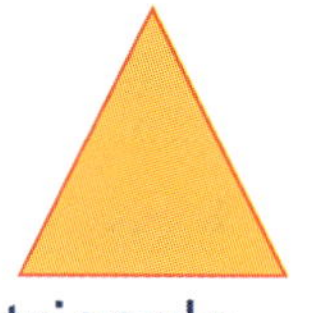

triangle
3 sides
3 corners

square
4 equal sides
4 corners

rectangle
2 equal long sides
and 2 equal short sides,
like a stretched square

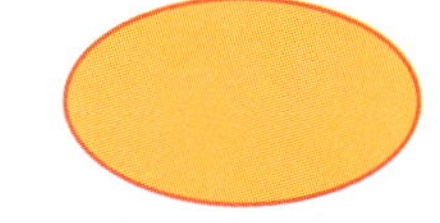

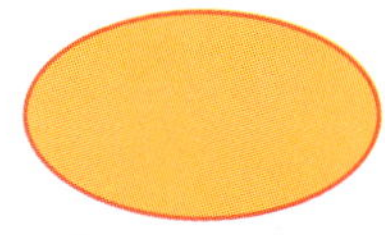

oval
1 curved side, like
a squashed circle

pentagon
5 sides
5 corners

hexagon
6 sides
6 corners

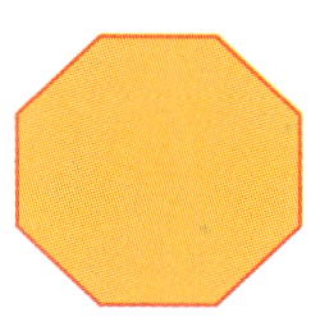

octagon
8 sides
8 corners

quadrilaterals
4 sides
4 corners

parallelogram
two sets of parallel lines
opposite sides equal

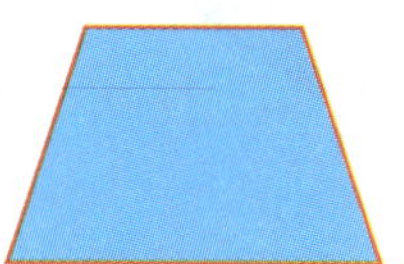

trapezium
one set of
parallel lines

rhombus
all sides equal
(a diamond)

kite
two pairs of
equal sides

All of the blue shapes are quadrilaterals.

3D (three-dimensional) objects

Solid objects are three-dimensional.
They have length, width and height.

sphere

A sphere is curved and round.

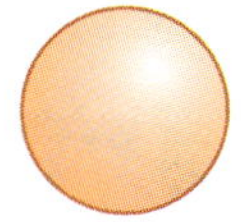

cube

A cube has 6 identical faces,
8 vertices and 12 straight edges.

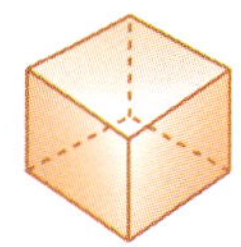

cylinder

A cylinder has 2 circular flat surfaces
and 1 curved surface.

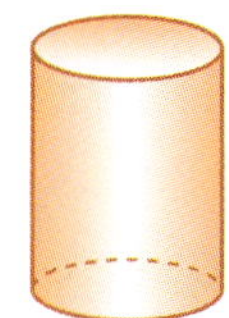

cone

A cone has 1 circular flat surface
and 1 curved surface.

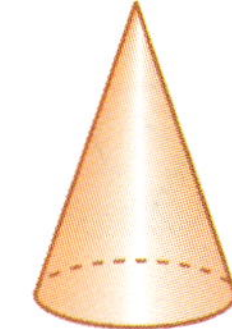

pyramid

A pyramid has triangular
faces joined around a base.

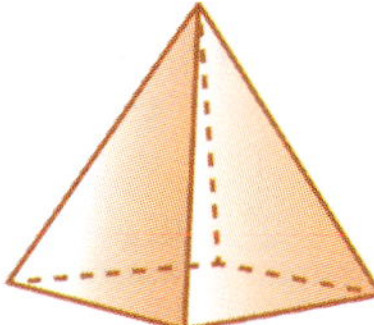

prism

A prism has rectangular faces
joining two identical bases.

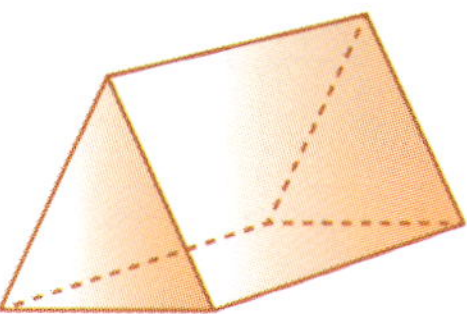

Counting

Even numbers end in 0, 2, 4, 6 or 8.
Odd numbers end in 1, 3, 5, 7 or 9.

1 Use the hundred chart to answer the questions.

a Count by 2s. Colour these numbers yellow.

b Starting at 100, count backwards by 10s. Draw a cross on these numbers.

c Circle every second even number up to 80. What do you notice?

Hundred chart

1	2	3	4	5	6	7	8	9	10
11	12	13	14	15	16	17	18	19	20
21	22	23	24	25	26	27	28	29	30
31	32	33	34	35	36	37	38	39	40
41	42	43	44	45	46	47	48	49	50
51	52	53	54	55	56	57	58	59	60
61	62	63	64	65	66	67	68	69	70
71	72	73	74	75	76	77	78	79	80
81	82	83	84	85	86	87	88	89	90
91	92	93	94	95	96	97	98	99	100

d Start at 8 and count on by tens until you reach 98. Write this pattern.

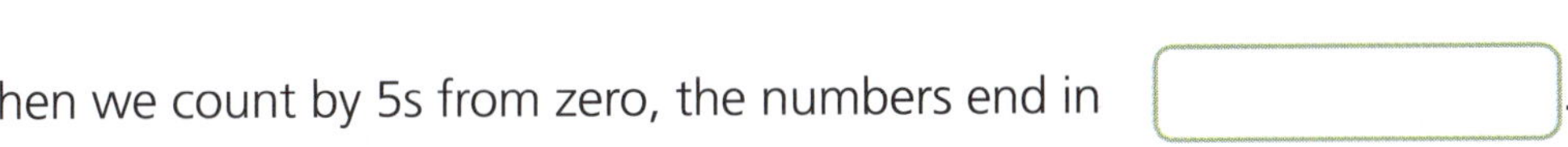

2 When we count by 2s from zero, the numbers end in ______.

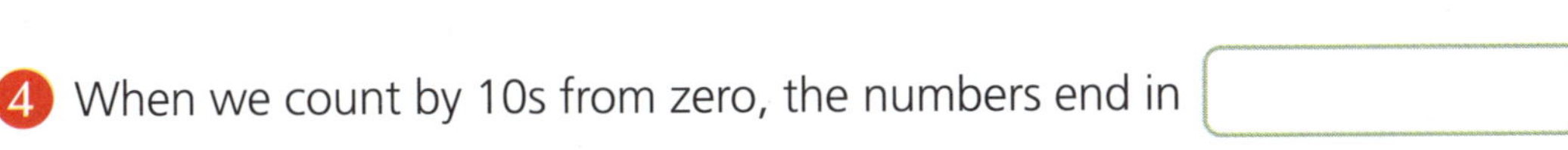

3 When we count by 5s from zero, the numbers end in ______.

4 When we count by 10s from zero, the numbers end in ______.

5 Continue each pattern using the rule given. Use a calculator to check.

a Add 5. 5, 10, 15, ___, ___, ___, ___, ___

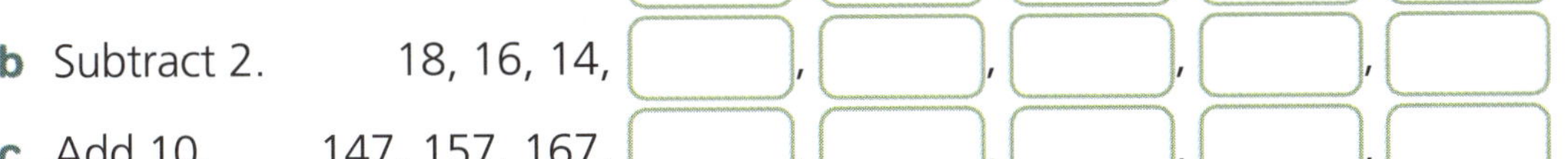

b Subtract 2. 18, 16, 14, ___, ___, ___, ___, ___

c Add 10. 147, 157, 167, ___, ___, ___, ___, ___

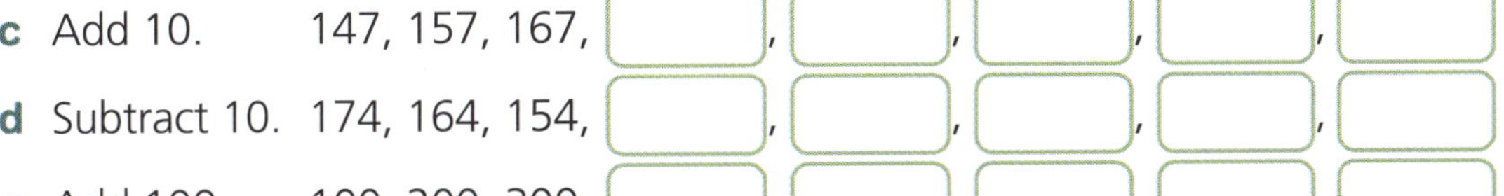

d Subtract 10. 174, 164, 154, ___, ___, ___, ___, ___

e Add 100. 100, 200, 300, ___, ___, ___, ___, ___

6 Show your answers to Questions 5**c** and 5**d** on the number lines.

a

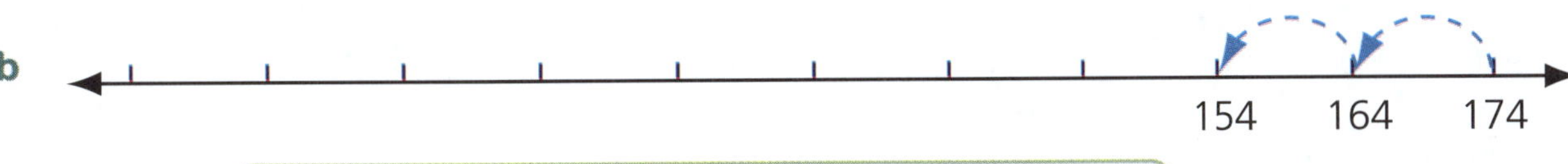

The rule is ______.

b

154 164 174

The rule is ______.

1:02 Counting

Five 20c coins make $1.
Ten 10c coins make $1.
Twenty 5c coins make $1.

1 a Count on from 76 to 94 by 2s.

b Count backwards from 1000 by 100s.

c Count on from 645 to 690 by 5s.

d Count backwards from 500 to 400 by 10s.

You could use a calculator to check your answers.

2 Write the missing numbers.

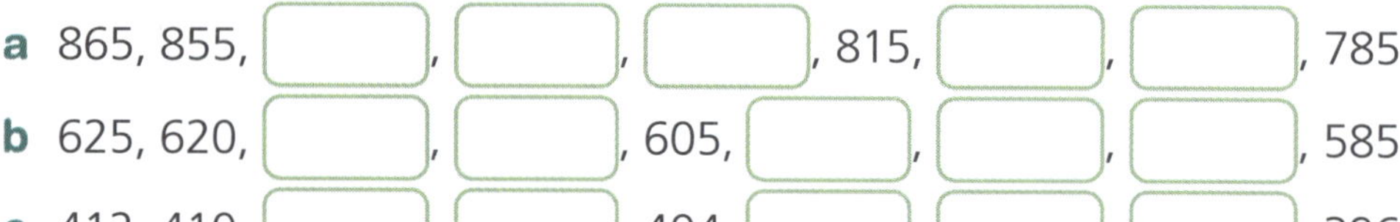

a 865, 855, ___, ___, ___, 815, ___, ___, 785

b 625, 620, ___, ___, 605, ___, ___, ___, 585

c 412, 410, ___, ___, 404, ___, ___, ___, 396

3 Count by 2s and write the first 20 numbers you count. Circle every second number and discuss the pattern.

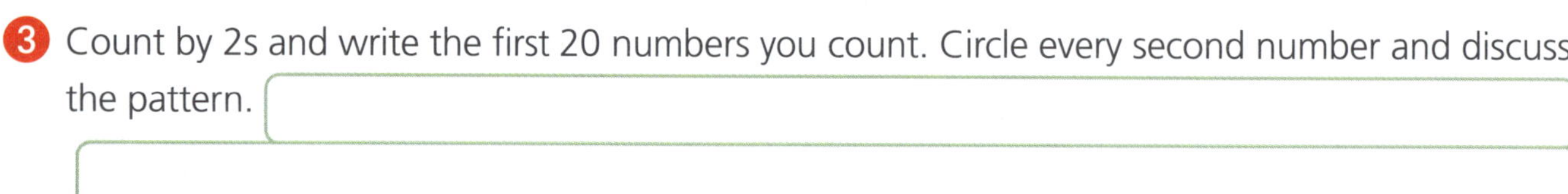

4 Count by 5s and write the first 20 numbers you count. Circle every second number and discuss the pattern.

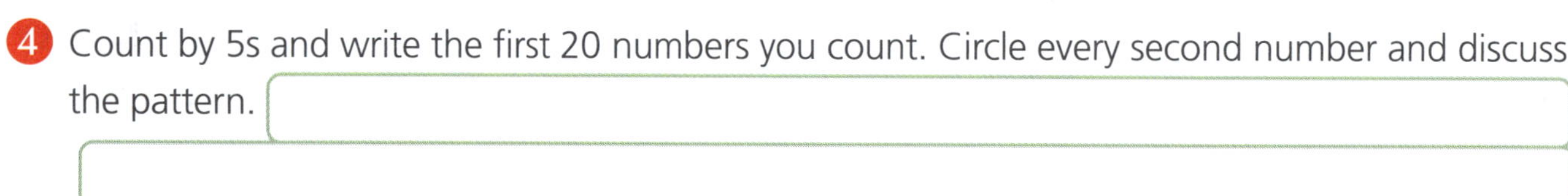

5 If you have to count 300 ten-cent coins, what is the best counting strategy to make sure you count them correctly?

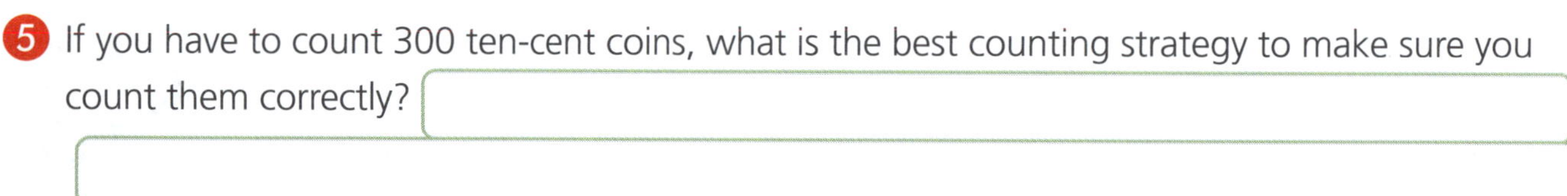

6 Show your answers to Questions 1**a** and 1**b** on the number line.

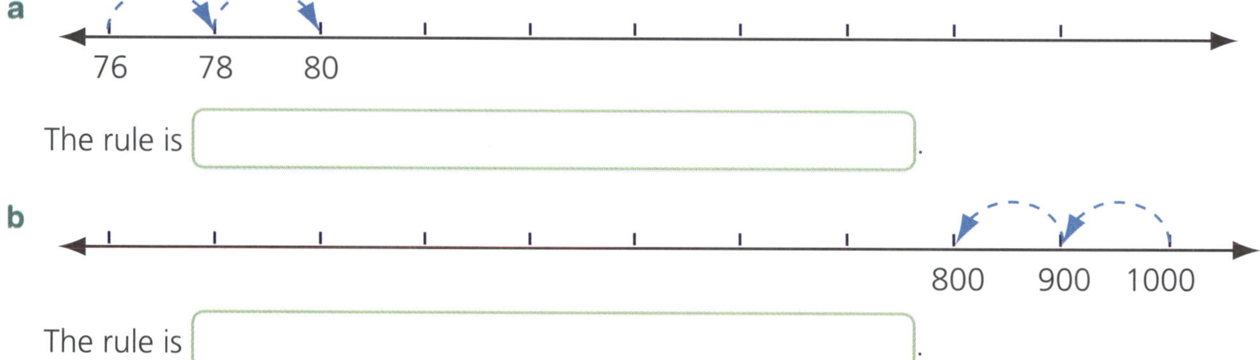

c Try to do Question 1**c** on your own number line.

 • *AUSTRALIAN SIGNPOST MATHS NSW 3* • ISBN 9780655709046

1:03 Numbers to 1000

two hundred and thirty-eight

hundreds tens ones

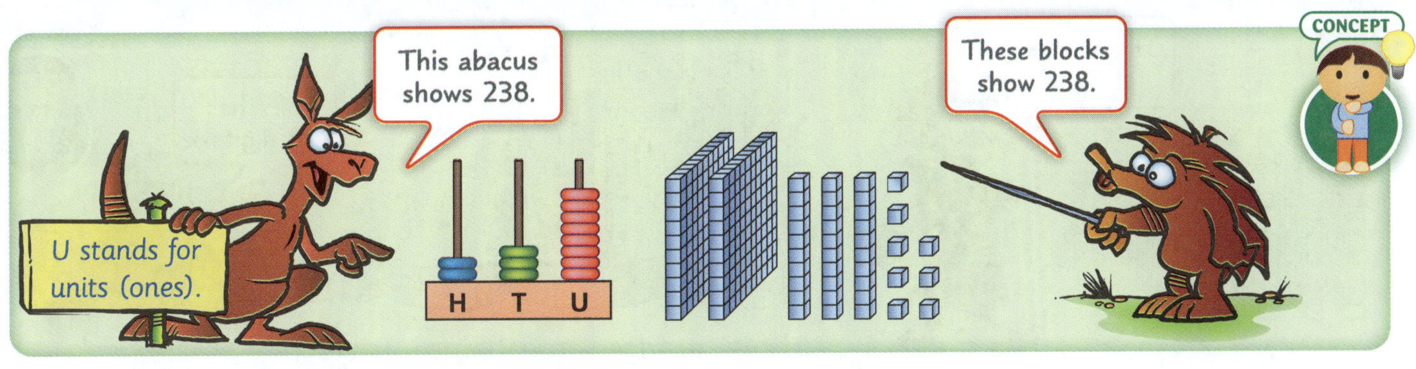

1 Write the number shown by the place-value blocks or abacus.

a b c d

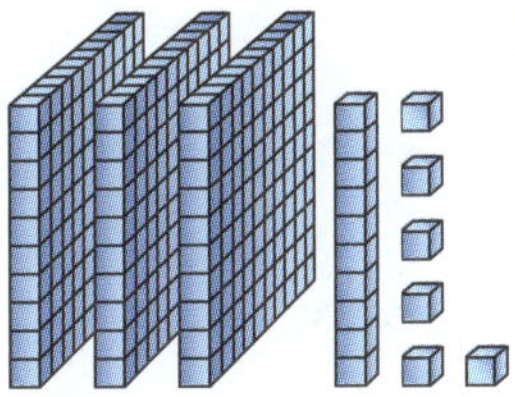

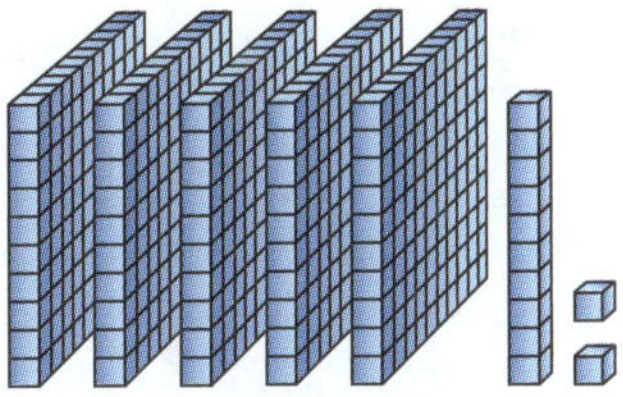

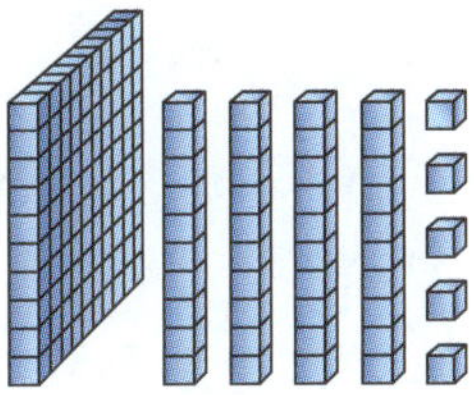

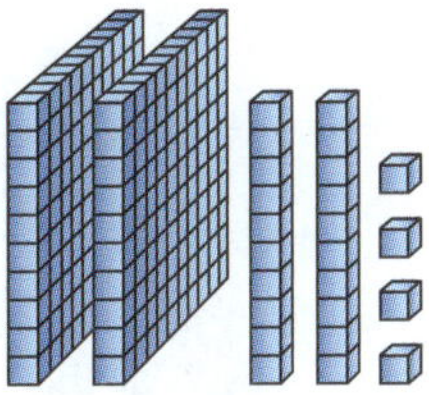

e f g h

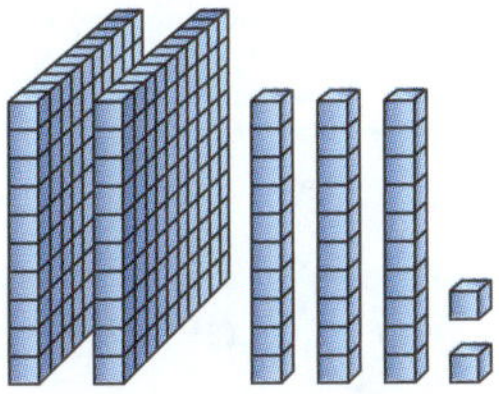

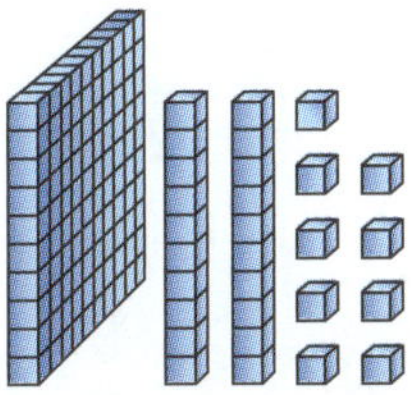

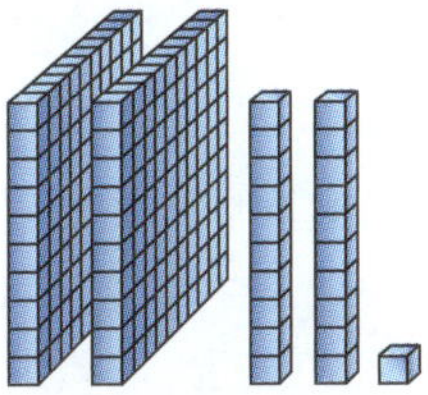

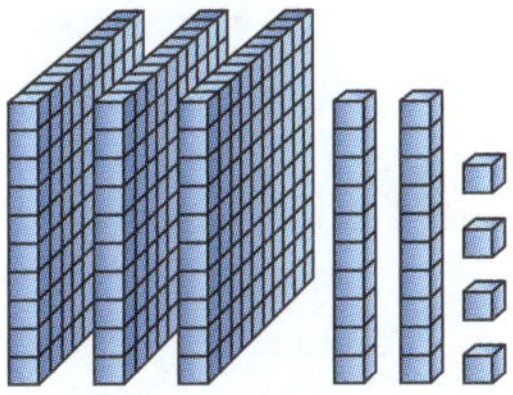

i j k l

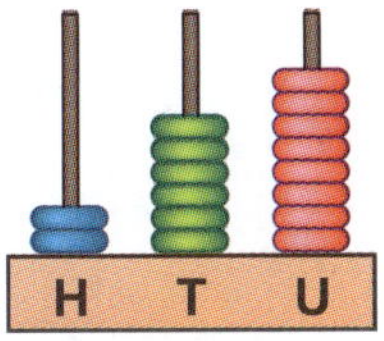

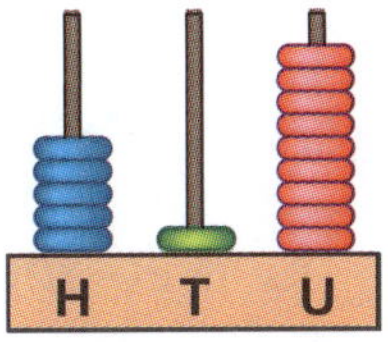

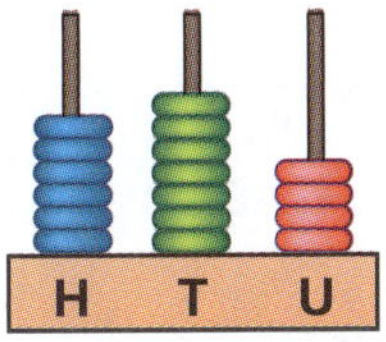

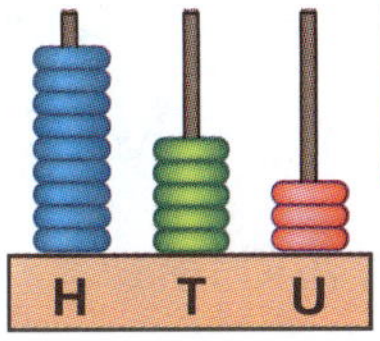

The abacus was invented thousands of years ago.

2 Which number is larger?

a 169 or 346
b 723 or 481
c 962 or 503
d 375 or 634
e 257 or 572
f 491 or 914

3 Write these in order from smallest to largest.

a 137, 653, 446 ____, ____, ____
b 974, 237, 491 ____, ____, ____
c 819, 106, 567 ____, ____, ____
d 683, 749, 250 ____, ____, ____

1:04 Numbers to 1000

Order from smallest (1) to largest (5).
380, 38, 308, 803, 83

1. Write the numeral, fill in the numeral expander and write the number in words.

a hundreds tens ones

b hundreds tens ones

2. How many digits are in each numeral?

a 39	b 256	c 970	d 56	e 498
f 13	g 7	h 520	i 1000	j 777

3. Write these numbers as numerals.

a two hundred and sixty

b one hundred and fifty-two

c nine hundred and forty

d seven hundred and eighteen

e six hundred and seventy-nine

f five hundred and thirty-four

g eight hundred and sixty-eight

h three hundred and six

4. Write the numbers before and after.

a ___, 999, ___

b ___, 863, ___

c ___, 659, ___

d ___, 306, ___

e ___, 499, ___

f ___, 709, ___

ACTIVITY

- Use place-value blocks to model these numbers.
  - 216
  - 525
  - 848
  - 634
  - 967
  - 388
  - 793
  - 364
  - 190
  - 572
  - 451
  - 1000

1:05 Numbers to 1000

247 = 2 hundreds, 4 tens and 7 ones
= 2 hundreds and 47 ones
= 24 tens and 7 ones

1 Complete the numeral expanders.

a 479

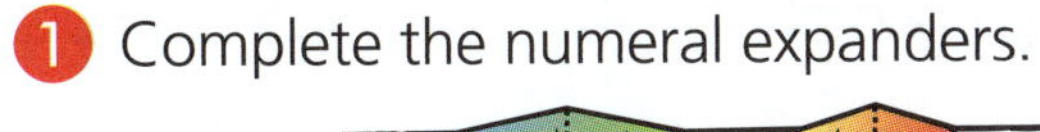
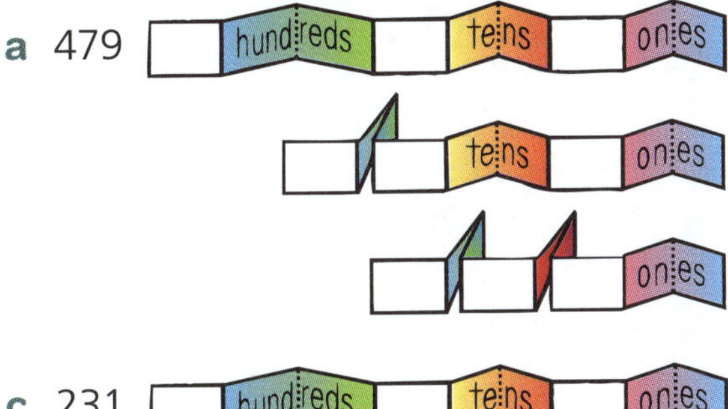

b 568

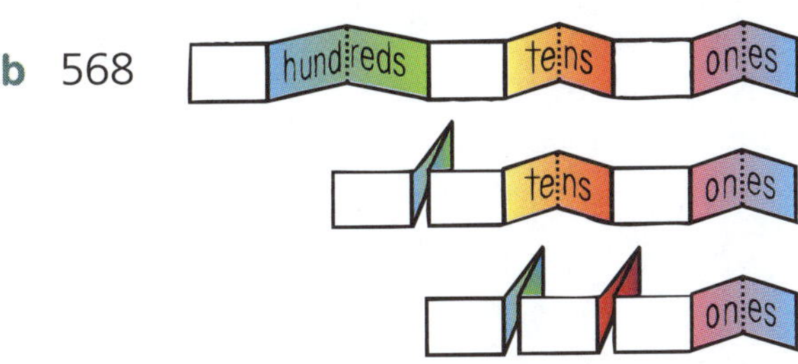

c 231

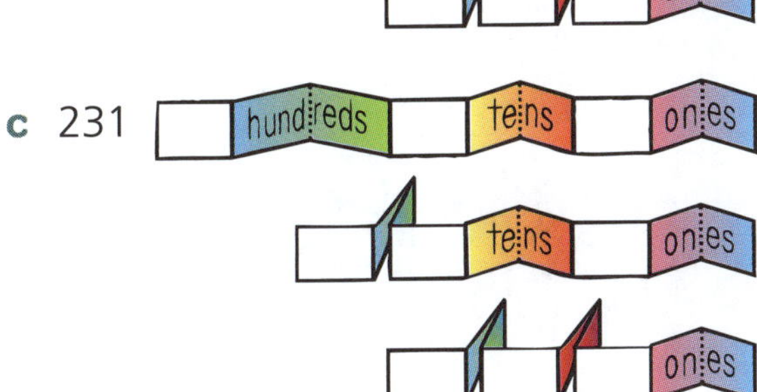

d 307

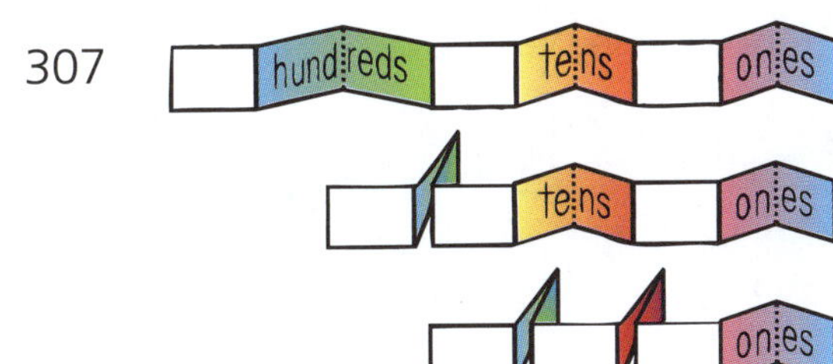

2 Write each number as a numeral.

a six hundred and thirty-two

b eight hundred and seventeen

c four hundred and twenty-nine

d seven hundred and sixty-three

e two hundred and thirty-eight

f five hundred and sixty-two

g nine hundred and forty

h three hundred and fifty-one

3 Write each number in words.

a 106

b 607

c 310

d 841

- Use concrete materials to show the numbers in Question 3. Explain your answer to a partner.

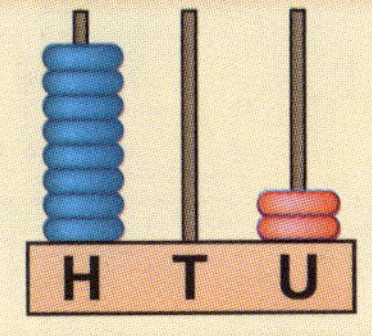

Rounding to the nearest 10

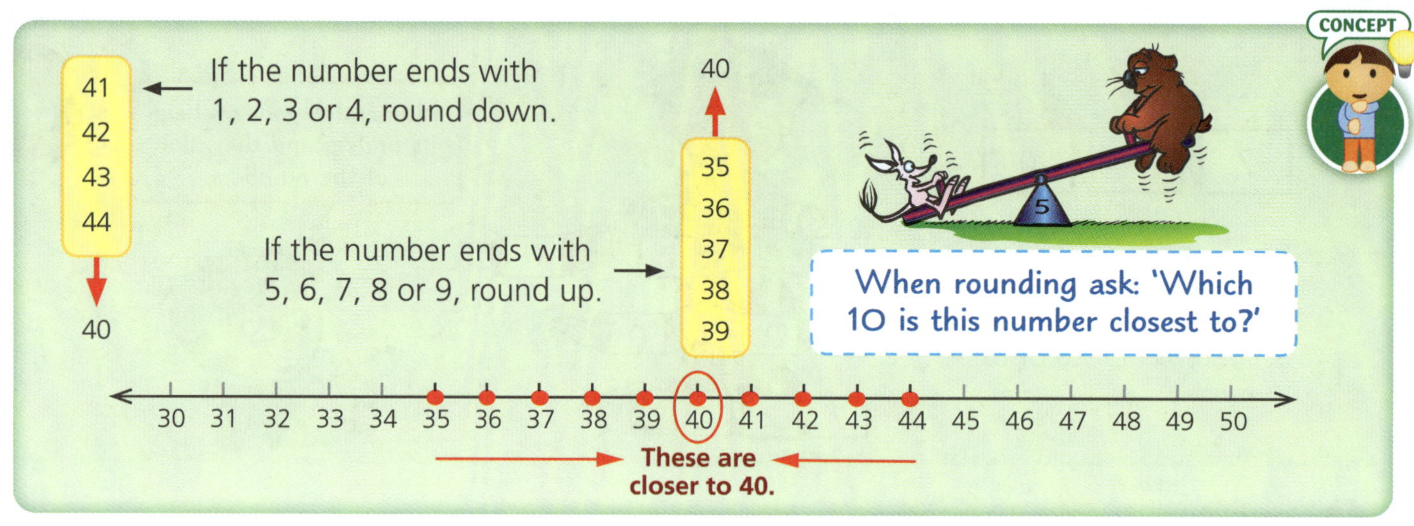

1 a Is 12 closer to 10 or 20? ☐ b Is 77 closer to 70 or 80? ☐

c Is 21 closer to 20 or 30? ☐ d Is 89 closer to 80 or 90? ☐

e Is 33 closer to 30 or 40? ☐ f Is 106 closer to 100 or 110? ☐

2 Round to the nearest 10.

a 24 ☐ b 36 ☐ c 63 ☐ d 47 ☐

e 92 ☐ f 74 ☐ g 59 ☐ h 81 ☐

i 103 ☐ j 115 ☐ k 123 ☐ l 127 ☐

3 a Circle the numbers that round to 60.

57 58 67 68 64

61 69 62 65 52 56

Digits below 5 are rounded down.

b Circle the numbers that round to 190.

199 187 186 197 194 183

193 185 189 188 191

4 Round off each number to the nearest 10. (77 + 41 becomes 80 + 40, and 92 – 38 becomes 90 – 40.)

a 56 + 23 ☐ b 42 – 17 ☐ c 133 – 26 ☐

d 72 + 69 ☐ e 118 – 34 ☐ f 241 – 55 ☐

g 54 + 78 ☐ h 665 – 46 ☐ i 447 – 118 ☐

 • *AUSTRALIAN SIGNPOST MATHS NSW 3* • ISBN 9780655709046

1:07 Rounding to the nearest 100

closer to 100 | closer to 200
100 150 200

150 rounds up to 200.

1
a Is 186 closer to 100 or 200? ☐
b Is 392 closer to 300 or 400? ☐
c Is 529 closer to 500 or 600? ☐
d Is 613 closer to 600 or 700? ☐
e Is 435 closer to 400 or 500? ☐
f Is 264 closer to 200 or 300? ☐
g Is 756 closer to 700 or 800? ☐
h Is 348 closer to 300 or 400? ☐

2 Round these numbers to the nearest hundred.

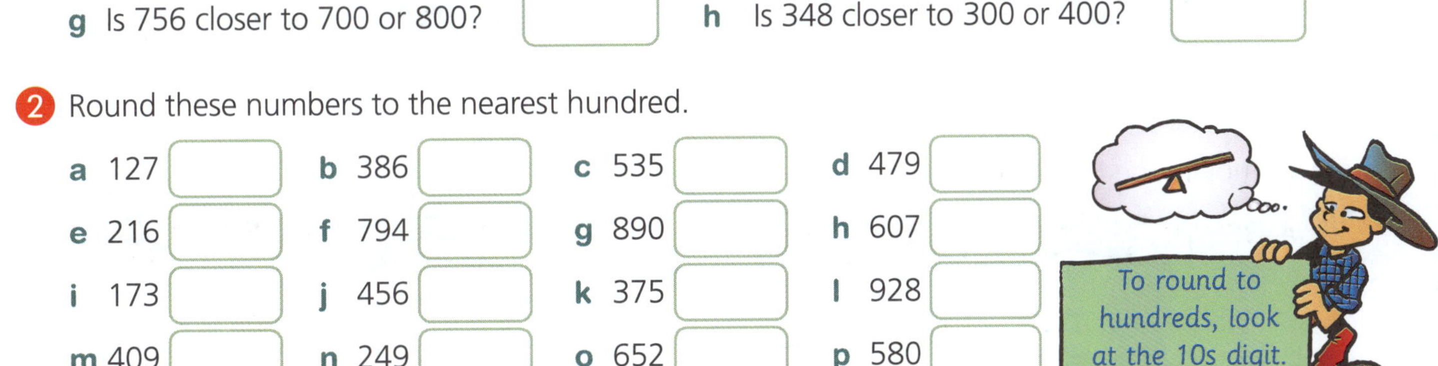

a 127 ☐	b 386 ☐	c 535 ☐	d 479 ☐
e 216 ☐	f 794 ☐	g 890 ☐	h 607 ☐
i 173 ☐	j 456 ☐	k 375 ☐	l 928 ☐
m 409 ☐	n 249 ☐	o 652 ☐	p 580 ☐

3
a Circle the numbers that round to 200.
b Circle the numbers that round to 500.

a					b				
264	163	296	220	186	569	467	416	456	575
217	237	125	143	205	483	590	532	439	521

4 Answer true or false for each statement.

a 974 rounds off to 900. ☐
b 426 rounds off to 500. ☐
c 396 rounds off to 400. ☐
d 399 rounds off to 400. ☐
e 37 tens is less than 371. ☐
f 3 hundred is more than 305. ☐
g 679 is less than 68 tens. ☐
h 409 is more than 4 hundred. ☐

5 Round off each number to the nearest 100, then add them to estimate the answer.

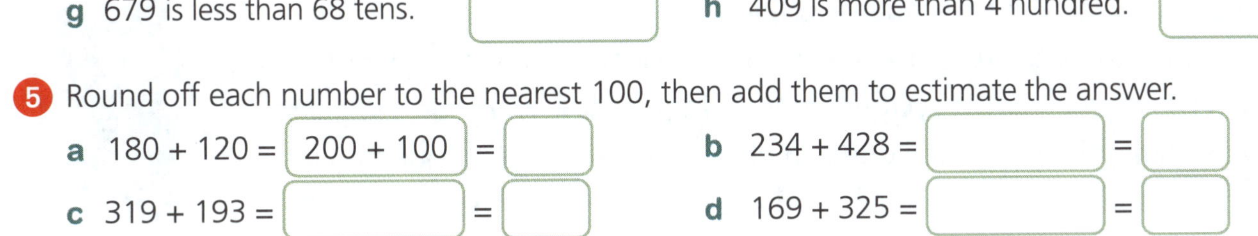

a 180 + 120 = 200 + 100 = ☐
b 234 + 428 = ☐ = ☐
c 319 + 193 = ☐ = ☐
d 169 + 325 = ☐ = ☐

 ISBN 9780655709046

1:08 Numbers to 1000

Order from smallest (1) to largest (3).

421
42 tens
4 hundreds

1 Write the number shown by each abacus.

a
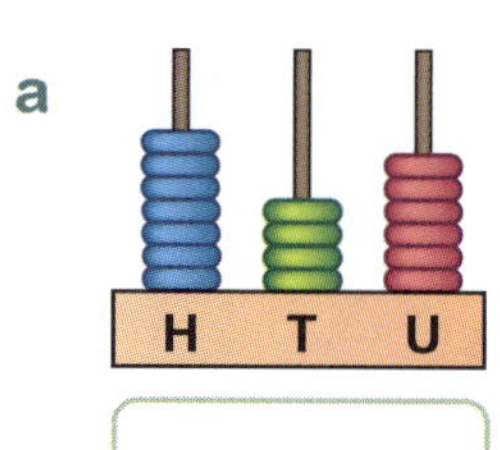

b
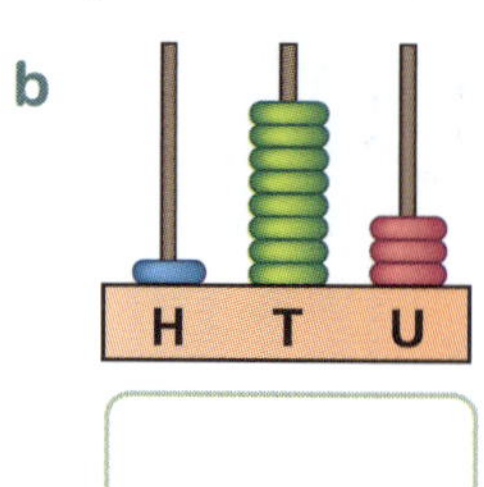

c
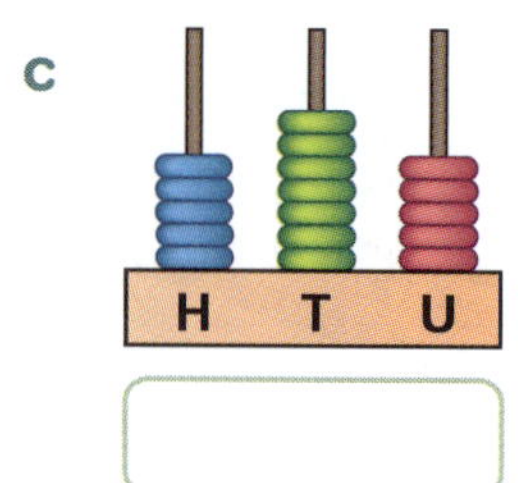

d
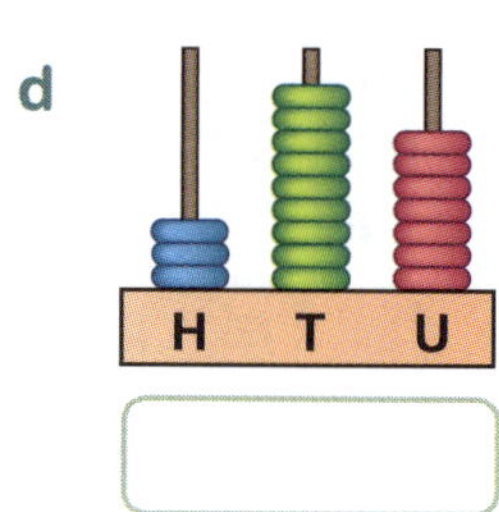

2 Write the numeral, fill in the numeral expander and write the number in words.

a
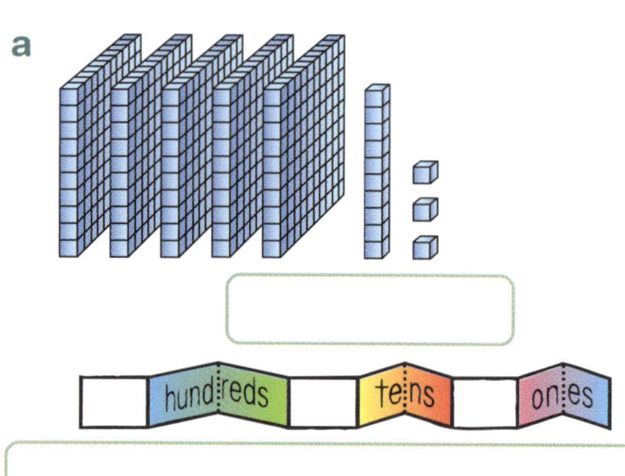

hundreds tens ones

b
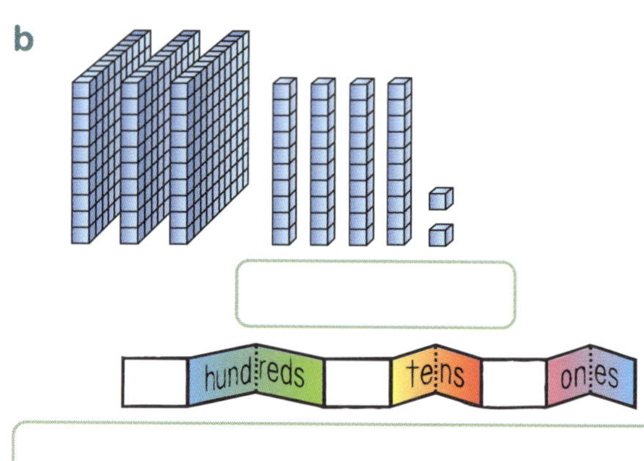

hundreds tens ones

3 Complete the numeral expanders.

a 375 hundreds tens ones

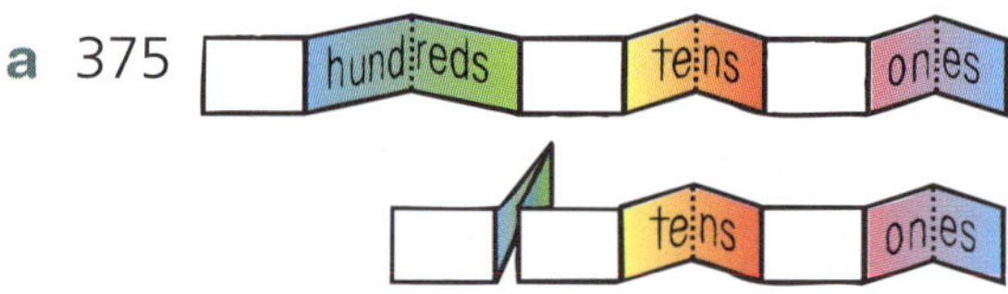

b 198 hundreds tens ones

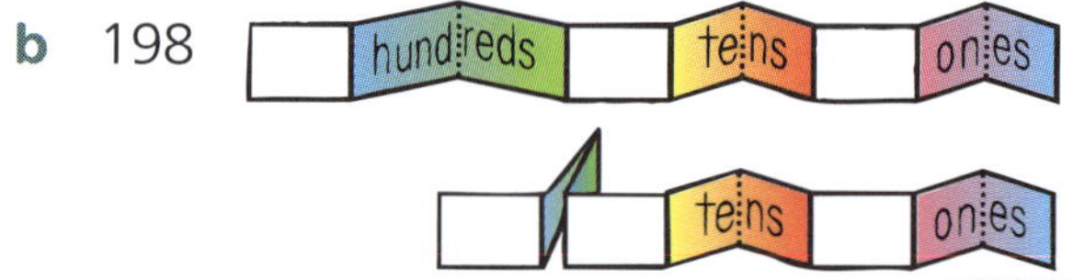

4 Round each number to the nearest hundred.

a 378 **b** 842 **c** 296

d 419 **e** 675 **f** 324

g 906 **h** 547 **i** 752

This rounds to 600.

567

Higher or lower

- One player records a secret 3-digit number and says the boundaries for the number, such as 'between 200 and 300'.
- Other players mark the boundaries on number lines.
- Players take turns to guess the number. After each guess, the holder of the number says whether the secret number is **higher** or **lower** than the guess.
- Players mark this clue for the guess (**higher** or **lower**) on their number lines.
- The game continues until someone guesses the secret number exactly.

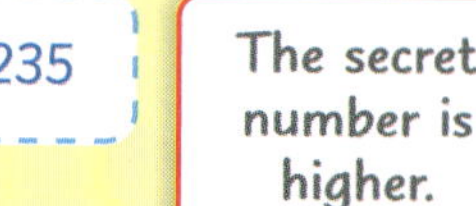

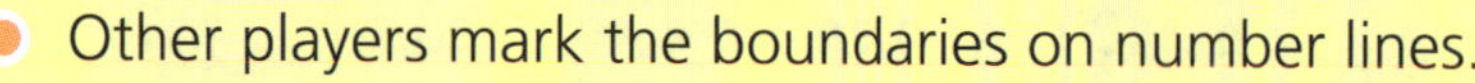

 • *AUSTRALIAN SIGNPOST MATHS NSW 3* • ISBN 9780655709046

Numbers to 1000

8	hundreds	3	tens	4	ones
83	tens	4	ones		

1 Position these numbers where they belong on each number line.

a 20 40 — number line: 5, 10

b 30 60 — number line: 5, 10

c 25 50 — number line: 5, 10

d 35 70 — number line: 5, 10

2 Complete each pattern and write the rule.

a 330, 340, 350, ____, ____, ____, ____, ____ Rule: ____

b 780, 770, 760, ____, ____, ____, ____, ____ Rule: ____

c 277, 377, 477, ____, ____, ____, ____, ____ Rule: ____

d 956, 856, 756, ____, ____, ____, ____, ____ Rule: ____

e 268, 278, 288, ____, ____, ____, ____, ____ Rule: ____

3 863 can be written as 86 tens and 3 ones. Partition these numbers in the same way.

a 472 ____ **b** 529 ____

c 836 ____ **d** 547 ____

637 can be partitioned and written as:

- 6 hundreds and 37 ones — 6 hundreds 3 7 ones
- 63 tens and 7 ones — 6 3 tens 7 ones
- 637 ones — 6 3 7 ones

4 Write these numbers in three different ways using partitioning.

a 561

____

____

____

b 937

____

____

____

Number and algebra

1:10 Fractions of a group

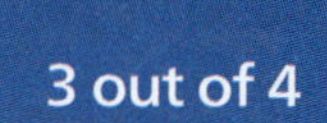
$\frac{2}{4}$ 2 out of 4
$\frac{3}{4}$ 3 out of 4

CONCEPT

We can put groups into a line to help us find the fraction of the group.

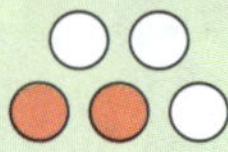 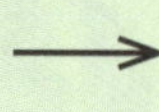 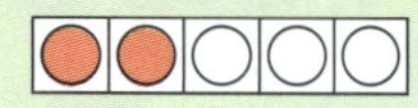  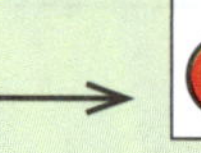   

2 out of 5 are coloured. That's $\frac{2}{5}$.

3 out of 6 are coloured. That's $\frac{3}{6}$ or $\frac{1}{2}$.

1

Group	Number coloured	Total in group	Fraction coloured
			$\frac{4}{5}$

2

a 
fraction coloured ☐ fraction not coloured ☐

b 
fraction coloured ☐ fraction not coloured ☐

c 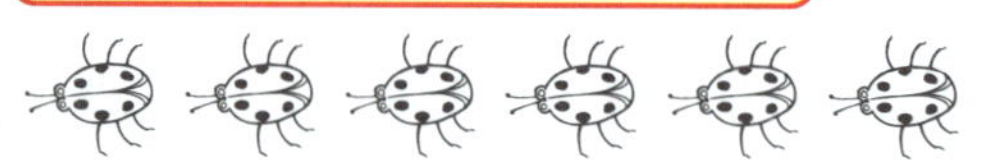
fraction coloured ☐ fraction not coloured ☐

d
fraction coloured ☐ fraction not coloured ☐

e
fraction coloured ☐ fraction not coloured ☐

f
fraction coloured ☐ fraction not coloured ☐

3 Colour part of each group to match the fraction.

$\frac{2}{5}$ and $\frac{3}{5}$ makes 1 whole.

a 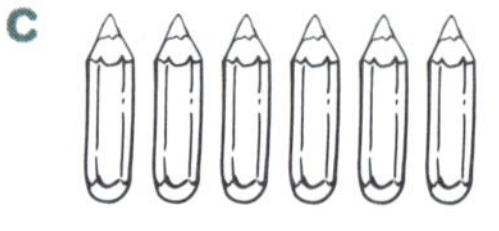 $\frac{3}{4}$

b     $\frac{7}{8}$

c 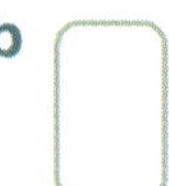 $\frac{5}{6}$

d   $\frac{2}{5}$

e $\frac{3}{3}$

4 What fraction of these groups in Question 3 is not coloured?

a ☐ b ☐ c ☐ d ☐

1:11 Fractions of a whole

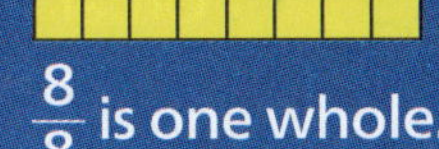

$\frac{8}{8}$ is one whole. $\frac{3}{8}$ $\frac{7}{8}$

The **d**enominator is written **d**own on the bottom.

1 How much of each shape has been coloured?

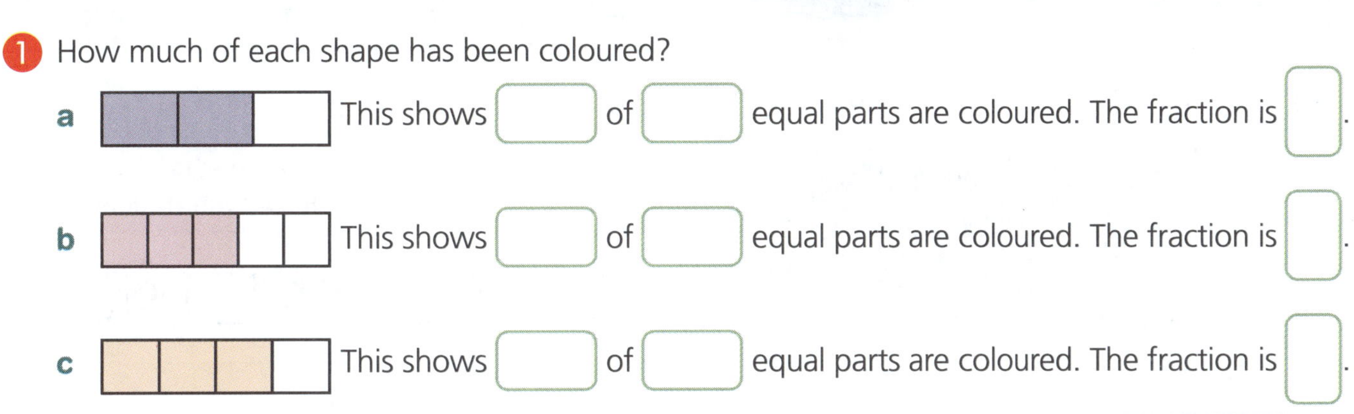

a This shows ☐ of ☐ equal parts are coloured. The fraction is ☐.

b This shows ☐ of ☐ equal parts are coloured. The fraction is ☐.

c This shows ☐ of ☐ equal parts are coloured. The fraction is ☐.

2 What fraction of each shape has been coloured?

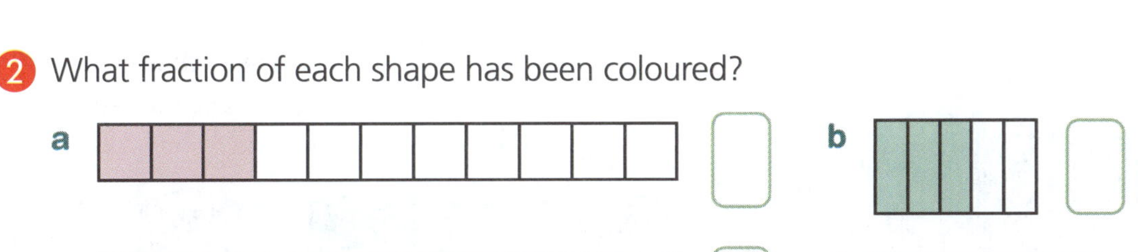

a ☐ b ☐

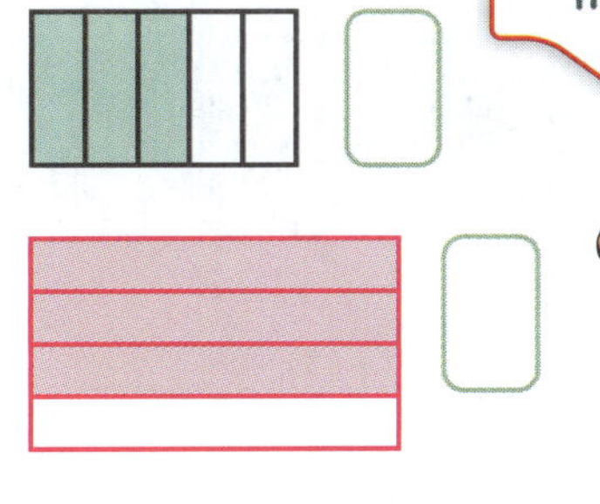

c ☐ d ☐

Fractions are not whole numbers.

3 Colour part of each shape to match the fraction.

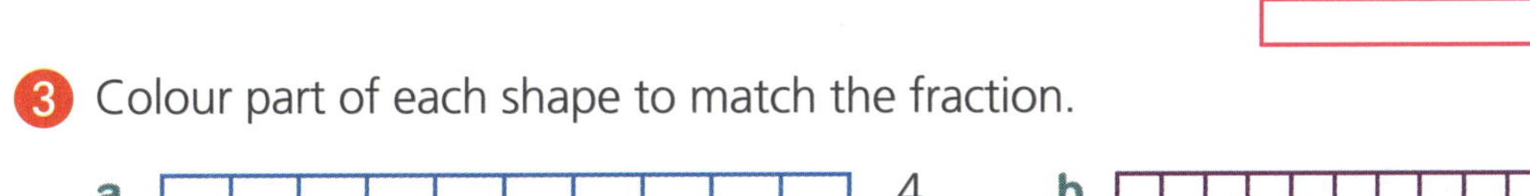

a $\frac{4}{10}$ b $\frac{8}{10}$

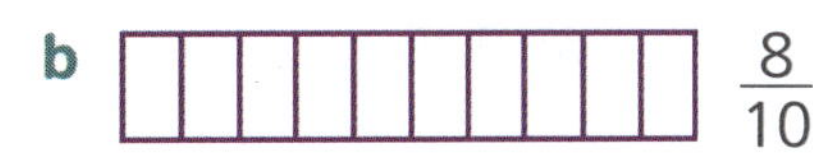
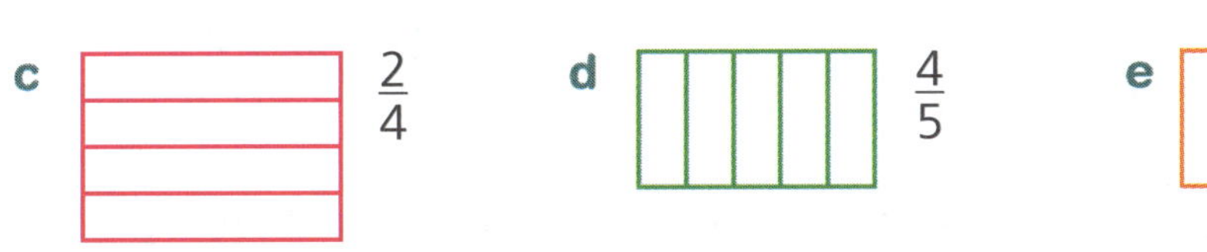
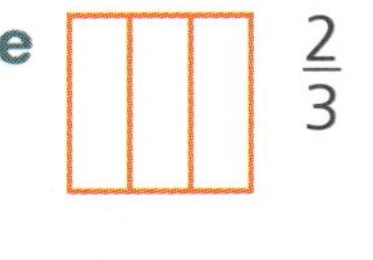

c $\frac{2}{4}$ d $\frac{4}{5}$ e $\frac{2}{3}$

Make thirds of a length

- Cut 3 equal lengths of paper.
- Stick the ends together without gaps or overlaps.
- Label each third with $\frac{1}{3}$. Colour $\frac{1}{3}$ of your length.

You could use paper to make fifths of a length too.

1:12 Numbers to 10 000

Order from smallest (1) to largest (3).

100
10 000
1000

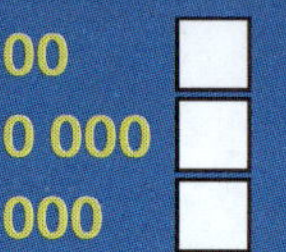

CONCEPT

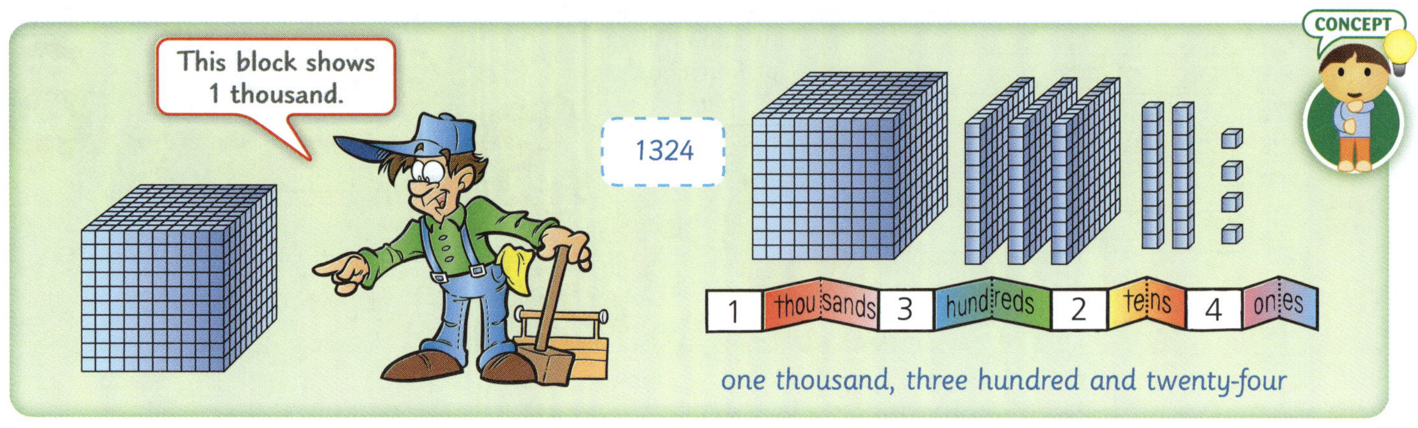

1 Write the numeral, fill in the numeral expander and write the number in words.

2 How many digits are in each numeral?

a 39 ____	b 1307 ____	c 9 ____	d 85 ____
e 1000 ____	f 99 ____	g 2469 ____	h 1325 ____

FUN SPOT

Digit game

- Each player uses 4 numeral cards to make a number on a place-value chart.
- Players get one numeral card at a time. Before they can see the next card, they must put the card they have onto the place-value chart.
- The player with the largest number at the end wins.

Thousand	Hundreds	Tens	Ones
6	4	3	0

 ISBN 9780655709046

Numbers to 10 000

Why would we use 'U' for 'units' instead of 'O' for 'ones'?

CONCEPT

1. Write the number shown as a numeral.

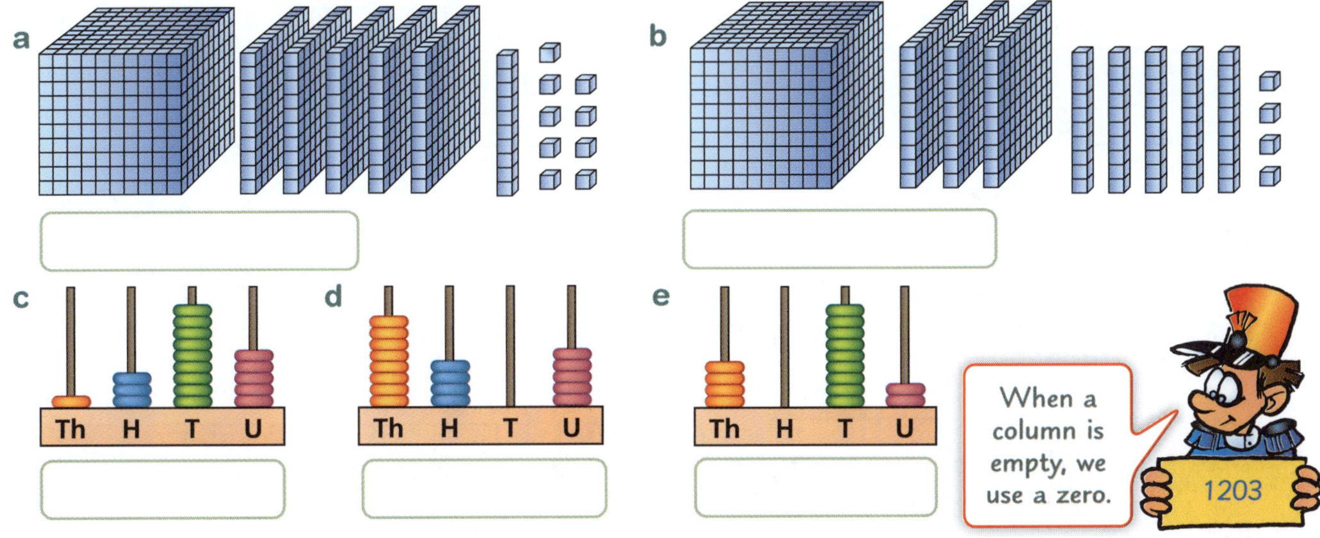

2. Write the numeral for each number.
   - a five thousand, eight hundred and thirty-seven
   - b six thousand, nine hundred and two
   - c four thousand, one hundred and eighty-nine

3. Circle the larger number.
   - a 1365 or 2547
   - b 3128 or 4263
   - c 5409 or 4149
   - d 2157 or 2010
   - e 4312 or 4196
   - f 7256 or 10 000

Comparing numbers

1. Compare the digits in the largest column.
2. If these are the same, compare digits in the next column on the right.

INVESTIGATION

- This is **one thousand, one hundred and eleven**

100 is ten

1000 is ten

1111 is 11 hundreds and 11.

1:14 Fractions

How many hamburgers are in $\frac{3}{4}$ of my group?

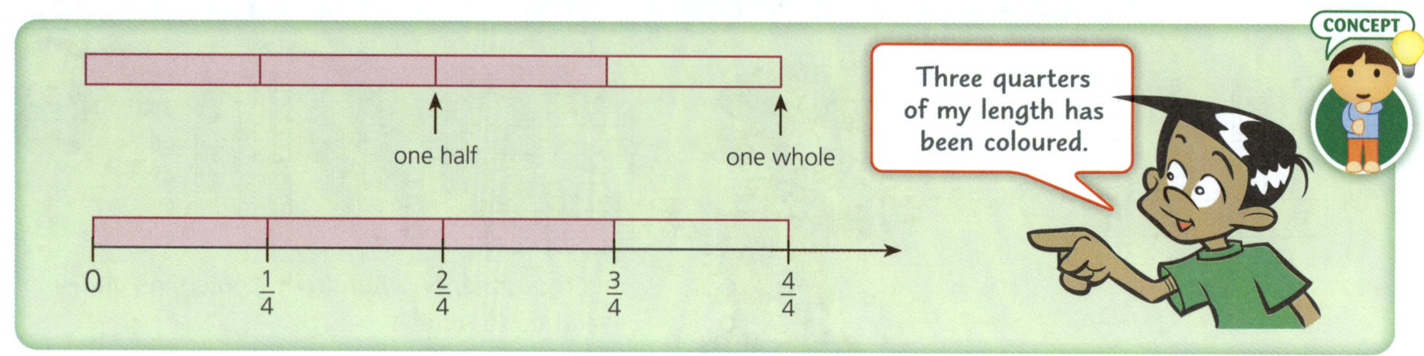

1 Colour the fraction given for each strip.

a 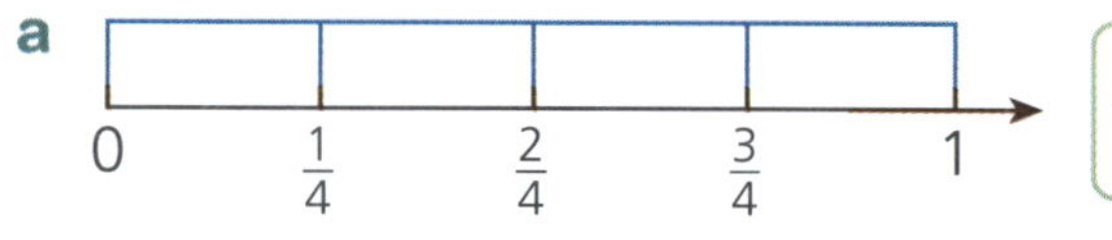 $\frac{2}{4}$

b 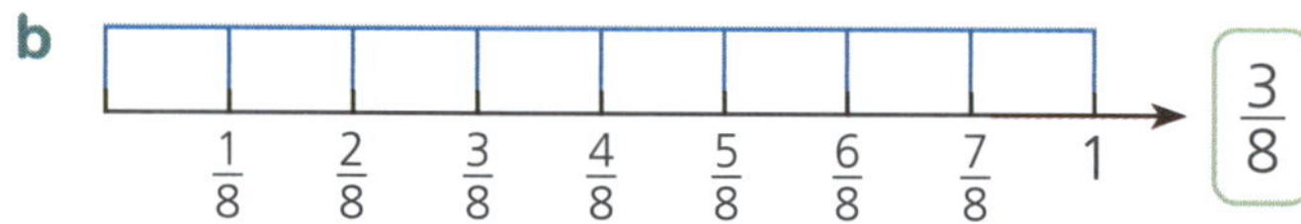 $\frac{3}{8}$

c 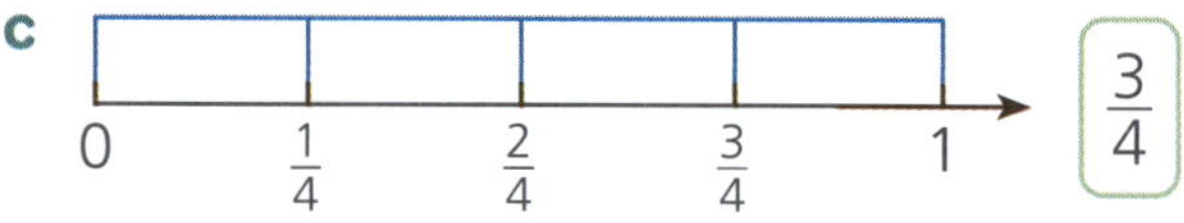 $\frac{3}{4}$

d 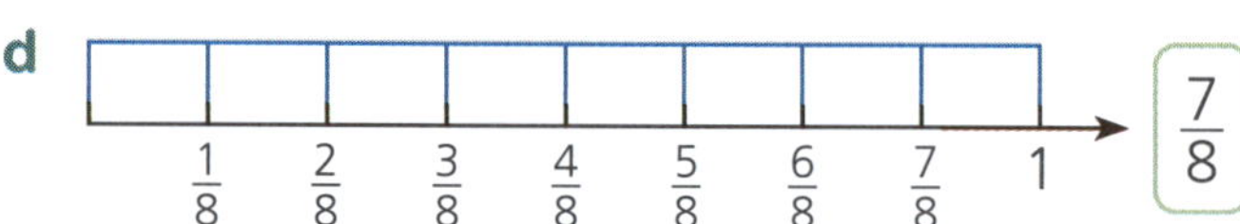 $\frac{7}{8}$

e 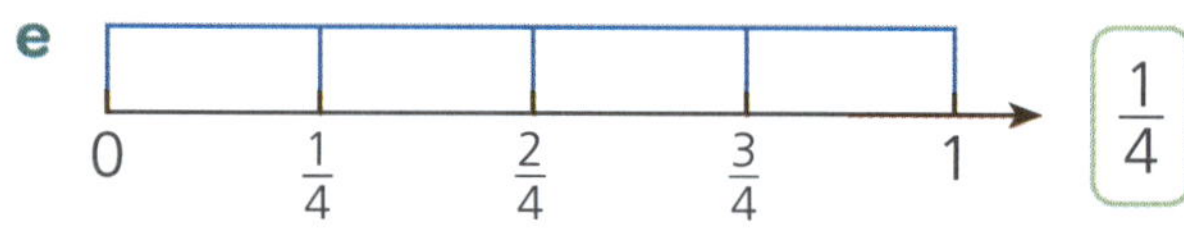 $\frac{1}{4}$

f 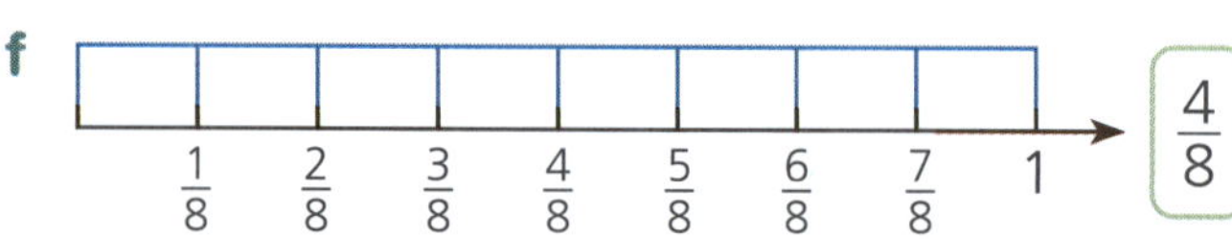 $\frac{4}{8}$

g 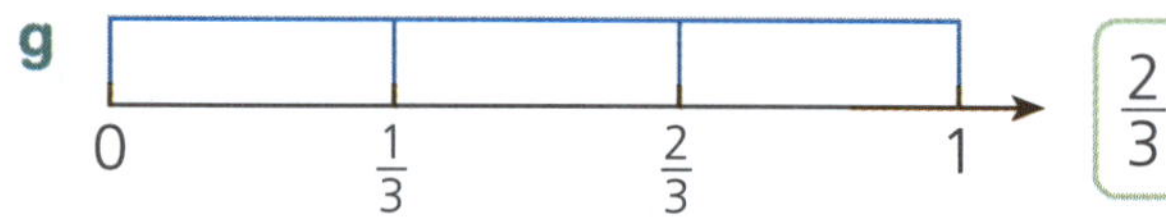 $\frac{2}{3}$

h 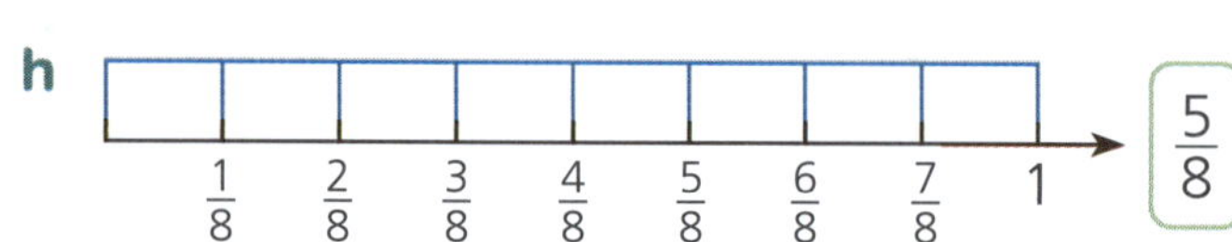 $\frac{5}{8}$

2 Write the fraction that is not coloured in each part of Question 2.

a  **b**  **c**  **d**  **e**  **f**  **g**  **h** 

3 Colour the fraction given for each strip.

a 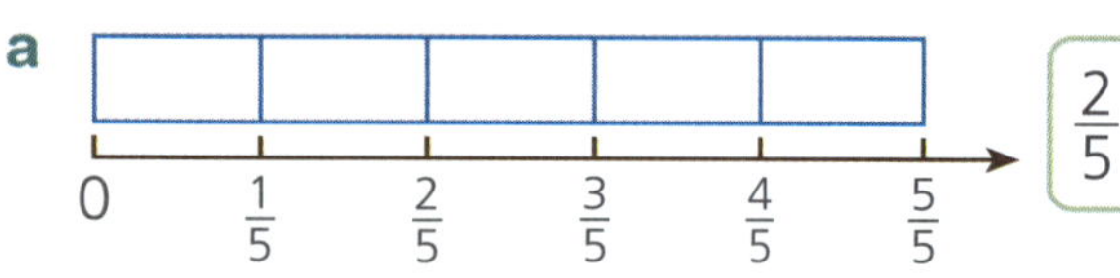 $\frac{2}{5}$

b 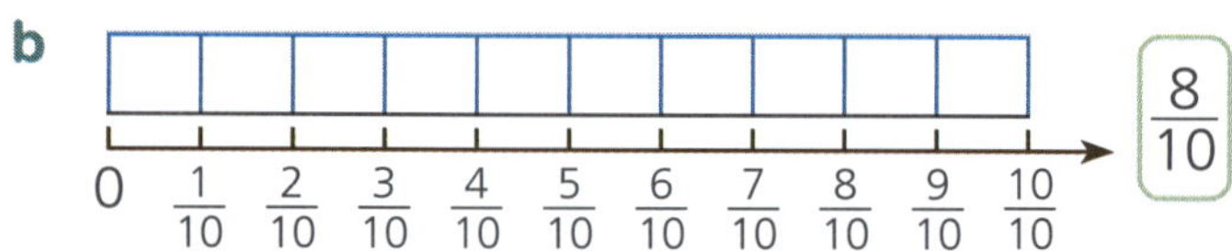 $\frac{8}{10}$

c 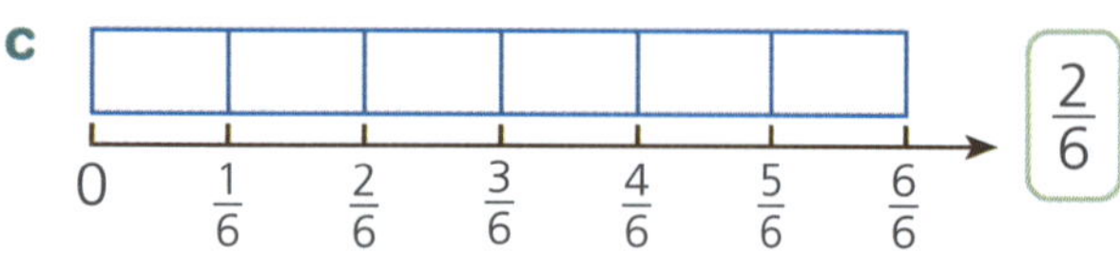 $\frac{2}{6}$

d 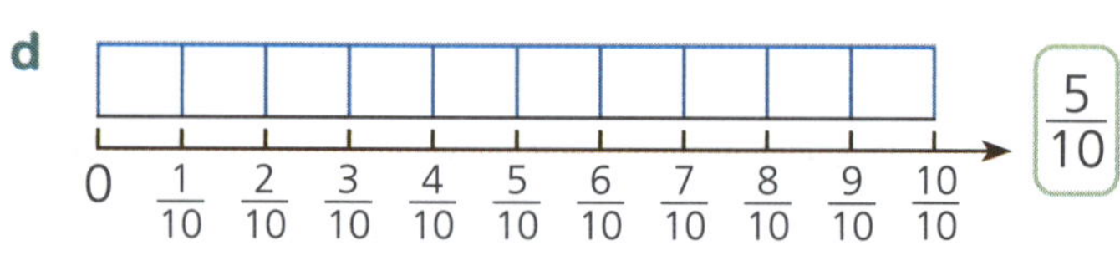 $\frac{5}{10}$

4 Write the missing fractions for these bars.

a 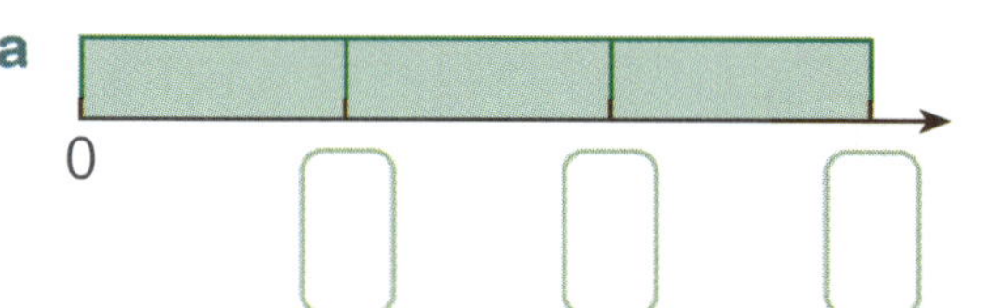

b 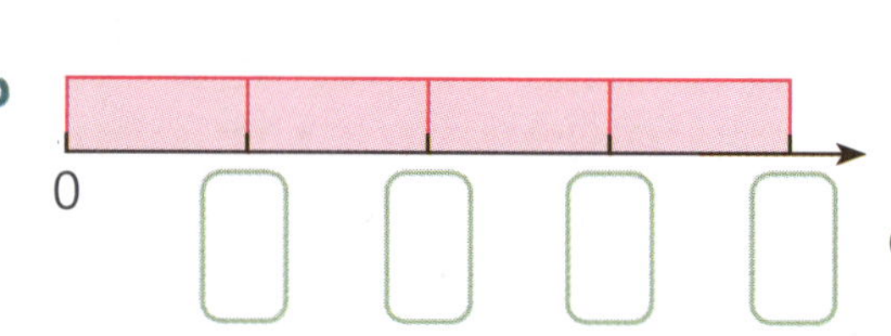

 • *AUSTRALIAN SIGNPOST MATHS NSW 3* • ISBN 9780655709046

Fractions

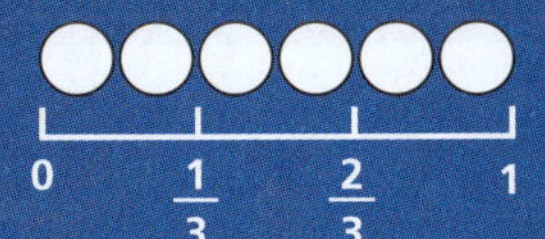

How many balls are in $\frac{2}{3}$ of my group?

1 Colour the fraction given for each strip.

a 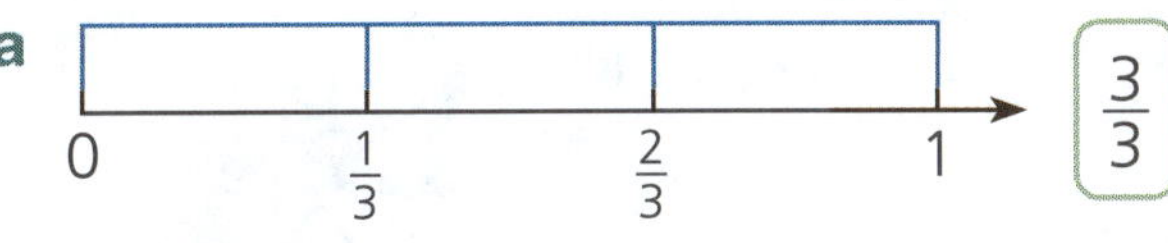

b 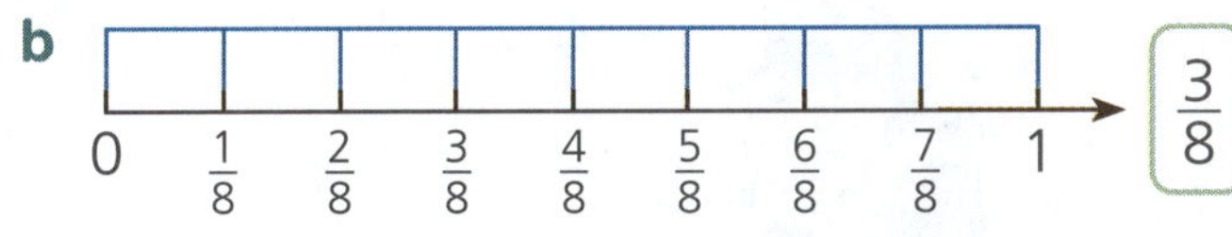

c 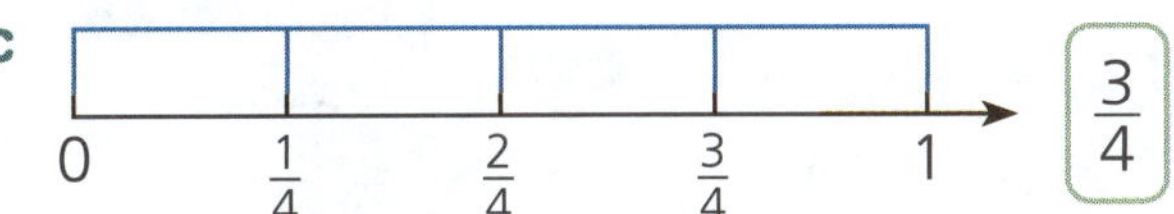

d 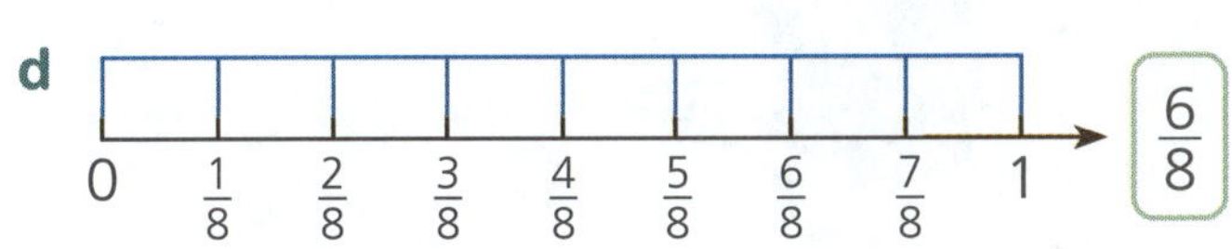

2 Write the fraction that is not coloured in each part of Question 1.

a  b 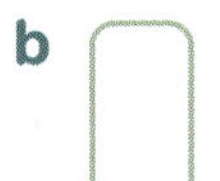 c 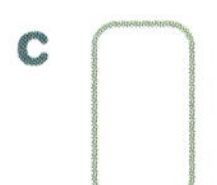 d 

3 Write the missing fractions for these lengths.

a 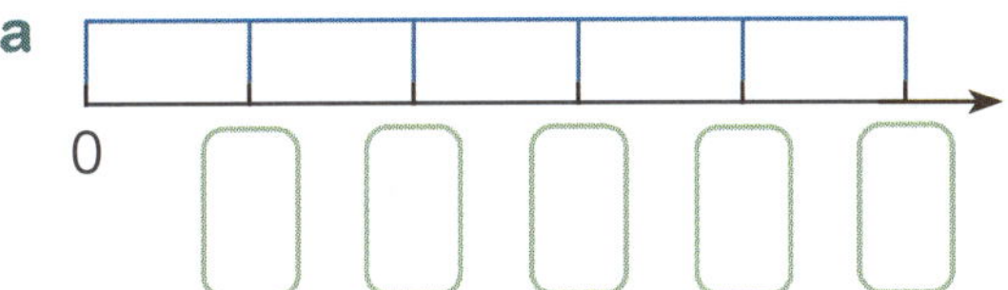

b 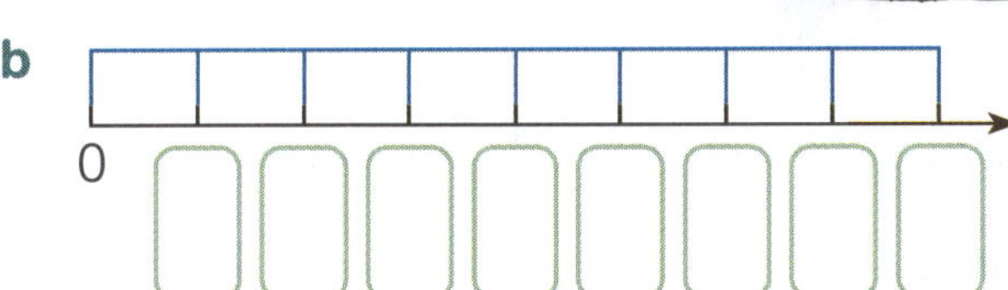

4 I have coloured part of each strip. What fraction do I need to colour to make 1?

a 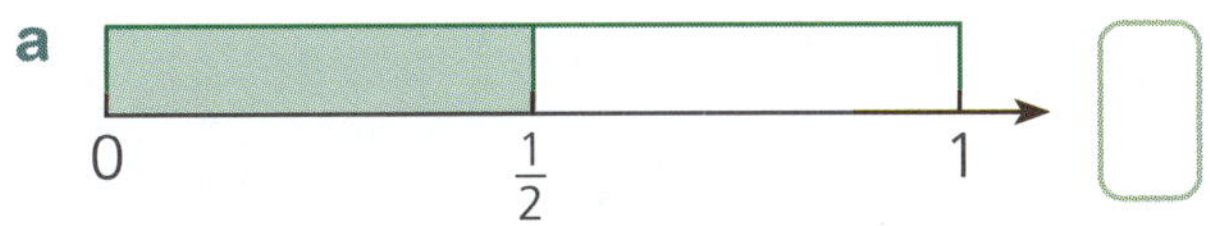

b 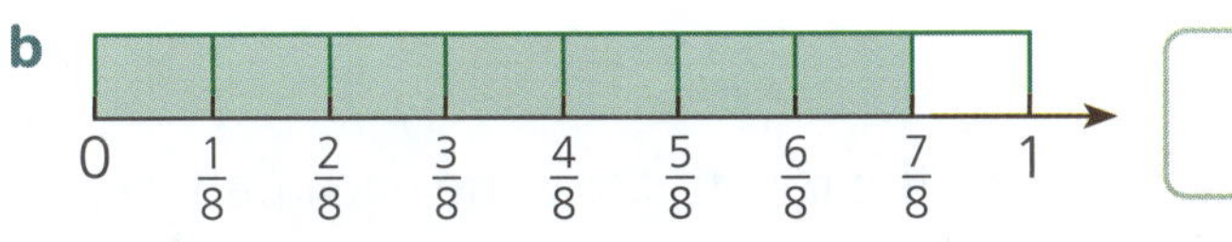

c 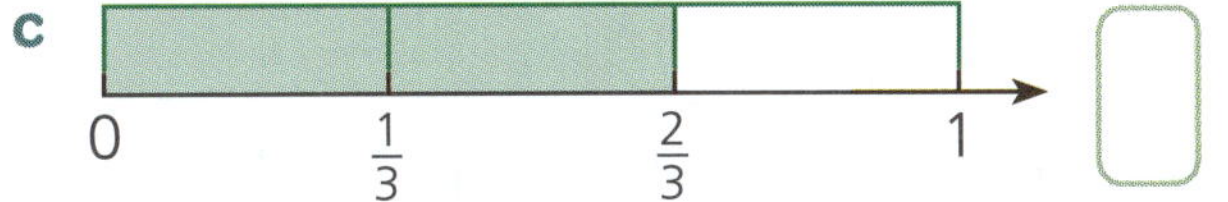

d 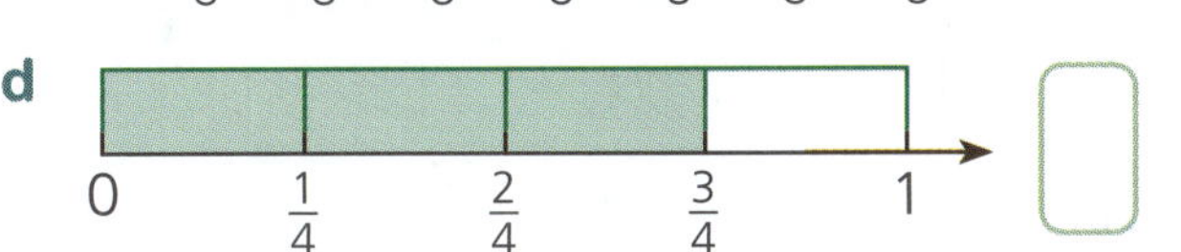

5 Only a fraction of each strip of paper is shown. Draw the rest to show the whole length.

a 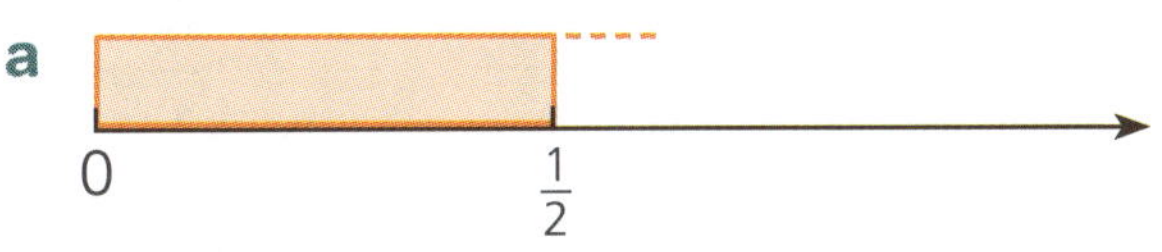

b 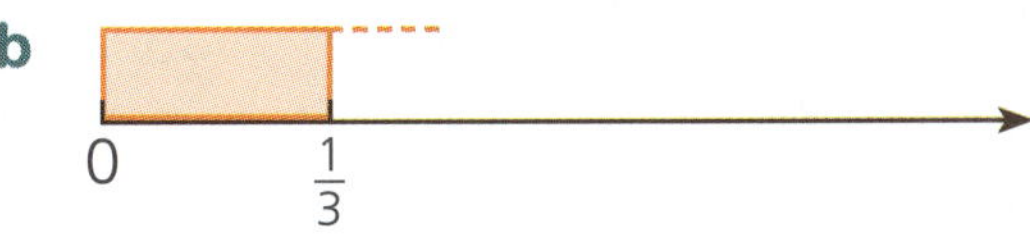

c 

d 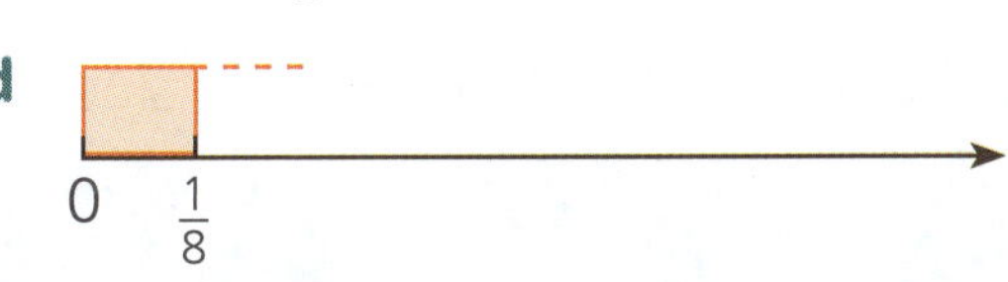

6 I have 8 counters in a row. 

a If I remove 2, what fraction have I taken? ☐ What fraction do I have left? ☐

b If I remove 4, what fraction have I taken? ☐ What fraction do I have left? ☐

1:16 What's the rule?

11, 11 + 3, 14 + 3, 17 + 3, ...
11, 14, 17, 20, ...

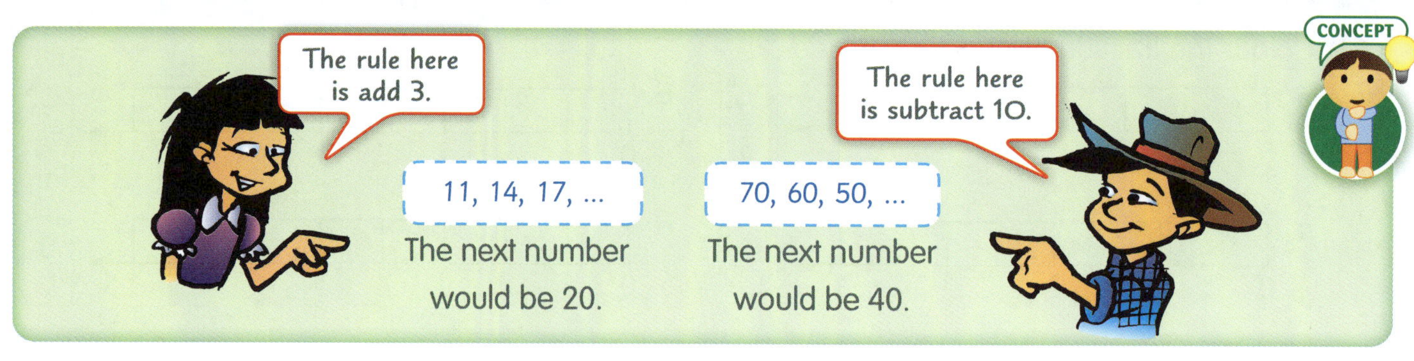

1. Write the next number in each pattern.

a 1, 3, 5, …		**b** 7, 10, 13, …		**c** 10, 20, 30, …	
d 20, 16, 12, …		**e** 33, 32, 31, …		**f** 44, 33, 22, …	
g 10, 14, 18, …		**h** 75, 70, 65, …		**i** 38, 46, 54, …	

2. Write the rule for each pattern in Question 1.

a		**b**		**c**	
d		**e**		**f**	
g		**h**		**i**	

3. Follow the rule to continue each pattern.

a	Add 6.	21, ___, ___, ___	**b**	Subtract 1.	41, ___, ___, ___
c	Subtract 2.	74, ___, ___, ___	**d**	Add 8.	34, ___, ___, ___
e	Add 20.	23, ___, ___, ___	**f**	Subtract 4.	40, ___, ___, ___
g	Multiply by 2.	3, ___, ___, ___	**h**	Add 15.	5, ___, ___, ___
i	Subtract 10.	63, ___, ___, ___	**j**	Multiply by 2.	1, ___, ___, ___

4. Write the pattern for the number of sides, then write the rule.

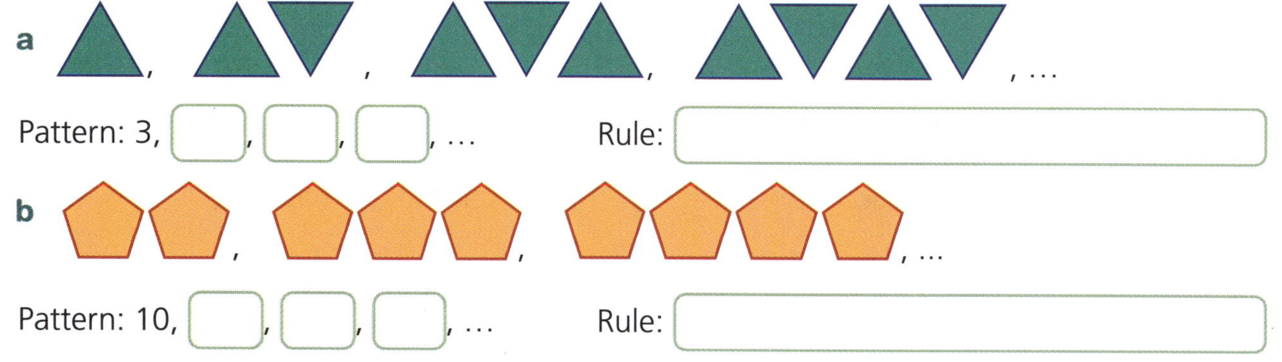

a Pattern: 3, ___, ___, ___, … Rule: ______

b Pattern: 10, ___, ___, ___, … Rule: ______

 • *AUSTRALIAN SIGNPOST MATHS NSW 3* • ISBN 9780655709046

1:17 Number patterns

10, 8, 6, 4, 2, 0
The rule is take away 2.

1 Complete each number pattern and discuss the rule for each.

a 2, 4, 6, ___, ___, ___, ___, ___, ___, ___

b 4, 8, 12, ___, ___, ___, ___, ___, ___, ___

c 5, 10, 15, ___, ___, ___, ___, ___, ___, ___

These are the multiples of 2, 4 and 5.

2 Write the first five numbers in each number pattern and discuss the rule for each.

a Start at 423 and count by tens. ___, ___, ___, ___, ___

b Start at 423 and count by hundreds. ___, ___, ___, ___, ___

c Start at 1220 and count by tens. ___, ___, ___, ___, ___

d Start at 1220 and count by hundreds. ___, ___, ___, ___, ___

3 Count by fives and circle each number you count.
Count by tens and draw an X on each number you count.
Count by fours and colour each number you count.
Discuss the pattern formed by the circles, Xs and colour.

1	2	3	4	5	6	7	8	9	10
11	12	13	14	15	16	17	18	19	20
21	22	23	24	25	26	27	28	29	30
31	32	33	34	35	36	37	38	39	40
41	42	43	44	45	46	47	48	49	50
51	52	53	54	55	56	57	58	59	60

4 Describe each number pattern.

a 125, 130, 135, 140

b 790, 690, 590, 490

ICT

- Press these keys on a calculator:

5 + + =

- Keep pressing the = key and record the answers.
- Clear the calculator and repeat the exercise, but this time press:

7 + + 10 =

Discuss your answers.

 • *AUSTRALIAN SIGNPOST MATHS NSW 3* • ISBN 9780655709046

1:18 Numbers to 10 000

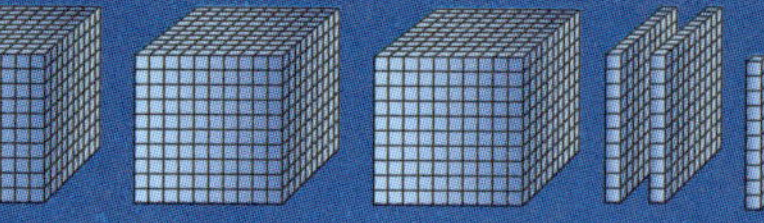

1 Write the number shown.

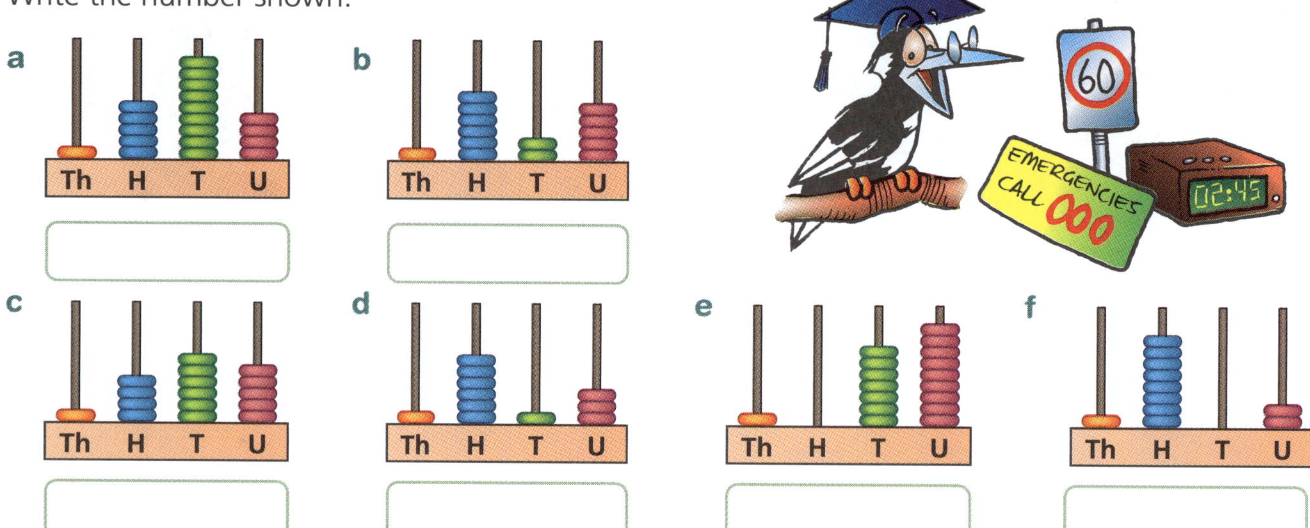

2 Write the numeral, fill in the numeral expander and write the number in words.

3 How many digits are in each number?

a 147 ___ b 21 ___ c 1945 ___ d 439 ___

4 Complete these patterns.

a 980, 990, 1000, ___, ___, ___, ___, ___, ___

b 4340, 4350, 4360, ___, 4380, 4390, ___, 4410, ___, ___

c 7605, 7705, 7805, ___, ___, 8105, 8205, 8305, ___, ___

d 1423, 1323, 1223, ___, ___, ___, ___, ___, ___

5 Write the number after:

a 346 ___ b 679 ___ c 999 ___ d 1316 ___

e 4876 ___ f 3207 ___ g 2649 ___ h 3640 ___

i 2199 ___ j 5010 ___ k 9999 ___ l 1001 ___

 • *AUSTRALIAN SIGNPOST MATHS NSW 3* • ISBN 9780655709046

Place value to 10 000

3800 is closer to 4000 than to 3000.
3400 is closer to 3000 than to 4000.

CONCEPT

1720 is the same as
17 hundreds and 2 tens,
or 17 hundreds and 20 ones,
or 172 tens.

1 Complete the numeral expanders.

a 1479

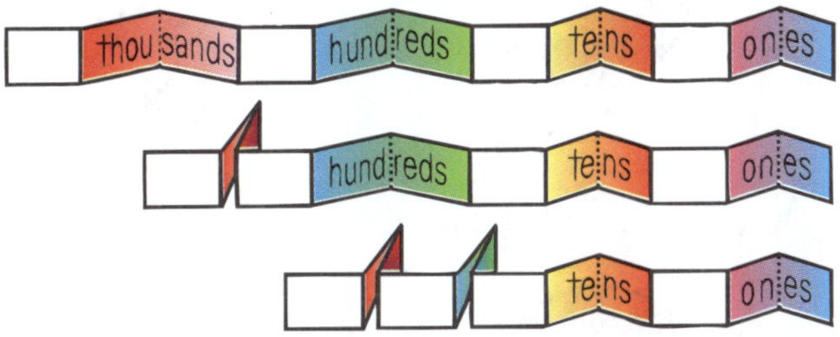

☐ thousands ☐ hundreds ☐ tens ☐ ones
☐ ☐ hundreds ☐ tens ☐ ones
☐ ☐ ☐ tens ☐ ones

b 3568

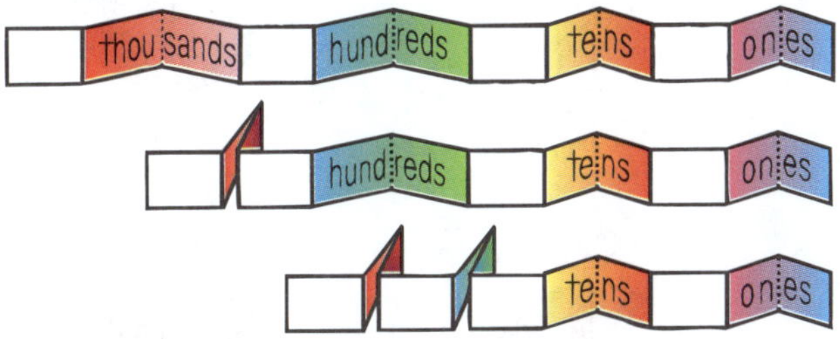

☐ thousands ☐ hundreds ☐ tens ☐ ones
☐ ☐ hundreds ☐ tens ☐ ones
☐ ☐ ☐ tens ☐ ones

c 4231

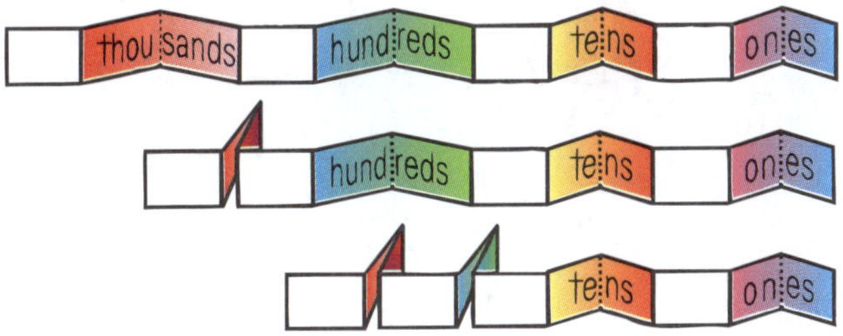

☐ thousands ☐ hundreds ☐ tens ☐ ones
☐ ☐ hundreds ☐ tens ☐ ones
☐ ☐ ☐ tens ☐ ones

d 2307

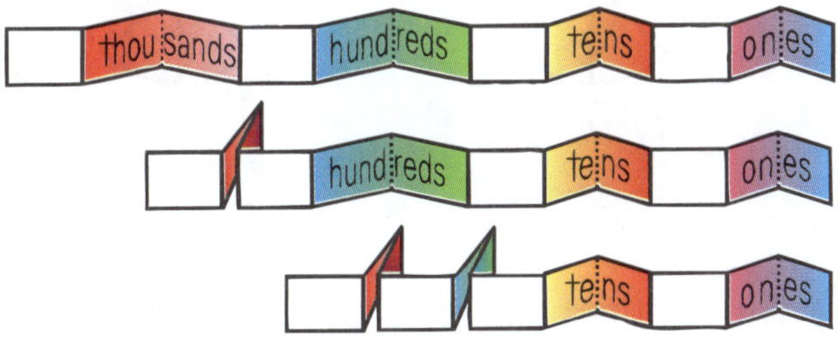

☐ thousands ☐ hundreds ☐ tens ☐ ones
☐ ☐ hundreds ☐ tens ☐ ones
☐ ☐ ☐ tens ☐ ones

2 Write the numeral for each number.

a five thousand, seven hundred and sixty-three ☐

b eight thousand, nine hundred and fifty-six ☐

c six thousand, two hundred and seventy-five ☐

d four thousand, six hundred and forty-nine ☐

e nine thousand, five hundred and eighty-two ☐

3 Write each number in words.

a 6824 ☐

b 2319 ☐

4 Round each number to the nearest thousand.

a 4695 ☐ **b** 3126 ☐ **c** 9538 ☐

Fractions with circles

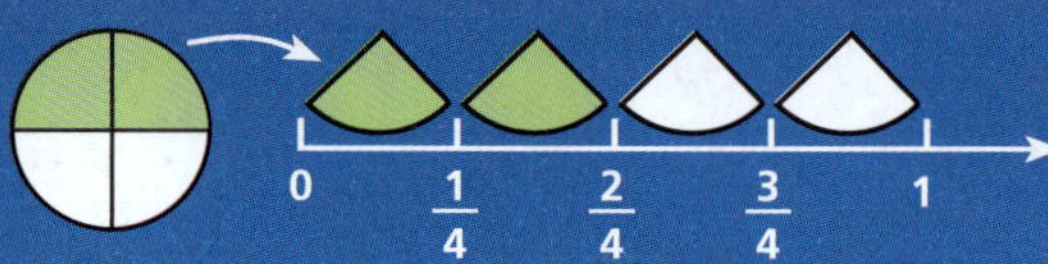

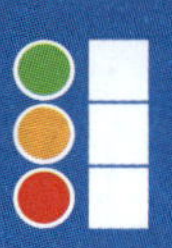

1 Write each fraction, then circle the smallest fraction in each row.

1 out of 6.
That's $\frac{1}{6}$.

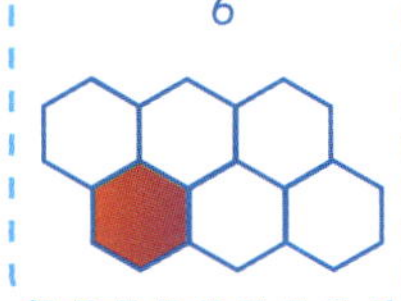

a
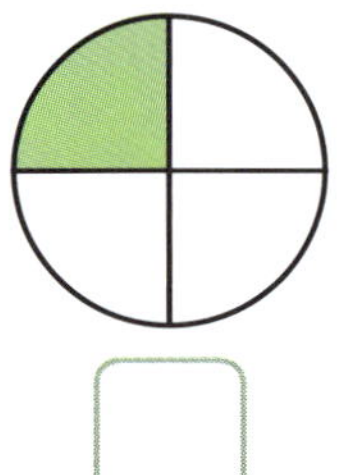

b
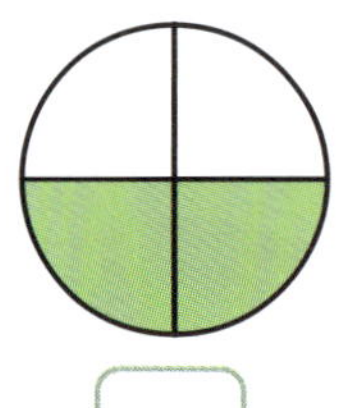

c
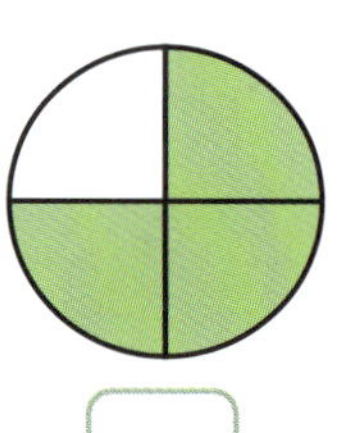

d
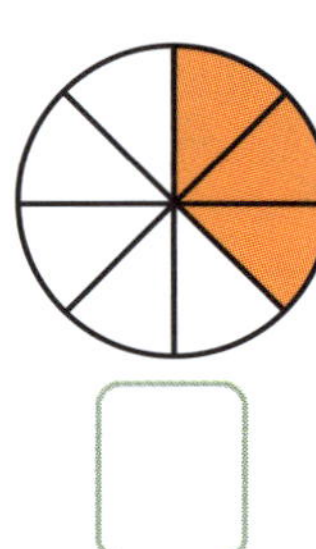

e
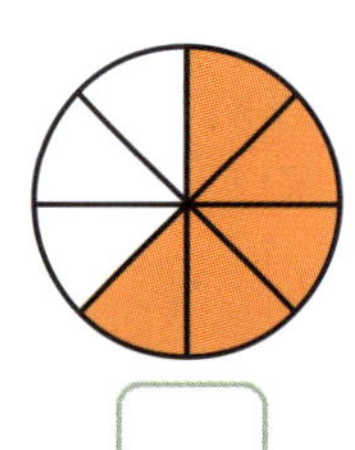

f
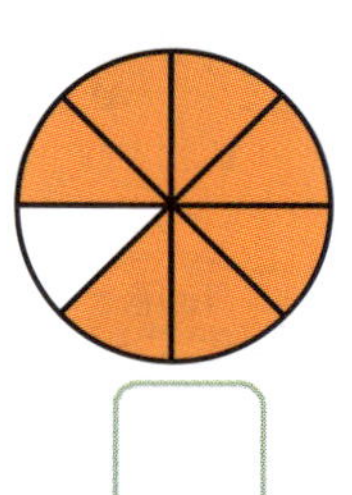

We can compare fractions of shapes if the shapes are the same.

Quarter past, quarter to, half past... We use fractions with clocks!

2 The minute hand starts at 12 and turns clockwise. What fraction of a full turn has the minute hand made when it is pointing to the:

a 3? 

b 6? 

c 9?

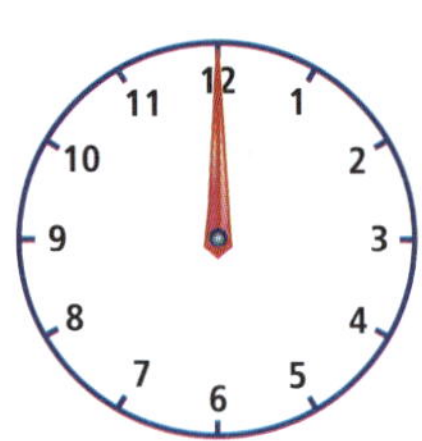

INVESTIGATION

- Show how you would share these cakes equally among the guests.

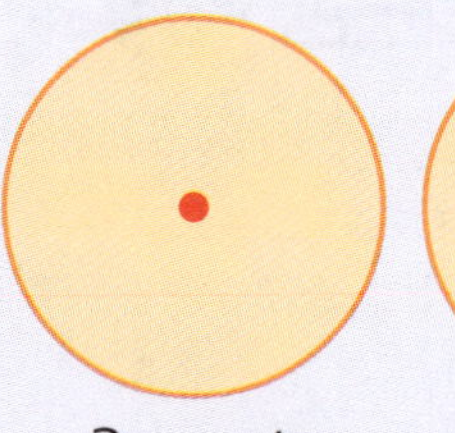
3 guests

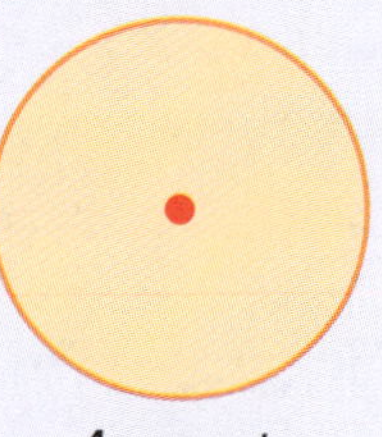
4 guests

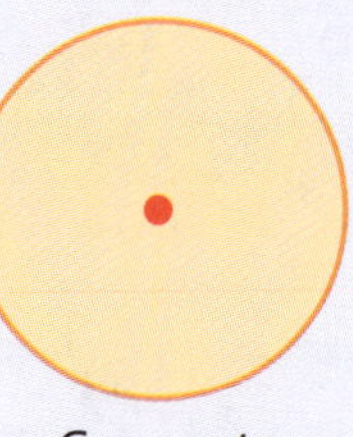
6 guests

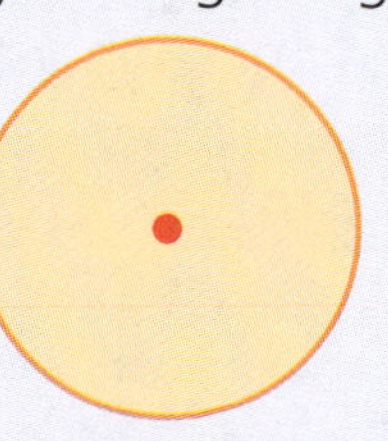
8 guests

Circle *smaller* or *larger*.

The more guests there are, the *smaller / larger* the pieces will be.

1:21 Using fractions

Four quarters of a pizza makes a whole pizza.

1 Divide each picture to match the number of parts.

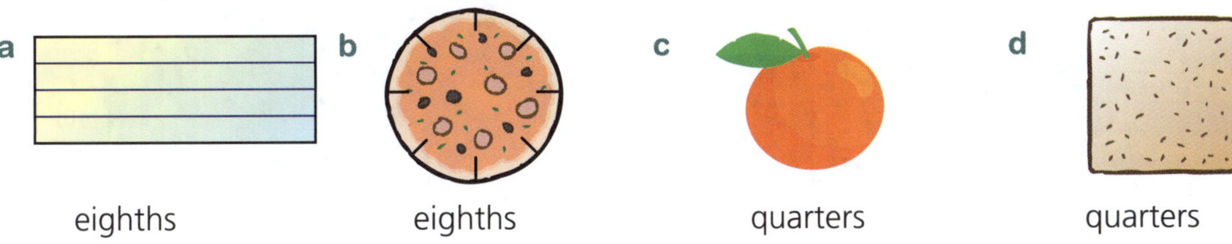

a eighths b eighths c quarters d quarters

2 Colour the time it would take to run the laps. One lap takes 5 minutes (shown in part **a**).

a 9 laps b 3 laps c 6 laps d 12 laps

3 Write the number of quarter-pizzas that would be in:

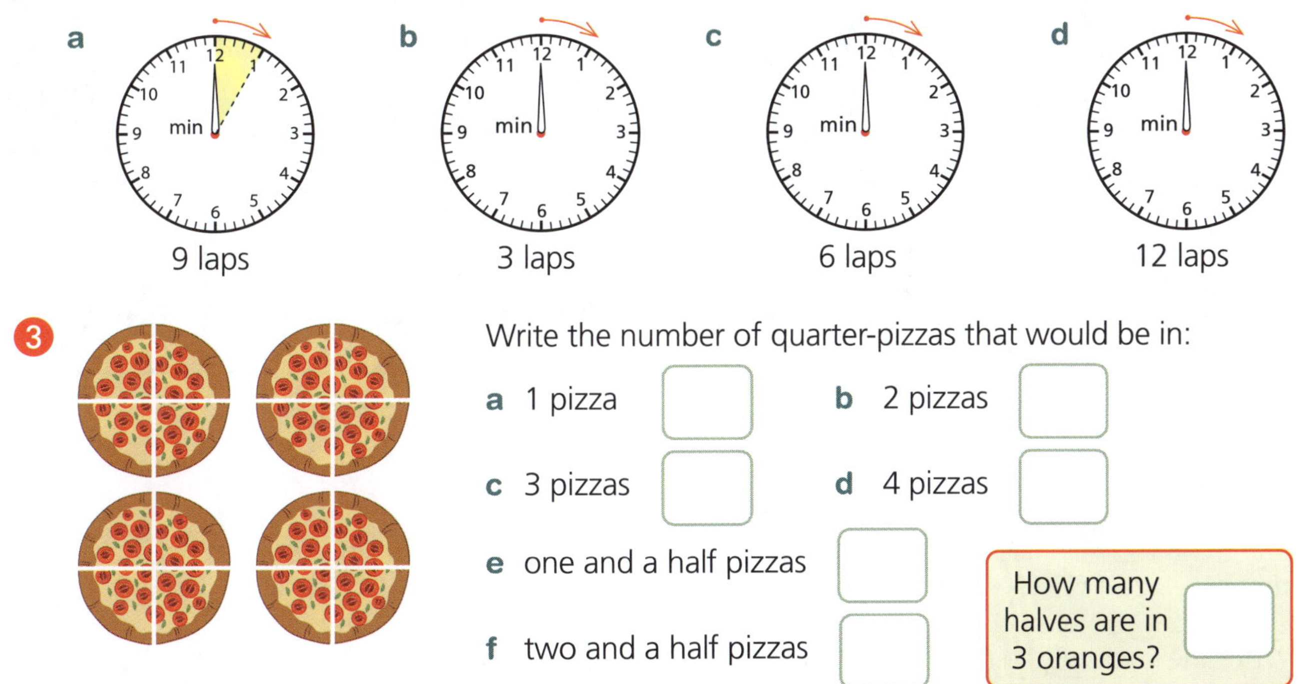

a 1 pizza ☐ **b** 2 pizzas ☐

c 3 pizzas ☐ **d** 4 pizzas ☐

e one and a half pizzas ☐

f two and a half pizzas ☐

How many halves are in 3 oranges? ☐

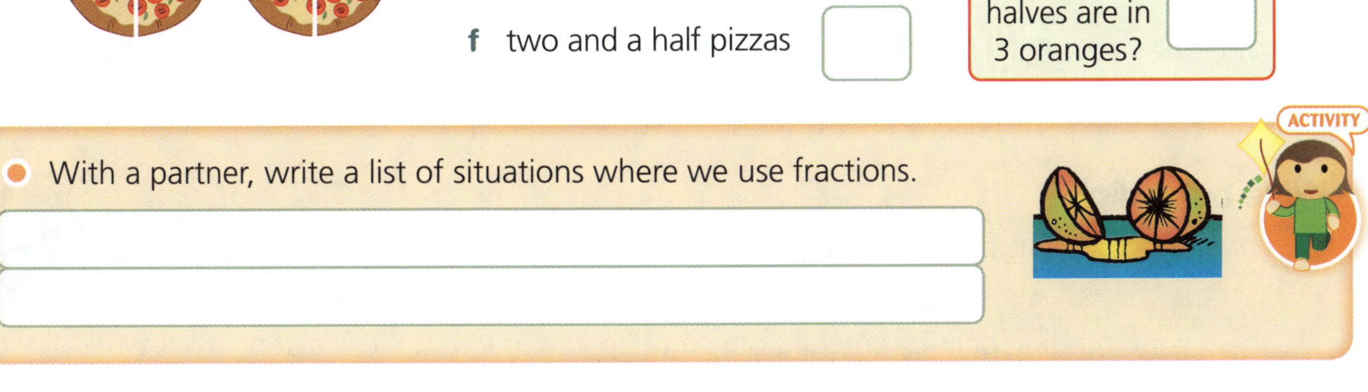

- With a partner, write a list of situations where we use fractions.

 • *AUSTRALIAN SIGNPOST MATHS NSW 3* • ISBN 9780655709046

Numbers to 10 000

1 Write the number shown.

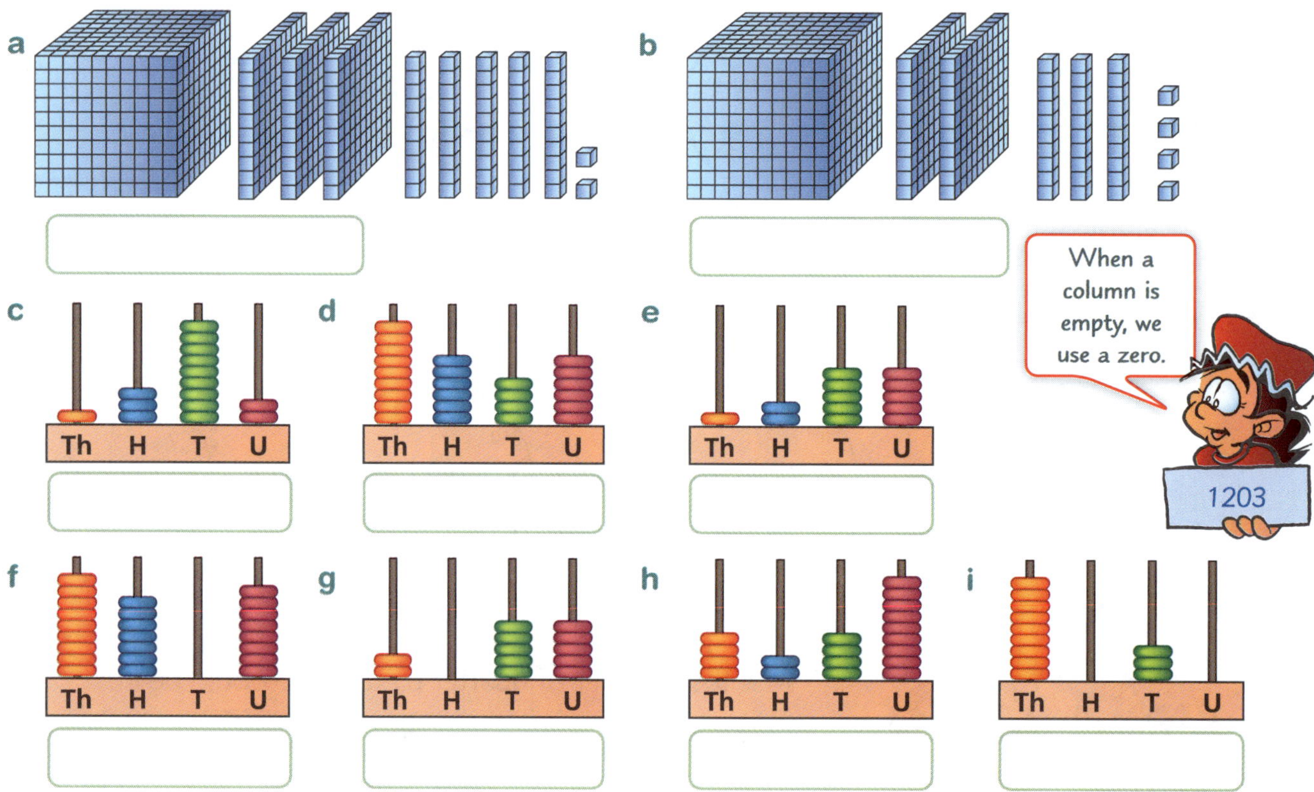

2 Circle the largest number in each group.

a 327, 237, 723 **b** 569, 669, 965 **c** 631, 613, 603

d 1246, 1264, 1216 **e** 2375, 2735, 2753 **f** 4194, 4094, 4049

3 Write the value of the 6 in each number.

a 3659 **b** 6125 **c** 4968

Wipe out a digit

- Enter a 4-digit number into a calculator.
- Your partner selects any digit to be **wiped out** – that is, changed to zero.
- Try to wipe out that digit by entering only **one** operation into the calculator. Did it work?
- Take turns with your partner. Score 1 point for each successful wipe out.

1:23 Numbers to 10 000

9076 = 9000 + 70 + 6

9 thousands, 7 tens and 6 ones

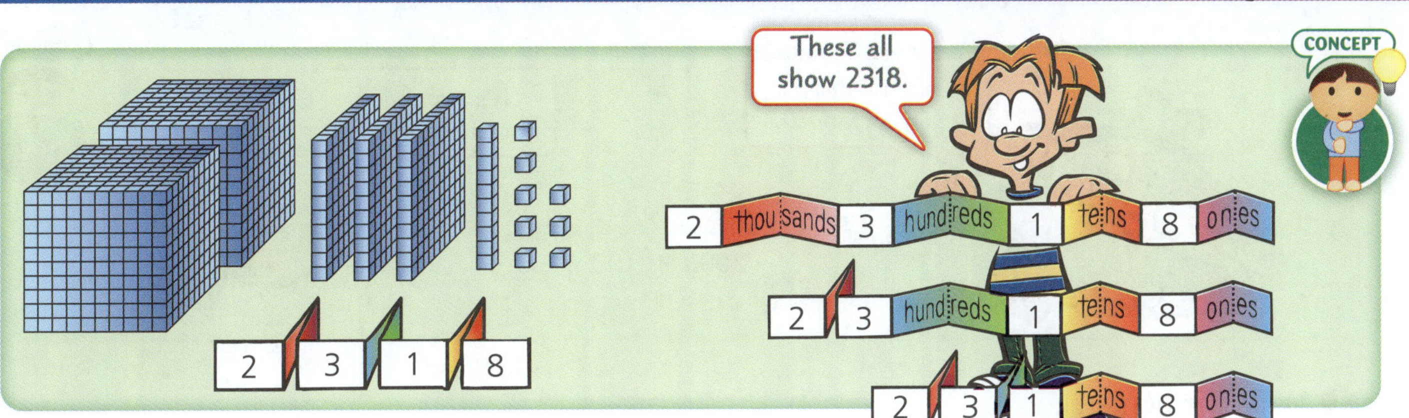

1 Complete the numeral expanders.

a 1764

b 3795

c 4013

d 9658

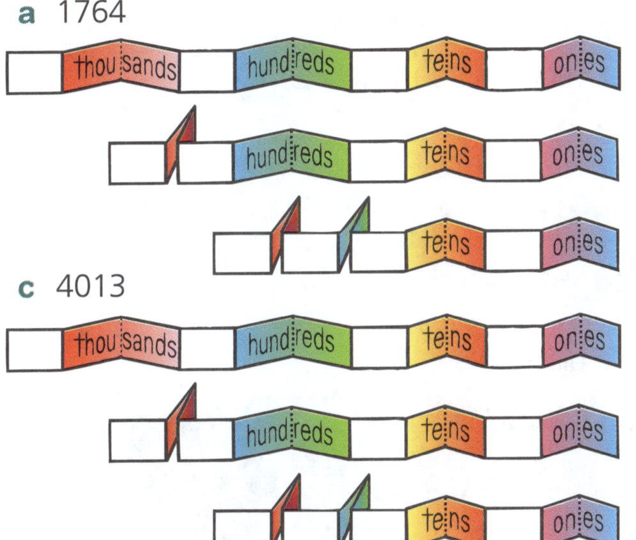

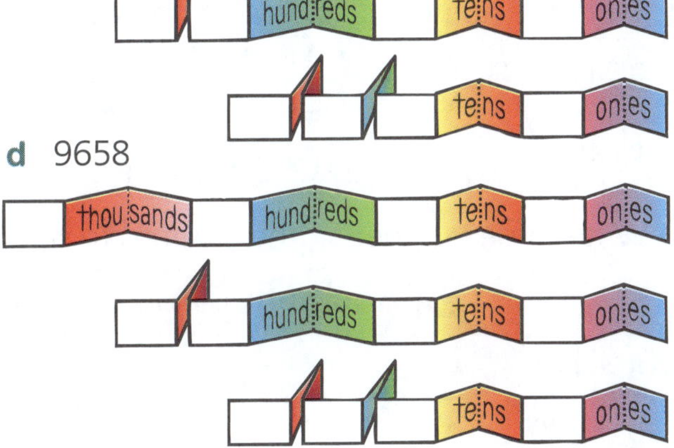

2 How many hundreds could be taken from each number?

a 1576 ☐ b 1253 ☐ c 2301 ☐

d 6192 ☐ e 7471 ☐ f 9368 ☐

3 How many tens could be taken from each number?

a 1742 ☐ b 1624 ☐

c 4906 ☐ d 7264 ☐

4 Write the numeral.

a one thousand, two hundred and ten ☐

b five thousand, six hundred and forty-one ☐

c six thousand, three hundred and one ☐

d two thousand, five hundred and sixteen ☐

5 a 3000 = ☐ tens

= ☐ hundreds

b 700 = ☐ tens

= ☐ hundreds

Expanded notation

2100 = 2000 + 100
2130 = 2000 + 100 + 30

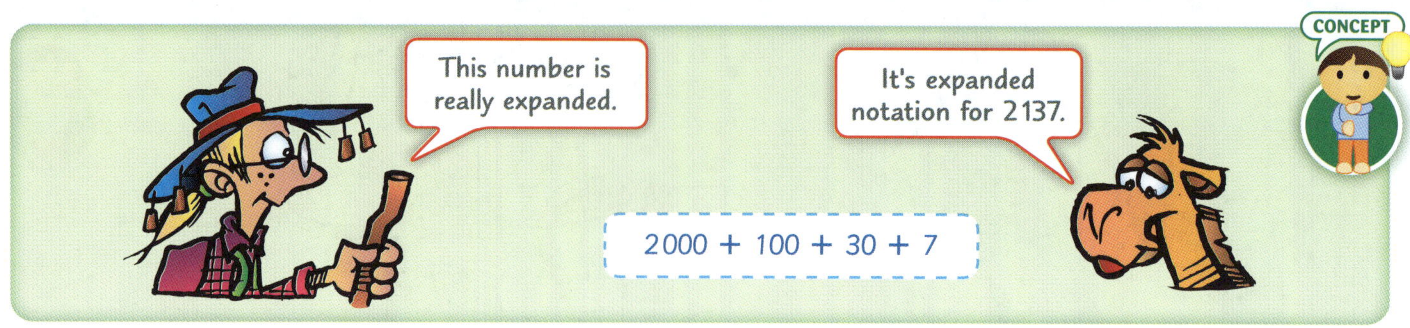

1 Write the numeral.

a 3000 + 700 + 60 + 9 ______ **b** 4000 + 600 + 30 + 7 ______
c 2000 + 500 + 80 + 1 ______ **d** 5000 + 400 + 70 + 6 ______
e 3000 + 900 + 50 + 8 ______ **f** 6000 + 800 + 40 + 3 ______

2 Write the number in expanded notation.

a 4247 ______ **b** 3169 ______
c 2675 ______ **d** 5192 ______

3 Write these numbers in the columns to show the place value.

	Thousands	Hundreds	Tens	Units
a 4378				
b 6249				
c 3821				
d 5873				

4 Write the value of each red digit.

a 2**9**16 ______ **b** **4**037 ______ **c** 627**9** ______ **d** 56**8**4 ______
e **3**690 ______ **f** 869**5** ______ **g** 2**6**70 ______ **h** 58**3**6 ______

5 Write the number before.

a 967 ______ **b** 1236 ______ **c** 2191 ______ **d** 4630 ______
e 5729 ______ **f** 6310 ______ **g** 3400 ______ **h** 7020 ______

Dicey numbers

- Take turns to roll four dice.
- Record the highest 4-digit number made by the dice.
- State the numbers before and after that number.

6655

Fractions of a group

2 out of 3 squares are coloured.

That's $\frac{2}{3}$.

CONCEPT

I drew 12 counters and circled each quarter. Each quarter has 3 counters.

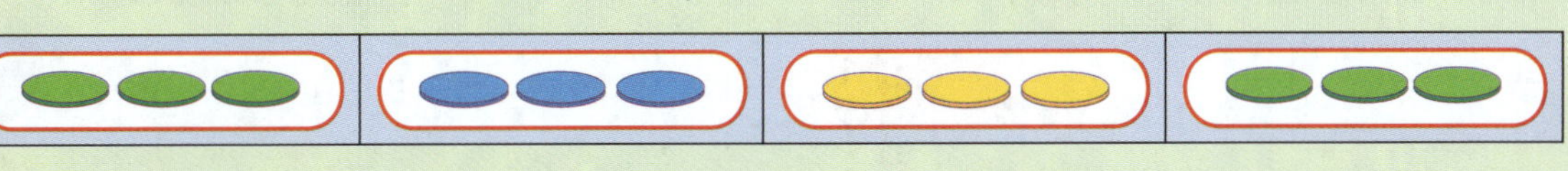

One quarter of my group is 3 counters. $\frac{1}{4}$ of 12 is 3.

Two quarters of my group is 6 counters. $\frac{2}{4}$ of 12 is 6.

Three quarters of my group is 9 counters. $\frac{3}{4}$ of 12 is 9.

Four quarters of 12 = ☐

Each group is a fraction of the whole group.

1 **a** Draw a line to cut this group of balls into halves. Circle one half of the balls.

b What is $\frac{1}{2}$ of 6? ☐

$\frac{1}{4}$ means 1 out of 4 equal parts.

2 **a** Draw lines to cut this group of stars into quarters. Circle one quarter of the group.

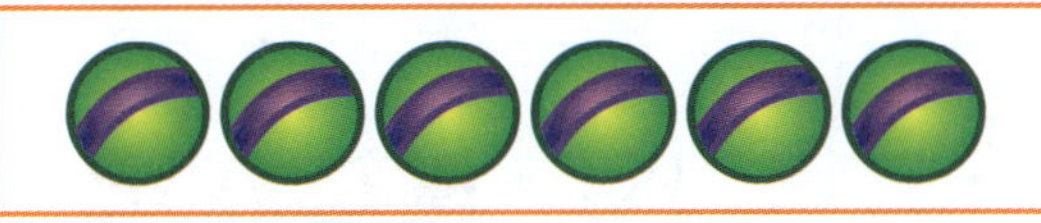

b What is $\frac{1}{4}$ of 8? ☐

c What is $\frac{2}{4}$ of 8? ☐

d What is $\frac{3}{4}$ of 8? ☐

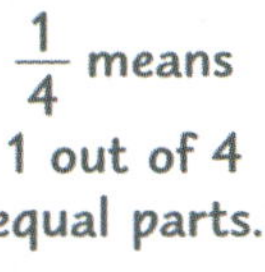

3 **a** Draw lines to cut this group of pencils into quarters. Circle one quarter of the group.

b What is $\frac{1}{4}$ of 16? ☐

c What is $\frac{2}{4}$ of 16? ☐

4 **a** Draw lines to cut this group of pears into thirds. Circle one third of each group.

b What is $\frac{1}{3}$ of 9? ☐

c What is $\frac{2}{3}$ of 9? ☐

d What is $\frac{3}{3}$ of 9? ☐

If 3 people shared the pears, each person would get one third.

5 What fraction of each row of apples has been eaten?

a 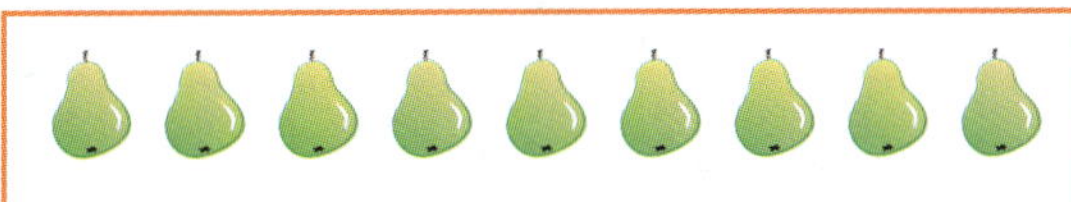 ☐ out of ☐ or ☐

b  ☐ out of ☐ or ☐

 • *AUSTRALIAN SIGNPOST MATHS NSW 3* • ISBN 9780655709046

1:26 Fractions of a whole

Fractions do not always appear in a straight line.

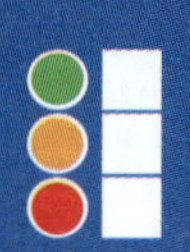

CONCEPT

This rectangle was cut and placed on a number line. It is easier to find the fraction coloured.

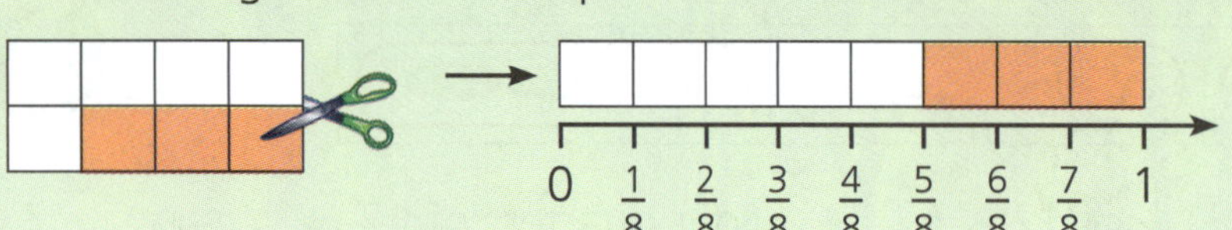

5 out of 8 or $\frac{5}{8}$ are not coloured.

3 out of 8 or $\frac{3}{8}$ are coloured.

1 What fraction of each shape is coloured?

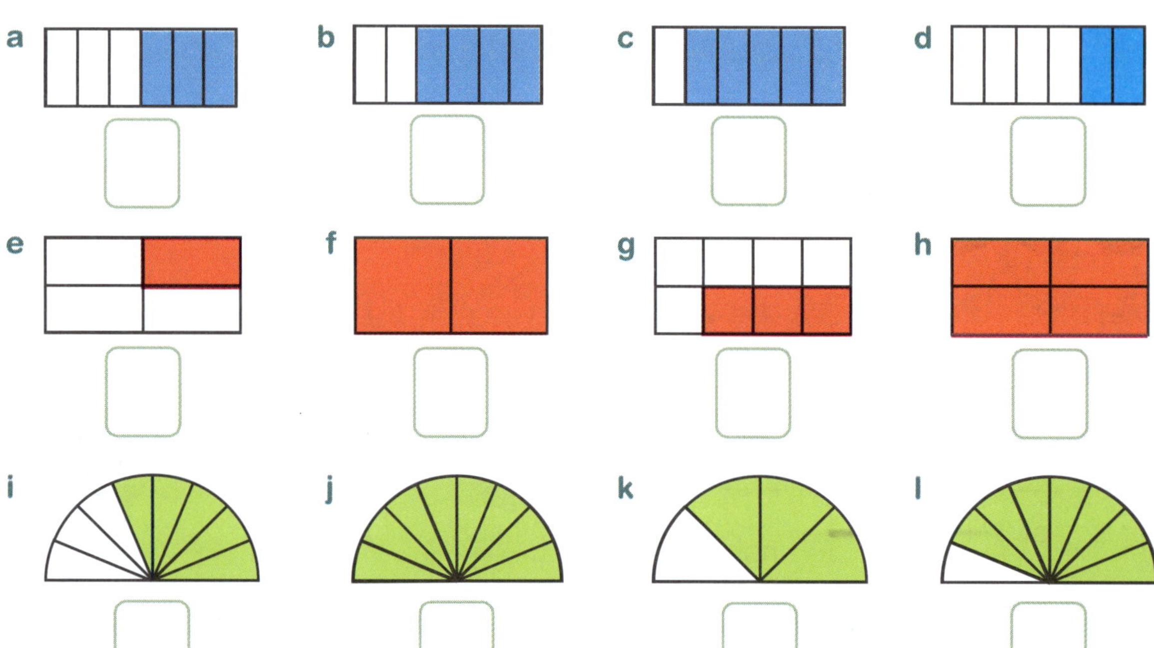

2 Colour part of each shape to match the fraction.

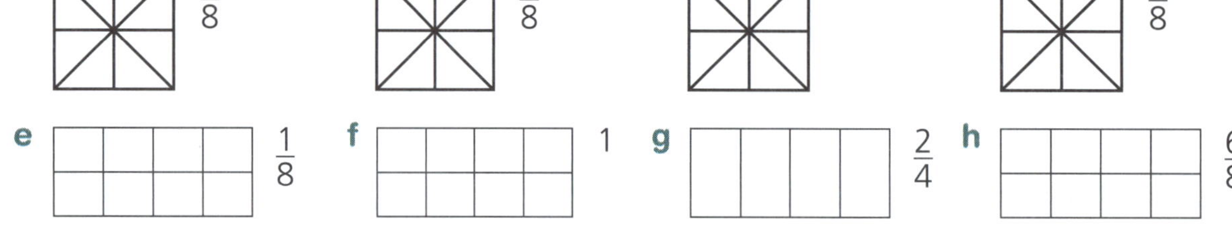

3 Draw lines to make:

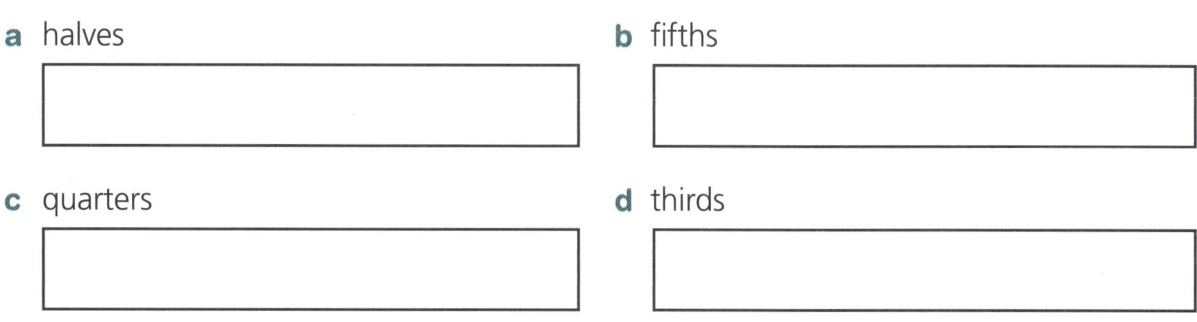

 ISBN 9780655709046

1:27 Numbers to 10 000

6 thousands 8 hundreds 3 tens 4 ones

68 hundreds 34 ones

CONCEPT

8132 can be partitioned and written as:

- 8 thousands and 132 ones
- 81 hundreds and 32 ones
- 813 tens and 2 ones
- 8132 ones

1 Complete the numeral expanders.

a 3726

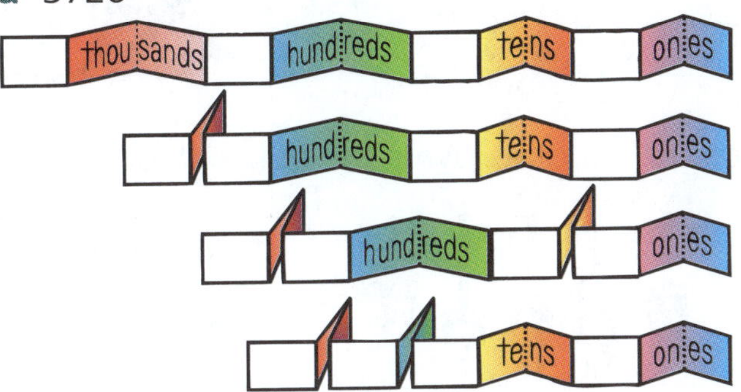

b 8915

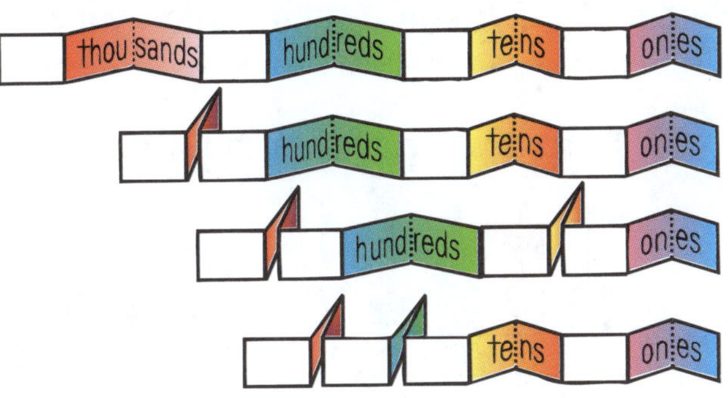

2 Write these numbers in different ways using partitioning.

a 6218

b 3274

3 4391 can be written as 43 hundreds and 91 ones. Partition these numbers in the same way.

a 7123

b 9362

c 6217

d 8592

e 1975

f 2546

4 Complete each pattern and write the rule.

a 750, 760, 770, ___, ___, ___, ___, ___ Rule: ___

b 1140, 1130, 1120, ___, ___, ___, ___, ___ Rule: ___

c 1230, 1330, 1430, ___, ___, ___, ___, ___ Rule: ___

d 4729, 4629, 4529, ___, ___, ___, ___, ___ Rule: ___

e 5297, 5287, 5277, ___, ___, ___, ___, ___ Rule: ___

1:28 Numbers over 10 000

45 thousand
45 000

123 thousand
123 000

CONCEPT

Thousands	Hundreds, Tens, Ones
75	248
19	783
140	529

75 248

Leave a space to the right of the thousands digit.

75 thousand, 2 hundred and forty-eight
19 thousand, 7 hundred and eighty-three
140 thousand, 5 hundred and twenty-nine

75 248 = 7 ten thousands, 5 thousands, 2 hundreds, 4 tens and 8 ones
= 70 000 + 5000 + 200 + 40 + 8

1 **T Th** stands for tens of thousands. **U** stands for units or ones. Write the numeral for:

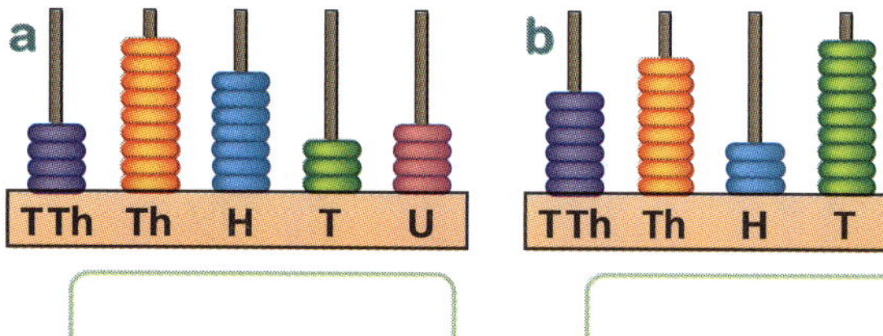

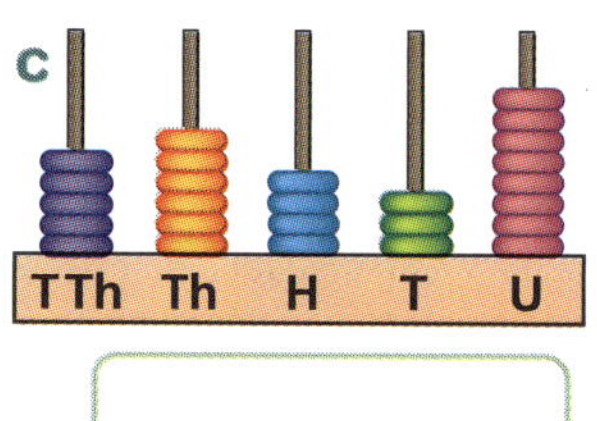

62 530 is also 6253 tens or 625 hundreds and 30 ones.

2 Read these numbers aloud and then write them in figures on the place-value chart. Tick the largest number. Circle the smallest number.

a twenty-six thousand, three hundred and twenty-four
b thirty-five thousand, one hundred and sixty-two
c eighty-two thousand, nine hundred and seventy
d fifty-two thousand, eight hundred and fourteen
e seventy-four thousand, two hundred and sixty

T Thous	Thous	Hund	Tens	Ones

3 Write the numeral for:

a 30 000 + 4000 + 500 + 20 + 8
b 60 000 + 7000 + 900 + 30 + 4
c 50 000 + 8000 + 400 + 60 + 2
d 90 000 + 2000 + 700 + 40 + 8
e 80 000 + 2000 + 300 + 50 + 9
f 40 000 + 8000 + 600 + 70 + 3

4 Write these as 'thousands' and 'hundreds, tens, ones':

a The library paid $47 500 for a painting of Perth.
b The population of Geelong was 263 280 in 2020.
c In 2021 there were 984 000 Aboriginal and Torres Strait Islander people living in Australia.

Thousands	Hundreds, Tens, Ones

 • *AUSTRALIAN SIGNPOST MATHS NSW 3* • ISBN 9780655709046

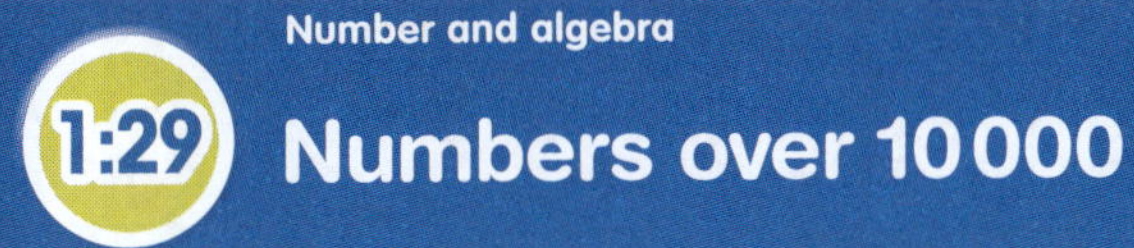

Number and algebra

1:29 Numbers over 10 000

49 620 = 49 000 + 620
270 539 = 270 000 + 539

1. Write the numeral for:
   - a 50 000 + 8000 + 400 + 30 + 7 ☐
   - b 50 000 + 400 + 30 + 7 ☐
   - c 80 000 + 1000 + 500 + 20 + 6 ☐
   - d 10 000 + 4000 + 200 + 1 ☐
   - e 30 000 + 5000 + 800 + 30 + 2 ☐
   - f 70 000 + 2000 + 600 ☐
   - g 400 000 + 60 000 + 2000 + 900 + 30 + 7 ☐

2. Circle the smallest number in each group.
   - a 34 728, 38 274, 87 352
   - b 15 906, 90 651, 51 960
   - c 79 207, 97 207, 97 702
   - d 75 098, 69 999, 70 789
   - e 112 403, 87 345, 60 913
   - f 56 920, 105 206, 49 502

3. Put in order from smallest to largest.
   - a 50 712, 51 270, 50 752, 9752 ☐
   - b 75 098, 69 999, 70 789, 508 970 ☐

4. How many digits are in:
   - a 76 084 ☐
   - b 4073 ☐
   - c 76 830 ☐
   - d 116 777 ☐

5. Complete the numeral expanders for the number 213 605.

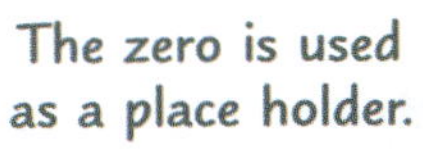

6. Complete.
   - a 1 hundred = ☐ tens
   - b 1 thousand = ☐ hundreds
   - c 1 ten thousand = ☐ thousands
   - d 1 hundred thousand = ☐ ten thousands

2:01 Arrays

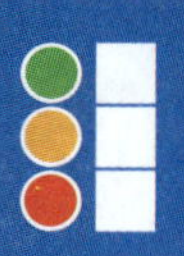

2 rows of 4 = 8
4 columns of 2 = 8
8 is a multiple of 2.

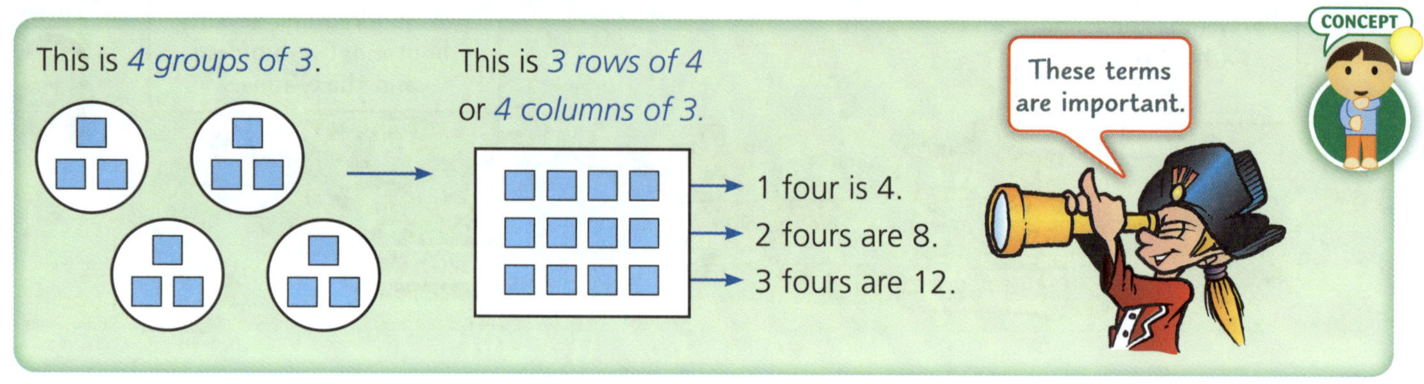

1 Describe each array using the terms above. For example, 7 columns of 2.

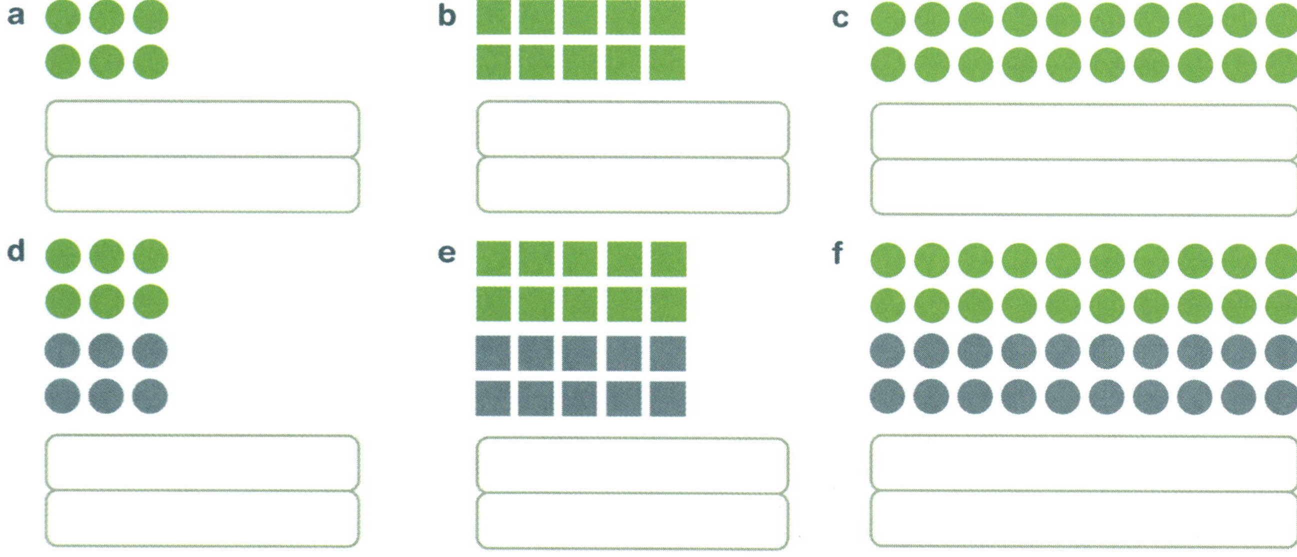

- Compare arrays **a** and **d**. Discuss what you noticed.
- Compare arrays **b** and **e**. Compare arrays **c** and **f**.

2 Describe these arrays in different ways and write the total number of dots. Some of the dots have been covered.

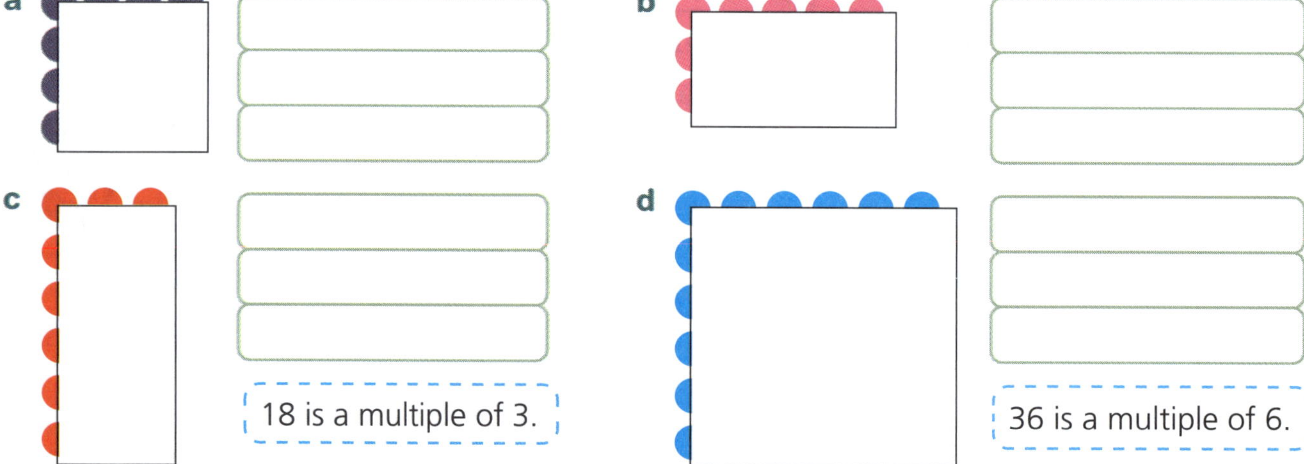

2:02 Square numbers

3 × 3 = 9
2 × 2 = 4
1 × 1 = 1

1 Draw squares which are the length of each coloured side. Describe each array below.

a

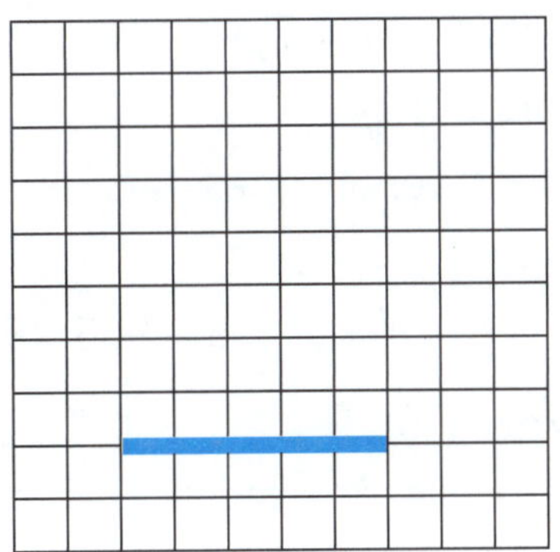

☐ rows of ☐ = ☐
☐ × ☐ = ☐

b

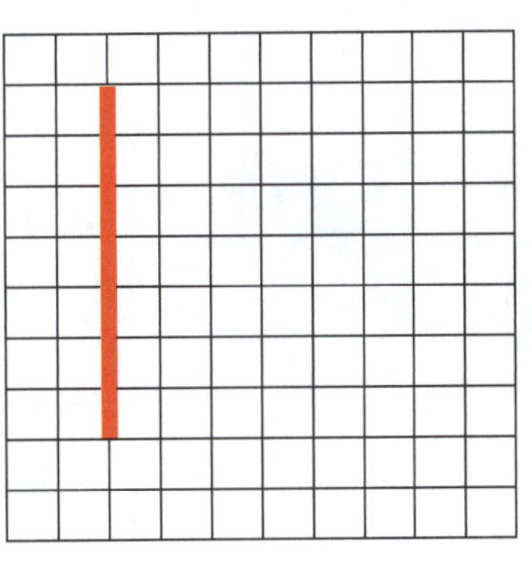

Area of red square
= ☐ small squares

c

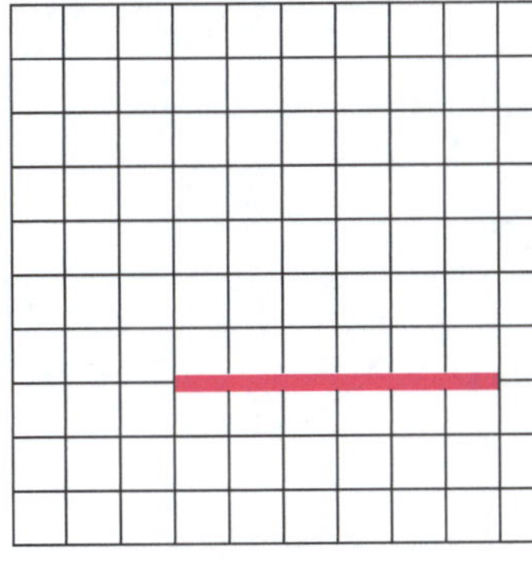

☐ rows of ☐ = ☐
☐ × ☐ = ☐

d

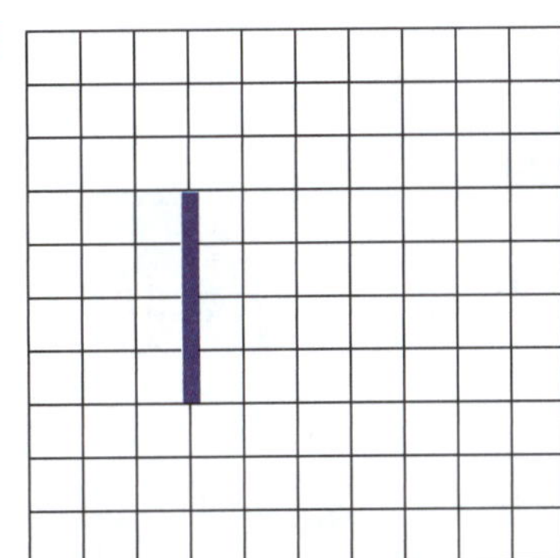

Area of purple square
= ☐ small squares

e

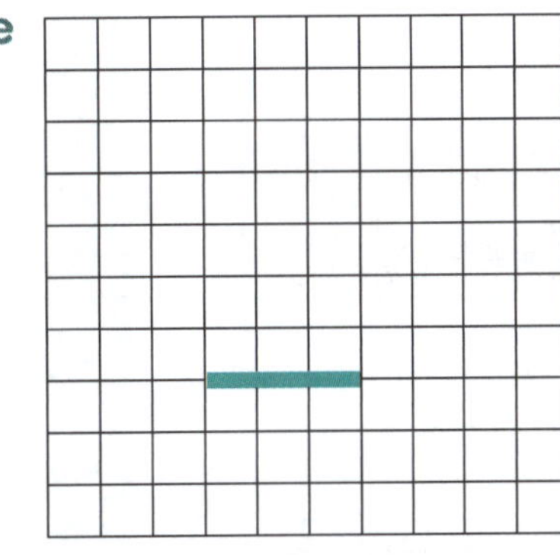

☐ rows of ☐ = ☐
☐ × ☐ = ☐

f

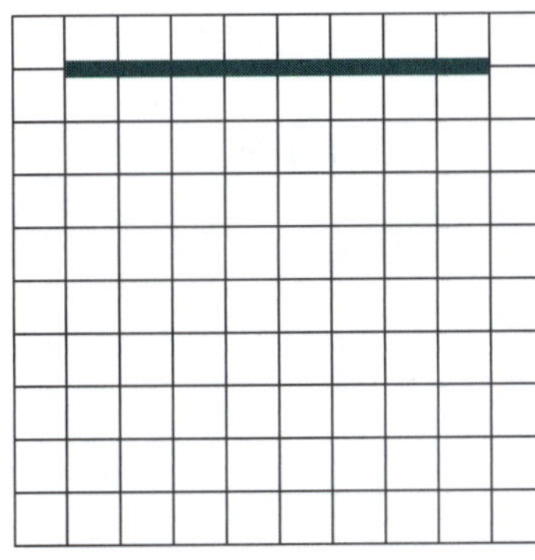

Area of green square
= ☐ small squares

CONCEPT

The result of multiplying a number by itself is called a **square number**.

2 a Here we have 3 rows of 3 counters.
3 × 3 = ☐

b What shape does this array look like?
☐

c Make square arrays using 4, 9, 16 and 25 counters.

3 List all of the square numbers up to 100.

4 Use place-value blocks or a calculator to find at least seven more square numbers.

5 Explain why the numbers 1, 4, 9 and 16 are called square numbers .

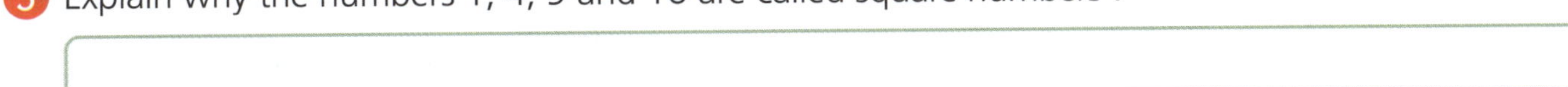

2:03 Addition and subtraction

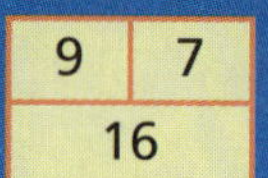

9 + 7 = 16   16 − 9 = 7
7 + 9 = 16   16 − 7 = 9

1 Complete the additions and subtractions. Discuss any patterns you can see.

a 4 + 1 = ☐
1 + 4 = ☐
5 − 4 = ☐
5 − 1 = ☐

b 4 + 2 = ☐
2 + 4 = ☐
6 − 4 = ☐
6 − 2 = ☐

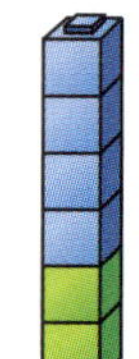

4	
6	

c 1 + 9 = ☐
9 + 1 = ☐
10 − 1 = ☐
10 − 9 = ☐

9	
10	

d 2 + 8 = ☐
8 + 2 = ☐
10 − 2 = ☐
10 − 8 = ☐

8	
10	

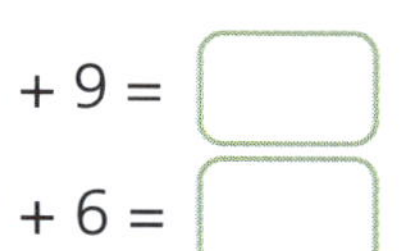

e 6 + 9 = ☐
9 + 6 = ☐
15 − 6 = ☐
15 − 9 = ☐

2 Colour matching pairs the same.
For example: 6 + 7 = 7 + 6
(The 13s are blue.)
Show the answers to these and their partners.
4 + 8, 9 + 7, 8 + 9, 7 + 8, 5 + 9, 6 + 5, 5 + 7

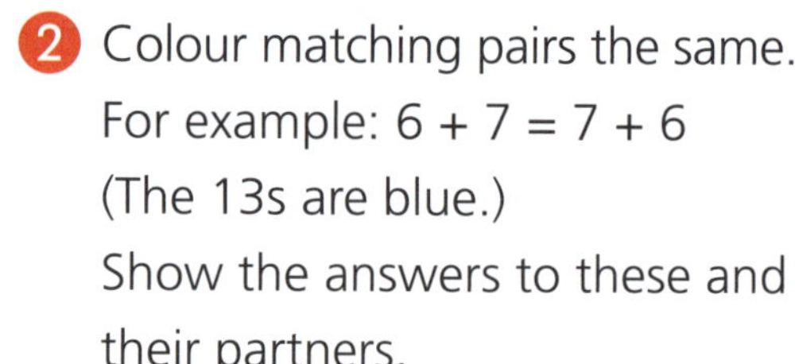

+	0	1	2	3	4	5	6	7	8	9	10
0											
1											
2						7					
3											
4											
5			7								
6								13			
7							13				
8											
9											
10											

3 Use the number line to complete the number facts. Look for patterns.

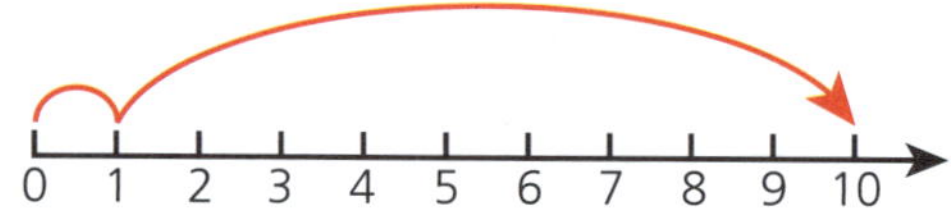

a 1 + 9 = ☐
2 + 8 = ☐
3 + 7 = ☐
4 + 6 = ☐
5 + 5 = ☐
6 + 4 = ☐
7 + 3 = ☐
8 + 2 = ☐
9 + 1 = ☐

b 10 − 9 = ☐
10 − 8 = ☐
10 − 7 = ☐
10 − 6 = ☐
10 − 5 = ☐
10 − 4 = ☐
10 − 3 = ☐
10 − 2 = ☐
10 − 1 = ☐

See Extra Support 1–4 (Number facts).

 AUSTRALIAN SIGNPOST MATHS NSW 3 • ISBN 9780655709046

Number facts, ×2

$2 \times 6 = 6 \times 2$
Double 6 is the same as 6 twos.

1 Use the number models to complete the multiplications.

Learn your × 2 tables.

6 groups of 2 is the same as 3 groups of 4.

Multiple: 6; 2, 3

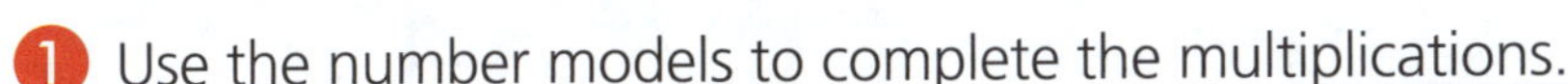
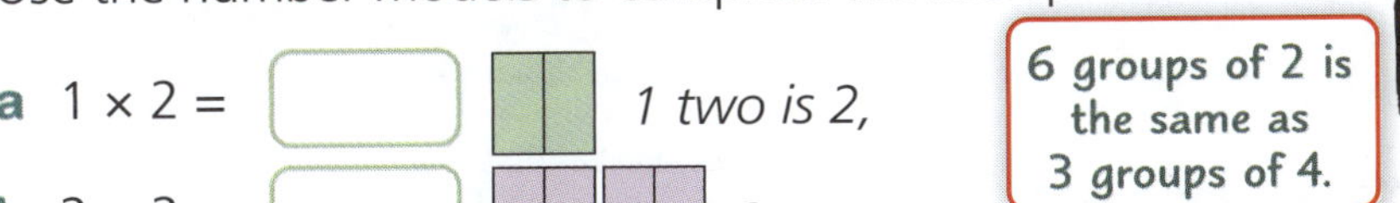
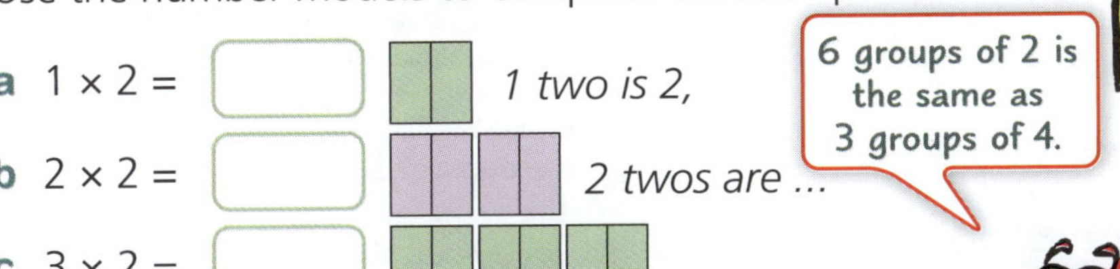
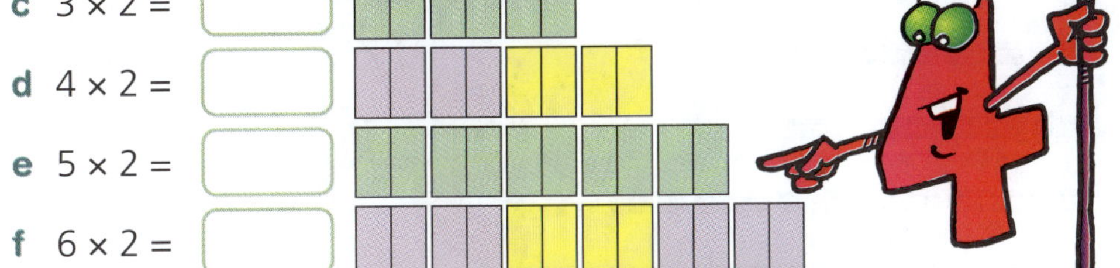
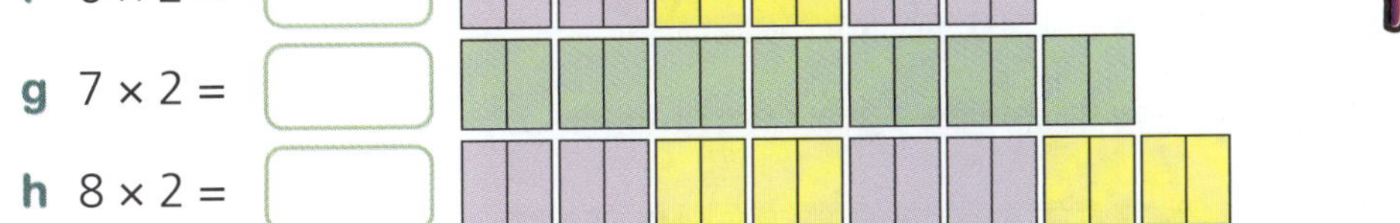

a $1 \times 2 =$ ☐ *1 two is 2,*

b $2 \times 2 =$ ☐ *2 twos are …*

c $3 \times 2 =$ ☐

d $4 \times 2 =$ ☐

e $5 \times 2 =$ ☐

f $6 \times 2 =$ ☐

g $7 \times 2 =$ ☐

h $8 \times 2 =$ ☐

i $9 \times 2 =$ ☐

j $10 \times 2 =$ ☐

k $1 \times 4 =$ ☐

l $2 \times 4 =$ ☐

m $3 \times 4 =$ ☐

n $4 \times 4 =$ ☐

o $5 \times 4 =$ ☐

2 **a** $8 \times 2 =$ ☐, $3 \times 2 =$ ☐, 8×2 plus $3 \times 2 = 11 \times 2 =$ ☐

b $7 \times 2 =$ ☐, $5 \times 2 =$ ☐, 7×2 plus $5 \times 2 = 12 \times 2 =$ ☐

c $4 \times 2 =$ ☐, $9 \times 2 =$ ☐, 4×2 plus $9 \times 2 = 13 \times 2 =$ ☐

d $10 \times 2 =$ ☐, $6 \times 2 =$ ☐, 10×2 minus $6 \times 2 = 4 \times 2 =$ ☐

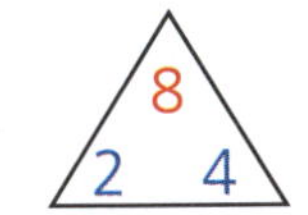

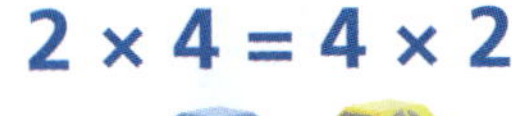

3 **a** 6×2 plus $2 = 7 \times 2 =$ ☐

b 7×2 plus $2 = 8 \times 2 =$ ☐

c 10×2 plus $2 = 11 \times 2 =$ ☐

d 11×2 plus $2 = 12 \times 2 =$ ☐

◀ This is 6×2 plus 2.

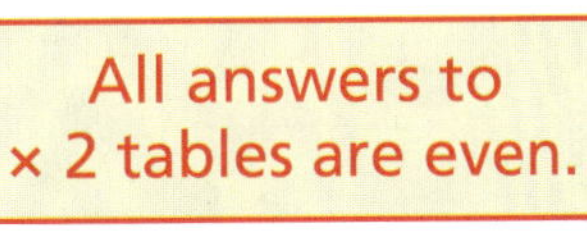

4 **a**

	3	10	2	1	5	4	7	9	8	6
× 2	6	20								

b

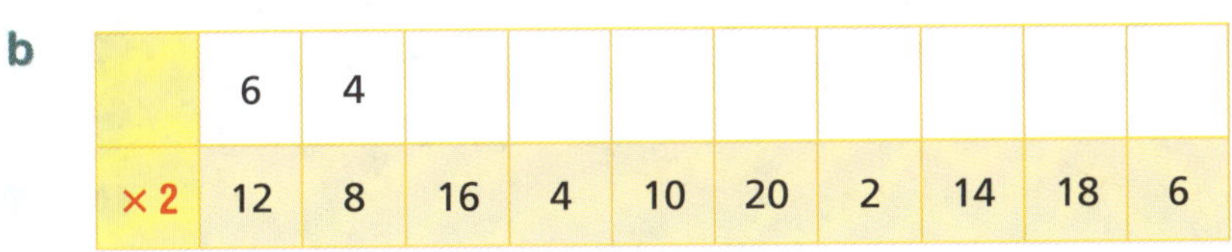

	6	4								
× 2	12	8	16	4	10	20	2	14	18	6

c

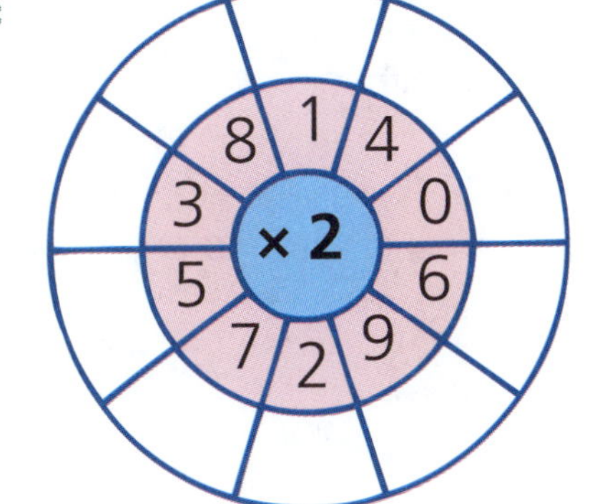

2:05 Number facts, ×5, ×10

3 × 5 = 5 × 3
Three 5s are the same as five 3s.

1 Use the number models to complete the multiplications.

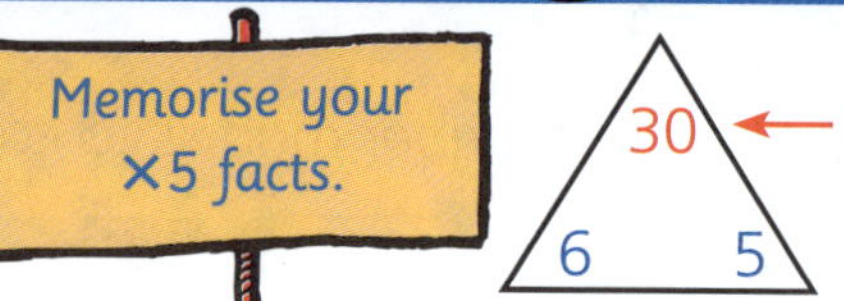

a 1 × 5 = ☐ *1 five is 5,*

b 2 × 5 = ☐ *2 fives are …*

c 3 × 5 = ☐

d 4 × 5 = ☐

e 5 × 5 = ☐

f 6 × 5 = ☐

g 7 × 5 = ☐

h 8 × 5 = ☐

i 9 × 5 = ☐

j 10 × 5 = ☐

6 groups of 5 is the same as 3 groups of 10.

k 1 × 10 = ☐

l 2 × 10 = ☐

m 3 × 10 = ☐

n 4 × 10 = ☐

o 5 × 10 = ☐

2 Use the place-value blocks to complete the multiplications.

a
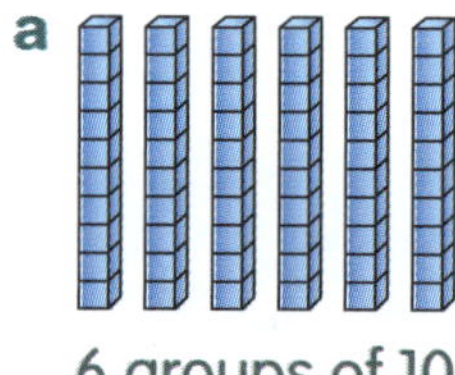

6 groups of 10

$$\begin{array}{r} 10 \\ \times \quad 6 \\ \hline \square \end{array}$$

b
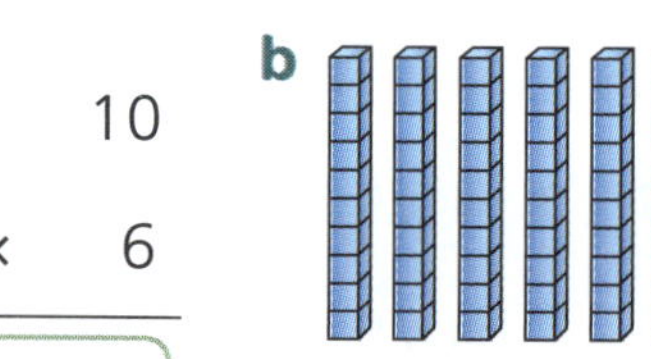
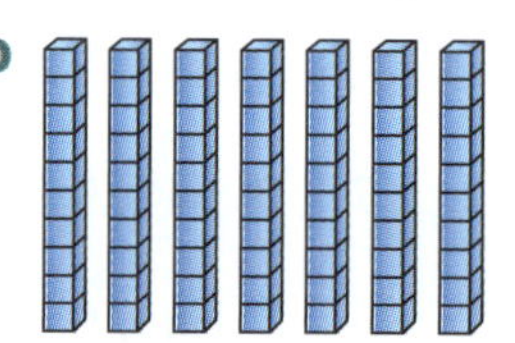
7 groups of 10

$$\begin{array}{r} 10 \\ \times \quad 7 \\ \hline \square \end{array}$$

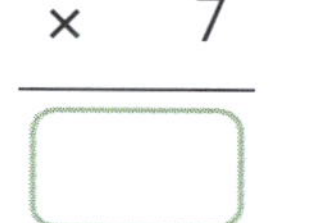

c
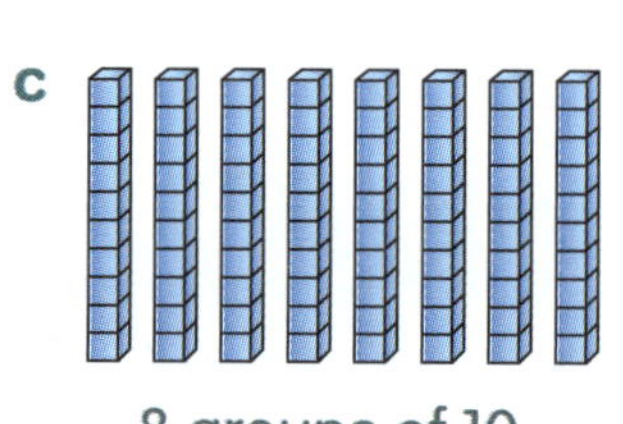
8 groups of 10

$$\begin{array}{r} 10 \\ \times \quad 8 \\ \hline \square \end{array}$$

d
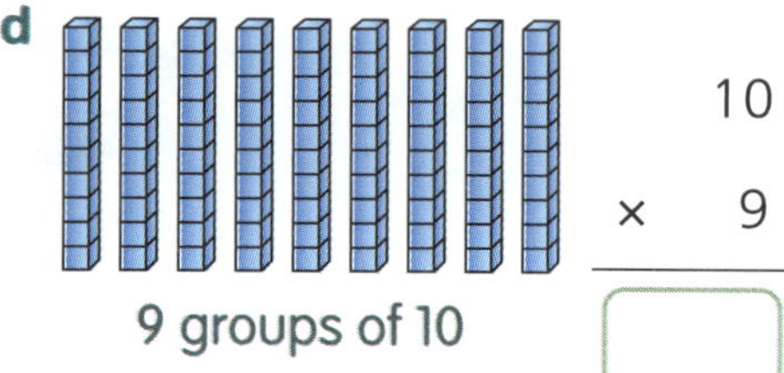
9 groups of 10

$$\begin{array}{r} 10 \\ \times \quad 9 \\ \hline \square \end{array}$$

e
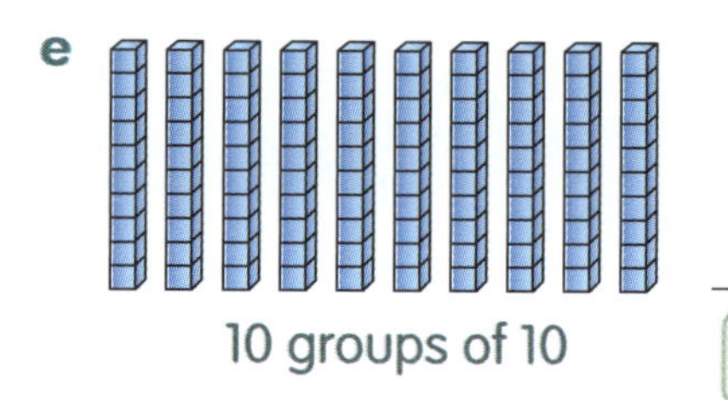
10 groups of 10

$$\begin{array}{r} 10 \\ \times \quad 10 \\ \hline \square \end{array}$$

3 a

	3	10	2	1	5	4	7	9	8	6
× 10										

b

	3	10	2	1	5	4	7	9	8	6
× 5										

c Is 3 × 5 half of 3 × 10? ☐

d Is 5 × 5 half of 10 × 5? ☐

e Does 7 fives equal 6 fives plus 1 five? ☐

 • *AUSTRALIAN SIGNPOST MATHS NSW 3* • ISBN 9780655709046

2:06 Multiplication facts

1 + 1 + 1 + 1 + 1 + 1 = 6 × 1 = 6
0 + 0 + 0 + 0 + 0 + 0 = 6 × 0 = 0

True or false?

- Any number multiplied by 1 always gives that number.
- Any number multiplied by 0 always gives zero.

Five empty bowls means that I have no food.

5 × 0 = 0

INVESTIGATION

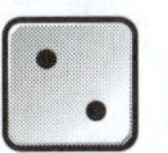

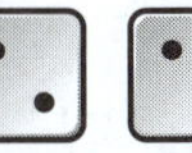

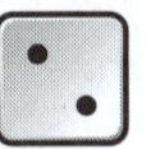
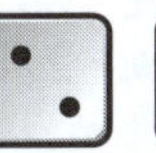

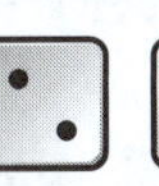

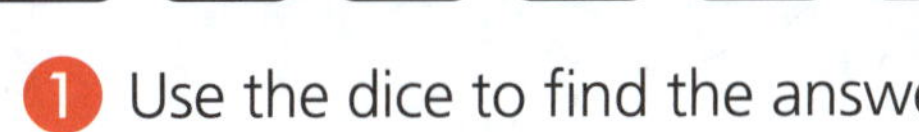

1 Use the dice to find the answers.

a 6 × 2 =	b 7 × 5 =	c 7 × 2 =	d 8 × 10 =
e 7 × 10 =	f 8 × 2 =	g 5 × 5 =	h 10 × 5 =
i 9 × 2 =	j 6 × 5 =	k 6 × 10 =	l 9 × 10 =
m 8 × 5 =	n 11 × 2 =	o 9 × 5 =	p 11 × 5 =

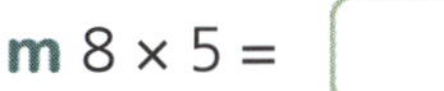

2 Complete each pair of multiplication facts.

a 2 × 1 =	b 2 × 5 =	c 2 × 10 =
1 × 2 =	5 × 2 =	10 × 2 =
d 1 × 5 =	e 5 × 0 =	f 5 × 10 =
5 × 1 =	0 × 5 =	10 × 5 =

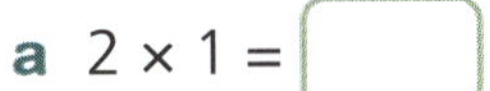

20 is a multiple of 10.

3 Measure the time you take to complete each set of multiplication facts. Write the time.

a	b	c	d
9 × 0 =	8 × 0 =	6 × 0 =	7 × 0 =
7 × 1 =	6 × 1 =	9 × 1 =	8 × 1 =
6 × 5 =	9 × 5 =	8 × 5 =	7 × 5 =
10 × 5 =	10 × 10 =	10 × 2 =	10 × 1 =
3 × 2 =	2 × 2 =	5 × 2 =	4 × 2 =
5 × 5 =	4 × 5 =	3 × 5 =	2 × 5 =
4 × 10 =	5 × 10 =	2 × 10 =	3 × 10 =
6 × 2 =	9 × 2 =	7 × 2 =	8 × 2 =
8 × 5 =	7 × 5 =	9 × 5 =	6 × 5 =
7 × 10 =	8 × 10 =	6 × 10 =	9 × 10 =
seconds	seconds	seconds	seconds

2, 5 and 10 times tables

Skip counting by 2:
2, 4, 6, 8, 10, 12, …
+2 +2 +2 +2 +2

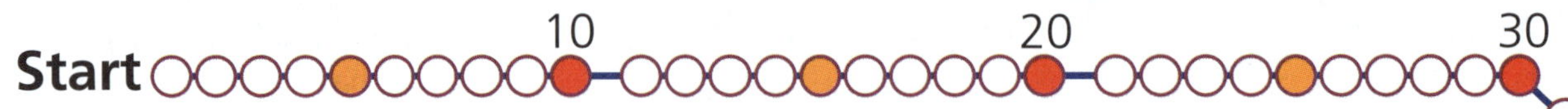

CONCEPT

5, 10, 15, 20, 25, 30, 35, 40, 45, 50
To skip count by 5, add 5.

10, 20, 30, 40, 50, 60, 70, 80, 90, 100
To skip count by 10, add 10.

Do you know your 2, 5 and 10 times tables?

5 × 2 = 2 × 5

40 50 60 70

1 Join each question to its answer using a pencil and ruler.

a

=	
2 × 2	0
4 × 2	2
0 × 2	4
1 × 2	6
3 × 2	8
7 × 2	10
5 × 2	12
10 × 2	14
9 × 2	16
6 × 2	18
8 × 2	20

b

=	
3 × 2	0
0 × 2	2
5 × 2	4
1 × 2	6
7 × 2	8
2 × 2	10
8 × 2	12
4 × 2	14
6 × 2	16
10 × 2	18
9 × 2	20

c

=	
1 × 10	0
3 × 10	10
0 × 10	20
5 × 10	30
2 × 10	40
7 × 10	50
4 × 10	60
6 × 10	70
10 × 10	80
9 × 10	90
8 × 10	100

×2
answers end in:
0, 2, 4, 6, or 8.

×10
answers end in:
0.

d

=	
4 × 10	70
2 × 10	20
7 × 10	40
3 × 10	90
9 × 10	30
1 × 10	60
6 × 10	10
10 × 10	50
5 × 10	80
8 × 10	100
0 × 10	0

e

=	
1 × 5	50
6 × 5	25
10 × 5	5
5 × 5	30
8 × 5	0
0 × 5	40
2 × 5	15
9 × 5	35
3 × 5	20
7 × 5	10
4 × 5	45

f

=	
0 × 5	0
6 × 5	15
3 × 5	30
8 × 5	20
4 × 5	25
10 × 5	40
5 × 5	10
2 × 5	50
1 × 5	35
7 × 5	45
9 × 5	5

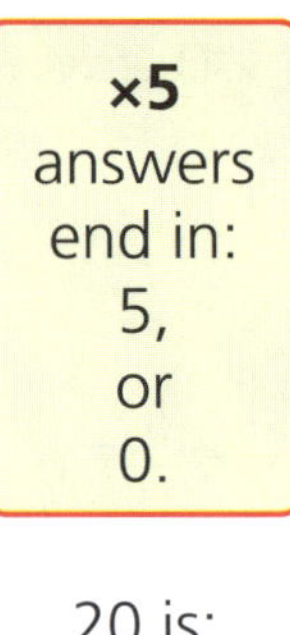

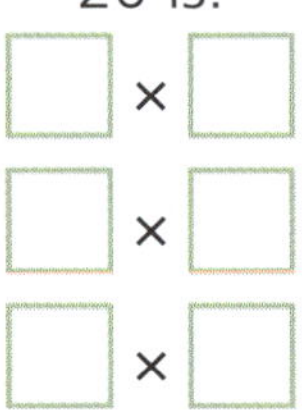

100 90 80

 • *AUSTRALIAN SIGNPOST MATHS NSW 3* • ISBN 9780655709046

Patterns in + and –

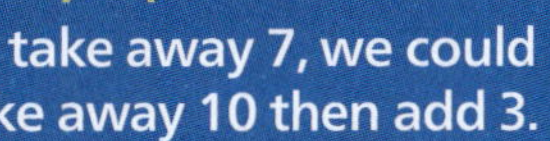
23 – 7 = ?
To take away 7, we could take away 10 then add 3.

INVESTIGATION

1 When we add 9, what happens to the tens and the ones digits?

Example: **37** + 9 = 37 + 10 – 1 = **46**

- The tens digit: ______
- The ones digit: ______

So, to add 9 we can add **10** and then subtract ____.

9
9 + 9 = 18
18 + 9 = 27
27 + 9 = 36
36 + 9 = 45
45 + 9 = 54

2 When we subtract 9, what happens to the tens and the ones digits?

Example: **42** – 9 = 42 – 10 + 1 = **33**

- The tens digit: ______
- The ones digit: ______

So, to subtract 9 we can subtract **10** and then add ____.

3 Race a partner to complete these. Use the strategy above.

a 7 + 9 = ____ b 16 + 9 = ____ c 28 + 9 = ____ d 42 + 9 = ____

e 17 – 9 = ____ f 34 – 9 = ____ g 99, 90, 81, ____, ____, ____, ____

4 Discuss and explore strategies for adding or subtracting 8. Race a partner to complete these.

a 6 + 8 = ____ b 19 + 8 = ____ c 53 + 8 = ____ d 75 + 8 = ____

e 23 – 8 = ____ f 67 – 8 = ____ g 32, 40, 48, ____, ____, ____, ____

52	?
61	

5 Complete the number sentence to find the answer.

a Heather has 23 pins. How many more does she need to have 32?

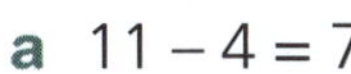
23 + ____ = 32

b Jack needs 55 cents. He has 40 cents. How much more does he need?

40 + ____ = 55

c 61 nails were lost. Luke found 52. How many are still missing?

52 + ____ = 61

6 Complete the patterns.

a 11 – 4 = 7
21 – 4 = 17
31 – 4 = ____
41 – 4 = ____
51 – 4 = ____

b 14 – 8 = 6
24 – 8 = 16
34 – 8 = ____
44 – 8 = ____
54 – 8 = ____

c 15 – 6 = 9
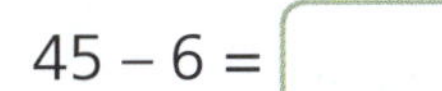
25 – 6 = 19
35 – 6 = ____
45 – 6 = ____
55 – 6 = ____

 • *AUSTRALIAN SIGNPOST MATHS NSW 3* • ISBN 9780655709046

2:09 Relating addition and subtraction

If 7 – 2 = 5 then 5 + 2 = 7.

CONCEPT

Jenny needed to find the difference in length between these two ribbons.

33 – 15 = ☐ can also be thought of as 15 + ☐ = 33.

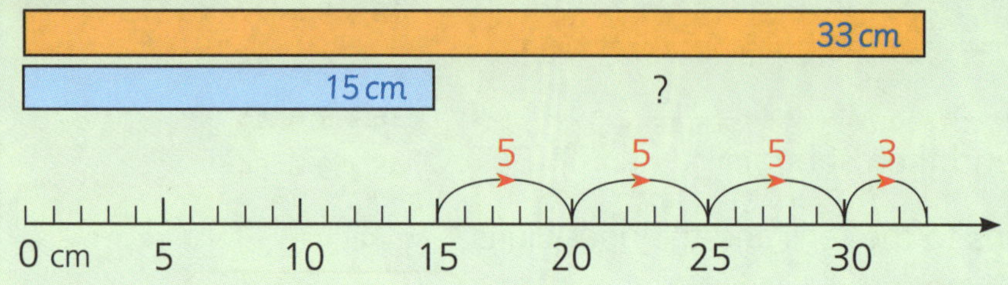

We subtract to find the difference or write 15 + ☐ = 33.

We count on from 15 until we reach 33.

The length difference between the two ribbons is 5 + 5 + 5 + 3 cm = 18 cm.

1 Find the length differences between ribbons.

a

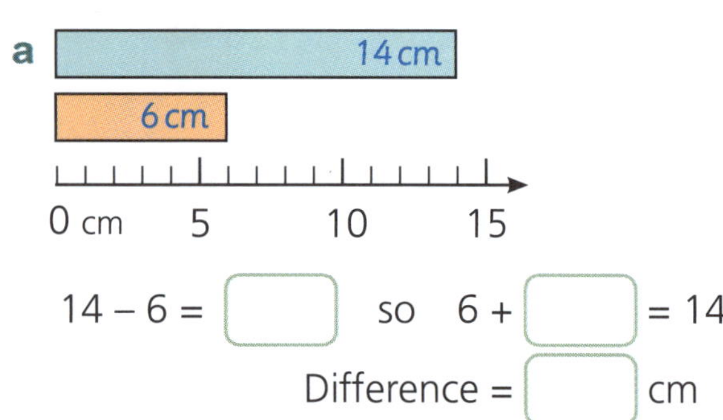

14 – 6 = ☐ so 6 + ☐ = 14

Difference = ☐ cm

b

20 cm

13 cm

0 cm 5 10 15 20

20 – 13 = ☐ so 13 + ☐ = 20

Difference = ☐ cm

c

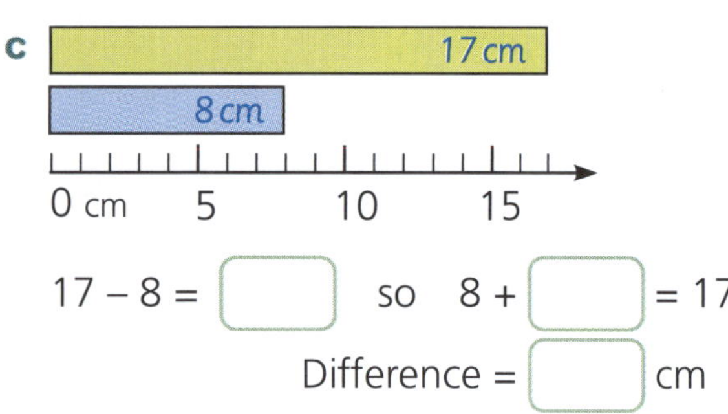

17 – 8 = ☐ so 8 + ☐ = 17

Difference = ☐ cm

d

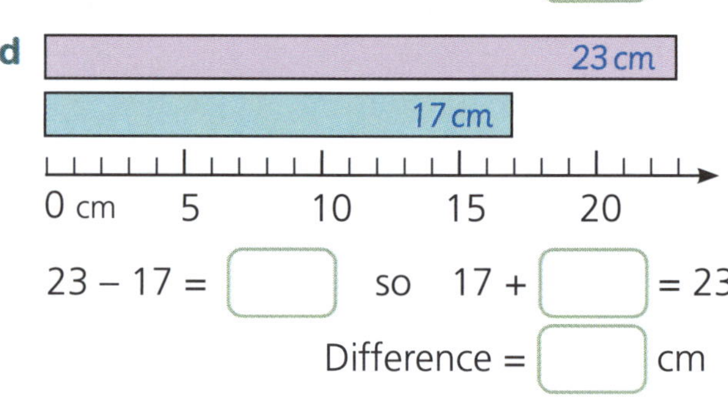

23 – 17 = ☐ so 17 + ☐ = 23

Difference = ☐ cm

2 Use these bar models to write three related number sentences.

a

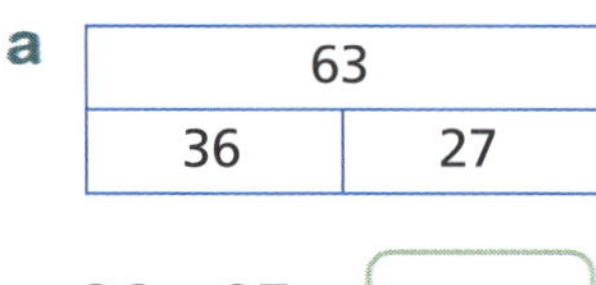

36 + 27 = ☐

63 – 36 = ☐

63 – 27 = ☐

b

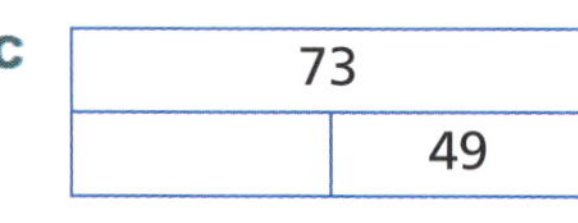

29 + ☐ = 67

67 – 29 = ☐

67 – ☐ = 29

c

73	
	49

☐ + 49 = 73

73 – 49 = ☐

73 – ☐ = ☐

ACTIVITY

- Compare pieces of paper cut to different centimetre lengths, or draw your own bar models. Write number sentences to match.

 • *AUSTRALIAN SIGNPOST MATHS NSW 3* • ISBN 9780655709046

Money

Add the notes, starting with the highest note and working to the lowest.

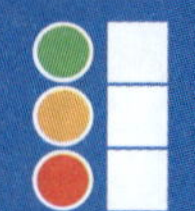

1 Write the total value of each group of banknotes.

a

b

c

d

2 Circle the larger amount.

a

b

c

3 $100 can be made using: ☐ $50 notes, or ☐ $20 notes, or ☐ $10 notes, or ☐ $5 notes.

4 Write the value of the banknotes in order from smallest to largest.

☐ ☐ ☐ ☐ ☐

2:11 Shopping

Can you list all of the coins and notes?

CONCEPT

To make an amount of money, start with the higher value coins or notes.

1 Use coins to make $1.65.

Steps:

Start with $1 and count on.

- Use 50c to make $1.50.
- Use 10c to make $1.60.
- Use 5c to make $1.65.

2 Use coins to make $3.85.

Steps:

Start with $2 and count on.

- Use $1 to make $3.
- Use 50c to make $3.50.
- Use 20c to make $3.70.
- Use 10c to make $3.80.
- Use 5c to make $3.85.

1 Colour the coins you could use to buy each item.

a Exercise Book 90c

b $1.85

c Mmm... Milk $2.70

d $3.60

e 12 coloured pencils $2.95

f $3.20

g $7.70

h $5.30

Make $5 using coins in four different ways.

FUN SPOT

2 Choose coins or notes to make each amount of money.

a $3.80

b $2.95

c $4.35

d $9.10

e $12.70

f $15.50

2:12 Money

$2 = ☐ $1 coins $2 = ☐ 20c coins

$2 = ☐ 50c coins $2 = ☐ 10c coins

1 Write the total value of each group of coins. Discuss which groups have an equal value.

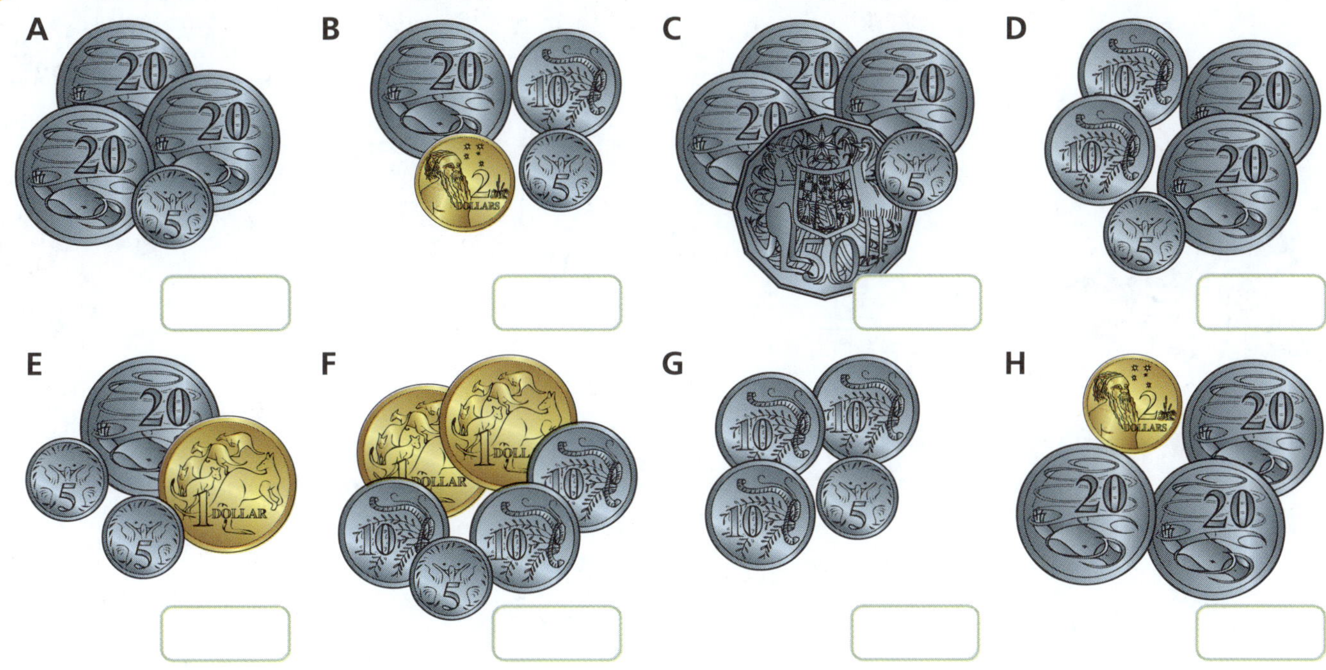

2 $1 is the same as 100 cents. How many cents in:

a $2? ☐ cents b $5? ☐ cents c $8? ☐ cents

3 Write the total value of the coins in:

a **A** and **D** ☐ b **E** and **F** ☐ c **C** and **G** ☐

4 Which group of banknotes is worth:

a the same as **P**? ☐ b the same as **T**? ☐

c less than **P**? ☐ d more than **Q**? ☐

M

N

O

P

Q

R

S

T

 • *AUSTRALIAN SIGNPOST MATHS NSW 3* • ISBN 9780655709046

2:13 Addition to 99

$34 + 23 = (30 + 20) + (4 + 3)$

Add tens.
Add ones.

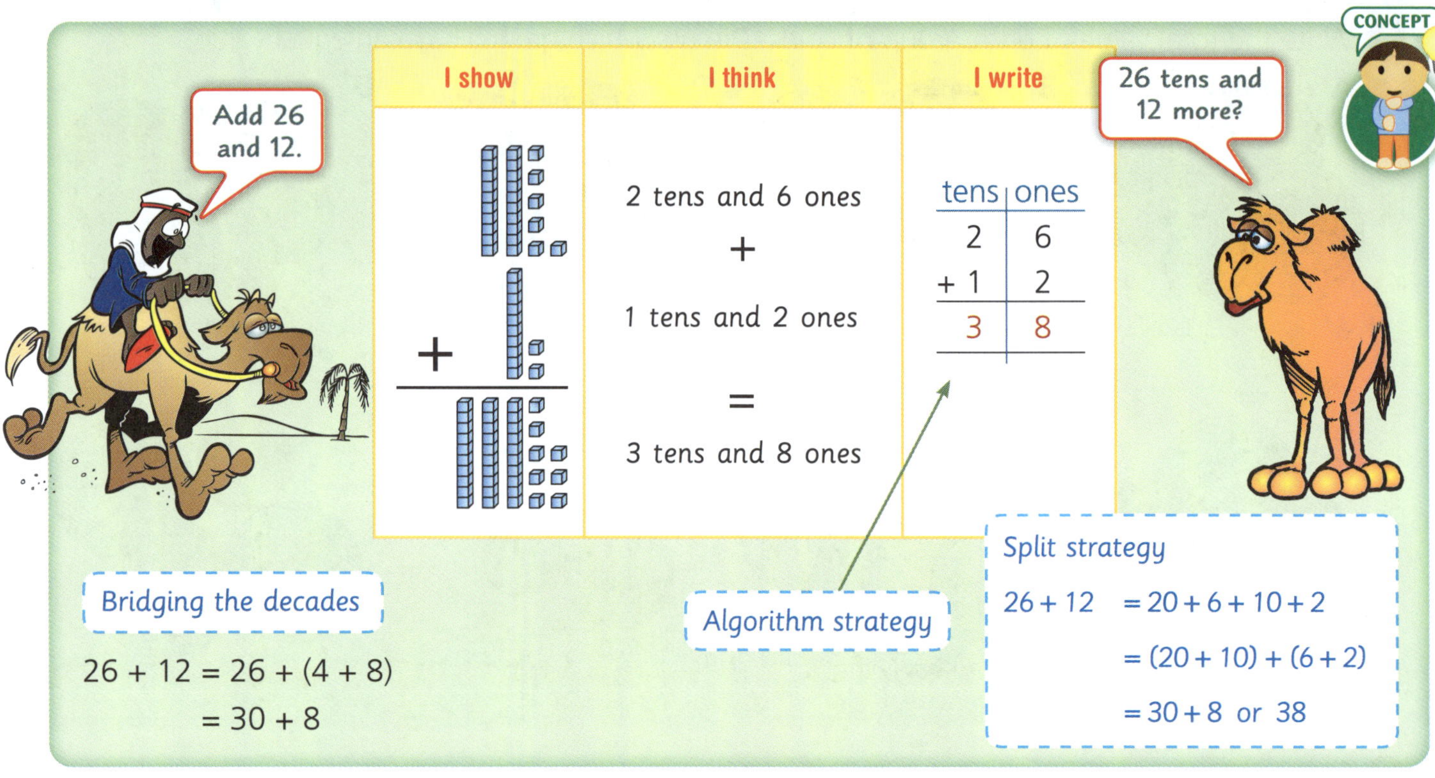

1. Model these problems and write them as number sentences.

a 5 eggs
12 eggs
How many eggs altogether?
☐ + ☐ = ☐

b 13 horses
32 horses
How many horses altogether?

☐ + ☐ = ☐

2. Use the split strategy or place-value blocks to answer these.

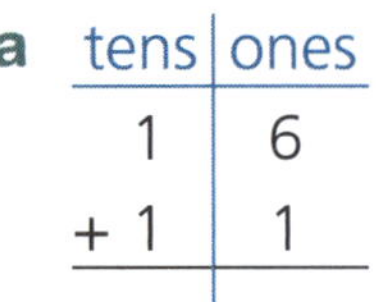

a

tens	ones
1	6
+ 1	1

b

tens	ones
2	0
+ 2	3

c

tens	ones
1	4
+ 2	3

d

tens	ones
3	1
+ 2	2

e

tens	ones
3	8
+ 1	0

f

tens	ones
1	7
+ 2	2

g

tens	ones
2	3
+ 2	5

h

tens	ones
1	4
+ 1	5

3. **a** 3 tens and 5 ones
+ 1 ten and 2 ones

b 2 tens and 4 ones
+ 2 tens and 5 ones

c 1 ten and 3 ones
+ 2 tens and 6 ones

4. **a** 36 + 62 ☐ **b** 51 + 37 ☐ **c** 25 + 43 ☐

 • *AUSTRALIAN SIGNPOST MATHS NSW 3* • ISBN 9780655709046

Jump strategy

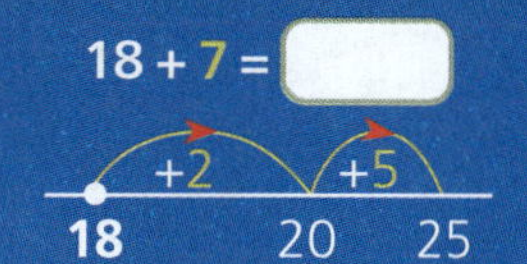

CONCEPT

Addition

35 + 19

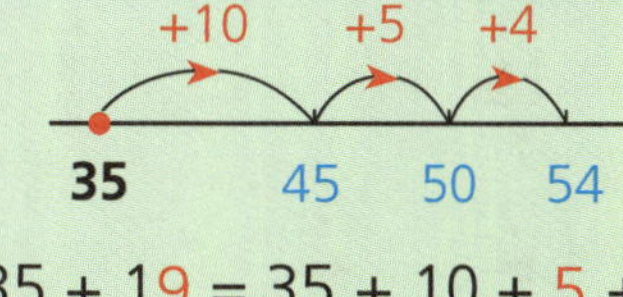

35 + 19 = 35 + 10 + 5 + 4
= 45 + 5 + 4
= 50 + 4 = 54

1 **a** 27 + 8 ☐

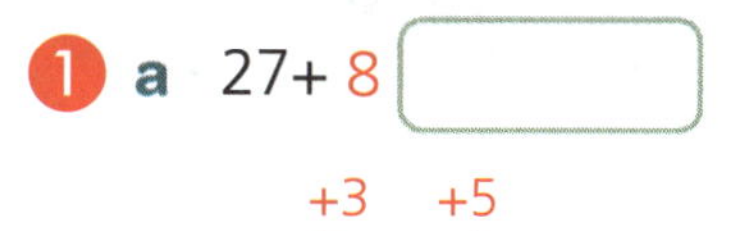

b 16 + 17 ☐

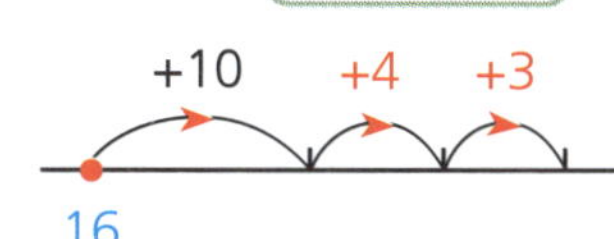

c 36 + 15 ☐

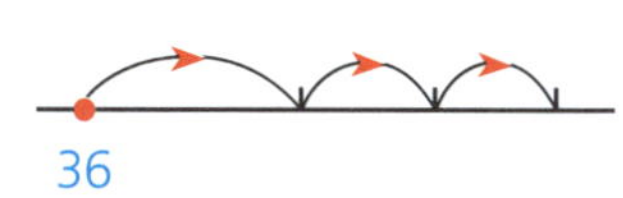

d 74 + 19 ☐

74

e 58 + 6 ☐

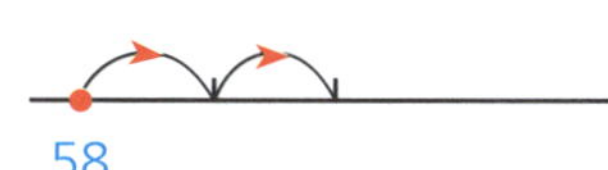

f 45 + 27 ☐

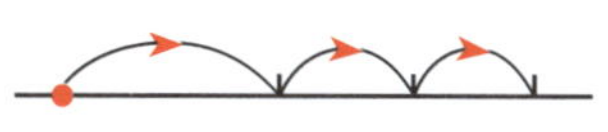

CONCEPT

Subtraction

31 – 14

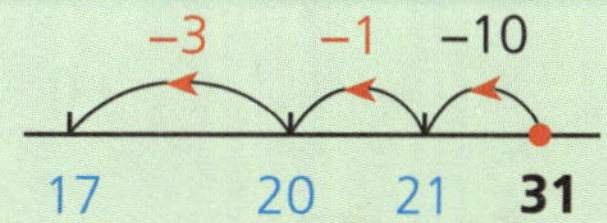

31 – 14 = 31 – 10 – 1 – 3
= 21 – 1 – 3
= 20 – 3 = 17

2 **a** 33 – 19 ☐

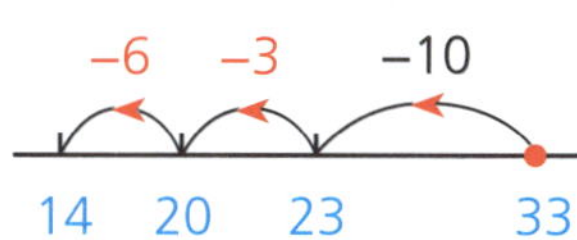

b 36 – 28 ☐

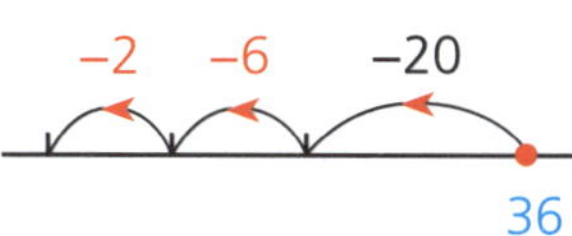

c 41 – 27 ☐

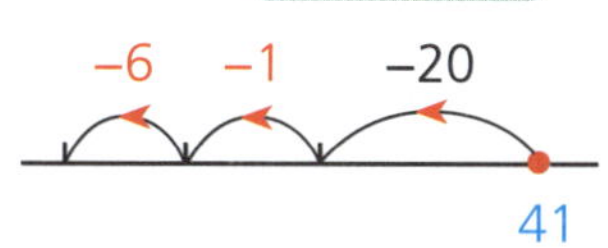

d 42 – 23 ☐

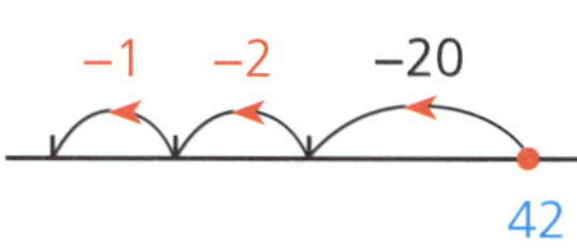

e 75 – 38 ☐

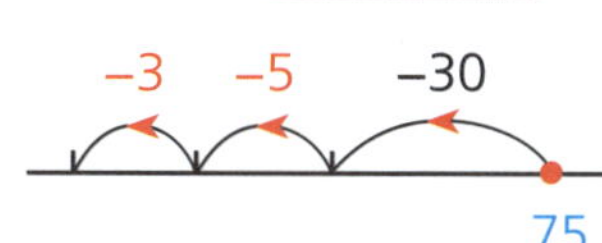

f 83 – 52 ☐

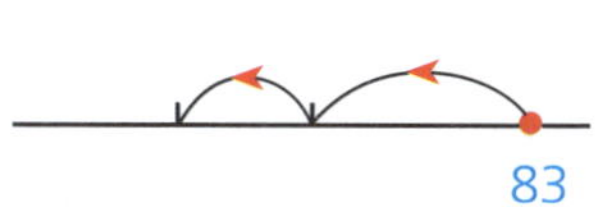

g 44 – 38 ☐

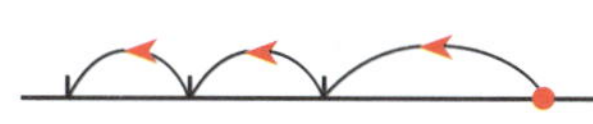

h 64 – 45 ☐

i 57 – 28 ☐

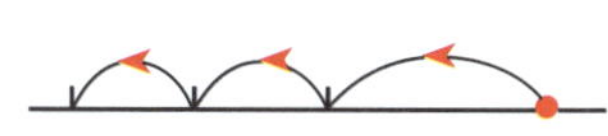

 • *AUSTRALIAN SIGNPOST MATHS NSW 3* • ISBN 9780655709046

Jump strategy

CONCEPT

Addition 43 + 29

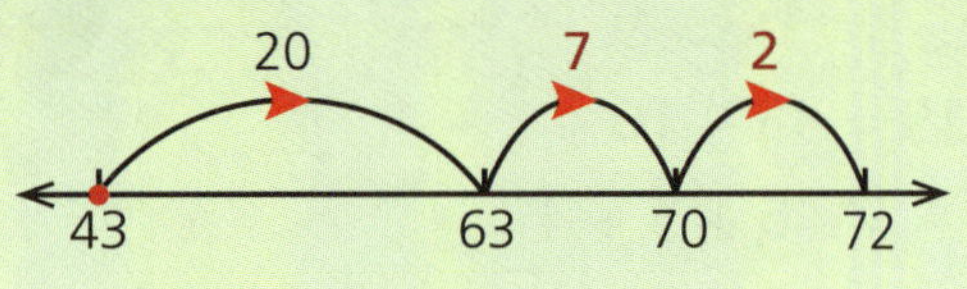

43 + 29 = 43 + 20 + 7 + 2
= 63 + 7 + 2
= 70 + 2 = 72

Subtraction 82 − 27

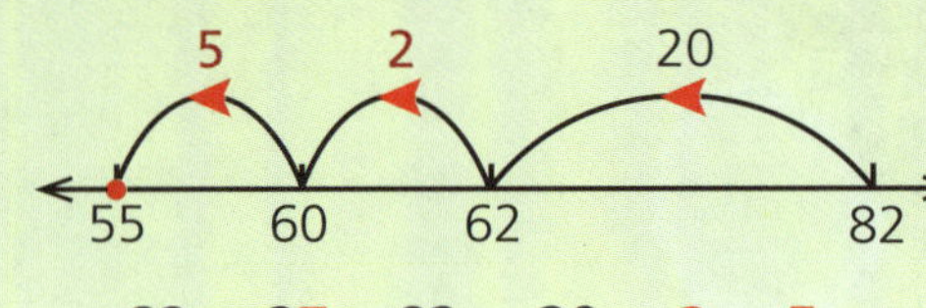

82 − 27 = 82 − 20 − 2 − 5
= 62 − 2 − 5
= 60 − 5 = 55

Learn the jump strategy.

1 a 72 + 19 ☐

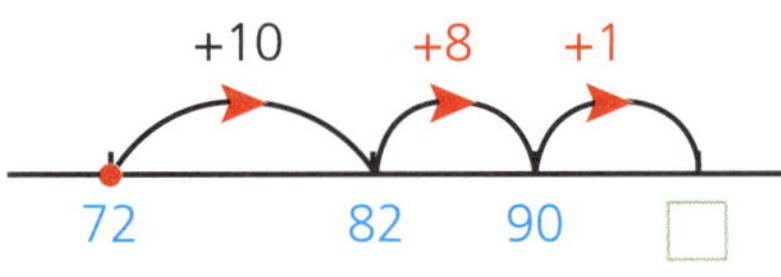

b 35 + 47 ☐

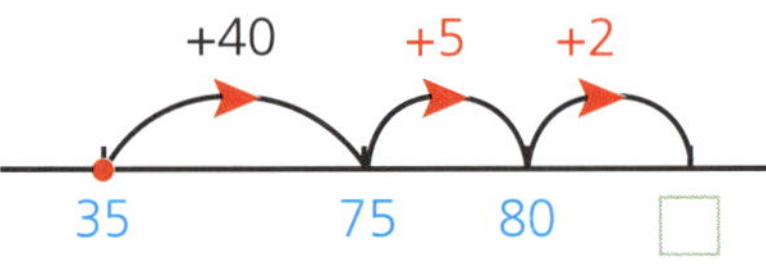

c 28 + 35 ☐

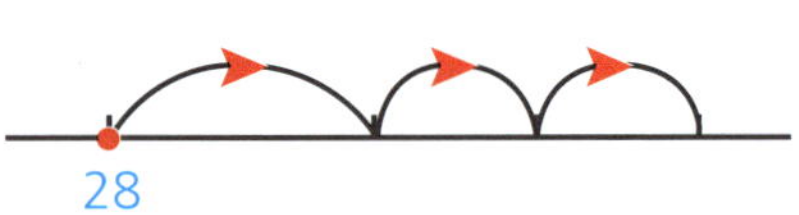

d 54 + 18 ☐

e 42 + 36 ☐

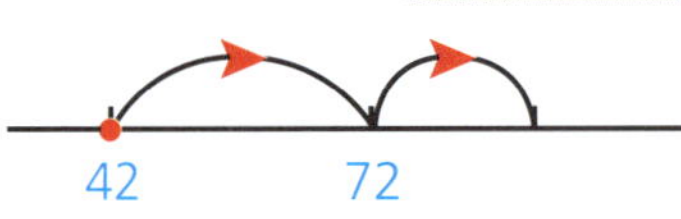

f 77 + 15 ☐

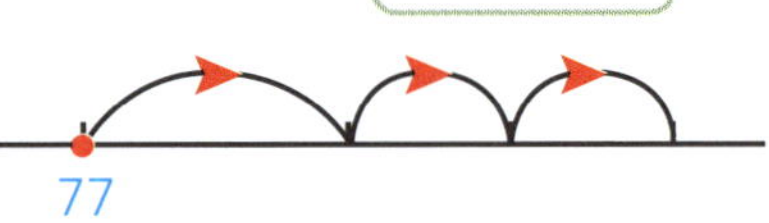

g 66 + 35 ☐

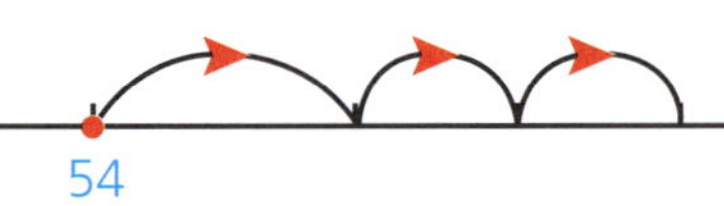

h 35 + 68 ☐

Work out the tens, then jump to the 10 above for addition or the 10 below for subtraction.

2 a 92 − 19 ☐

b 86 − 48 ☐

c 52 − 24 ☐

d 65 − 38 ☐

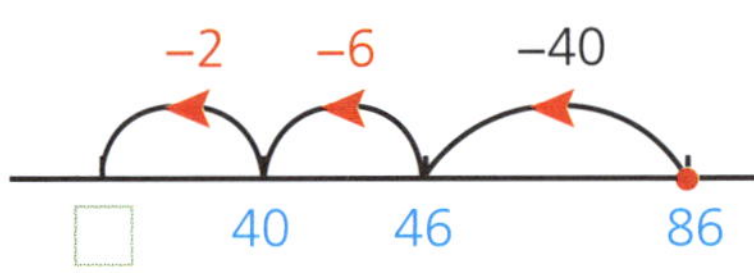

e 93 − 62 ☐

f 44 − 37 ☐

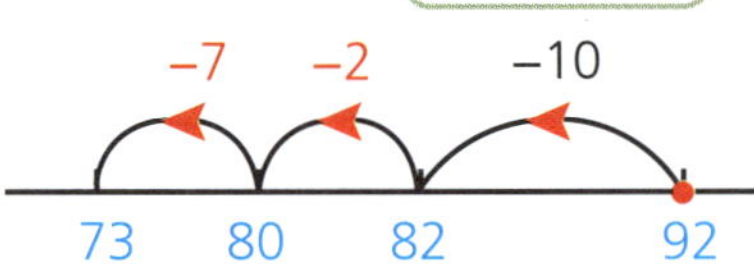

g 62 − 45 ☐

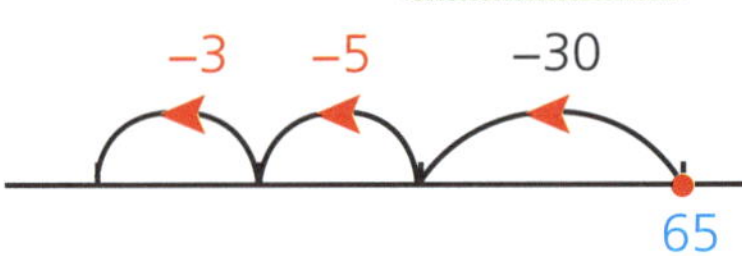

h 87 − 28 ☐

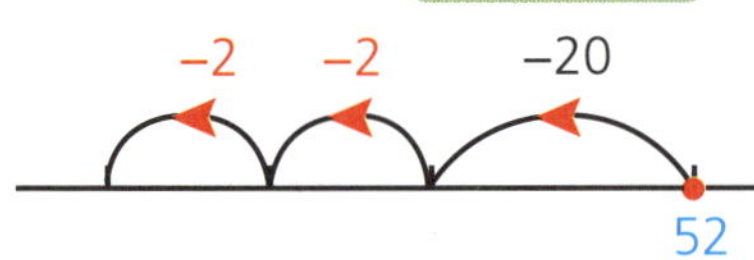

3 a 55 + 28 ☐

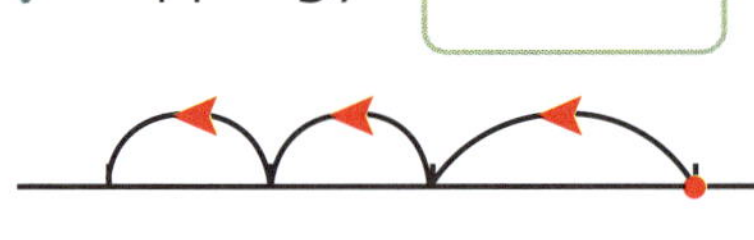

b 83 − 47 ☐

c 78 + 46 ☐

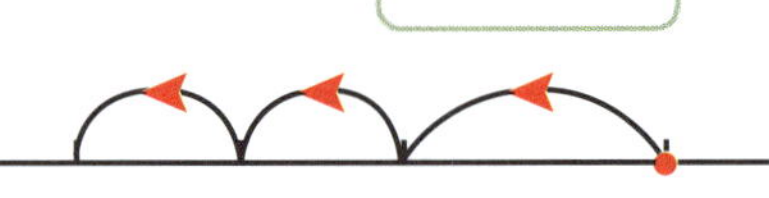

 • *AUSTRALIAN SIGNPOST MATHS NSW 3* • ISBN 9780655709046

Equalities

The = sign means 'the same as'.

True or false: 5 – 3 = 6 – 4?

CONCEPT

Elizabeth is standing at number 13. Max is standing at number 19.
The difference between their numbers is **19 – 13** = 6
They both move 3 steps back.
The difference between their numbers is now 16 – 10 = 6.
19 – 13 = 16 – 10 This number sentence has two equal sides.

1. Follow the instructions to write a number sentence that has two equal sides.

Add 3 to each part:	Subtract 2 from each part:	Subtract 10 from each part:
25 – 7 = 28 – ☐	21 – 12 = ☐ – ☐	20 – 12 = ☐ – ☐
27 – 17 = ☐ – ☐	32 – 22 = ☐ – ☐	30 – 17 = ☐ – ☐
36 – 27 = ☐ – ☐	51 – 32 = ☐ – ☐	20 – 19 = ☐ – ☐
64 – 47 = ☐ – ☐	64 – 42 = ☐ – ☐	40 – 18 = ☐ – ☐

2. Write the answer beside each number sentence in Question 1.
In each case, check each side of the number sentence. Discuss what you found.

3. Rewrite these problems to make them easier. Keep the difference constant by adding or subtracting the same amount to each number. Try to make the 2nd number a multiple of 10.

a 21 – 17 (Add 3.) ☐ – ☐
b 24 – 16 (Add 4.) ☐ – ☐
c 33 – 26 ☐ – ☐
d 31 – 23 ☐ – ☐
e 39 – 28 ☐ – ☐
f 38 – 17 ☐ – ☐
g 47 – 34 ☐ – ☐
h 49 – 27 ☐ – ☐

4. Rewrite each number sentence by subtracting 10, 20 or 30 from each side to make the number sentence easier to answer, e.g. 34 – 27 = 14 – 7 = 7. (I have subtracted 20 from each numeral.)

a 19 – 12 
b 27 – 15 ☐ – ☐
c 38 – 21 
d 36 – 18 ☐ – ☐
e 47 – 38 ☐ – ☐
f 51 – 34 

2:17 Mental strategies

Check your answers using the inverse operations, e.g. 3 + 4 = 7 so 7 − 4 = 3.

CONCEPT

Different types of questions need different strategies.

A	Using patterns	5 + 4 = 9 so 500 + 400 = 900
B	Changing the order	16 + 8 + 4 = 16 + 4 + 8 = 20 + 8 = 28
C	Bridging to 10s	45 + 8 = 45 + 5 + 3 = 50 + 3 = 53
D	Compensation	63 + 19 = 63 + 20 − 1 = 83 − 1 = 82
E	Split	23 + 35 = 20 + 30 + 3 + 5 = 50 + 8 = 58
F	Jump	58 + 23 (58 +20 78 +2 80 +1 81) 58 + 23 = 81

1 Using patterns

a 500 + 200 = ☐ b 200 + 700 = ☐ c 400 + 300 = ☐ d 200 + 400 = ☐

2 Changing the order

a 16 + 7 + 4 = ☐ b 27 + 4 + 3 = ☐ c 65 + 8 + 5 = ☐ d 28 + 4 + 2 = ☐

3 Bridging to 10s

a 38 + 8 = ☐ b 29 + 4 = ☐ c 37 + 6 = ☐ d 54 + 7 = ☐

4 Compensation

a 37 + 19 = ☐ b 63 + 29 = ☐ c 48 + 19 = ☐ d 25 + 39 = ☐

5 Split

a 32 + 41 = ☐ b 55 + 34 = ☐ c 23 + 16 = ☐

d 14 + 34 = ☐ e 36 + 21 = ☐ f 47 + 33 = ☐

Memorise the addition facts. See Extra Support on pages 164 to 167.

6 Jump

a 67 + 22 = ☐

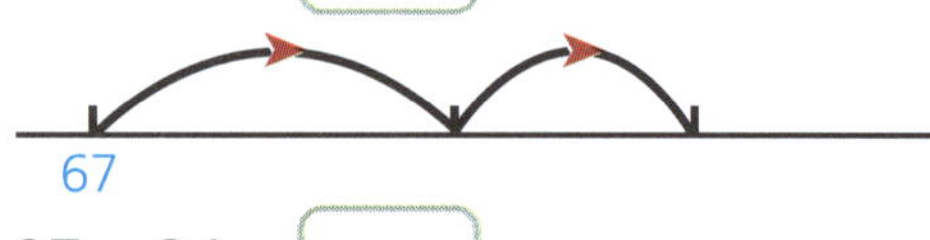

b 53 + 25 = ☐

c 27 + 34 = ☐

d 44 + 18 = ☐

INVESTIGATION

7 Complete the additions. Write the strategy you used (from **A** to **F** above).

a 51 + 37 = ☐ ☐ b 36 + 3 + 4 = ☐ ☐ c 44 + 9 = ☐ ☐

d 38 + 7 = ☐ ☐ e 300 + 500 = ☐ ☐ f 39 + 27 = ☐ ☐

Reflection: Were the strategies you used effective? Why or why not?

2:18 Number facts, ×3 extension

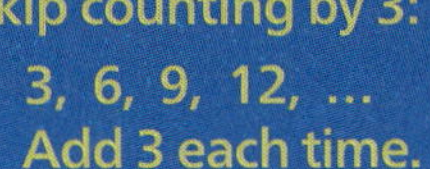

1 Use the number models to complete the multiplications. Practise counting by 3s.

a $1 \times 3 =$ ☐ *1 three is 3,*

b $2 \times 3 =$ ☐ *2 threes are …*

c $3 \times 3 =$ ☐

d $4 \times 3 =$ ☐

e $5 \times 3 =$ ☐

f $6 \times 3 =$ ☐

g $7 \times 3 =$ ☐

h $8 \times 3 =$ ☐

i $9 \times 3 =$ ☐

j $10 \times 3 =$ ☐

2 Write the answers. Remember that $3 \times 1 = 1 \times 3$.

a $3 \times 0 =$ ☐	b $0 \times 3 =$ ☐	c $3 \times 10 =$ ☐	d $10 \times 3 =$ ☐
e $3 \times 2 =$ ☐	f $2 \times 3 =$ ☐	g $3 \times 1 =$ ☐	h $1 \times 3 =$ ☐
i $3 \times 5 =$ ☐	j $5 \times 3 =$ ☐	k $8 \times 3 =$ ☐	l $4 \times 3 =$ ☐
m $9 \times 3 =$ ☐	n $6 \times 3 =$ ☐	o $3 \times 3 =$ ☐	p $7 \times 3 =$ ☐

3

a $5 \times 1 =$ ☐	b $1 \times 5 =$ ☐	c $5 \times 2 =$ ☐	d $2 \times 5 =$ ☐
e $5 \times 0 =$ ☐	f $0 \times 5 =$ ☐	g $5 \times 10 =$ ☐	h $10 \times 5 =$ ☐
i $2 \times 10 =$ ☐	j $10 \times 2 =$ ☐	k $5 \times 5 =$ ☐	l $10 \times 10 =$ ☐

4 a 3 pens in a set
8 sets
How many pens?

$$\begin{array}{r} 3 \\ \times\ 8 \\ \hline \square \end{array}$$

b 3 dollars per person
9 people
How many dollars?

$$\begin{array}{r} 3 \\ \times\ 9 \\ \hline \square \end{array}$$

5 Try to complete these tables from memory. Discuss: How are the × 5 and × 10 tables related?

a

	4	7	9	5	8	6
×3						

b

	4	7	9	5	8	6
×5						

c

	4	7	9	5	8	6
×2						

d

	4	7	9	5	8	6
×10						

×3 extension

3, 6, 9, 12, 15, 18, 21, 24, 27, 30
To skip count by 3, add 3.

Any number times 1 stays the same.

3 × 1 = 3 10 × 1 = 10

Any number times 0 is equal to 0.

3 × 0 = 3 10 × 0 = 0

1 Join each question to its answer, using a pencil and ruler.

a

	=	
0 × 3		6
1 × 3		3
2 × 3		0
3 × 3		9
4 × 3		15
5 × 3		18
6 × 3		12
7 × 3		27
8 × 3		21
9 × 3		24
10 × 3		30

b

	=	
3 × 3		0
0 × 3		3
5 × 3		6
1 × 3		9
7 × 3		12
2 × 3		15
8 × 3		18
4 × 3		21
6 × 3		24
10 × 3		27
9 × 3		30

c

	=	
1 × 3		9
3 × 3		3
0 × 3		0
5 × 3		21
2 × 3		12
7 × 3		15
4 × 3		6
6 × 3		27
10 × 3		24
9 × 3		18
8 × 3		30

×2 answers end in: 0, 2, 4, 6, or 8.

×10 answers end in: 0.

d

	=	
4 × 2		35
2 × 3		6
7 × 5		8
3 × 10		9
9 × 1		30
4 × 0		40
8 × 5		0
10 × 2		50
5 × 10		20
8 × 0		21
7 × 3		0

e

	=	
1 × 5		18
6 × 3		50
10 × 5		5
5 × 5		24
8 × 3		0
0 × 5		25
2 × 5		27
9 × 3		10
3 × 5		21
7 × 3		12
4 × 3		15

f

	=	
7 × 1		18
6 × 3		7
3 × 5		24
8 × 3		15
4 × 3		10
8 × 5		40
5 × 2		12
6 × 5		21
1 × 0		30
7 × 3		27
9 × 3		0

×5 answers end in: 5 or 0.

30 is:

	×	10
	×	3
	×	5

4 5 6 7

100 90 80

Multiplication facts

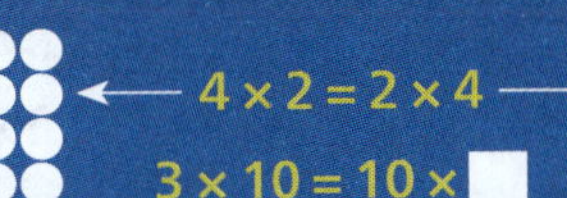

1 Complete each pair of multiplication facts.

a 5 × 10 = ☐
10 × 5 = ☐

b 2 × 5 = ☐
5 × 2 = ☐

c 2 × 10 = ☐
10 × 2 = ☐

d 1 × 5 = ☐
5 × 1 = ☐

e 5 × 0 = ☐
0 × 5 = ☐

f 2 × 6 = ☐
6 × 2 = ☐

2 Measure the time you take to complete each set of multiplication facts. Write the time.

a	**b**	**c**	**d**
9 × 0 = ☐	3 × 0 = ☐	6 × 0 = ☐	7 × 0 = ☐
7 × 1 = ☐	6 × 1 = ☐	9 × 1 = ☐	3 × 1 = ☐
6 × 2 = ☐	3 × 2 = ☐	8 × 2 = ☐	7 × 2 = ☐
10 × 5 = ☐	10 × 10 = ☐	6 × 2 = ☐	10 × 1 = ☐
3 × 2 = ☐	2 × 2 = ☐	5 × 2 = ☐	4 × 2 = ☐
5 × 5 = ☐	4 × 5 = ☐	3 × 2 = ☐	2 × 5 = ☐
4 × 10 = ☐	5 × 10 = ☐	2 × 10 = ☐	3 × 10 = ☐
4 × 2 = ☐	9 × 2 = ☐	7 × 2 = ☐	8 × 2 = ☐
8 × 2 = ☐	7 × 2 = ☐	9 × 2 = ☐	6 × 2 = ☐
7 × 10 = ☐	8 × 10 = ☐	6 × 10 = ☐	9 × 10 = ☐
☐ seconds	☐ seconds	☐ seconds	☐ seconds

 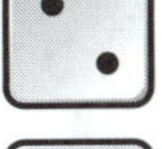    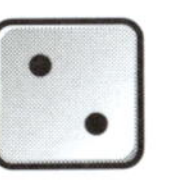      

3 Use the dice to find the answers.

a 2 × 2 = ☐	**b** 7 × 2 = ☐	**c** 1 × 2 = ☐	**d** 4 × 2 = ☐
e 3 × 5 = ☐	**f** 8 × 2 = ☐	**g** 5 × 5 = ☐	**h** 10 × 2 = ☐
i 9 × 2 = ☐	**j** 6 × 5 = ☐	**k** 3 × 2 = ☐	**l** 6 × 2 = ☐
m 8 × 5 = ☐	**n** 5 × 2 = ☐	**o** 9 × 5 = ☐	**p** 11 × 2 = ☐

2:21 Number facts, ×4

Skip count by 4:
4, 8, 12, 16, 20, 24, …
+4 +4 +4 +4 +4

1 Use the number models to complete the multiplications.

a 1 × 4 = ☐ *1 four is 4,*

b 2 × 4 = ☐ *2 fours are …*

c 3 × 4 = ☐

d 4 × 4 = ☐

e 5 × 4 = ☐

f 6 × 4 = ☐

g 7 × 4 = ☐

h 8 × 4 = ☐

i 9 × 4 = ☐

j 10 × 4 = ☐

Learn your × 4 facts.

The four times tables are double the 2 times tables. 3 × 2 = 6 so 3 × 4 = 12. 12 is double 6.

The answers to × **4** tables are always even (ending in 0, 2, 4, 6 or 8).

2
a 5 × 4 = ☐ b 1 × 4 = ☐ c 6 × 4 = ☐ d 2 × 4 = ☐
e 7 × 4 = ☐ f 9 × 4 = ☐ g 8 × 4 = ☐ h 3 × 4 = ☐
i 9 × 4 = ☐ j 6 × 4 = ☐ k 10 × 4 = ☐ l 4 × 4 = ☐

3 a

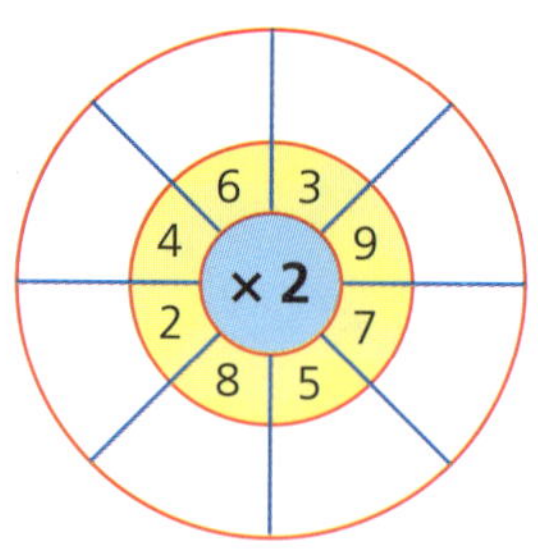

b

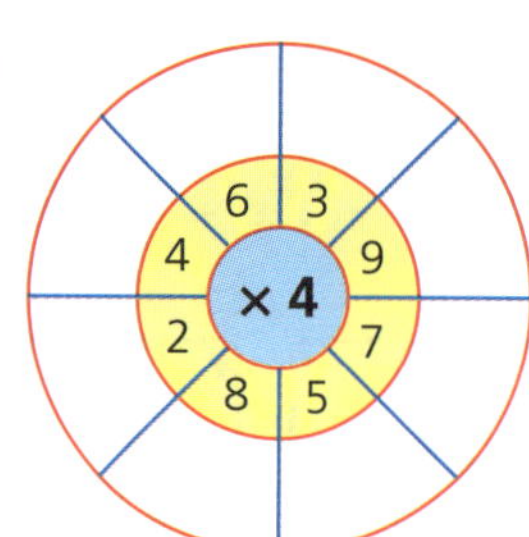

c

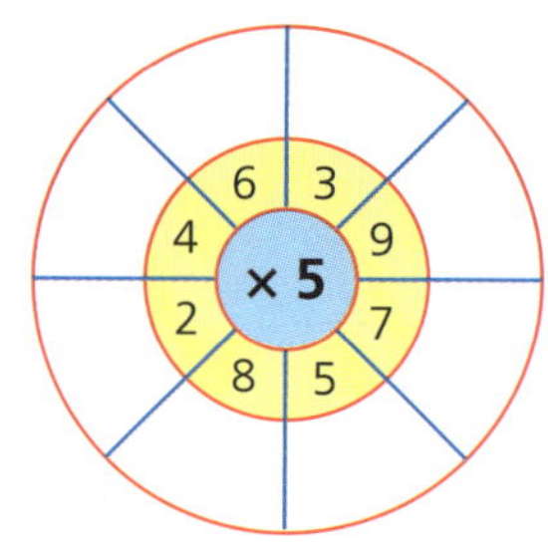

4
a **5 × 4 =** ☐ and **1 × 4 =** ☐ so **6 × 4 =** 20 + 4 = ☐
b **6 × 4 =** ☐ and **1 × 4 =** ☐ so **7 × 4 =** 24 + 4 = ☐

This is 5 × 4 plus 4.

5 Try to complete these tables from memory.

a

	2	1	5	10	3	4	8
× 4							

b

	4	6	8	5	9	7	3
× 4							

2:22 Times tables

2 × 4 means '2 groups of 4' or '2 rows of 4'.

Are you a tables champion?

4 threes is the same as 3 fours.

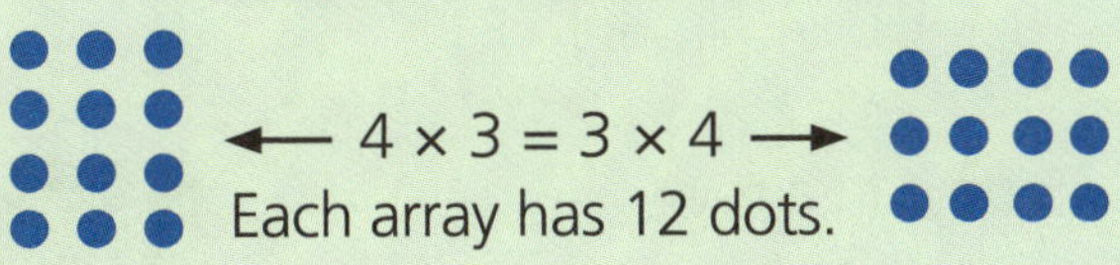

← 4 × 3 = 3 × 4 →

Each array has 12 dots.

Keep practising until you can recall all the facts on this page instantly.

1 Join each question to its answer using a pencil and ruler. You could practise your tables facts by rubbing out your answers and doing them again. Challenge your classmates.

a

	=
3 × 2	0
2 × 2	2
4 × 2	4
0 × 2	6
1 × 2	8
7 × 2	10
5 × 2	12
6 × 2	14
10 × 2	16
8 × 2	18
9 × 2	20

b

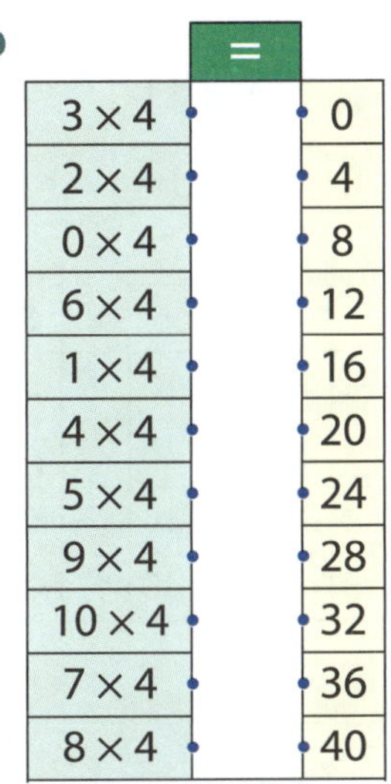

	=
3 × 4	0
2 × 4	4
0 × 4	8
6 × 4	12
1 × 4	16
4 × 4	20
5 × 4	24
9 × 4	28
10 × 4	32
7 × 4	36
8 × 4	40

c

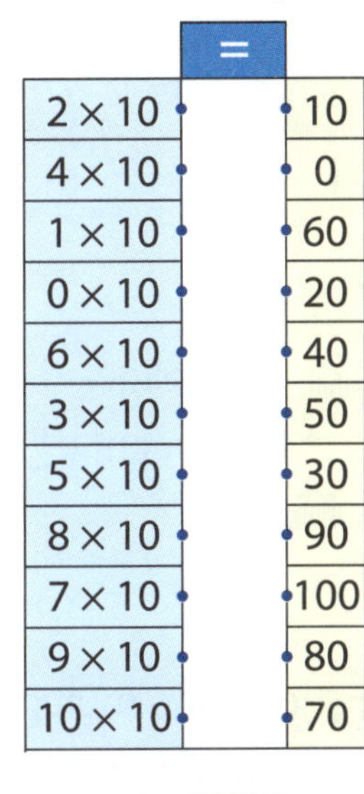

	=
2 × 10	10
4 × 10	0
1 × 10	60
0 × 10	20
6 × 10	40
3 × 10	50
5 × 10	30
8 × 10	90
7 × 10	100
9 × 10	80
10 × 10	70

d

	=
2 × 2	0
4 × 2	2
1 × 2	4
0 × 2	6
6 × 2	8
3 × 2	10
5 × 2	12
8 × 2	14
7 × 2	16
9 × 2	18
10 × 2	20

e

	=
0 × 5	45
9 × 5	40
8 × 5	0
6 × 5	15
3 × 5	30
5 × 5	10
4 × 5	5
7 × 5	25
2 × 5	20
1 × 5	50
10 × 5	35

f

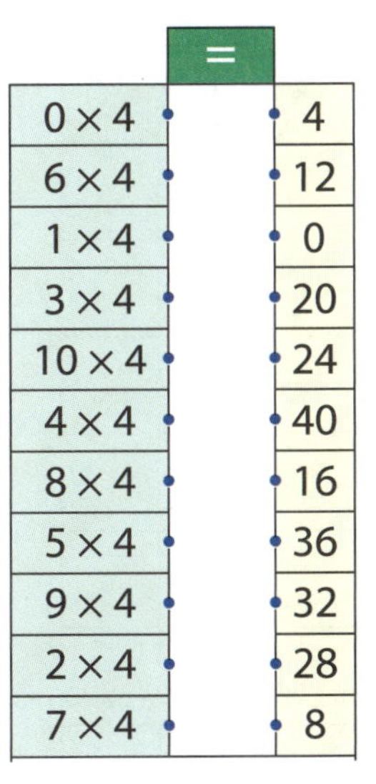

	=
0 × 4	4
6 × 4	12
1 × 4	0
3 × 4	20
10 × 4	24
4 × 4	40
8 × 4	16
5 × 4	36
9 × 4	32
2 × 4	28
7 × 4	8

g

	=
1 × 5	0
3 × 5	25
0 × 5	5
5 × 5	15
2 × 5	30
6 × 5	10
4 × 5	45
9 × 5	35
7 × 5	20
10 × 5	40
8 × 5	50

h

	=
6 × 5	20
4 × 5	28
7 × 4	30
8 × 4	36
5 × 5	45
9 × 4	32
9 × 5	25
5 × 4	35
7 × 5	20
4 × 4	40
8 × 5	16

Start 4 10 20 30 40 50

2 Try to complete these tables from memory.

a

	5	3	4	8	6	9	7
× 5							

b

	5	3	4	8	6	9	7
× 4							

 • *AUSTRALIAN SIGNPOST MATHS NSW 3* • ISBN 9780655709046

Number facts, multiplication

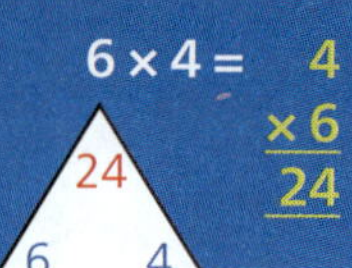

1 Write each problem as a number sentence or a vertical times table, and find the answer.

a 7 rows of 5 hats

b 4 groups of 10 pens

c 5 groups of 5 eggs

d 5 girls in a team
8 teams
How many girls?
×

e 5 boys in a row
6 rows
How many boys?
×

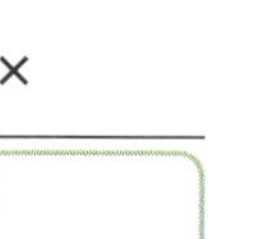

2

a 9 × 2 = ☐ **b** 4 × 5 = ☐ **c** 8 × 10 = ☐ **d** 7 × 2 = ☐

e 4 × 1 = ☐ **f** 6 × 2 = ☐ **g** 3 × 10 = ☐ **h** 5 × 2 = ☐

i 3 × 5 = ☐ **j** 3 × 1 = ☐ **k** 7 × 10 = ☐ **l** 8 × 0 = ☐

3 On this 50 chart:

- colour the multiples of two yellow
- colour the multiples of five green
- circle the multiples of four.

1	2	3	4	5	6	7	8	9	10
11	12	13	14	15	16	17	18	19	20
21	22	23	24	25	26	27	28	29	30
31	32	33	34	35	36	37	38	39	40
41	42	43	44	45	46	47	48	49	50

4 This multiplication grid shows the multiples of 2.
Write in the multiples of 4, 5 and 10.

×	0	1	2	3	4	5	6	7	8	9	10
0			0								
1			2								
2	0	2	4	6	8	10	12	14	16	18	20
3			6								
4			8								
5			10								
6			12								
7			14								
8			16								
9			18								
10			20								

Each table should be written twice, once across a row and once down a column.
2 × 10 = 10 × 2

5 Draw and describe an array that is a square number.

Example: 2 × 2 = 4 

 • *AUSTRALIAN SIGNPOST MATHS NSW 3* • ISBN 9780655709046

Problem solving

I invited 10 people, you invited 6.
How many will be there?

10	6
?	

Solve these problems.

My mum caught 37 prawns.
I caught 5 more than she did.
How many did we catch altogether?

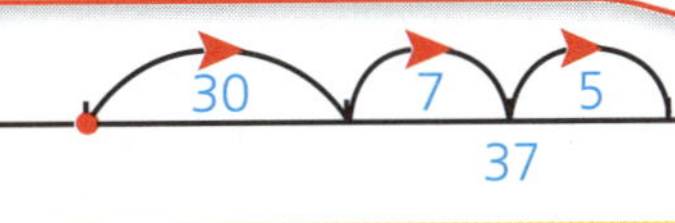

Find: How many altogether?

Working

Number sentence: 37 + (37 + 5)

Answer:

1. Holly had 43 football cards and bought 25 more. How many altogether?

   Find:

   Working

   Number sentence:

   Answer:

2. There are 3 rows of 5 bottles. How many bottles are there altogether?

   Find:

   Working

   Number sentence:

   Answer:

3. A farmer had 96 sheep but sold 28. How many did she have left?

   Find:

   Working

   Number sentence:

   Answer:

4. Marnie collected 54 aluminium cans before lunch and 37 in the afternoon. How many cans did she collect?

   Find:

   Working

   Number sentence:

   Answer:

5. Lee planted seeds in rows of 5. He planted 6 full rows and had 4 seeds left. How many seeds were there altogether?

   Find:

   Working

   Number sentence:

   Answer:

INVESTIGATION

6. Lauren and Justin want to play handball. For a handball court they need two squares next to each other.

   a How many different courts could they choose?

   b How many courts could all be used at the same time?

   c If they needed three squares in a row to make a court, how many courts could be used at the same time?

2:25 Inverse operations, × and ÷

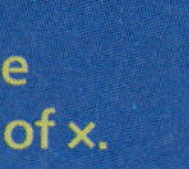
÷ is the opposite of ×.

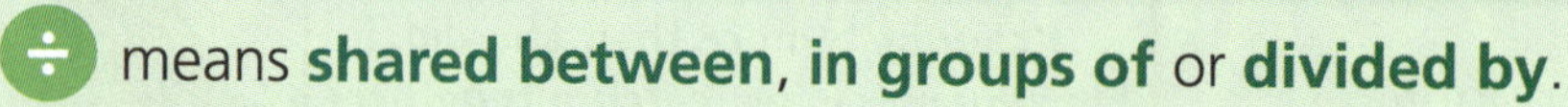
÷ means **shared between**, **in groups of** or **divided by**.

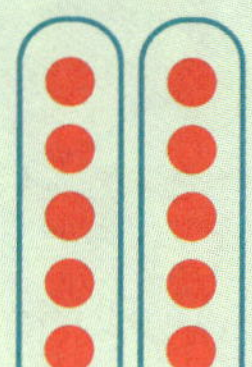

Double 5 = 10
Half 10 = 5
So,
5 (× 2) (÷ 2) = 5

12 ÷ 2 = 6
6 × 2 = 12
So,
12 (÷ 2) (× 2) = 12

CONCEPT

1

a 20 ÷ 10 × 10 = ☐ b 10 × 5 ÷ 5 = ☐ c 3 × 2 ÷ 2 = ☐
d 30 ÷ 5 × 5 = ☐ e 8 × 2 ÷ 2 = ☐ f 60 ÷ 10 × 10 = ☐

2

a
Half 14 = ☐
Double 7 = ☐
So, 14 ÷ 2 × 2 = ☐

b
15 ÷ 5 = ☐
3 × 5 = ☐
So, 15 ÷ 5 × 5 = ☐

c
4 × 10 = ☐
40 ÷ 10 = ☐
So, 4 × 10 ÷ 10 = ☐

d
4 × 5 = ☐
20 ÷ 5 = ☐
So, 4 × 5 ÷ 5 = ☐

e
5 × 2 = ☐
10 ÷ 2 = ☐
So, 5 × 2 ÷ 2 = ☐

f
20 ÷ 2 = ☐
10 × 2 = ☐
So, 20 ÷ 2 × 2 = ☐

3

a 6 × 2 ÷ 2 = ☐ b 10 ÷ 5 × 5 = ☐
c 30 ÷ 10 × 10 = ☐ d 4 ÷ 2 × 2 = ☐
e 8 × 5 ÷ 5 = ☐ f 50 ÷ 10 × 10 = ☐
g 9 × 2 ÷ 2 = ☐ h 7 × 5 ÷ 5 = ☐
i 45 ÷ 5 × 5 = ☐ j 6 × 10 ÷ 10 = ☐

FUN SPOT

- Make up your own inverse number sentences.
- Example: 8 (× 10) (÷ 10) (× 3) (÷ 3) (× 4) (× 2) (÷ 4) (÷ 2) = 8

☐

Relating × and ÷

How many could be given 2?

$12 \div 2 =$ ___

3 rows of 4 = 12 | $3 \times 4 = 12$
4 columns of 3 = 12 | $4 \times 3 = 12$
12 divided by 3 = 4 | $12 \div 3 = 4$
12 divided by 4 = 3 | $12 \div 4 = 12$

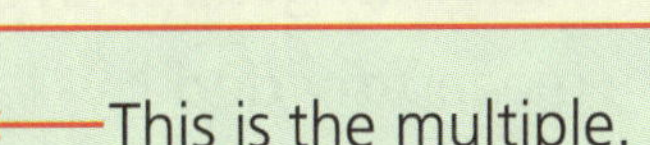

Multiplication and division facts are related.

CONCEPT

Triangle: 12 at top; 3 and 4 at bottom.
12 ← This is the multiple.
3, 4 ← These are multiplied together.

1 Link multiplication and division facts to answer these.

a

3 rows of ___ = ___
5 columns of ___ = ___
15 divided by ___ = ___
15 divided by ___ = ___

Triangle: 15; 3, 5

$3 \times 5 =$ ___
$5 \times 3 =$ ___
$15 \div 3 =$ ___
$15 \div 5 =$ ___

b

$2 \times 4 =$ ___
$4 \times 2 =$ ___
$8 \div 2 =$ ___
$8 \div 4 =$ ___

c

$4 \times 5 =$ ___
$5 \times 4 =$ ___
$20 \div 4 =$ ___
$20 \div 5 =$ ___

d

$2 \times 5 =$ ___
$5 \times 2 =$ ___
$10 \div 2 =$ ___
$10 \div 5 =$ ___

e

$3 \times 6 =$ ___
$6 \times 3 =$ ___
$18 \div 3 =$ ___
$18 \div 6 =$ ___

2 Complete these multiplication fact family triangles and complete the number sentences. The first one has been done for you.

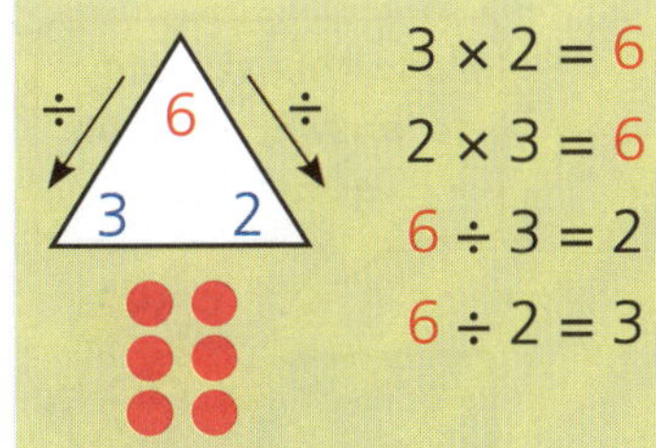

Triangle: 6; 3, 2 (÷ arrows)

$3 \times 2 = 6$
$2 \times 3 = 6$
$6 \div 3 = 2$
$6 \div 2 = 3$

a

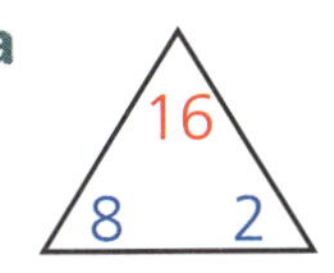

Triangle: 16; 8, 2

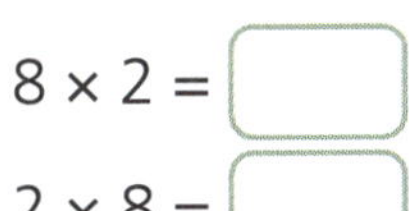

$8 \times 2 =$ ___
$2 \times 8 =$ ___
$16 \div 2 =$ ___
$16 \div 8 =$ ___

b

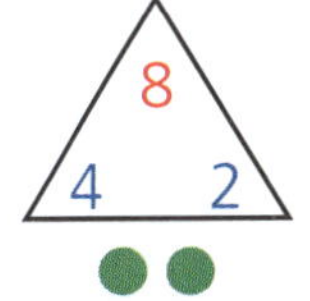

Triangle: 8; 4, 2

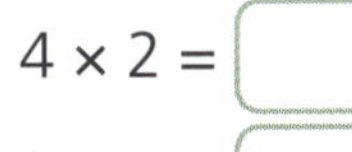

$4 \times 2 =$ ___
$2 \times 4 =$ ___
$8 \div 4 =$ ___
$8 \div 2 =$ ___

c

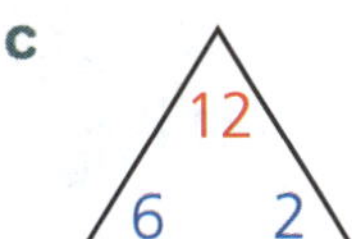

Triangle: 12; 6, 2

$6 \times 2 =$ ___
$2 \times 6 =$ ___
$12 \div 6 =$ ___
$12 \div 2 =$ ___

d

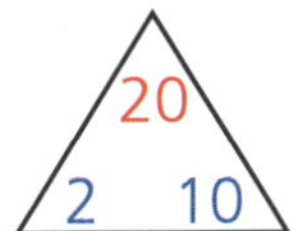

Triangle: 20; 2, 10

$10 \times 2 =$ ___
$2 \times 10 =$ ___
$20 \div 2 =$ ___
$20 \div 10 =$ ___

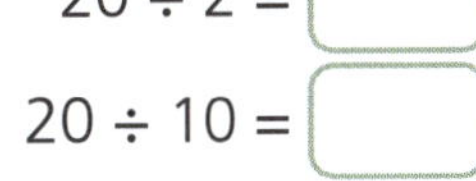

2:27 × and ÷ fact families

÷ is the opposite of ×. 5 × 10 = 50
50 ÷ 10 = 5

CONCEPT

÷ means **shared** between
means **in groups of**
means **divided by**

15 shared into 3 rows ...

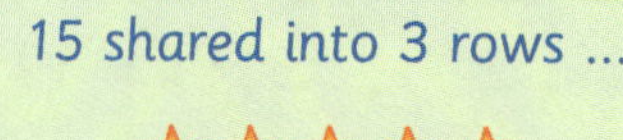
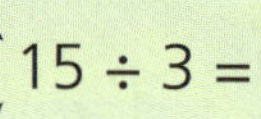

Groups of 3 in 15 ...

15 ÷ 3 =

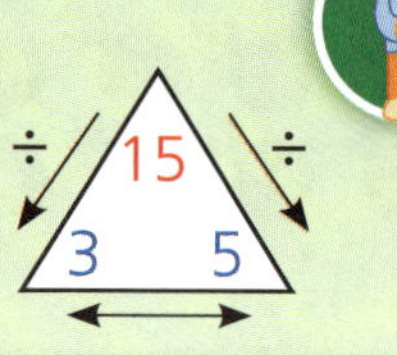

1 Link multiplication and division facts to answer these.

a

2 × 6 =
6 × 2 =
12 ÷ 2 =
12 ÷ 6 =

b

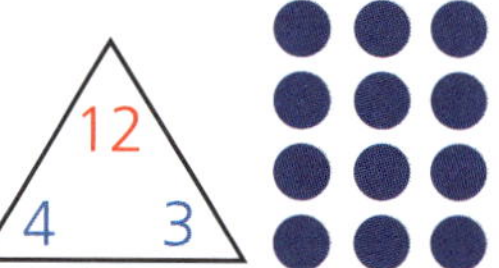

4 × 3 =
3 × 4 =
12 ÷ 4 =
12 ÷ 3 =

c

15
5 3

5 × 3 =
3 × 5 =
15 ÷ 5 =
15 ÷ 3 =

d

5 × 4 =
4 × 5 =
20 ÷ 5 =
20 ÷ 4 =

e

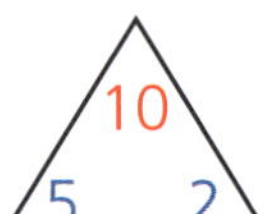

5 × 2 =
2 × 5 =
10 ÷ 5 =
10 ÷ 2 =

f

30
3 10

3 × 10 =
10 × 3 =
30 ÷ 3 =
30 ÷ 10 =

g

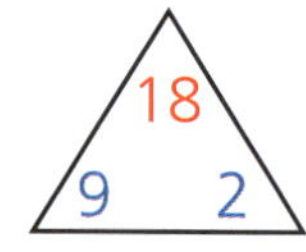

9 × 2 =
2 × 9 =
18 ÷ 9 =
18 ÷ 2 =

h

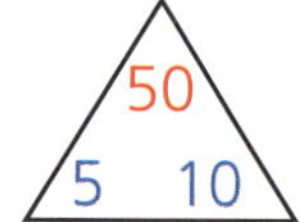

5 × 10 =
10 × 5 =
50 ÷ 5 =
50 ÷ 10 =

2 Write the fact families for these triangles.

a

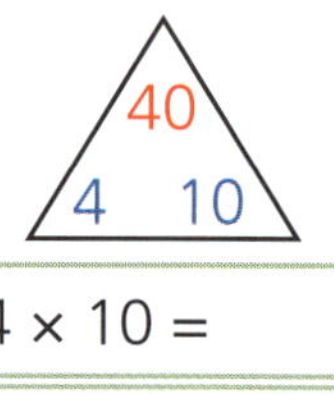

4 × 10 =

b

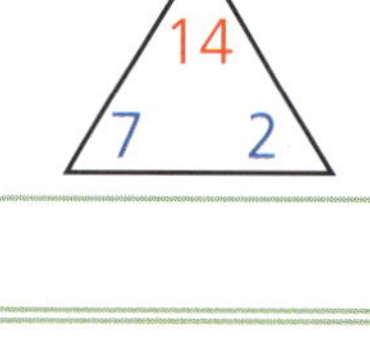

c

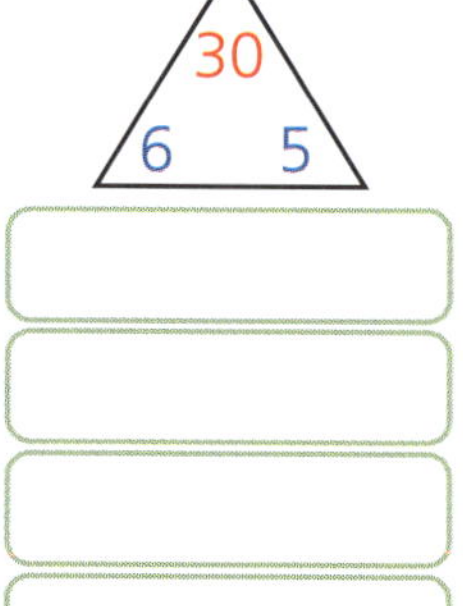

3 How would you find the answer to 18 ÷ 3?

 • *AUSTRALIAN SIGNPOST MATHS NSW 3* • ISBN 9780655709046

2:28 Relating × and ÷

6 fours
6 × 4

How many 4s in 24?
Share 24 among 4.
24 ÷ 4

5 groups of 4 make ☐. 5 × 4 = 20

How many groups of 4 in 20? ☐ 20 ÷ 4 = 5

1 Complete each question and write the related number sentences.

a 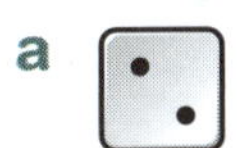      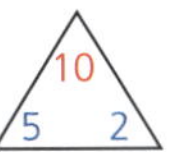

5 groups of 2 make ☐.

How many 2s in 10? ☐

5 × 2 = ☐ 10 ÷ 2 = ☐

b       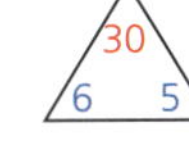

6 groups of 5 make ☐.

How many 5s in 30? ☐

6 × 5 = ☐ 30 ÷ 5 = ☐

c 

5 × 5 = ☐

25 ÷ 5 = ☐

5 × ☐ = 25

d 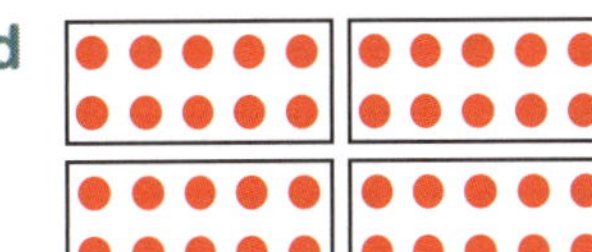

4 × 10 = ☐

40 ÷ 10 = ☐

☐ × 10 = 40

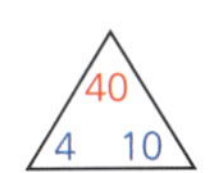

e 

7 × 5 = ☐

35 ÷ 5 = ☐

☐ × 5 = 35

f    

8 × 2 = ☐

16 ÷ 2 = ☐

☐ × 2 = 16

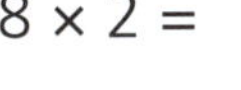

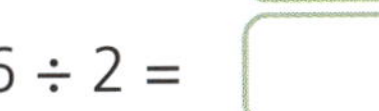

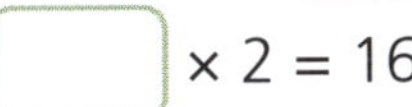

If you share 35 squares between 5 students, how many is each given? ☐

2
a 9 × 4 = 36 so 36 ÷ 4 = ☐
b 6 × 4 = 24 so 24 ÷ 4 = ☐
c 4 × 4 = 16 so 16 ÷ 4 = ☐
d 7 × 4 = 28 so 28 ÷ 4 = ☐
e 5 × 4 = 20 so 20 ÷ 4 = ☐
f 8 × 4 = 32 so 32 ÷ 4 = ☐
g 10 × 4 = 40 so 40 ÷ 4 = ☐

3
a 6 × 5 = 30 so 30 ÷ 5 = ☐
b 7 × 2 = 14 so 14 ÷ 2 = ☐
c 9 × 5 = 45 so 45 ÷ 5 = ☐
d 7 × 10 = 70 so 70 ÷ 10 = ☐
e 7 × 5 = 35 so 35 ÷ 5 = ☐
f 10 × 5 = 50 so 50 ÷ 5 = ☐
g 8 × 5 = 40 so 40 ÷ 5 = ☐

4 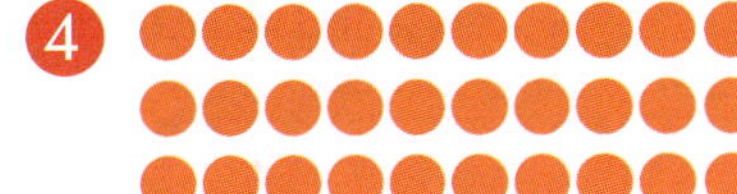

a 30 balls are shared among 3 people, how many is each given? ☐

b 30 balls are shared among 10 people, how many is each given? ☐

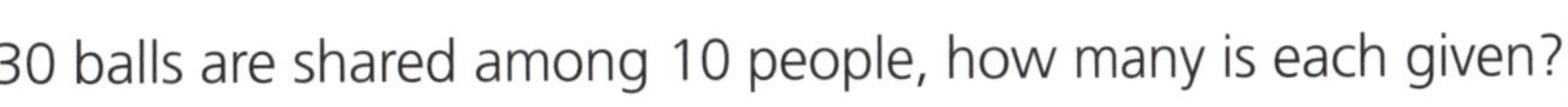

2:29 Linking × and ÷

5 × 2 = 10, so:
there are 5 twos in 10 and 2 fives in 10.
10 ÷ 2 = 5 and 10 ÷ 5 = 2.

CONCEPT

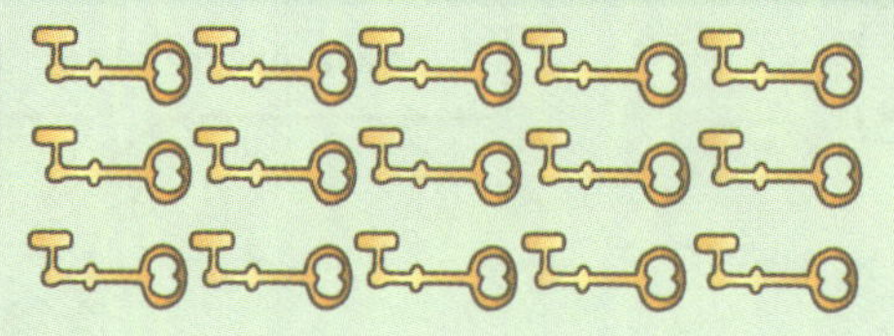

For 15 ÷ 5, ask:
What × 5 = 15?

Grouping: How many groups of 5 keys can be made from 15?
Sharing: 15 keys are shared by 5 people. What is each share?

1 a What is 4 groups of 5? ☐ 4 × 5 = ☐
b How many 5s in 20? ☐ 20 ÷ 5 = ☐
c Share 20 among 4. ☐ 20 ÷ 4 = ☐

2 a What is 3 groups of 8? ☐ 3 × 8 = ☐
b How many 8s in 24? ☐ 24 ÷ 8 = ☐
c Share 24 among 3. ☐ 24 ÷ 3 = ☐

3 Write the multiplication fact families for these triangles.

a
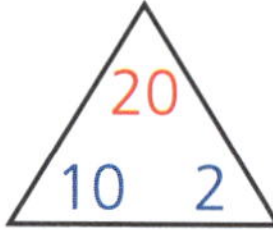

10 × 2 =
2 × 10 =
20 ÷ 2 =
20 ÷ 10 =

b
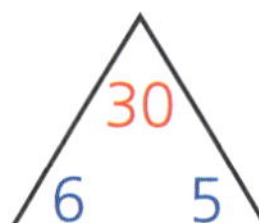

☐
☐
☐
☐

c
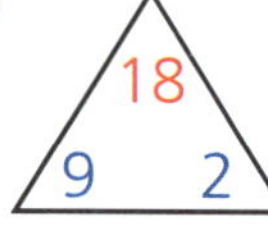

☐
☐
☐
☐

CONCEPT

10 × 5 = 50 → 50 ÷ 5 = 10, 50 ÷ 10 = 5

For 50 ÷ 5 = ?, ask: ☐ × 5 = 50, 5 × ☐ = 50

4 Use the first number sentence to complete the others.

a 5 × 2 = 10
10 ÷ 2 = ☐
10 ÷ 5 = ☐

b 10 × 3 = 30
30 ÷ 3 = ☐
30 ÷ 10 = ☐

c 7 × 2 = 14
14 ÷ 2 = ☐
14 ÷ 7 = ☐

d 9 × 4 = 36
36 ÷ 4 = ☐
36 ÷ 9 = ☐

5 Use the first number sentence to complete the others.

a 12 ÷ 3 = 4
☐ × 3 = 12
3 × ☐ = 12

b 35 ÷ 5 = 7
☐ × 5 = 35
5 × ☐ = 35

c 50 ÷ 10 = 5
☐ × 10 = 50
10 × ☐ = 50

d 80 ÷ 10 = 8
☐ × 10 = 80
10 × ☐ = 80

÷ facts from × facts

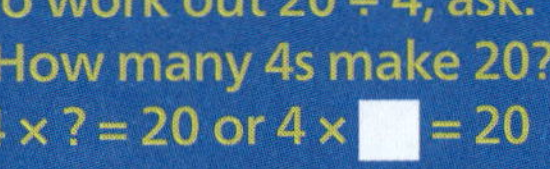

CONCEPT

To find how many 5s in 15, ask:
What multiplied by 5 gives 15?

Groups of 5 in 15:

Answer: 3

1
a $8 \div 2 = ?$ ☐ × 2 = 8 Answer = ☐
b $50 \div 5 = ?$ ☐ × 5 = 50 Answer = ☐
c $50 \div 10 = ?$ ☐ × 10 = 50 Answer = ☐
d $20 \div 5 = ?$ ☐ × 5 = 20 Answer = ☐
e $45 \div 5 = ?$ ☐ × 5 = 45 Answer = ☐
f $24 \div 4 = ?$ ☐ × 4 = 24 Answer = ☐
g $35 \div 5 = ?$ ☐ × 5 = 35 Answer = ☐
h $80 \div 10 = ?$ ☐ × 10 = 80 Answer = ☐

2 Use the first number sentence to complete the others.

a $2 \times 10 = 20$
20 ÷ 10 = ☐
20 ÷ 2 = ☐

b $6 \times 2 = 12$
12 ÷ 2 = ☐
12 ÷ 6 = ☐

c $3 \times 5 = 15$
15 ÷ 3 = ☐
15 ÷ 5 = ☐

d $8 \times 5 = 40$
40 ÷ 5 = ☐
40 ÷ 8 = ☐

3
a ☐ × 10 = 10
b ☐ × 2 = 20
c ☐ × 10 = 60
d ☐ × 4 = 36
e 5 × ☐ = 5
f 3 × ☐ = 30
g 4 × ☐ = 8
h 2 × ☐ = 16

4
a 10 ÷ 2 = ☐
b 8 ÷ 2 = ☐
c 14 ÷ 2 = ☐
d 12 ÷ 2 = ☐
e 25 ÷ 5 = ☐
f 30 ÷ 5 = ☐
g 40 ÷ 5 = ☐
h 45 ÷ 5 = ☐
i 20 ÷ 10 = ☐
j 80 ÷ 10 = ☐
k 90 ÷ 10 = ☐
l 70 ÷ 10 = ☐

5
a How many groups of 2 are in 10? ☐ 10 ÷ 2 = ☐
b Is there a whole number answer to how many groups of 10 are in 2? ☐
c Is 10 ÷ 2 equal to 2 ÷ 10? ☐

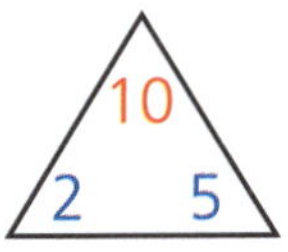

ACTIVITY

Number line jumps

- One person draws a number line starting at zero that shows several equal jumps.
- The other person writes multiplication and division number sentences to match the picture.

This shows 6 × 5 = 30 and 30 ÷ 5 = 6.

0 5 10 15 20 25 30 35 40 45 50

2:31 × and ÷ tables

10 ÷ 2 can mean:
'How many 2s are in 10?' or 'How many in each share if 10 is shared by 2?'

Start 10 20 30 40 50 60 70 80 90 100

If 4 × 5 = 20 then
- 20 ÷ 5 (How many 5s in 20?) = 4
- 20 ÷ 4 (20 shared by 4) = 5 (each)

Multiplication is the opposite of division.

12 ÷ 3 × 3 = 12

30 ÷ 5 × 5 = 30

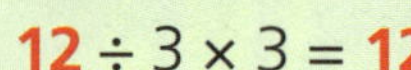

1 Join each question to its answer using a pencil and ruler.

a

	=	
2 × 5		0
4 × 5		5
0 × 5		20
1 × 5		10
3 × 5		35
7 × 5		25
5 × 5		15
10 × 5		45
9 × 5		50
6 × 5		40
8 × 5		30

b

	=	
3 × 4		4
0 × 4		20
5 × 4		0
1 × 4		8
7 × 4		32
2 × 4		16
8 × 4		12
4 × 4		28
6 × 4		36
10 × 4		24
9 × 4		40

c

	=	
6 × 10		25
9 × 2		3
5 × 5		40
3 × 1		18
8 × 5		60
9 × 10		14
7 × 2		35
7 × 5		20
8 × 1		90
4 × 5		40
8 × 5		8

15
5 3

5 × 3 = 15
3 × 5 = 15
15 ÷ 5 = 3
15 ÷ 3 = 5

×10 answers end in: 0.

d

	=	
4 ÷ 2		8
60 ÷ 10		3
16 ÷ 2		9
30 ÷ 10		2
18 ÷ 2		6
70 ÷ 10		1
6 ÷ 6		7
50 ÷ 10		4
20 ÷ 2		0
8 ÷ 2		5
0 ÷ 10		10

e

	=	
20 ÷ 5		7
14 ÷ 2		2
10 ÷ 5		10
10 ÷ 1		9
45 ÷ 5		4
0 ÷ 2		0
30 ÷ 5		1
40 ÷ 5		6
5 ÷ 5		5
5 ÷ 1		8
15 ÷ 5		3

f

	=	
30 ÷ 5		0
32 ÷ 4		6
0 ÷ 5		3
8 ÷ 4		8
15 ÷ 5		2
28 ÷ 4		4
45 ÷ 5		10
20 ÷ 4		7
50 ÷ 5		9
16 ÷ 4		1
5 ÷ 5		5

×5 answers end in: 5, or 0.

20 is:

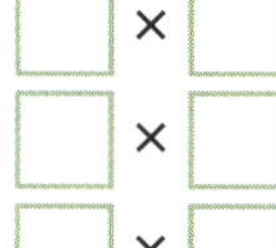

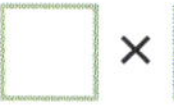

☐ × ☐
☐ × ☐
☐ × ☐

 • *AUSTRALIAN SIGNPOST MATHS NSW 3* • ISBN 9780655709046

Problem solving

Skip counting by 5:
5, 10, 15, 20, 25, 30, 35, 40, 45, 50

Solve these problems.

1. Davis had 100 bones. He gave his dog 40 of them. How many were left?

Find:

Number sentence: ___ = ___

Answer:

?	40
100	

Find: How many bones were left?
Number sentence: 100 – 40 = ___
Answer: There were ___ bones left.

2. Ten pies are needed to fill one tray. Three trays are filled. How many pies are there?

Find:

Number sentence: ___ = ___

Answer:

3. Corina had 24 apricots. She gave 2 to each friend until no apricots were left. How many friends were given apricots?

Find:

Number sentence: ___ = ___

Answer:

4. In a library, one shelf holds 24 books. Another shelf holds 55. How many books do these shelves hold altogether?

Find:

Number sentence: ___ = ___

Answer:

5. At the first stop, 15 people got off the bus. At the second stop, 10 people got off. At the third, 8 got off. How many people got off altogether?

Find:

Number sentence: ___ = ___

Answer:

6. 5 boys shared 45 books equally. How many did each boy have?

Find:

Number sentence: ___ = ___

Answer:

7. How many rows of bottles could you make if you had 45 bottles and you put 5 bottles in each row?

Find:

Number sentence: ___ = ___

Answer:

8. Discuss ways of solving these problems in your head.

a 1000 – 101 = ___ **b** 1000 – 110 = ___ **c** 1000 – 410 = ___

d 1000 – 510 = ___ **e** 1000 – 302 = ___ **f** 1000 – 802 = ___

g Could you use place value to find your answers quickly? ___

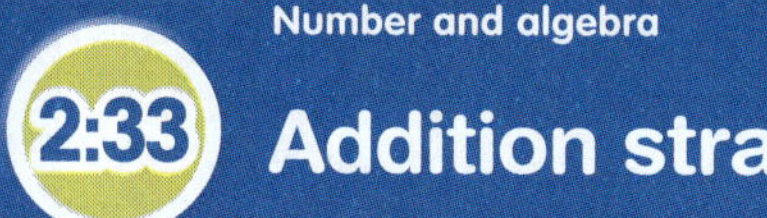

2:33 Addition strategies

Using strategies is like playing with numbers.

CONCEPT

- Knowing that 7 + 3 = 10, means that 27 + 3 = 30.
  Knowing that 2 + 8 = 10, means that 152 + 8 = 160.
- 27 **+ 8 + 3** = 27 **+ 3** **+ 8** = 30 **+ 8** = 38
  345 **+ 6 + 5** = 345 **+ 5** **+ 6** = 350 **+ 6** = 356

1 a 3 + 7 = 10 so 153 + 7 = ☐ b 4 + 6 = 10 so 674 + 6 = ☐

c 252 + 9 + 8 = 252 + 8 + 9 = ☐ d 174 + 7 + 6 = 174 + 6 + 7 = ☐

e 28 + 5 + 2 ☐ f 79 + 7 + 1 ☐ g 56 + 9 + 4 ☐

h 277 + 2 + 3 ☐ i 146 + 5 + 4 ☐ j 782 + 3 + 8 ☐

CONCEPT

	Question	Bridging to 10	Change the order	Add
A	36 **+ 9**	36 **+ 4 + 5**		40 **+ 5** = 45
B	315 **+ 8**	315 **+ 5 + 3**		320 **+ 3** = 323
C	36 **+ 9** + 13	36 **+ 4 + 5** + 13	40 + 13 **+ 5**	53 **+ 5** = 58
D	508 **+ 4** + 61	508 **+ 2 + 2** + 61	510 + 61 **+ 2**	571 **+ 2** = 573

2 a 52 **+ 9** = 52 **+ 8** **+ 1** = ☐ b 877 **+ 8** = 877 **+ 3** **+ 5** = ☐

c 25 + 8 ☐ d 66 + 6 ☐ e 87 + 9 ☐ f 38 + 6 ☐

g 17 + 7 ☐ h 66 + 7 ☐ i 25 + 8 ☐ j 88 + 7 ☐

k 288 + 5 ☐ l 516 + 9 ☐ m 873 + 8 ☐ n 356 + 9 ☐

o 52 **+ 9** + 13 = 52 **+ 8** **+ 1** + 13 = 60 + 13 **+ 1** = ☐

p 838 **+ 5** + 41 = 838 **+ 2** **+ 3** + 41 = 840 + 41 **+ 3** = ☐

q 534 **+ 8** + 23 = 534 **+ 6 + 2** + 23 = 540 + 23 **+ 2** = ☐

Working:

2:34 Subtraction strategies

Ask yourself, which strategy should I use?

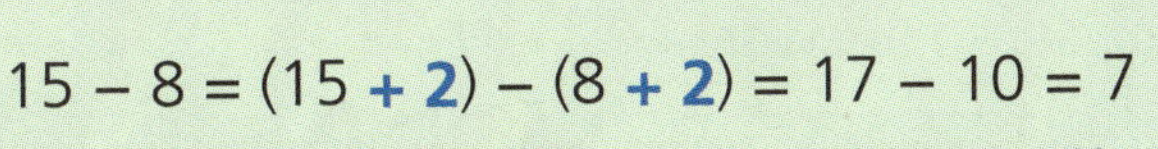
15 − 8 = (15 + 2) − (8 + 2) = 17 − 10 = 7

15 − 8 and 17 − 10 have a constant difference.

- 781 − 49 = (781 + 1) − (49 + 1) = 782 − 50 = 732

We made the second number easier to take away.

1
- a 24 − 9 = (24 + 1) − (9 + 1) = 25 − 10 = ☐
- b 61 − 17 = (61 + 3) − (17 + 3) = 64 − 20 = ☐
- c 74 − 39 = (74 + 1) − (39 + 1) = 75 − 40 = ☐
- d 598 − 39 = (598 + 1) − (39 + 1) = 599 − 40 = ☐
- e 962 − 78 = (962 + 2) − (78 + 2) = 964 − 80 = ☐

2
- a 73 − 18 = ☐
- b 47 − 29 = ☐
- c 62 − 37 = ☐
- d 288 − 69 = ☐
- e 461 − 48 = ☐

CONCEPT

Use patterns • 12 − 8 = 4 so 42 − 8 = 34 • 16 − 9 = 7 so 536 − 9 = 527

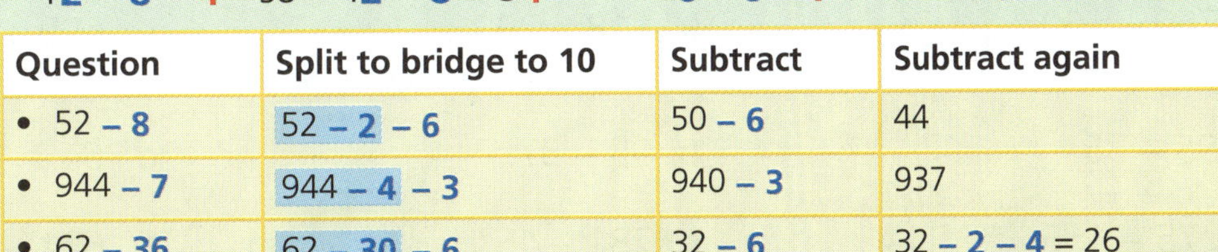

	Question	Split to bridge to 10	Subtract	Subtract again
Bridge to last 10	• 52 − 8	52 − 2 − 6	50 − 6	44
Bridge to last 10	• 944 − 7	944 − 4 − 3	940 − 3	937
Jump strategy	• 62 − 36	62 − 30 − 6	32 − 6	32 − 2 − 4 = 26

3
- a 13 − 7 = 6 so 53 − 7 = ☐
- b 14 − 6 = 8 so 74 − 6 = ☐
- c 14 − 6 = 8 so 754 − 6 = ☐
- d 11 − 4 = 7 so 641 − 4 = ☐
- e 15 − 8 = 7 so 365 − 8 = ☐
- f 16 − 7 = 9 so 526 − 7 = ☐
- g 34 − 9 = 34 − 4 − 5 = 30 − 5 = ☐
- h 52 − 8 = 52 − 2 − 6 = 50 − 6 = ☐
- i 181 − 8 = 181 − 1 − 7 = 180 − 7 = ☐
- j 493 − 7 = 493 − 3 − 4 = 490 − 4 = ☐
- k 82 − 9 ☐
- l 56 − 7 ☐
- m 36 − 8 ☐
- n 41 − 6 ☐
- o 27 − 8 ☐
- p 66 − 9 ☐
- q 71 − 25 ☐
- r 66 − 18 ☐

Working:

Levelling and constant difference

485 + ☐ = 500

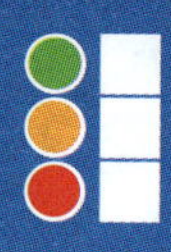

CONCEPT

- We can adjust questions like this to make them easier to answer.

Amy's jottings

485 + 365 +
15 + 350
(485 + 15 = 500)
500 + 350 = 850
Answer: 850

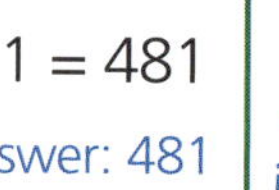

842 − 361 −
700 + 140 + 2
−300 −60 −1
400 + 80 + 1 = 481
Answer: 481

John's jottings

It is useful to jot down your thinking when solving a problem.

Make your own jottings on paper to answer these problems. Reflect on the strategies you use.

1 a 84 + 23 ☐ b 98 + 42 ☐ c 85 + 35 ☐
d 145 + 35 ☐ e 75 + 145 ☐ f 162 + 198 ☐
g 445 + 335 ☐ h 180 + 325 ☐ i 285 + 645 ☐
j 760 + 160 ☐ k 518 + 290 ☐ l 699 + 248 ☐

2 a 95 − 35 ☐ b 95 − 37 ☐ c 64 − 18 ☐
d 275 − 115 ☐ e 781 − 45 ☐ f 671 − 98 ☐
g 915 − 609 ☐ h 765 − 445 ☐ i 405 − 285 ☐
j 459 − 297 ☐ k 865 − 195 ☐ l 605 − 315 ☐

Add the answer to the number taken away to check your answers to Question 2.

3 a How many students came to the library last week if 221 came on Monday, 135 on Tuesday, 126 on Wednesday, 85 on Thursday and 231 on Friday? ☐

Number sentence:

b How many visits to the local park occurred last week if there were 380 on Sunday, 27 on Monday, 132 on Tuesday, 180 on Wednesday, 54 on Thursday, 17 on Friday and 151 on Saturday? ☐

Number sentence:

Change from $2

CONCEPT

To give change, we count on from the price paid.

Example: What is the change from $2 if the cost is 35c?

35c

- Count on from 35c.
- 35c and 5c makes 40c, and 10c makes 50c, and 50c makes $1, and $1 makes $2.
- The change is 5c + 10c + 50c + $1 = **$1.65**.

1 Colour the coins to show the change from $2.

2 Use the coins to count on and find the change.

	Cost	Money given	Coins counted	Total change
a	45c	60c	5c, 10c	15c
b	65c	80c		
c	55c	$1		
d	$1.75	$2		

Coins

3 What is the change from $2 if the item costs:

a 70c? ______ **b** $1.40? ______ **c** 45c? ______ **d** $1.05? ______

2:37 Problem solving

Reflect on the effectiveness of the strategies you use.

1 I was given five of these number cards. 1 2 3 4 5 6
The total of the numbers on my cards was 18. What were my numbers?
The 5 cards were ______.
Hint: What is the total of all of the cards?

You could use trial and error for Q1 and 2.

2 Daren must pay $5 for each light globe and $2 for each battery.
How much change will he have from $20 if he bought:

Check your answers.

a 2 batteries and 2 light globes? ______ **b** 3 light globes and 2 batteries? ______
c 1 battery and 2 light globes? ______ **d** 1 light globe and 5 batteries? ______

3 I had a collection of stars. Some had 5 points.
Some had 6 points.
I could see 21 points on my star collection.
How many of each type could I have?

5-point star 6-point star

Number of 5-point stars ______ Number of 6-point stars ______

4 **a** How could you throw a total of 24 on this dartboard using 3 darts?
______ or ______

b Can I throw a total of 21 on this dartboard using 3 darts? ______
Explain why or why not. ______
______

4 6 8 10 8 6 4

INVESTIGATION

5 Rachel put 20 chairs in front of the stage in 2 rows of 10 chairs, as shown. Use 20 counters to find other ways to arrange the chairs in equal rows. Write the ways you found.

2 × 10	

Stage

2 × 10

6 List ways that 30 chairs can be arranged in equal rows.

 ISBN 9780655709046

Number and algebra

2:38 Addition to 99, no trading

The split strategy:
34 + 23
= (30 + 20) + (4 + 3)

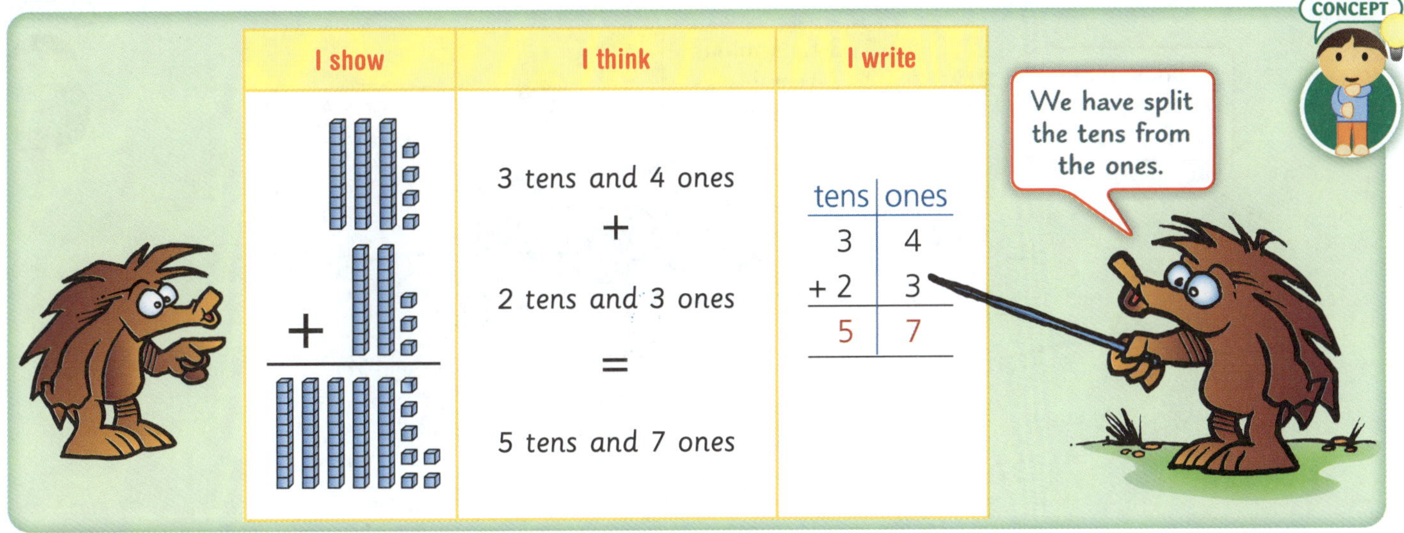

1 Use the split strategy to answer these. Use another mental strategy to check your answers.

a

tens	ones
3	2
+ 2	6

b

tens	ones
4	3
+ 3	5

c

tens	ones
3	7
+ 4	0

d

tens	ones
6	4
+ 2	5

e

tens	ones
5	6
+ 4	0

f

tens	ones
4	2
+ 3	5

g

tens	ones
5	3
+ 3	6

h

tens	ones
7	3
+ 2	5

i

tens	ones
\$6	6
+ \$2	3

j

tens	ones
\$7	5
+ \$2	2

k

tens	ones
\$4	8
+ \$3	1

l

tens	ones
\$5	4
+ \$3	5

2

a 4 tens and 6 ones
\+ 4 tens and 2 ones

b 5 tens and 4 ones
\+ 3 tens and 3 ones

c 2 tens and 4 ones
\+ 5 tens and 5 ones

d 7 tens and 3 ones
\+ 1 ten and 6 ones

e 6 tens and 0 ones
\+ 2 tens and 9 ones

f 3 tens and 1 one
\+ 4 tens and 7 ones

3

a I paid \$35 for a shirt and \$61 for pants. How much did I spend? ☐

b There are 11 girls and 18 boys in our class. How many are in our class? ☐

c 15 horses and 42 cows are on our farm. How many animals altogether? ☐

d I saved \$53. Alana saved \$24. How much did we save? ☐

 • *AUSTRALIAN SIGNPOST MATHS NSW 3* • ISBN 9780655709046

2:39 Subtraction, no trading

$37 - 24$
$= (30 - 20) + (7 - 4)$

tens	ones
3	7
– 2	4
1	3

1 Model the word problem using place-value blocks. Write a number sentence.

a 36 badges, 4 sold.
How many are left?

b 55 birds, 23 fly away.
How many remain?

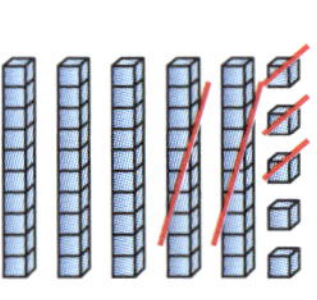

c 47 girls, 5 boys.
How many more girls than boys?

d 68 needed, 34 collected.
How many more to collect?

34	?
68	

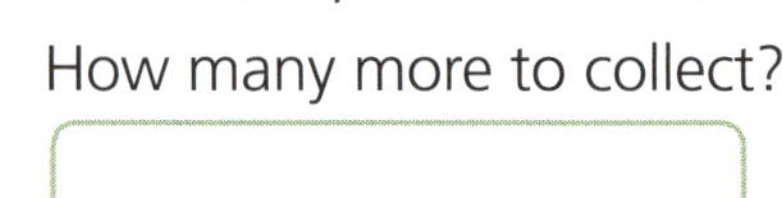

e 76 books, 42 covered.
How many more to cover?

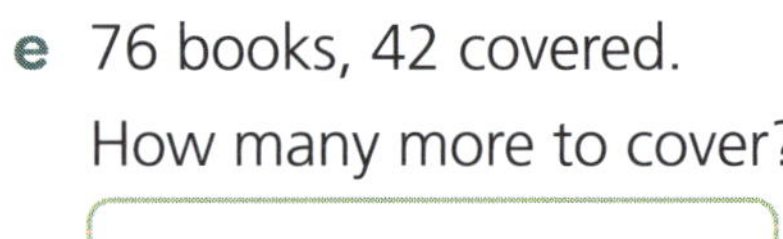

f 59 grapes, 46 eaten.
How many are left?

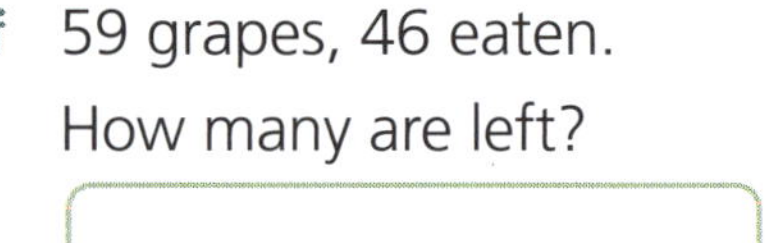

2

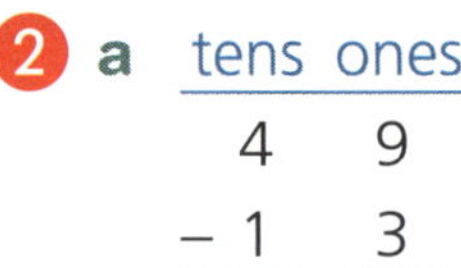

	tens	ones
a	4	9
	– 1	3

	tens	ones
b	7	5
	– 4	4

	tens	ones
c	5	7
	– 3	4

	tens	ones
d	6	9
	– 4	2

	tens	ones
e	5	6
	– 2	1

	tens	ones
f	4	8
	– 1	4

	tens	ones
g	6	7
	– 2	5

	tens	ones
h	7	4
	– 4	0

	tens	ones
i	\$9	4
	– \$3	1

	tens	ones
j	\$6	3
	– \$2	3

	tens	ones
k	\$8	5
	– \$8	1

	tens	ones
l	\$7	4
	– \$2	2

3 Use mental strategies to check your answers in Question 2.

 ISBN 9780655709046

2:40 Addition to 99 with trading

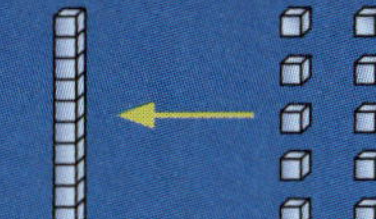
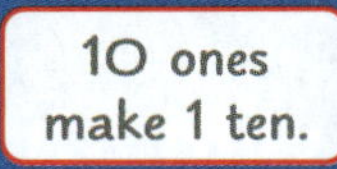

CONCEPT

45 + 27

	tens	ones
	1	
+	4	5
	2	7
	7	2

The 10 ones are shown as 1 ten.

Steps

1 5 ones + 7 ones = **12** ones

2 Trade **10 ones for 1 ten** and write the **2** that is left.

3 (**1** + 4 + 2) tens = 7 tens

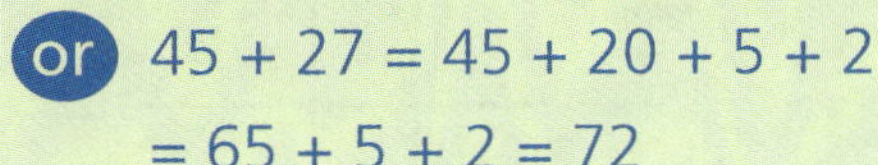

or 45 + 27 = 45 + 20 + 5 + 2
= 65 + 5 + 2 = 72

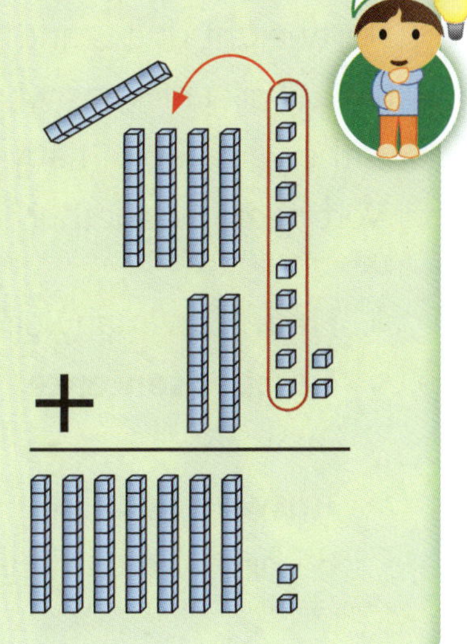

1 Trade ten ones for one ten in each addition. Use mental strategies to check your answers.

a tens ones: 2 4 + 7

b tens ones: 1 8 + 1 5

c tens ones: 3 5 + 6

d tens ones: 4 6 + 1 9

e tens ones: 1 3 + 5 8

f tens ones: 2 7 + 4 7

g tens ones: 1 4 + 7 6

h tens ones: 4 8 + 3 4

i tens ones: 3 6 + 3 6

j tens ones: 4 9 + 9

k tens ones: 5 6 + 3 8

l tens ones: 5 8 + 1 8

m tens ones: $ 5 + $8 9

n tens ones: $5 4 + $2 9

o tens ones: $2 7 + $3 3

p tens ones: $6 9 + $2 8

2 Write a number sentence including the answer for each number story.

a Myah has 4 cats and 29 mice. How many animals has she altogether?

b Mark has 16 canaries and 27 budgies. How many birds does he have?

c Flynn has 65 ants and 28 bees. How many insects has he altogether?

d I have 57 five-cent coins and 26 ten-cent coins. How many do I have?

See Extra Support 5 (Addition problems to 99).

2:41 Addition with trading

14 ones is the same as 1 ten and 4 ones.

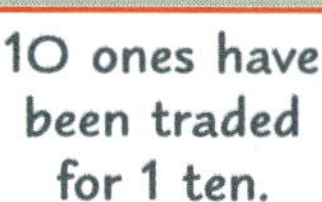

Thirty-eight ducks and twenty-six chickens were in the yard. How many birds were there altogether?

- **Find:** How many birds?
- **Number sentence:** 38 + 26 = ☐
- **Answer:** 64 birds were in the yard.

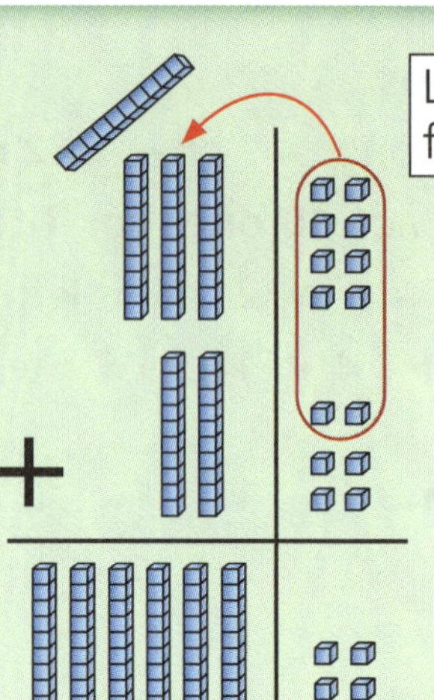

Learn the tables facts on page 167.

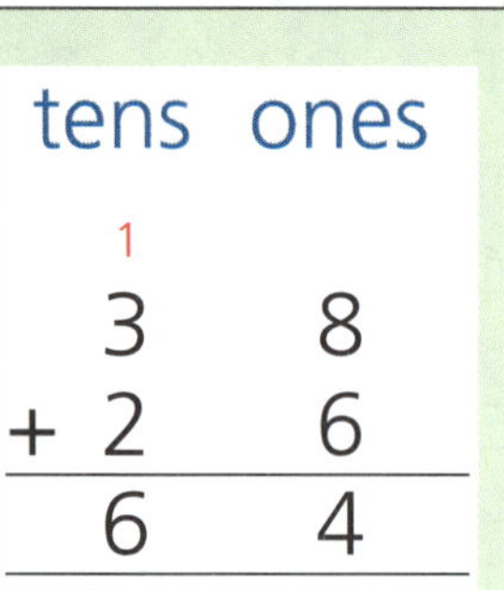

1 Complete the additions and show the trading. Check your answers using a mental strategy.

a tens ones
  1 2
+ 2 8

b tens ones
  3 3
+ 3 9

c tens ones
  4 5
+ 1 6

d tens ones
  2 7
+ 3 4

e tens ones
  6 5
+ 2 8

f tens ones
  1 1
+ 5 9

g tens ones
  3 6
+ 5 7

h tens ones
  2 4
+ 2 8

i tens ones
  7 7
+ 1 7

j tens ones
  6 6
+ 2 9

k tens ones
  4 5
+ 3 7

l tens ones
  2 8
+ 5 4

m tens ones
  $4 6
+ $ 8

n tens ones
  $ 7
+ $8 9

o tens ones
  $2 6
+ $6 4

p tens ones
  $4 9
+ $3 1

2 a How many students are in both classes if there are 27 in class 3P and 26 in class 3N? ☐

b We collected 43 cans on Monday and 37 on Tuesday. How many have we collected? ☐

c I have 35 stamps. Peter has 2 more than me. How many stamps altogether? ☐

d I had 3 cards less than 50. I was given 46 more cards. How many do I have now? ☐

See Extra Support 5 (Addition problems to 99).

2:42 Addition with 2-digit numbers

21
= 20 + 1
= 2 tens + 1 one

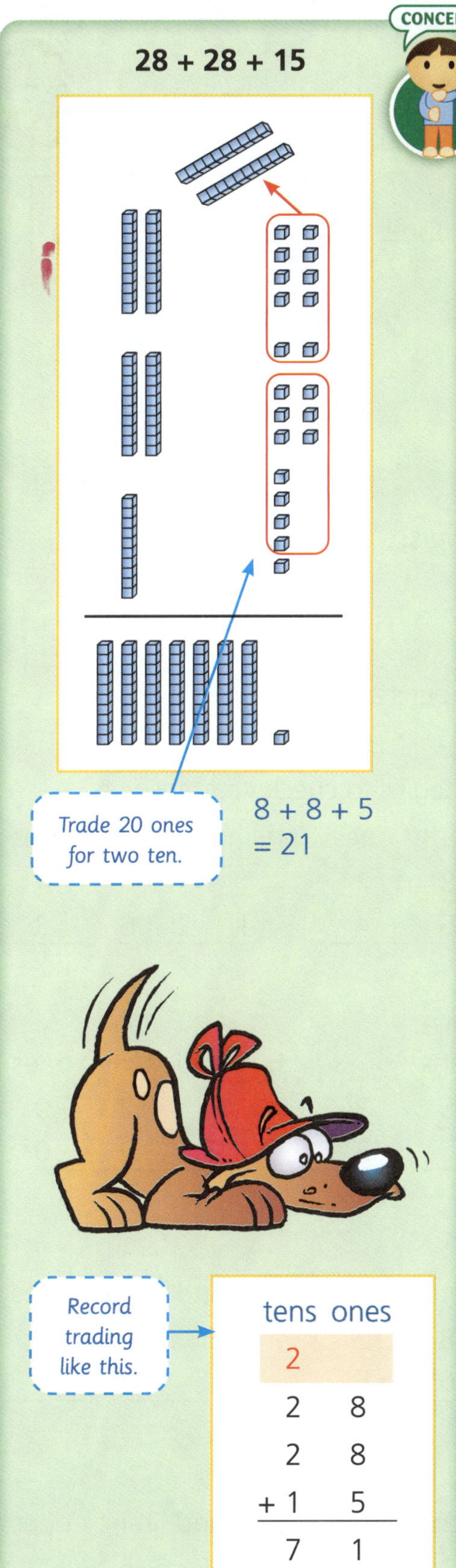

1

a

tens	ones
2	1
	7
+ 4	5

b

tens	ones
1	6
1	2
+ 1	7

c

tens	ones
2	5
3	9
+ 1	9

d

tens	ones
	7
2	1
+ 3	7

e

tens	ones
3	1
2	7
+ 1	5

f

tens	ones
4	5
1	7
+ 1	8

g

tens	ones
2	7
1	7
+ 2	7

h

tens	ones
5	8
	7
+ 2	8

2 Circle the answer. Adding 3 odd numbers gives an **odd / even** answer.

3

a

tens	ones
2	6
2	4
1	7
+ 1	6

b

tens	ones
3	2
2	3
1	4
+	1

c

tens	ones
2	5
3	7
1	4
+ 1	5

d

tens	ones
1	5
1	5
1	5
+ 1	5

e

tens	ones
1	3
3	7
1	4
+ 1	6

f

tens	ones
5	5
	7
2	9
+	3

See Extra Support 5 (Addition problems to 99).

 • *AUSTRALIAN SIGNPOST MATHS NSW 3* • ISBN 9780655709046

2:43 Addition, trading for 100

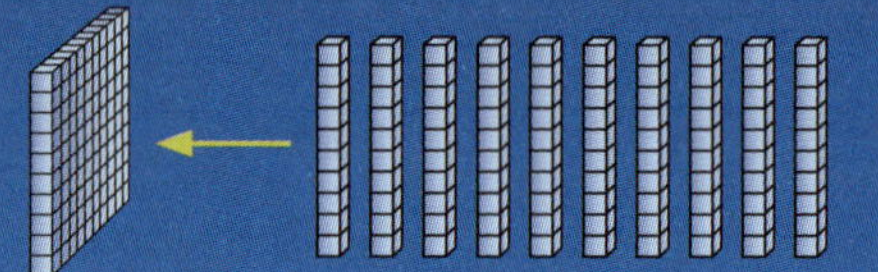

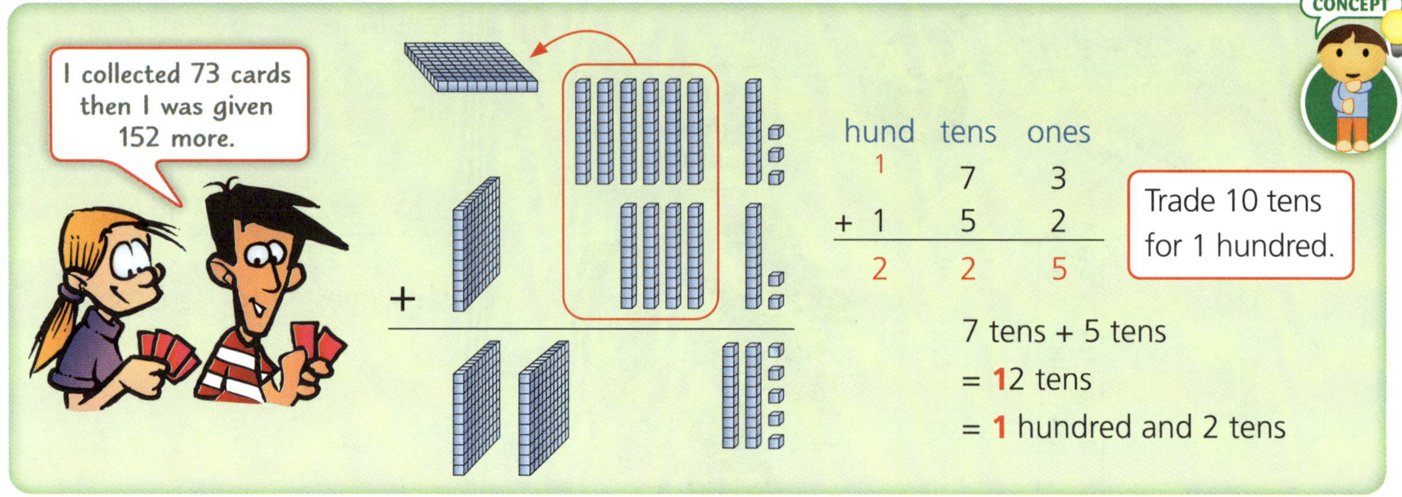

1 Model these problems with place-value blocks. Fill in the answers.

a 62 books,
144 books. ☐ + ☐ = ☐
How many books altogether? ☐

b 173 pens,
251 pens. ☐ + ☐ = ☐
How many pens altogether? ☐

2 Trade 10 tens for 1 hundred in each addition. Use mental strategies to check your answers.

a

hund	tens	ones
	5	3
+	5	2

b

hund	tens	ones
	7	6
+ 4	3	1

c

hund	tens	ones
2	8	2
+	5	4

d

hund	tens	ones
1	6	4
+	6	3

e

hund	tens	ones
	8	0
+ 6	3	9

f

hund	tens	ones
	9	2
+ 5	9	6

g

hund	tens	ones
2	5	3
+	7	2

h

hund	tens	ones
	2	9
+ 3	9	0

i

hund	tens	ones
	8	3
+ 7	4	5

j

hund	tens	ones
6	3	7
+	8	1

k

hund	tens	ones
4	8	2
+	6	5

l

hund	tens	ones
8	9	4
+	4	3

m

hund	tens	ones
2	5	5
+ 2	5	4

n

hund	tens	ones
1	8	3
+ 3	5	4

o

hund	tens	ones
7	3	6
+ 1	9	2

p

hund	tens	ones
5	4	7
+ 2	8	0

See Extra Support 6–10 (Addition with trading).

2:44 Addition to 999 with one trade

Trade 10 ones for 1 ten.
Trade 10 tens for 1 hundred.

CONCEPT

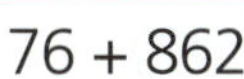

hund	tens	ones
1		
	7	6
+ 8	6	2
9	3	8

7 tens + 6 tens
= 13 tens
= 1 hundred + 3 tens

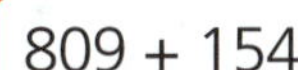

hund	tens	ones
	1	
8	0	9
+ 1	5	4
9	6	3

9 ones + 4 ones
= 13 ones
= 1 ten + 3 ones

1 Use trading to find the answers. Use mental strategies to check your answers.

a

hund	tens	ones
	6	8
+	9	1

b

hund	tens	ones
	2	7
+ 8	1	5

c

hund	tens	ones
5	4	2
+	7	6

d

hund	tens	ones
1	3	6
+	3	7

e

hund	tens	ones
1	6	0
+ 2	9	9

f

hund	tens	ones
	7	5
+ 4	8	2

g

hund	tens	ones
2	8	2
+ 3	9	2

h

hund	tens	ones
	3	9
+ 4	4	6

i

hund	tens	ones
	8	8
+ 8	9	0

j

hund	tens	ones
3	3	7
+ 2	4	8

k

hund	tens	ones
2	2	2
+ 5	5	8

l

hund	tens	ones
8	1	4
+	5	6

m

hund	tens	ones
1	7	2
+ 4	4	0

n

hund	tens	ones
	7	9
+ 8	1	4

o

hund	tens	ones
3	0	8
+ 1	8	2

p

hund	tens	ones
5	3	6
+	8	3

2 Use trading to find the answers.

a

hund	tens	ones
$ 2	3	5
+$ 2	3	5

b

hund	tens	ones
$	3	5
+$ 7	9	0

c

hund	tens	ones
$ 2	6	0
+$ 6	4	7

d

hund	tens	ones
$ 4	3	7
+$ 3	1	7

3 Test your answers to Questions 1 and 2 by rounding the numbers and adding.

See Extra Support 6–10 (Addition with trading).

Addition, two trades

Trade 10 ones for one ten.
Trade 10 tens for one hundred.

1 Use trading to find the answers. Use mental strategies to check your answers.

	hund	tens	ones
a		4	9
+		7	9

	hund	tens	ones
b		3	4
+	7	8	6

	hund	tens	ones
c	4	6	8
+		3	6

	hund	tens	ones
d	1	4	5
+		5	5

	hund	tens	ones
e	1	7	6
+	3	5	6

	hund	tens	ones
f	2	7	2
+	5	3	8

	hund	tens	ones
g	5	1	8
+		8	4

	hund	tens	ones
h	7	3	4
+	1	8	6

	hund	tens	ones
i	6	2	4
+	1	9	7

	hund	tens	ones
j	3	7	5
+	2	7	5

	hund	tens	ones
k	2	8	7
+	3	3	3

	hund	tens	ones
l	4	7	5
+	2	6	9

	hund	tens	ones
m	4	4	9
+	3	5	7

	hund	tens	ones
n	6	7	5
+		7	6

	hund	tens	ones
o	1	2	6
+	7	7	4

	hund	tens	ones
p		5	3
+	8	7	9

2
a Alan has 46 birds in one aviary and 178 in the other. How many birds does he have?
b Each packet of coloured paper has 156 sheets. How many sheets are in 2 packets?
c 99 meals were provided today and 98 yesterday. How many meals were provided?
d 286 cows were on one boat and 88 on the other. How many cows were on the boats?

See Extra Support 6–10 (Addition with trading).

 • *AUSTRALIAN SIGNPOST MATHS NSW 3* • ISBN 9780655709046

2:46 Subtraction with trading to 99

60 = 5 tens + 10

tens	ones
5	10
~~6~~	~~0~~
–	8
5	2

tens	ones
5	10
~~6~~	~~0~~
– 3	8
2	2

1. Show how one ten can be traded for 10 ones.

a tens ones
5 0

b tens ones
7 0

c tens ones
4 0

d tens ones
9 0

2. Use the method above or place-value blocks to answer these.

a tens ones
6 0
– 4

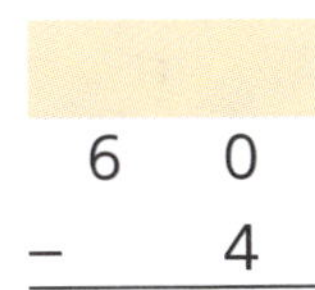

b tens ones
8 0
– 7

c tens ones
5 0
– 6

d tens ones
9 0
– 8

e tens ones
\$7 0
– \$5 6

f tens ones
\$4 0
– \$2 7

g tens ones
\$8 0
– \$3 5

h tens ones
\$9 0
– \$4 2

3. **a** tens ones
6 0
– 4 4

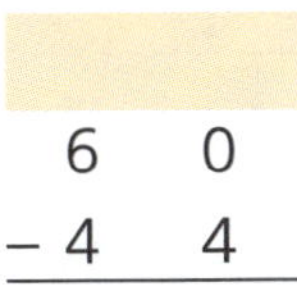

b tens ones
8 0
– 2 7

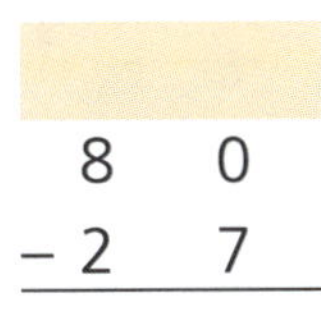

c tens ones
5 0
– 3 6

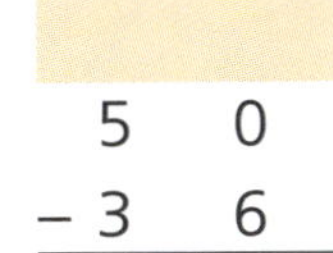

d tens ones
9 0
– 7 8

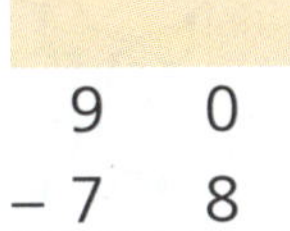

4. Use written algorithms on your own paper to find the answers to:

a \$70 – \$17 ☐ **b** \$80 – \$46 ☐ **c** \$50 – \$28 ☐

See Extra Support 11–17 (Subtraction with 3 digits).

Subtraction with trading

23 = 2 tens + 3 ones
= 1 ten + 13 ones

Trade 1 ten.

Trading down

Problem 23 cups, 9 used. How many left? You can't take 9 ones from 3 ones.		tens ones 2 3 – 9
Trading Trade to get more ones. You now have 1 ten and 13 ones.		tens ones [1 13] ~~2~~ ~~3~~ – 9
Ones 13 ones take away 9 ones equals 4 ones.		tens ones [1 13] ~~2~~ ~~3~~ – 9 4
Tens 1 ten take away 0 tens equals 1 ten.		tens ones [1 13] ~~2~~ ~~3~~ – 9 1 4

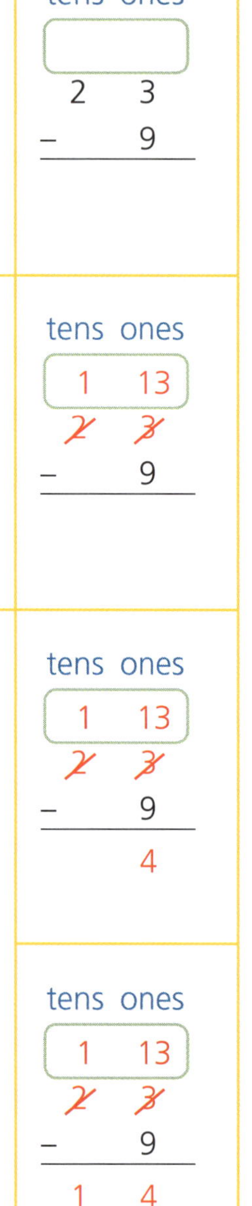

1 Show trading down 1 ten.

a tens ones
3 4

b tens ones
5 7

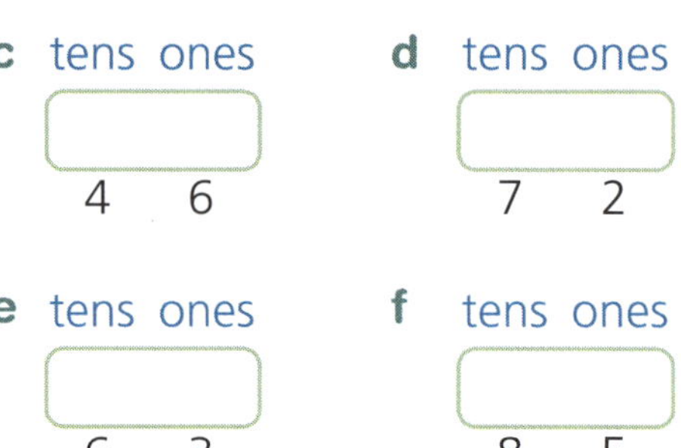

c tens ones
4 6

d tens ones
7 2

e tens ones
6 3

f tens ones
8 5

2 Use place-value blocks to do these.
Estimate your answer first.

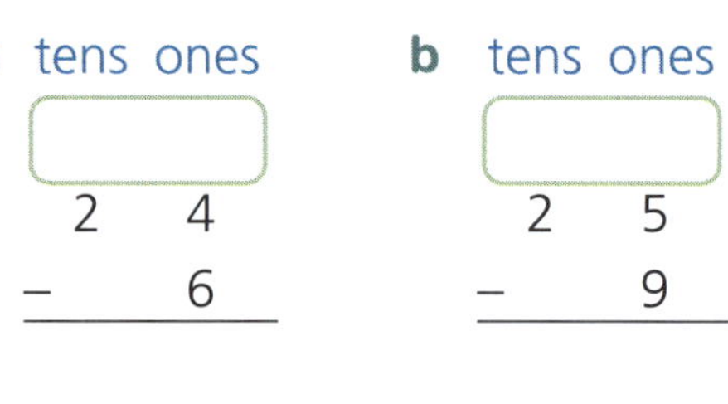

a tens ones
2 4
– 6

b tens ones
2 5
– 9

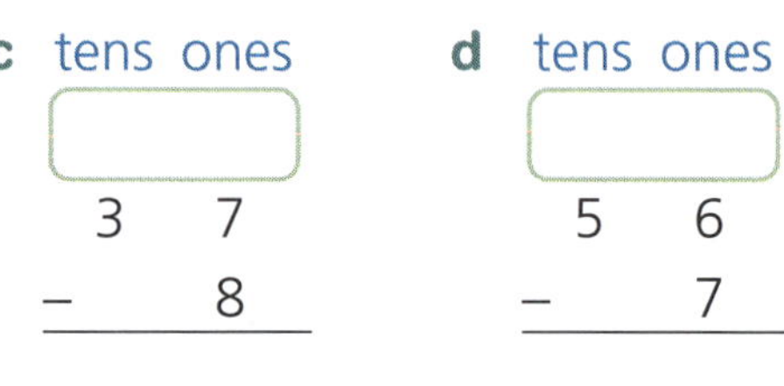

c tens ones
3 7
– 8

d tens ones
5 6
– 7

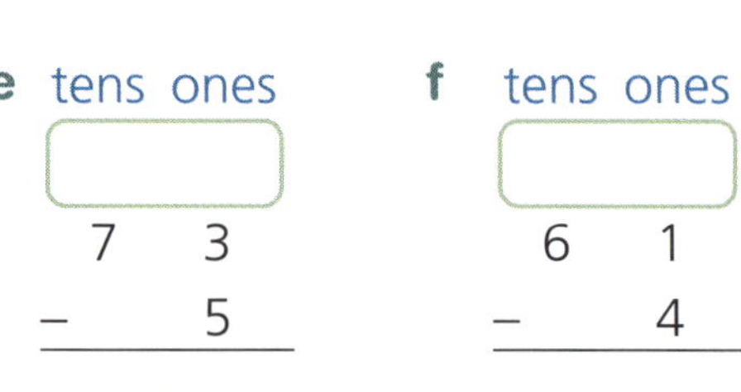

e tens ones
7 3
– 5

f tens ones
6 1
– 4

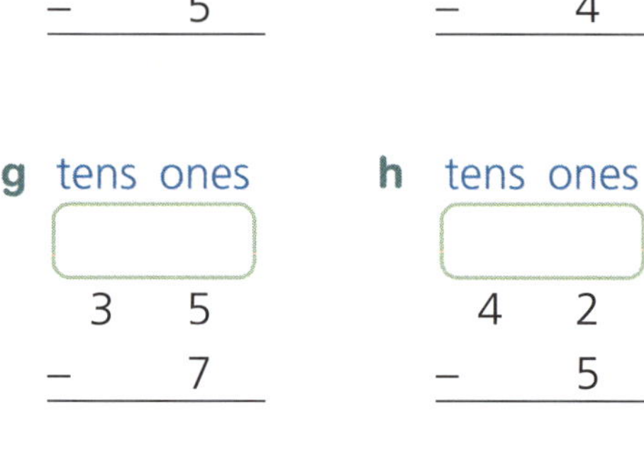

g tens ones
3 5
– 7

h tens ones
4 2
– 5

ACTIVITY

Make up number stories for Question 2 parts **g** and **h**. Use mental strategies to check your answers.

See Extra Support 11–17 (Subtraction with 3 digits).

Subtraction with trading

34 = 3 tens + 4 ones
= 2 tens + 14 ones

Trading down		
Problem 34 birds, 18 leave. How many stay? You can't take 8 ones from 4 ones.		tens ones 3 4 − 1 8
Trading Trade to get more ones. You now have 2 tens and 14 ones.		tens ones 2 14 ~~3~~ ~~4~~ − 1 8
Ones 14 ones take away 8 ones equals 6 ones.		tens ones 2 14 ~~3~~ ~~4~~ − 1 8 6
Tens 2 tens take away 1 ten equals 1 ten.		tens ones 2 14 ~~3~~ ~~4~~ − 1 8 1 6

1 Show trading down 1 ten.

a tens ones
[ ]
4 5

b tens ones
[ ]
2 7

c tens ones
[ ]
3 1

d tens ones
[ ]
7 2

2 Use place-value blocks to do these.
Estimate your answer first.

a tens ones
[ ]
5 6
− 1 8

b tens ones
[ ]
8 3
− 2 9

c tens ones
[ ]
6 2
− 3 4

d tens ones
[ ]
3 7
− 1 8

e tens ones
[ ]
4 1
− 2 7

f tens ones
[ ]
6 5
− 3 6

g tens ones
[ ]
7 4
− 4 9

h tens ones
[ ]
9 2
− 3 5

See Extra Support 11–17 (Subtraction with 3 digits).

Checking subtraction by addition

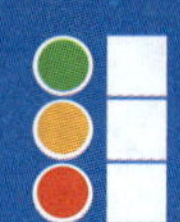

1 Complete each problem and check the answer.

a The teacher had 36 frogs. 14 got away. How many were left?

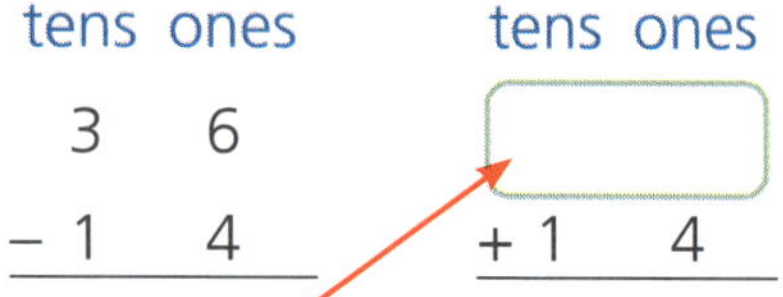

☐ frogs were left.

b James had $87. He spent $42. How much did he have left?

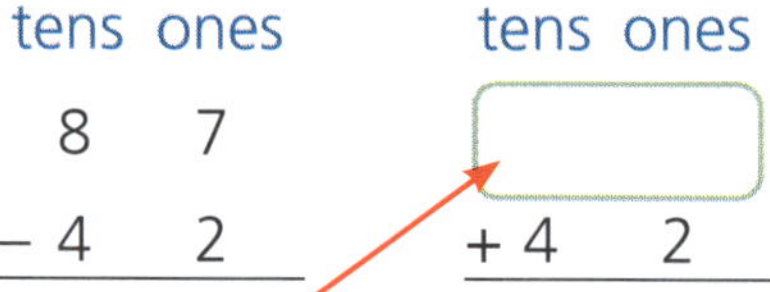

Addition is the inverse of subtraction.

James had $ ☐ left.

c 47 flowers were given to Kaylee. She gave away 9. How many were left?

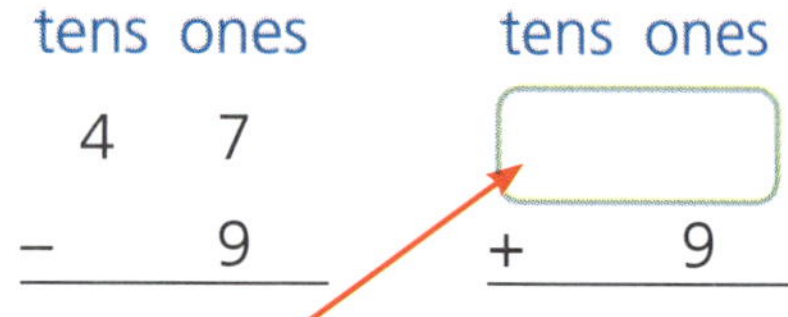

Kaylee had ☐ flowers left.

d The zoo has 24 emus and 8 koalas. How many more emus than koalas?

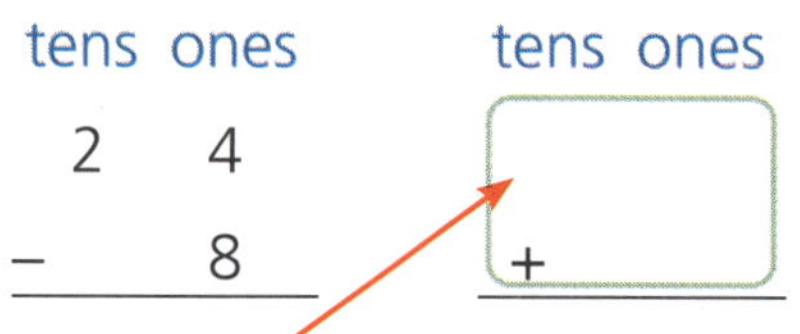

There are ☐ more emus.

To find the distance, you subtract.

2 Find the distance between the places on each sign.

a

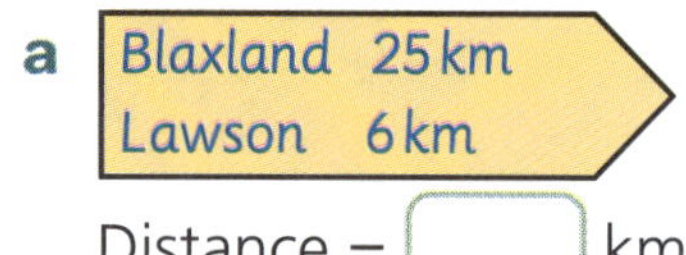

Distance = ☐ km

b Mackay 41 km
Clairview 7 km

Distance = ☐ km

c Horsham 8 km
Nhill 36 km

Distance = ☐ km

3 Use the signpost to find these distances:

Caves	79 km
Gumnut	44 km
Bellus	17 km
Dunnart	5 km

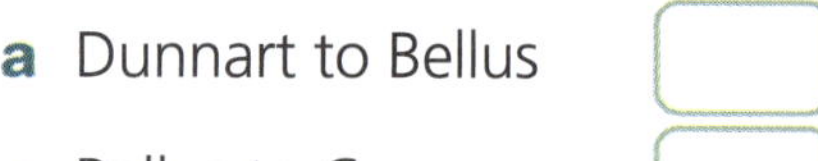

a Dunnart to Bellus ☐

b Dunnart to Caves ☐

c Bellus to Caves ☐

d Gumnut to Caves ☐

e Dunnart to Gumnut ☐

f Bellus to Gumnut ☐

 • *AUSTRALIAN SIGNPOST MATHS NSW 3* • ISBN 9780655709046

3:01 Revision of length

Estimate using personal benchmarks, then measure.

- We can compare the height, width and thickness of books by placing them side by side.

This book is 2 handspans wide.

- Measure your handspan to the nearest centimetre. ☐ cm

This could be a personal benchmark for length.

1 List the books Ⓐ, Ⓑ and Ⓒ in order from least to most, according to:

a width ☐ **b** thickness ☐ **c** height ☐

2 Find 3 picture books of different sizes. Place them side by side to compare the length and height of each. Visualise handspans to estimate, then measure the height of each.

Book	Estimate the height in handspans	Measure the height in handspans	Measure the height using a ruler
A	handspans	handspans	cm
B	handspans	handspans	cm
C	handspans	handspans	cm

Order the books from shortest to tallest: ☐

3 Use the same procedure to estimate these objects in your classroom.

Item	Estimate the height in handspans	Measure the height in handspans	Measure the height using a ruler
D length of desk	handspans	handspans	cm
E width of desk	handspans	handspans	cm
F height of desk	handspans	handspans	cm

Order these objects from shortest to tallest: ☐

4 Does using your handspans as your personal benchmark make estimating easier? ☐

 • *AUSTRALIAN SIGNPOST MATHS NSW 3* • ISBN 9780655709046

3:02 Length and width

How can we compare the length of two objects?

- The longer side is called the **length.**
- The shorter side is called the **width.**
- This rectangle is 4 cm long and 2 cm wide.

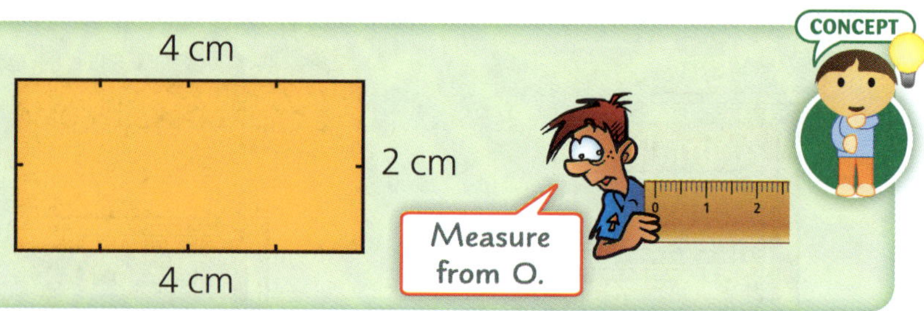

1 Write the length (L) and width (W) of each shape.

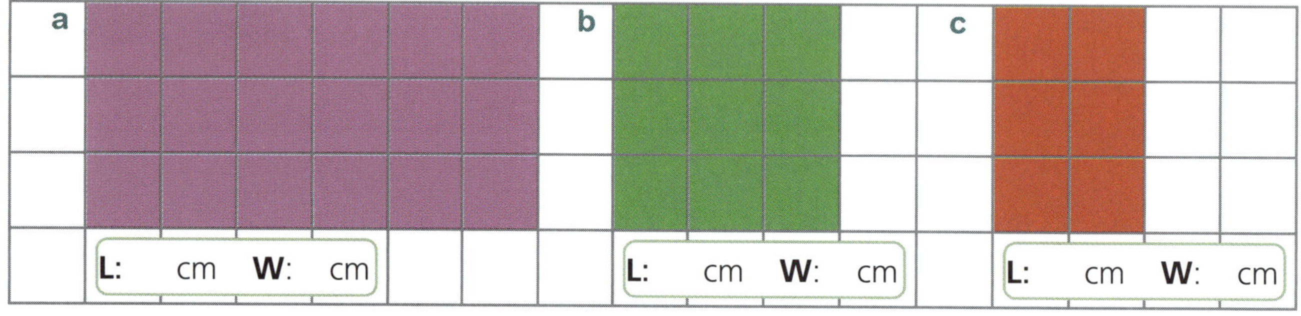

- Compare the rectangles above.

2 Use a ruler to measure the length and width of each shape.

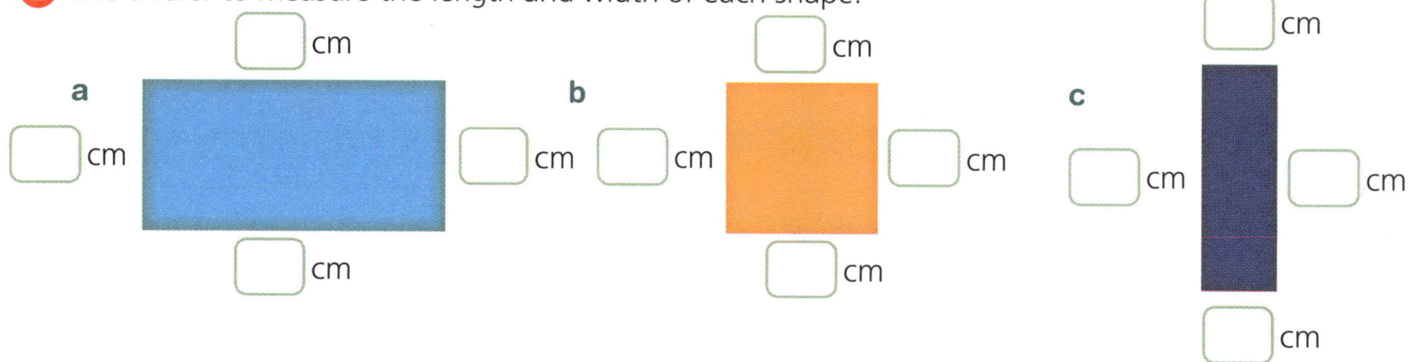

3 Use a ruler to measure to the nearest centimetre:

a the length and width of the cover of this book. length = ☐ cm width = ☐ cm

b the length and width of the concept box above. length = ☐ cm width = ☐ cm

- Use a ruler to measure the length and width of other objects to the nearest centimetre. Record one of them here.

Object	Length	Width

Measuring with centimetres

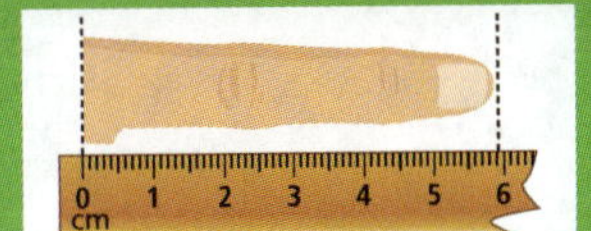

1 Write the length (L) and width (W) of each shape.

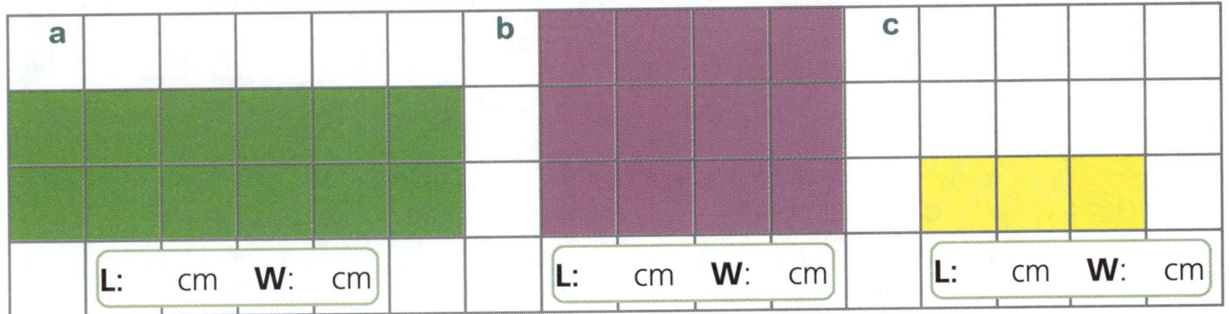

- Compare the rectangles above.

2 Estimate, then use a ruler to measure the sides of each shape. Write your measurements.

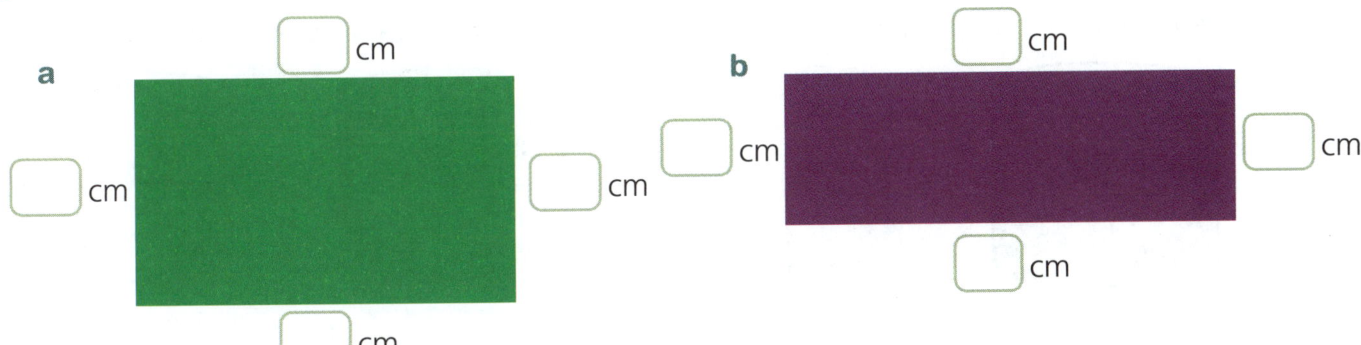

Make your own measuring tape.

You will need: centimetre grid paper, scissors and a pencil.

A paper ruler can measure curved objects.

1 Cut a long strip of 1 cm grid paper.
2 Write numbers to show centimetre marks.
3 Mark the halfway point for each centimetre.

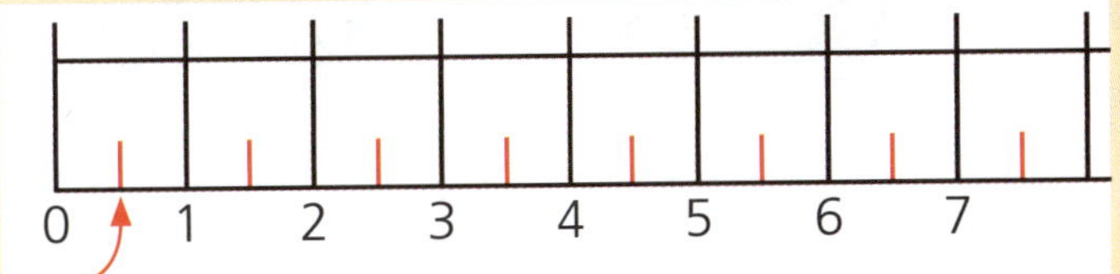

Use your paper ruler to measure an item in your classroom, then around these body parts. Use your halfway points to help you round to the nearest centimetre. Compare your results.

Draw and label one item	Measurement
	Length: cm
	Width: cm
	Height: cm

Measure around these	Measurement
your wrist	
your ankle	
your pointing finger	

3:04 Clocks

There are 60 minutes in one hour,
30 minutes in half an hour
and 15 minutes in a quarter of an hour.

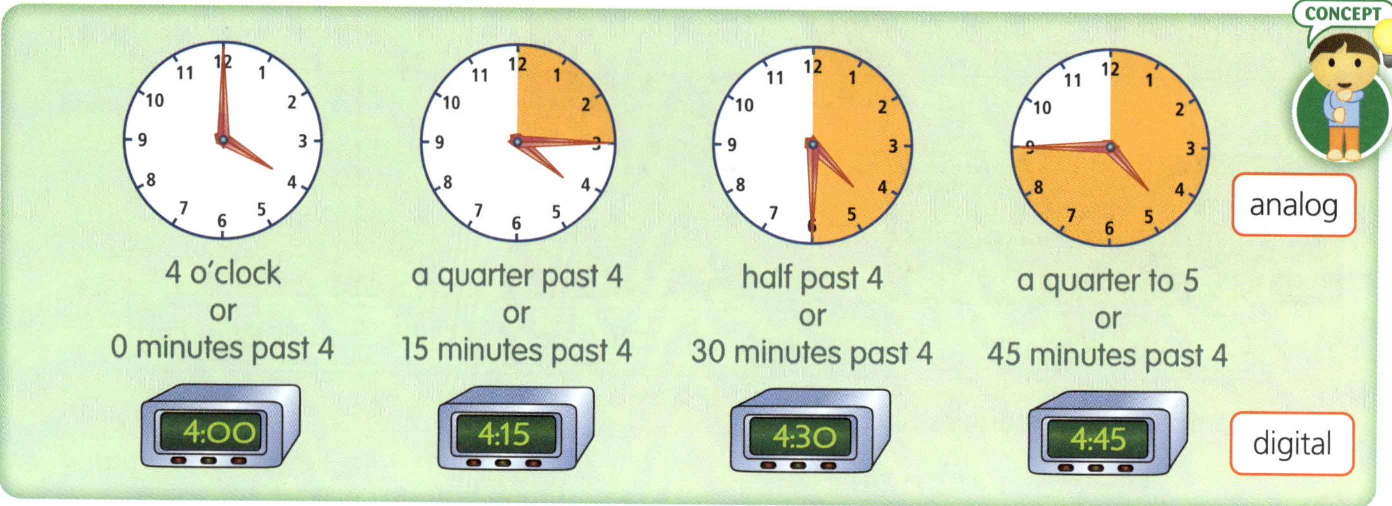

1 Write the time shown, using the words *o'clock*, *half past*, *quarter past* or *quarter to*.

2 Show the time given.

a a quarter past 10

b a quarter to 8

c 4 o'clock

d half past 7

3 Discuss and record how long these events take.

a assembly ______ minutes

b eating a biscuit ______ minutes

c library lesson ______ minutes

d eating a sandwich ______ minutes

 • *AUSTRALIAN SIGNPOST MATHS NSW 3* • ISBN 9780655709046

Analog time

Ten past 5
10 minutes past 5
5:10

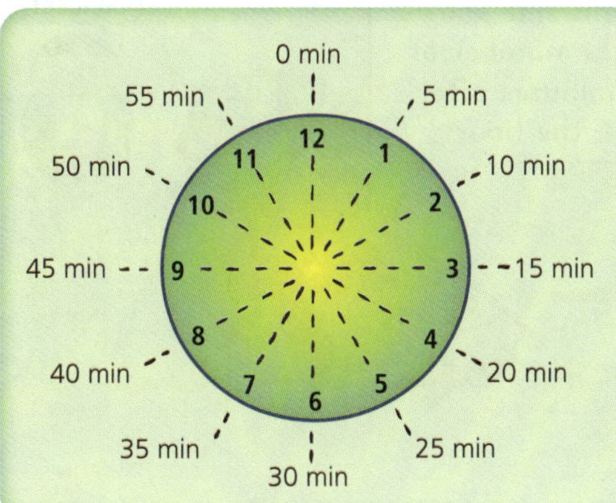

It takes 5 minutes for the minute hand to move from one numeral to the next.

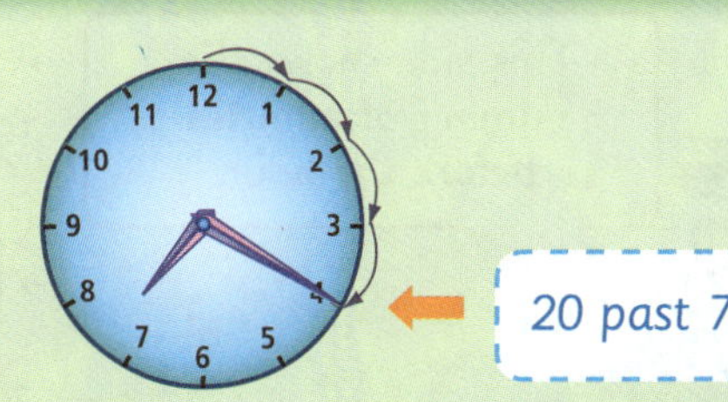

CONCEPT

- The hour hand has passed 7.
- The minute hand has moved 5, 10, 15, 20 minutes from 12.
- The time is **20 past 7**.

1 Write the time shown.

a 
☐ minutes past ☐

b 
☐ minutes past ☐

c 
☐ minutes past ☐

d 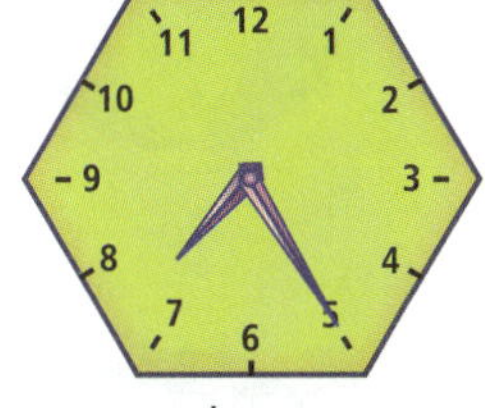
☐ minutes past ☐

e 
☐ past ☐

f 
☐ past ☐

g 
☐ past ☐

h 
☐ past ☐

CONCEPT

50 minutes past 2

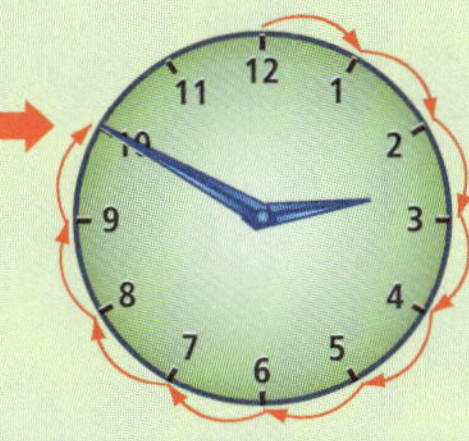

- The hour hand has passed 2.
- The minute hand has moved 5, 10, 15, … 50 minutes from 12.
- The time is **50 minutes past 2**.

2 Write the time shown.

a 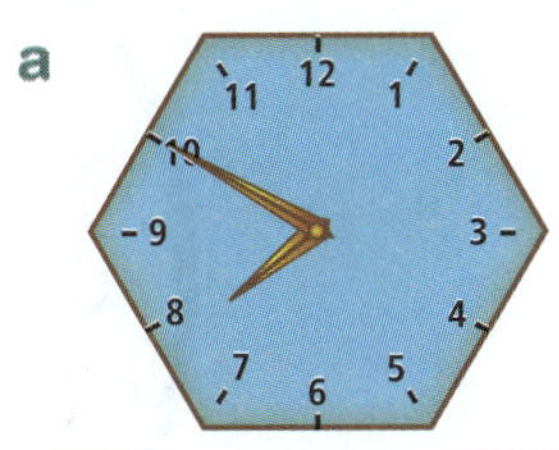
☐ past ☐
☐ minutes to ☐

b 
☐ past ☐
☐ minutes to ☐

c 
☐ past ☐
☐ to ☐

d 
☐ past ☐
☐ to ☐

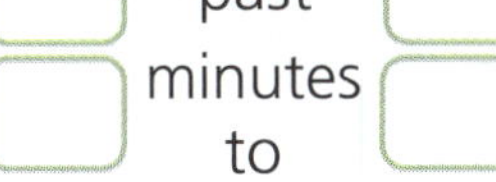

 • *AUSTRALIAN SIGNPOST MATHS NSW 3* • ISBN 9780655709046

3:06 Analog time

10 minutes after 25 past the hour would be … [ ] to the hour

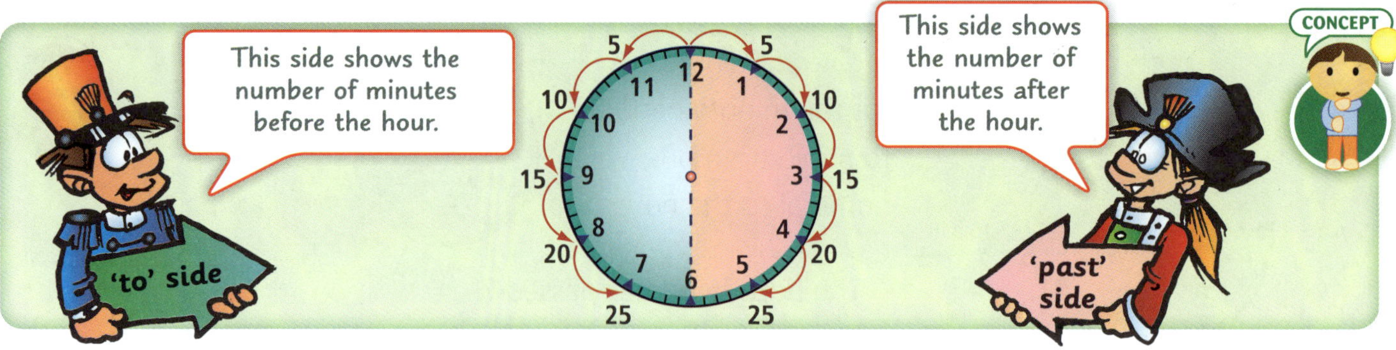

1 Complete the label for each time shown.

2 Complete the clocks to show the given times.

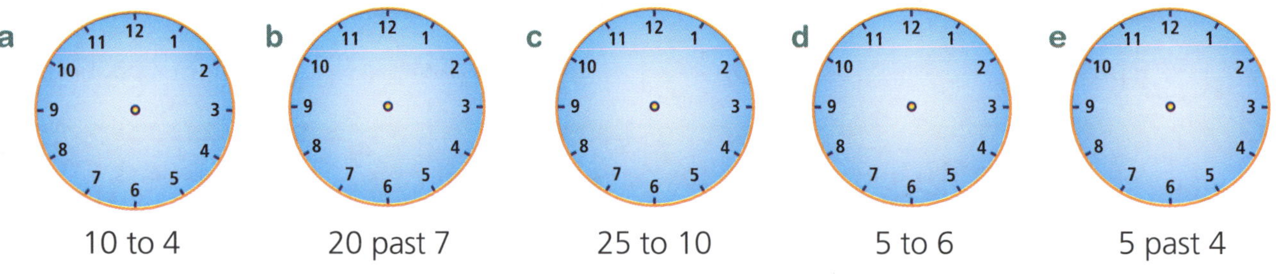

3 Write the time that is five minutes after:

a 5 past 8		b 10 past 7		c 10 to 12	
d 15 past 6		e 20 to 8		f 15 to 3	
g 20 past 3		h 25 to 3		i 5 to 9	

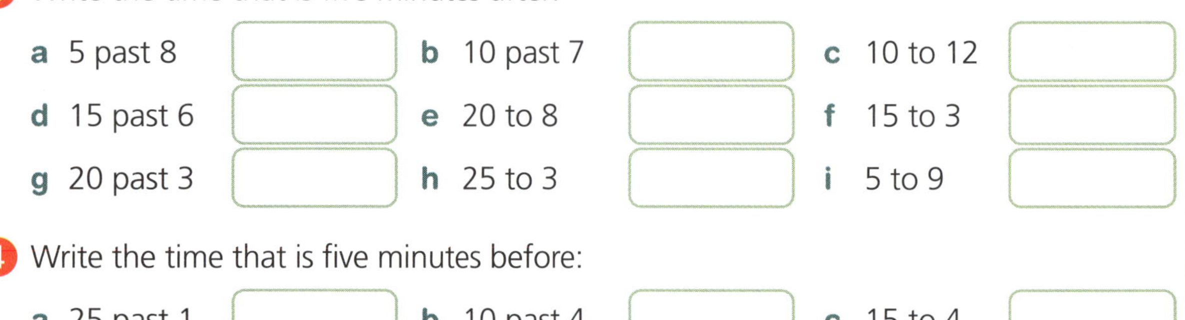

4 Write the time that is five minutes before:

a 25 past 1		b 10 past 4		c 15 to 4	
d 10 to 5		e 20 past 6		f 25 to 8	
g 15 past 10		h 20 to 11		i 5 past 2	

 ISBN 9780655709046

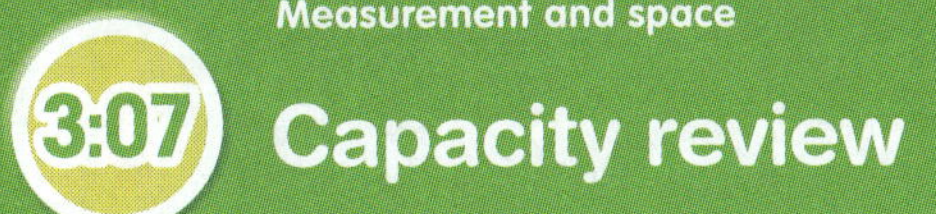

Capacity review

We can use full cups as an informal unit.

CONCEPT

Capacity is how much a container can hold.
This full jug has been poured into these two cups.

If **more than** one and a half cups are used, round to two cups. If **less than** one and a half cups are used, round to 1 cup.

1 Dipping into water:

A
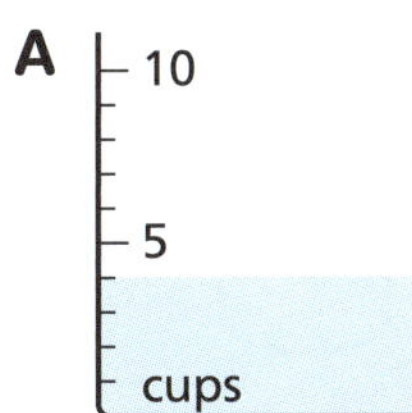

B
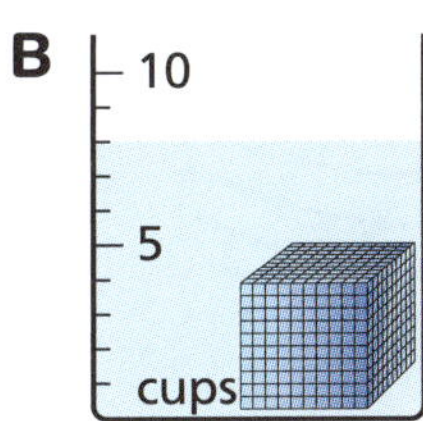

C
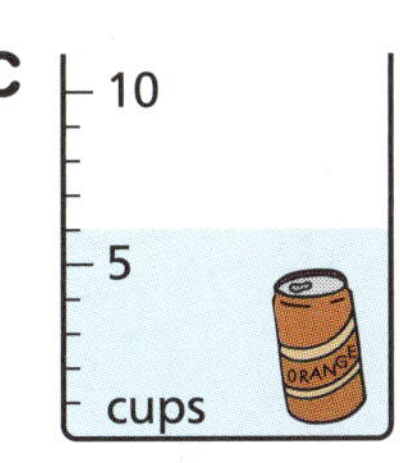

What's your capacity?

a What is the volume of water in container **A**? ☐ cups

b What is the volume of the 1000 block in **B**? ☐ cups

c What would the volume of two 1000s blocks be? ☐ cups

d What is the volume of the can in **C**? ☐ cups

e What would the volume of three cans be? ☐ cups

f How many cans would be the same volume as one 1000s block? ☐ cans

g How many cans would be the same volume as two 1000s block? ☐ cans

You could investigate and compare the volume of other objects using this method.

ACTIVITY

2 Choose containers and measure the capacity of each.
Use a full cup each time. Record your results in the table below.

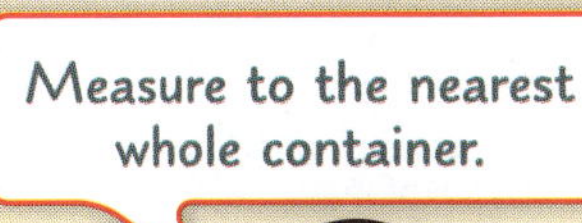

a

	Container	Estimate	Measure
A		cups	cups
B			
C			
D			

b Order the capacities **A**, **B**, **C** and **D** from smallest to largest.

☐

 • *AUSTRALIAN SIGNPOST MATHS NSW 3* • ISBN 9780655709046

3:08 Estimating the litre

A formal unit is a unit that everybody uses.

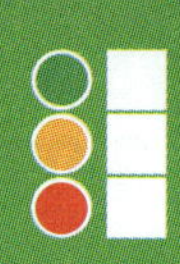

CONCEPT

- The litre is a formal unit for measuring capacity.
- **L** is short for **litre**.
  We write 1 litre as 1 L.

1 Colour in blue the containers that hold more than 1 litre.
Colour in red the containers that hold less than 1 litre.

2 Look at the pictures below. What is the total capacity of each pair of containers?

a drink bottle and esky ______ **b** storage box and bin ______

c esky and storage box ______ **d** bin and watering can ______

e Order the capacities **A**, **B**, **C**, **D** and **E** from largest to smallest. ______

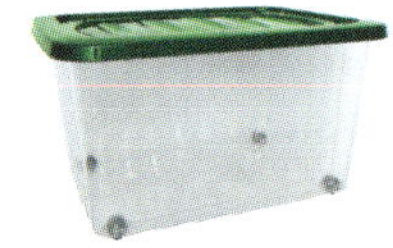
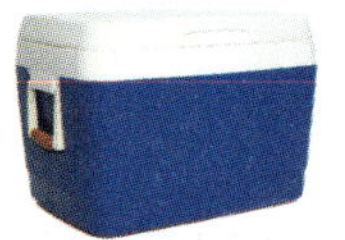

A drink bottle: 1 L | **B** storage box: 50 L | **C** esky: 10 L | **D** watering can: 9 L | **E** bin: 25 L

ACTIVITY

3 Use these two different containers to fill a 1 litre carton.
Write the number of containers needed to completely fill the carton.

Container	Estimated number to fill 1 L	Measured number to fill 1 L
one standard measuring cup		
small takeaway container		

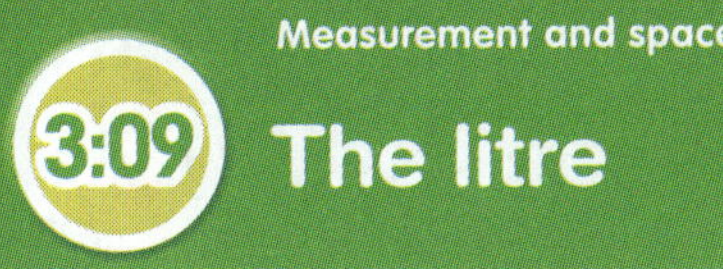

The litre

How many cups would we need to fill a litre?

1

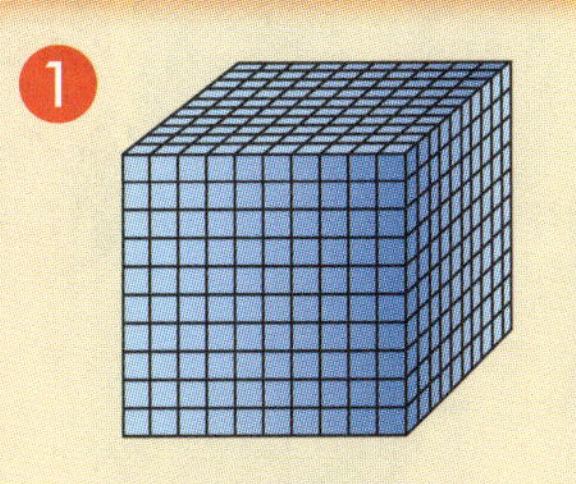

1000 block

1 litre measure

Compare a 1 litre measure with a 1000 block. Do they have about the same volume? ______

- 1 litre of water has the same volume as a 1000 block.

2 Compare a 1 L, 2 L and 3 L milk container.
Discuss the shape and size of each container.

3 Capacity of a bucket

Use a 1 L, 2 L and 3 L milk container to find the capacity of a bucket.

Unit	Estimate	Measure
1 L milk container	containers	
2 L milk container	containers	
3 L milk container	containers	

4 Make a 3 L measuring container

- Estimate where the 1 L, 2 L and 3 L marks would be on a 3 L milk container.
- Use a funnel to pour 1 L of water into your 3 L milk container.
- Label the 1 L mark on your 3 L container. Repeat and label the 2 L and 3 L marks.
- Discuss: Does 1 L of water always have the same shape? Why was there room left at the top or why did it overflow?

5 Use a funnel and your 3 L measuring container to measure the capacity of five containers. Fill a container with water.
Pour this water into the 3 L container. Record the closest litre mark.

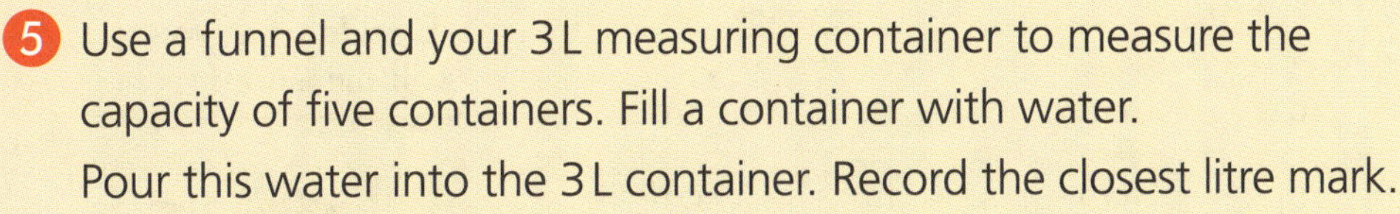

	Closer to 1 L	Closer to 2 L	Closer to 3 L
Containers			

3:10 Metres and centimetres

cm is short for centimetres.
1 metre = 100 centimetres
1m = 100 cm

CONCEPT

Caleb's desk has a length of 160 centimetres or 1 m 60 cm.

The width of the desk is 104 centimetres or 1 m 4 cm.

160 cm = 100 cm + 60 cm = 1 m 60 cm	104 cm = 100 cm + 4 cm = 1 m 4 cm

1 Convert these measurements to short form (3 metres 37 centimetres = 3 m 37 cm).

a 1 metre 25 centimetres ☐ m ☐ cm **b** 2 metres 34 centimetres ☐ m ☐ cm

c 5 metres 9 centimetres ☐ m ☐ cm **d** 7 metres 96 centimetres ☐ m ☐ cm

e 8 metres 42 centimetres ☐ m ☐ cm **f** 4 metres 22 centimetres ☐ m ☐ cm

2 Convert these measurements to metres and centimetres.

Partition the hundreds from the tens and ones, to do this.

a 119 cm = ☐ m ☐ cm **b** 345 cm = ☐ m ☐ cm

c 481 cm = ☐ m ☐ cm **d** 738 cm = ☐ m ☐ cm

e 405 cm = ☐ m ☐ cm **f** 801 cm = ☐ m ☐ cm

3 Convert these measurements to centimetres.

a 1 m 28 cm = ☐ cm **b** 3 m 14 cm = ☐ cm **c** 6 m 42 cm = ☐ cm

d 5 m 73 cm = ☐ cm **e** 5 m 30 cm = ☐ cm **f** 6 m 80 cm = ☐ cm

Order the lengths **a** to **f**, from shortest to longest. a,

ACTIVITY

4 a Find lengths longer than 1 metre. Use a personal benchmark to estimate, then use a tape measure to measure each to the nearest centimetre. Record your results.

	Object	Estimate		Width	
A		m	cm	m	cm
B		m	cm	m	cm
C		m	cm	m	cm
D		m	cm	m	cm

Decide what you will measure first.

b Order lengths **A** to **D** from shortest to longest.

 • *AUSTRALIAN SIGNPOST MATHS NSW 3* • ISBN 9780655709046

Recording length

1 m 17 cm
= 100 cm + 17 cm
= 117 cm

1 Write the lengths in short form.

a 1 metre 70 centimetres ☐ m ☐ cm **b** 3 metres 36 centimetres ☐ m ☐ cm

c 4 metres 26 centimetres ☐ m ☐ cm **d** 7 metres 13 centimetres ☐ m ☐ cm

e 6 metres 83 centimetres ☐ m ☐ cm **f** 5 metres 42 centimetres ☐ m ☐ cm

2 **a** Which of these lengths is longest? ☐ **b** Which of these lengths is shortest? ☐

3 Would you use metres (m) or centimetres (cm) to measure the following things?

a the height of your house ☐ **b** the length of an eraser ☐

c the length of your hair ☐ **d** the width of your room ☐

e the width of your thumb ☐ **f** the length of a pencil ☐

g the length of a path ☐ **h** the height of your desk ☐

4 Convert these measurements to centimetres.

a 4 m 84 cm = ☐ cm **b** 9 m 53 cm = ☐ cm **c** 1 m 72 cm = ☐ cm

d 3 m 92 cm = ☐ cm **e** 7 m 30 cm = ☐ cm **f** 2 m 5 cm = ☐ cm

Order the lengths **a** to **f**, from shortest to longest. c,

5 Convert these measurements to metres and centimetres.

a 187 cm = ☐ m ☐ cm **b** 426 cm = ☐ m ☐ cm

c 286 cm = ☐ m ☐ cm **d** 836 cm = ☐ m ☐ cm

e 806 cm = ☐ m ☐ cm **f** 572 cm = ☐ m ☐ cm

It is important to know how to convert measurements accurately.

Order the lengths **a** to **f**, from shortest to longest.

a,

3:12 Measuring distance

Which instruments would you use to measure a:
a spoon? b door? c path?

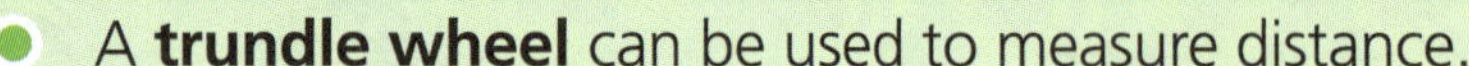

CONCEPT

- A **trundle wheel** can be used to measure distance.
  - Place the start arrow at the starting point.
  - Count how many clicks you hear to measure the distance. Each click is a measure of 1 metre.
  - Check the trundle wheel when you finish to add any extra centimetres to your metre count.
- Matthew used a trundle wheel to measure the length of a fence. He started at O and heard 7 clicks. When he finished measuring, the long blue pointer pointed to 5 cm. The fence was 7 m 5 cm long.

INVESTIGATION

1. Compare a metre ruler with your arm span. What did you find?

2. Place a metre ruler on the floor. How many of your steps make 1 metre? ☐
   Now roll a ball along the floor. It rolled ☐ steps. That is about ☐ metres.

3. a Use a trundle wheel to find the length of items longer than 2 metres. Complete the table. Use a personal benchmark (your step count or arm span) to visualise your estimate.

Object	Estimate	Measurement
the length of a path	m cm	m cm
the width of a classroom	m cm	m cm
	m cm	m cm
	m cm	m cm
	m cm	m cm

   b Compare your measurements with others and discuss the differences.

   c Which was the longest length? ☐ m cm

   d Which was the shortest length? ☐ m cm

   e Compare your measurements with your estimates. Were they close? ☐
   If your estimates were not close, discuss how you could improve your estimating skills.

Measuring length

Use your personal benchmark to estimate more accurately.

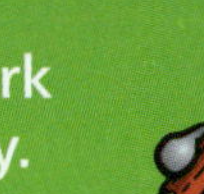

CONCEPT

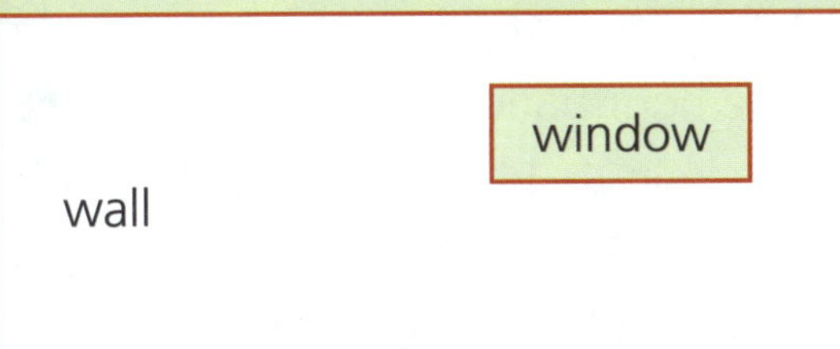

Daisy wanted to find the difference between the length of the wall and the length of the window.

Daisy's method:

Step 1: Measure each in metres and centimetres.
Step 2: Change the measurements to centimetres.
Step 3: Subtract the smaller from the larger.
Step 4: Convert this into metres and centimetres.
Step 5: Write a conclusion.

Daisy's working:

1: Wall: 6 m 28 cm Window: 2 m 10 cm
2: Wall: 628 cm Window: 210 cm
3: 628 cm – 210 cm = 418 cm
4: 418 cm = 4 m 18 cm
5: The wall was longer by 4 m 18 cm.

1 a Estimate, then measure these objects to the nearest centimetre. Convert each measurement to centimetres.

Compare the metres then the centimetres.

	Item	Estimate	Measurement	Convert to cm
A	blanket length	m cm	m cm	
B	blanket width	m cm	m cm	
C	table cloth length	m cm	m cm	
D	table cloth width	m cm	m cm	
E	tarpaulin length	m cm	m cm	
F	tarpaulin width	m cm	m cm	

b Which was the longest length? ☐ c Which was the shortest length? ☐

2 Use the last column above to find the difference between the length and width of each item.

a **A** and **B** ☐ cm or ☐ m ☐ cm b **C** and **D** ☐ cm or ☐ m ☐ cm c **E** and **F** ☐ cm or ☐ m ☐ cm

3 Use the last column above to find the difference between these lengths.

a **A** and **C** ☐ cm or ☐ m ☐ cm b **A** and **E** ☐ cm or ☐ m ☐ cm c **C** and **E** ☐ cm or ☐ m ☐ cm

3:14 Time, minutes past

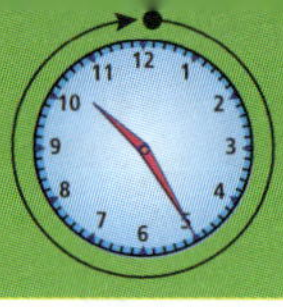

60 minutes makes 1 hour.

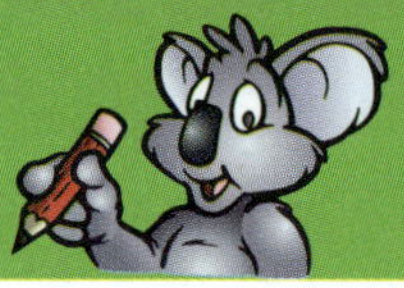

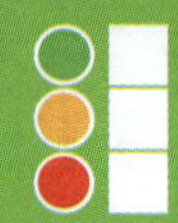

CONCEPT

- The hour hand has passed 1.
- The minute hand has moved 5, 10, 15, 20, 21, 22 minutes from 12.
- The time is **1:22** or **22 minutes past 1**.

1 Look carefully at each clock face and complete the labels.

a 10: ☐ ☐ past 10

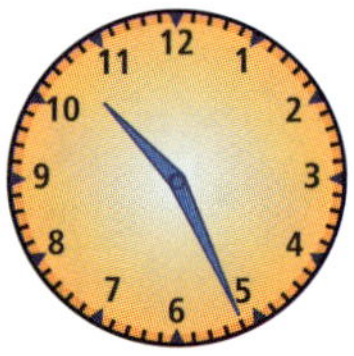

b 11: ☐ ☐ past 11

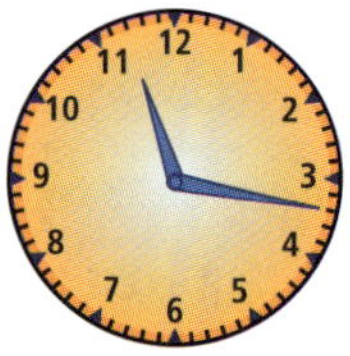

c 3: ☐ ☐ past 3

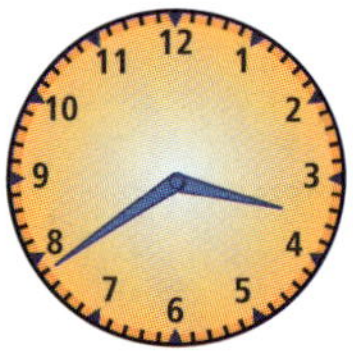

d 2: ☐ ☐ past 2

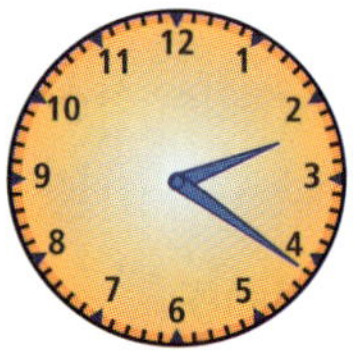

e 4: ☐ ☐ past 4

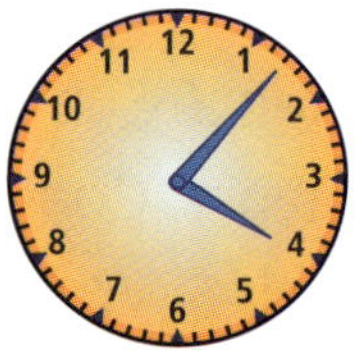

f 5: ☐ ☐ past 5

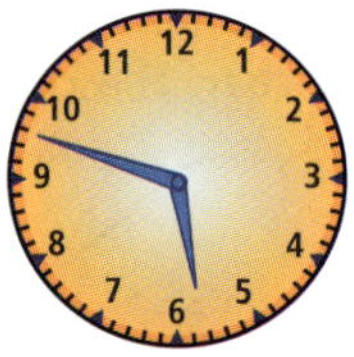

g 2: ☐ ☐ past 2

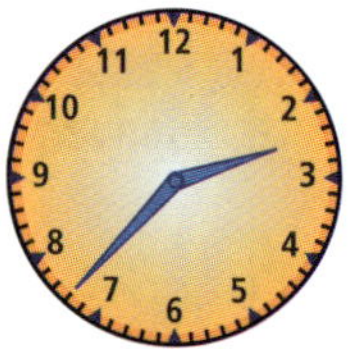

h 4: ☐ ☐ past 4

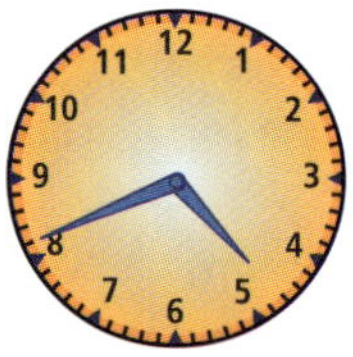

i 7: ☐ ☐ past 7

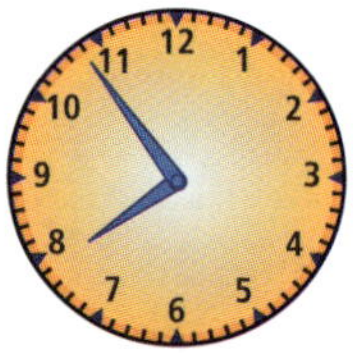

j 2: ☐ ☐ past 2

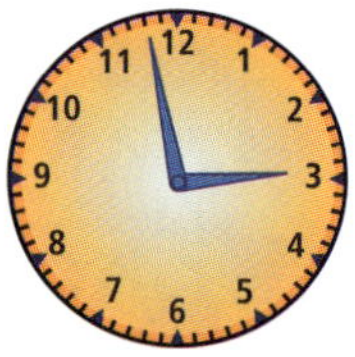

k 9:34 ☐ past ☐

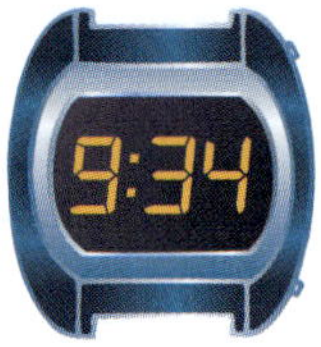

l 2:28 ☐ past ☐

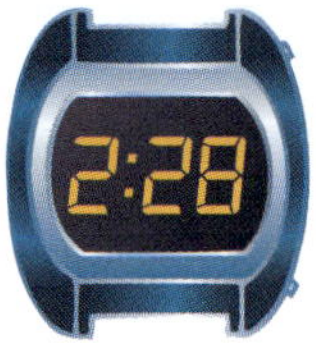

m 5:41 ☐ past ☐

n 8:47 ☐ past ☐

o 6:59 ☐ past ☐

2 Draw lines to join the same times together.

a

11:36	12 minutes past 6
6:12	57 minutes past 9
9:57	eleven thirty-six

b

1:43	26 minutes past 8
8:26	five-oh-seven
5:07	43 minutes past 1

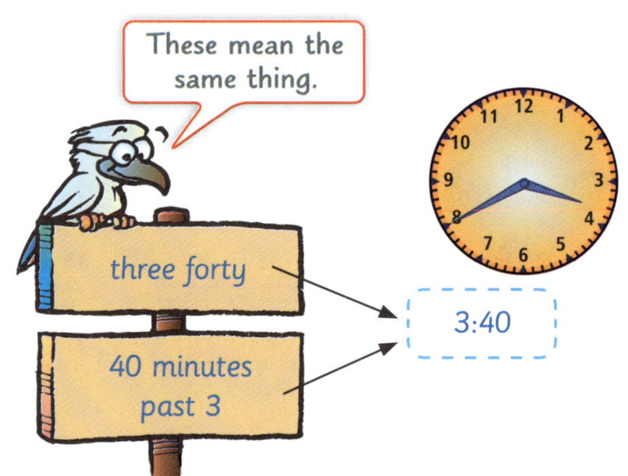

3:15 Time, minutes to

Analog clocks have 60 1-minute marks around the clock.
60 minutes = 1 hour

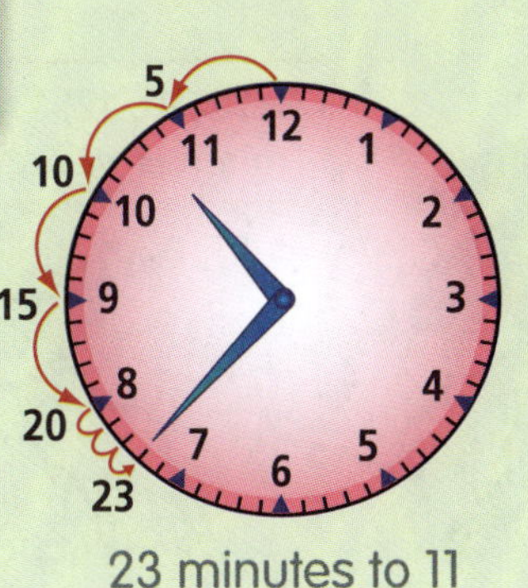

23 minutes to 11

- The hour hand is approaching 11.
- The minute hand has 23 minutes to go before it reaches the 12.
- The time is **23 to 11**.

1 Write the time shown.

a  ☐ to ☐

b  ☐ to ☐

c  ☐ to ☐

d  ☐ to ☐

e  ☐ to ☐

f  ☐ to ☐

g  ☐ to ☐

h  ☐ to ☐

2 Show the time given.

a 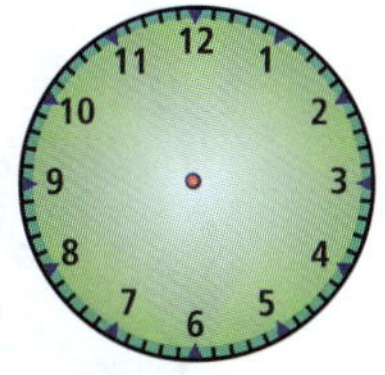
17 to 3

b 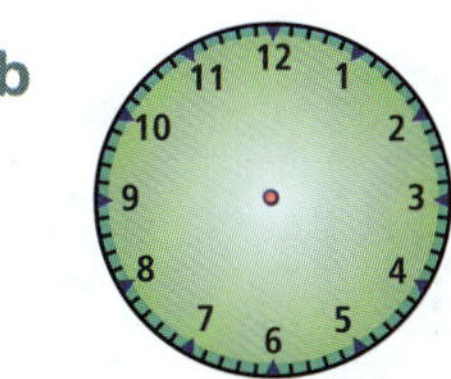
14 to 8

c 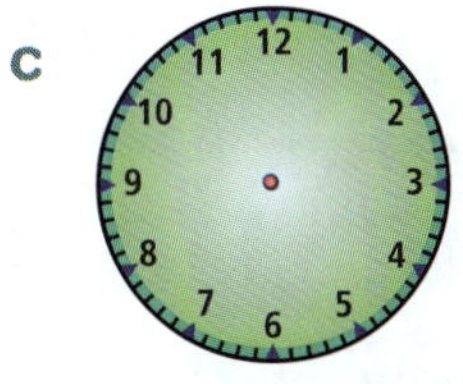
28 to 1

d 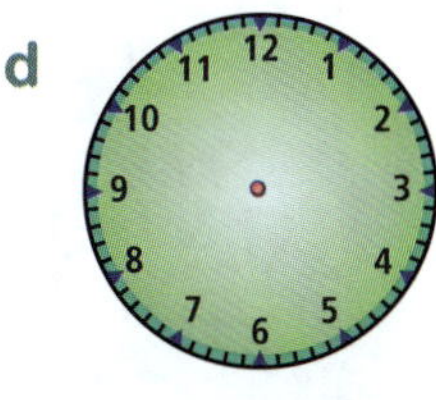
12 to 4

3 Write the time that is four minutes after.

a 20 to 6 ☐ b 15 to 9 ☐ c 25 to 3 ☐

d 20 to 10 ☐ e 25 to 11 ☐ f 10 to 7 ☐

4 About how many minutes do each of these events take?

a recess ☐ minutes b lunch  minutes c a game of soccer ☐ minutes

3:16 Time, minutes past and to

Count by 5s around the clock then count on the ones.

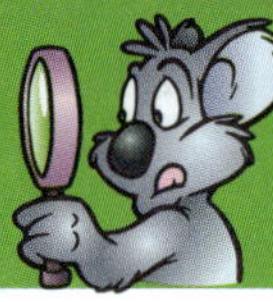

1 Write the time shown.

a ☐ past ☐
b ☐ to ☐
c ☐ past ☐
d ☐ past ☐
e ☐ to ☐
f ☐ past ☐
g ☐ to ☐
h ☐ to ☐

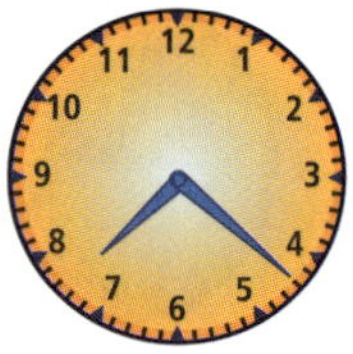

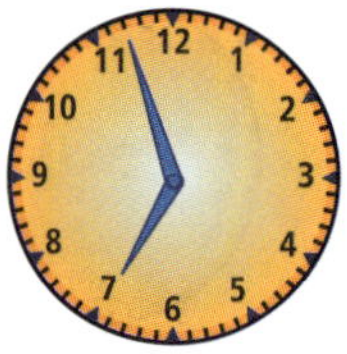

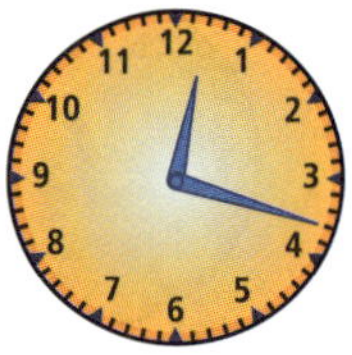

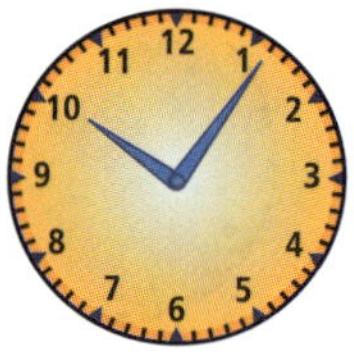

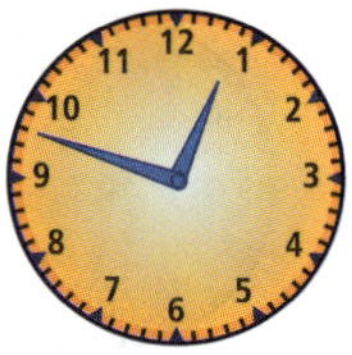

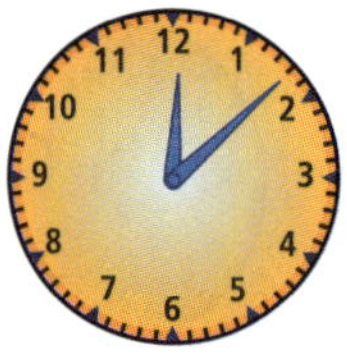

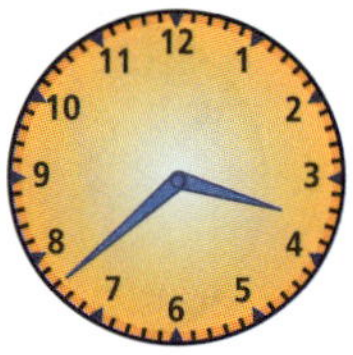

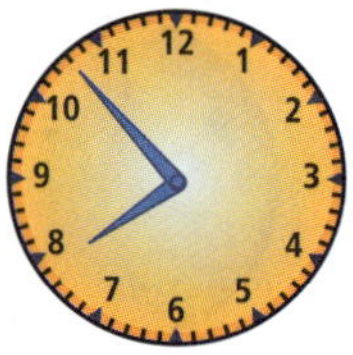

2 Write the time shown. When the number of minutes is more than 30, subtract from 60.

a 6:27 ☐ past ☐
b 7:18 ☐ past ☐
c 8:10 ☐ past ☐
d 4:54 ☐ to ☐
e 6:59 ☐ to ☐

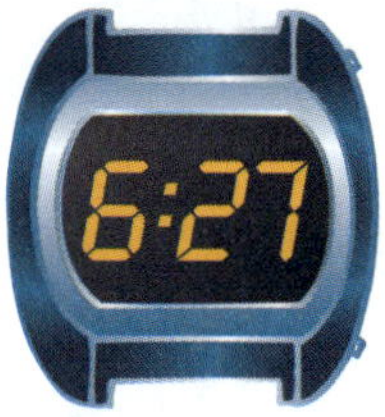

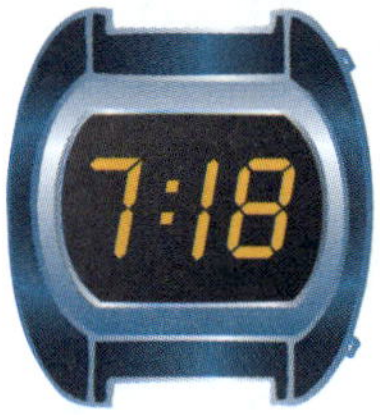

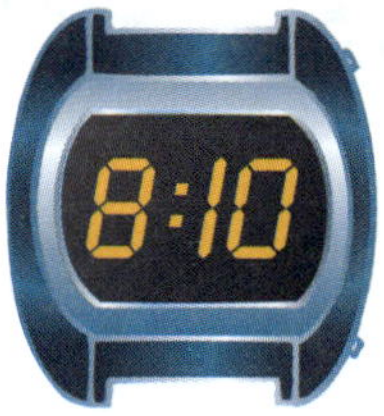

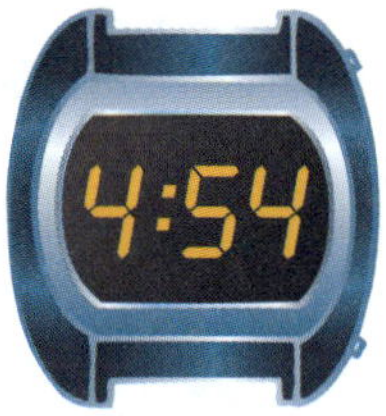

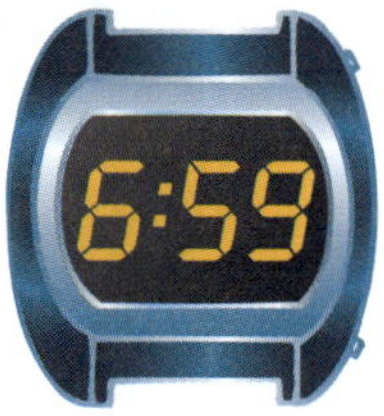

3 About how many minutes does it take to walk from your classroom to the:

a library? ☐ minutes b office? ☐ minutes c oval? ☐ minutes

4 How many minutes are there in:

a one hour? ☐ minutes b half an hour? ☐ minutes

c a quarter of an hour? ☐ minutes

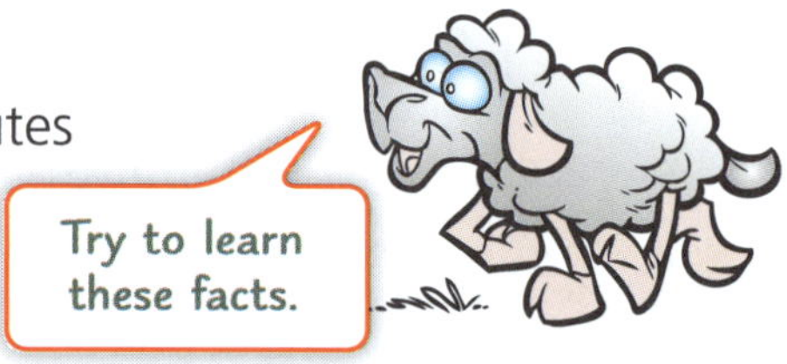

Try to learn these facts.

The kilogram

We can measure mass in kilograms.

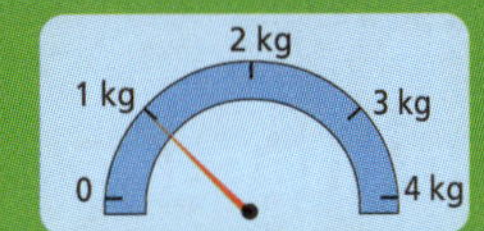

CONCEPT

1 litre of water has a mass of 1 kilogram.

ACTIVITY

1 **a** On one side of a balance scale, put a 1 kilogram mass. On the other side of the scale, put a bag of sand that you estimate to have the same mass.

b Does it balance? ______ Was the bag of sand lighter or heavier than 1 kg? ______

c Repeat this activity with stones instead of sand.

2 Estimate whether the items listed below are lighter than 1 kilogram. Use balance scales to check.

Item	Estimate (less than 1 kg?)	Measurement (less than 1 kg?)
3 pencils	yes	yes
10 books		
5 shoes		

Item	Estimate (less than 1 kg?)	Measurement (less than 1 kg?)
drink bottle	yes	yes
pencil case		
lunch box		

INVESTIGATION

3 **The mass of water**

On balance scales, place a milk container with 1 L of water on one side and a 1 kg mass with an identical milk container on the other side. Do they balance? ______

Discuss why or why not.

3:18 Comparing masses

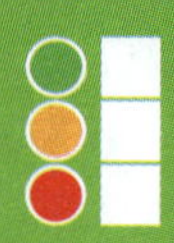

CONCEPT

ACTIVITY

1 Complete this table. Estimate first, then use a balance scale and a 1 kg mass to check.

Item	Less than 1 kg	About 1 kg	More than 1 kg
book			
large milk container			
full drink bottle			
vase			

2 Repeat this activity with other items in the classroom.
Draw each item on this chart to show where it belongs.

Less than 1 kg							
About 1 kg							
More than 1 kg							

3 Collect labels from packages that show kilograms. Display the labels on a chart.

4 Circle the items that would have a mass greater than 1 kilogram.

a television **b** ant **c** pair of socks **d** car battery
e football **f** dog collar **g** horse **h** ruler
i slice of bread **j** spoon **k** table **l** refrigerator

5 Circle the items that would be measured in kilograms.

a packet of jelly beans **b** bag of potatoes **c** suitcase of clothes
d jar of jam **e** packet of biscuits **f** a person
g packet of sultanas **h** packet of chips **i** sack of flour

3:19 Using the kilogram

Do you think 7 cockatoos would weigh more than 3 kg?

1 Use the short form to write these measurements.

a 3 kilograms ☐ b 10 kilograms ☐ c 8 kilograms ☐

d 5 kilograms ☐ e 7 kilograms ☐ f 11 kilograms ☐

2 Circle the items that would have a mass greater than 1 kilogram.

a bicycle b chair c nail d your teacher

e desk f marble g computer h brick

i matchbox j car tyre k large dog l golf ball

Flour 25 kg

ONIONS 20 kg

Grapes 3 kg

Meat 7 kg

Laundry Powder 4 kg

CHEESE 1 kg

3 Look at the pictures. What is the total mass of the items together?

a grapes and cheese ☐ b meat and grapes ☐

c flour and laundry powder ☐ d onions and meat ☐

e onions and grapes ☐ f cheese and meat ☐

g flour and onions ☐ h cheese and onions ☐

4 Circle the labels that are written correctly.

a 9 kg b 9 KG c 7 kg d 6 kg. e 11 Kg

f 14 kg g 3 kg h 17 kg i 21 kgs j 32 kg

Choose and check

ACTIVITY

- Choose 10 classroom items that you think are heavier than 1 kg. Use balance scales and a 1 kg mass to check.
- Choose 10 items that you think are lighter than 1 kg. Use balance scales to check.
- Without measuring, arrange six different items in order from lightest to heaviest. Use balance scales to check if you were right.

3:20 Mass problem solving

Always show the units in your answer.

1 a Zara's boat can only carry a mass of 30 kg or less.
Use the table to find which two creatures she can take with her.

	Mass
Zara	23 kg
dog	6 kg
duck	3 kg
pelican	2 kg

b What is the total mass of Zara and the three animals?

c How many pelicans would have the same mass as the dog?

d What is the difference in mass between Zara and the total mass of the 3 animals?

2 What is the difference in mass between these items?

a the fridge and the dishwasher

b the stove and the washing machine

c the fridge and the stove

d the stove and the dishwasher

Item	Mass
fridge	23 kg
washing machine	78 kg
dishwasher	18 kg
stove	69 kg

3 a What is the total mass of these products?

b How many packets of flour would have the same mass as the potatoes?

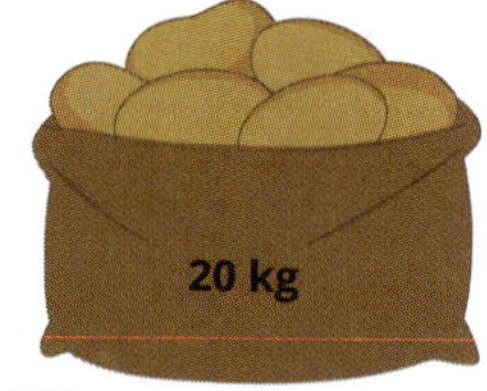

c Would 7 packets of washing powder be lighter than 2 sacks of potatoes?

d I had 3 sacks of potatoes and used half of them. What mass of potatoes do I have left?

- Write a problem of your own about the mass of these products. Share it with your class.

INVESTIGATION

4 Find the difference between the world record mass and my fruit's mass.

Fruit	My fruit's mass	World record mass*	Difference between the world record and my fruit
pineapple	18 kg	28 kg	28 kg – 18 kg = kg
cabbage	1 kg	62 kg	
watermelon	9 kg	118 kg	
squash	3 kg	981 kg	

* rounded down

- Find photos of the world record fruits.

 • *AUSTRALIAN SIGNPOST MATHS NSW 3* • ISBN 9780655709046

Area

This flag is 1 square centimetre.
It is a square with sides lengths of 1 cm.

1 

Books were used to cover this desk.

a Did the books cover the desk exactly?

b Estimate the amount of overhang.

c If we could cut the books, how many books would cover the table?

d Do you think a book would be a good unit of area?

Why or why not?

2 Shape **A** has 2 rows of 4 (or 4 columns of 2). Describe the area of shape:

a **B**

b **C**

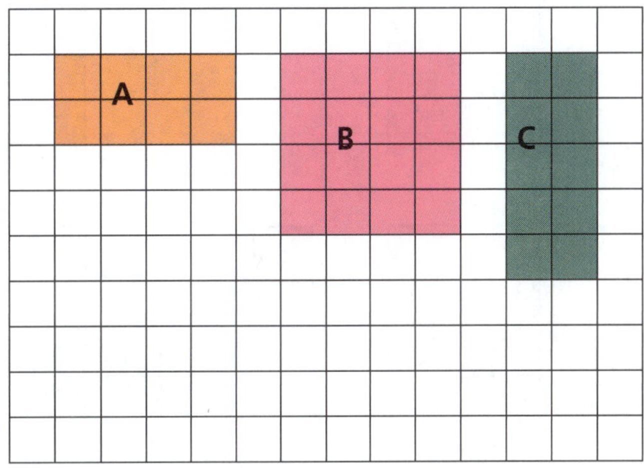

Draw a shape with:

c 3 rows of 4. Label it with a **D**.

d 2 columns of 2. Label it with an **E**.

Which shape has:

e the largest area?

f the smallest area?

3 A square with sides of 1 cm is called a square centimetre. Estimate then find the area of each.

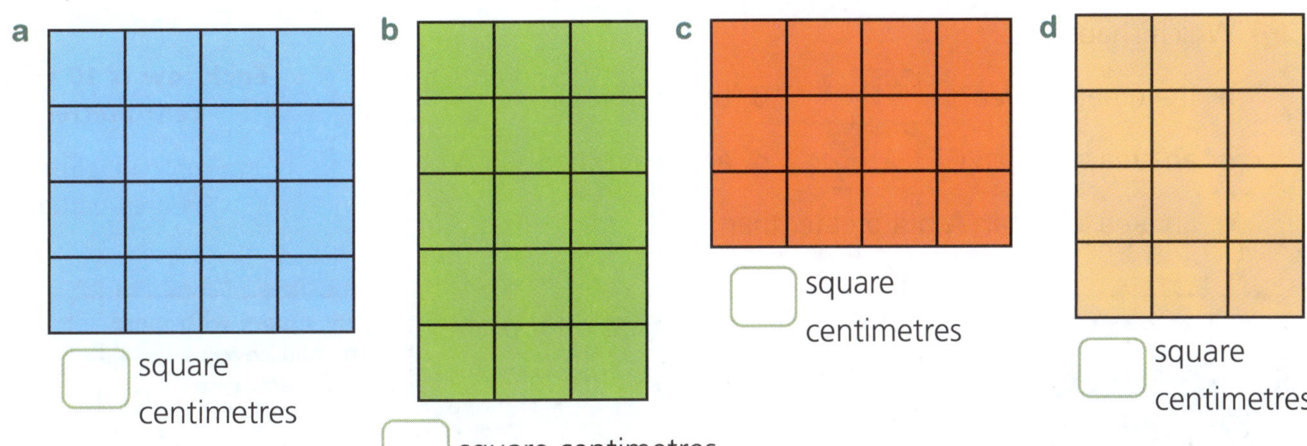

a square centimetres

b square centimetres

c square centimetres

d square centimetres

Visualise how many A4 sheets of paper cover the top of a desk, then use A4 sheets of paper to measure the area. Measure and compare other larger areas using this method.

Remember: no gaps, no overlaps.

3:22 Area using square centimetres

The bottom of a ones block is a square centimetre.

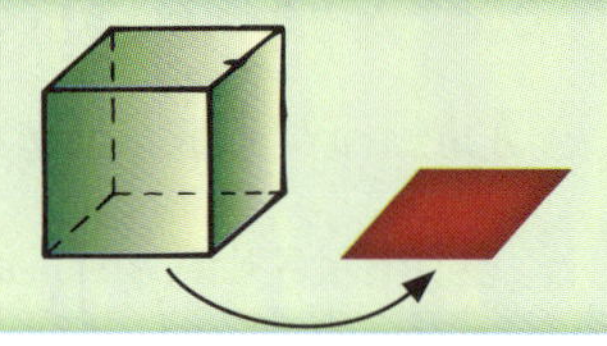

1. Each square on 1 cm grid paper is 1 square centimetre.
How many square centimetres make up the area of each shape?

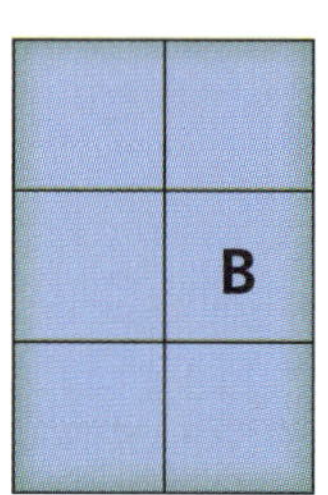

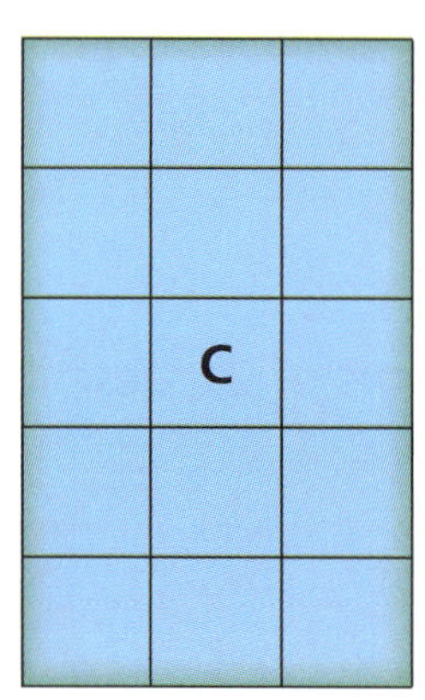

	Area
A	☐ square centimetres
B	☐ square centimetres
C	☐ square centimetres
D	☐ square centimetres
E	☐ square centimetres
F	☐ square centimetres

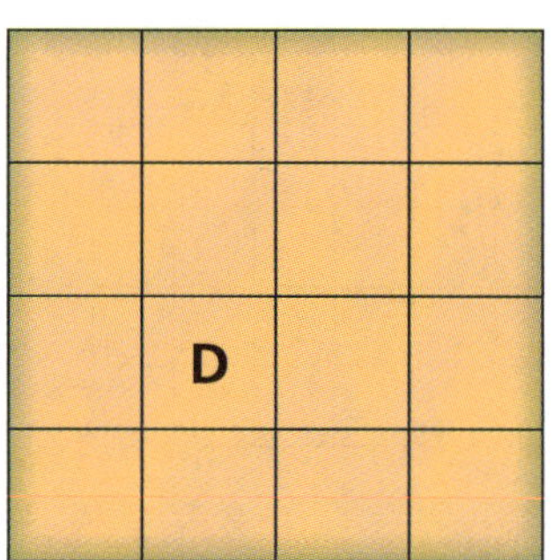

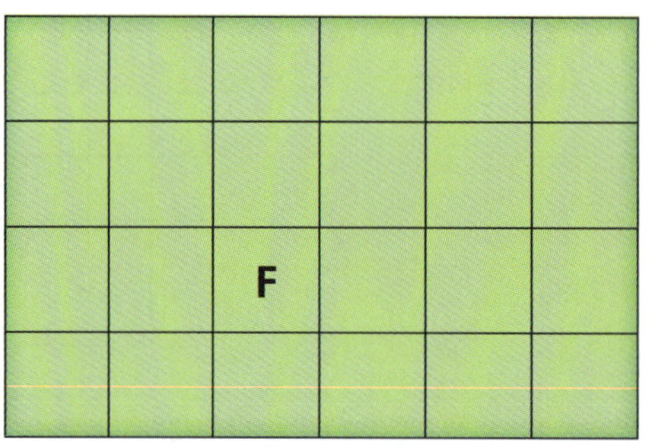

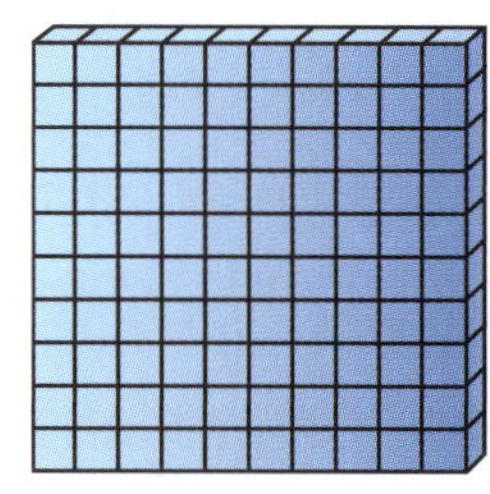

A hundreds block is a good personal benchmark for 100 square centimetres.

Each row is 10 square centimetres.

We can multiply to find the area quickly.

2. Which shape has:

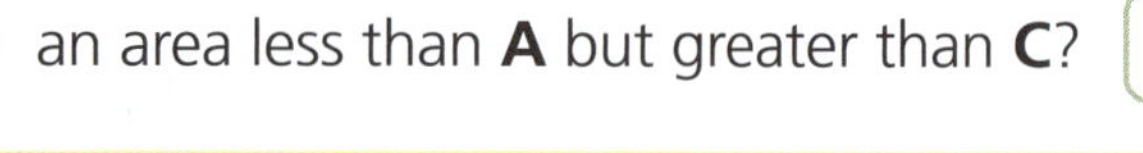

a the greatest area? ☐

b the least area? ☐

c an area less than **C**? ☐

d an area more than **A**? ☐

e an area less than **A** but greater than **C**? ☐

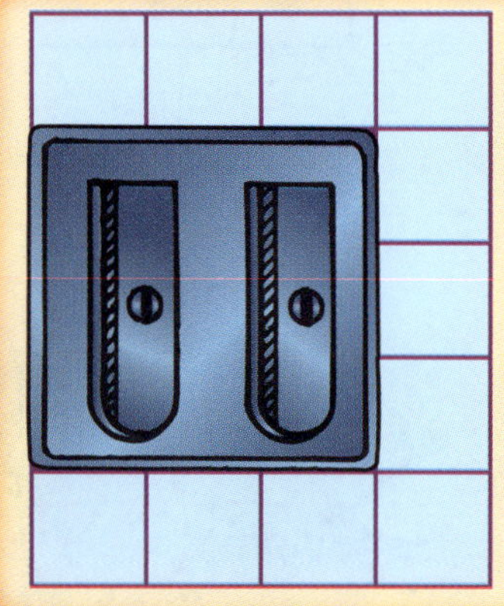

- Place small flat objects on top of 1 cm grid paper and trace around them.
- Estimate then find the number of square centimetres covered. Label each area measured.

sharpener: 9 square centimetres

Any square with more than half covered should be counted as one square.

 • *AUSTRALIAN SIGNPOST MATHS NSW 3* • ISBN 9780655709046

Square centimetres

3 rows of 5

The area of this array is 3 × 5 square centimetres.

1. Find the area of each rectangle. Order the areas **L**, **M** and **N** from smallest to largest. ☐

L ☐ square centimetres

M ☐ square centimetres

N ☐ square centimetres

2. **a** Estimate which area is largest, **X**, **Y** or **Z**. ☐

b Calculate the area of each rectangle.

X ☐ square centimetres

Y ☐ square centimetres

Z ☐ square centimetres

c Order the areas **X**, **Y** and **Z** from smallest to largest. ☐

3. **a** Describe each area as an array, then calculate the area.

A ☐ × ☐ squares

☐ square centimetres

B ☐

☐ square centimetres

C ☐

☐ square centimetres

b Order these areas, **A**, **B** and **C**, from smallest to largest. ☐

FUN SPOT

- Estimate the area of your hand. Estimate = ☐ square centimetres.
- Trace your hand on 1 cm grid paper. Count any square where more than half of the square is within your hand outline. Do not count any square where less than half is within your outline.
- Area = ☐ square centimetres

Compare the area of your hand with a hundreds block.

3:24 Area

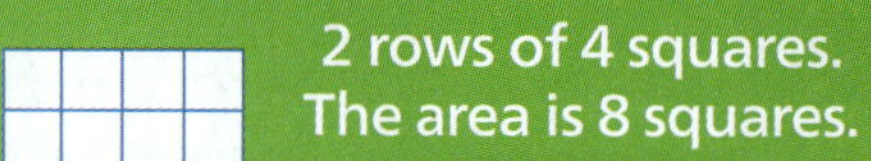

2 rows of 4 squares.
The area is 8 squares.

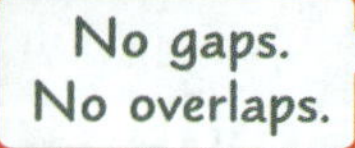

1. Describe each array. Calculate the area of each shape. Tick the larger area of each pair.

a

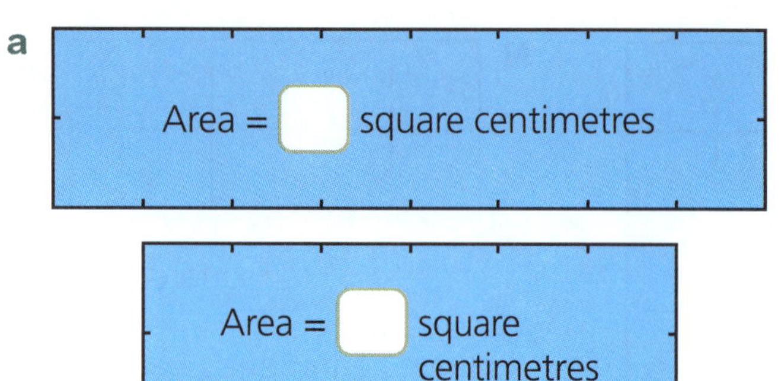

b

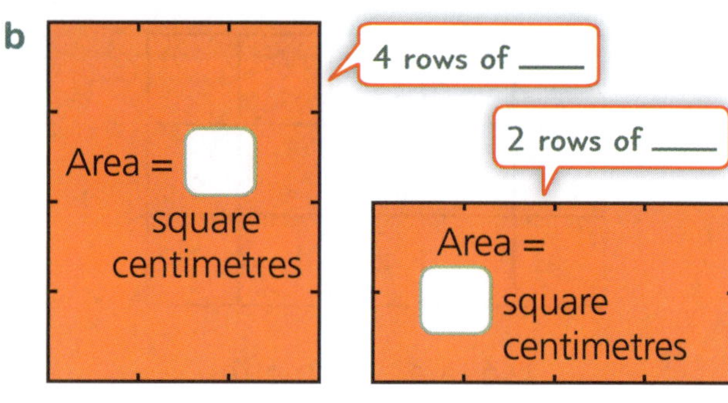

c

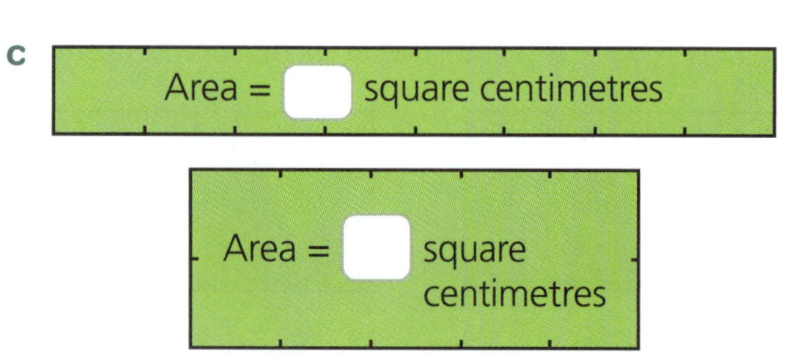

d

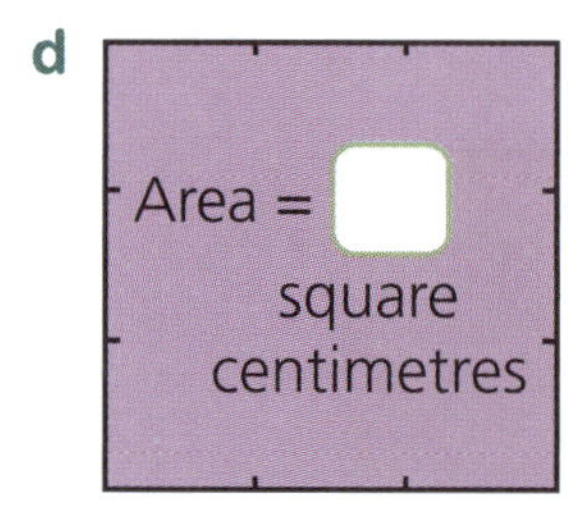

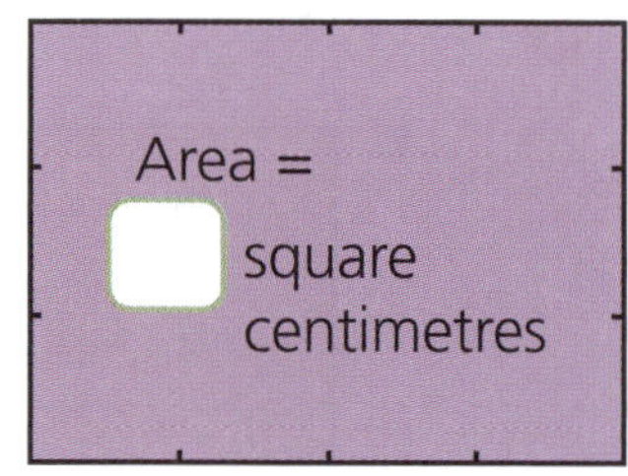

2. **a** **Estimate** the area of the cover of a book by visualising how many hundreds blocks would be needed to cover it. Estimate = ☐ blocks or ☐ square centimetres.

Use hundreds, tens and ones blocks to **measure** the cover of the book.
Area = ☐ blocks or ☐ square centimetres.

We could use photocopies of base 10 blocks.

Use this method to estimate then measure the area of:

b a poster

Estimate = ☐ blocks or ☐ square centimetres.

Area = ☐ blocks or ☐ square centimetres.

c the bottom surface of a tissue box.

Estimate = ☐ blocks or ☐ square centimetres.

Area = ☐ blocks or ☐ square centimetres.

A ones block covers 1 square centimetre.

A tens block covers 10 square centimetres.

A hundreds block covers 100 square centimetres.

ACTIVITY

Choose two rectangular areas in your classroom that are smaller than a hundreds block, for example, a sticky note or the surface of an eraser or calculator.
Use base ten blocks to measure the area of both and find the difference between them.

Area 1 = ☐ square centimetres Area 2 = ☐ square centimetres

The difference between the two areas is ☐ square centimetres.

 • *AUSTRALIAN SIGNPOST MATHS NSW 3* • ISBN 9780655709046

3:25 Using litres

- Find four containers, **A**, **B**, **C** and **D** that have a capacity greater than 1 L.
- Estimate how many litres each container holds.
- Use a 1 litre container to measure the capacity of each container, to the nearest litre. (You could place a line at the halfway mark.)
- Record your results in the table.
- Order the containers **A** to **D** from smallest capacity to largest capacity.

Make sure you fill your litre measure to the top each time.

Container	Estimated	Measured in L
A		
B		
C		
D		

1 Write each amount in short form.

a 2 litres
b 4 litres
c 1 litre
d 10 litres
e 7 litres
f 5 litres
g 19 litres
h 20 litres
i 14 litres

2

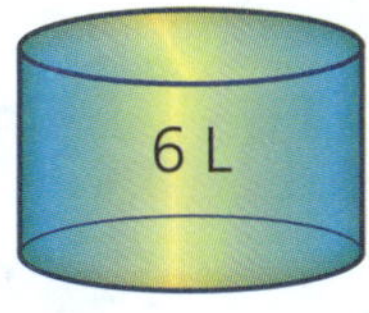

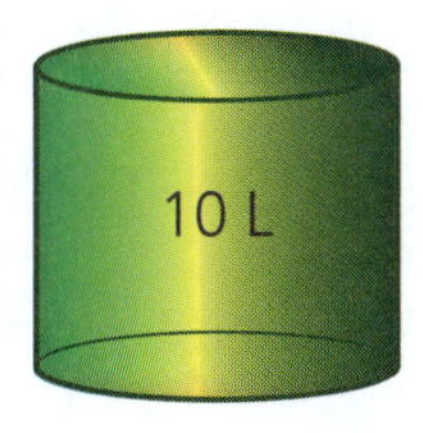

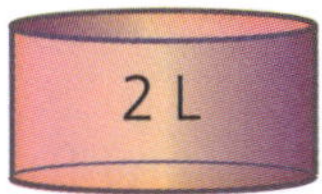

Write which of these containers would hold:

a the most water.
b the least water.
c more water than **A**.
d less water than **B**.
e What is the total capacity of these containers?
f How much water would be needed to fill both **A** and **C**?

3:26 Capacity problem solving

Underline the important parts of each problem.

1 It takes 6 cups to fill my water bottle to the top.

a How many half cups would it take to fill my water bottle to the top? [ ] half cups

b How many cups would it take to fill *5* water bottles? [ ] cups

2 I completed this chart after measuring the capacity of containers **A** to **D**.

	Container	Estimate	Measure
A	bottle	3 cups	4 cups
B	jug	5 cups	6 cups
C	vase	3 cups	3 cups
D	tub	34 cups	40 cups

a How many vases of water would I need to fill a jug? [ ]

b How many cups of water did I estimate it would take to fill a vase and a bottle? [ ] cups

c What was my estimate of the total number of cups of water needed to fill all of the containers? [ ] cups

What was the measure of the total number of cups of water needed to fill all of the containers? [ ] cups

How many more cups of water were needed than I estimated? [ ] cups

d How many bottles of water would I need to fill the tub? [ ] bottles

3

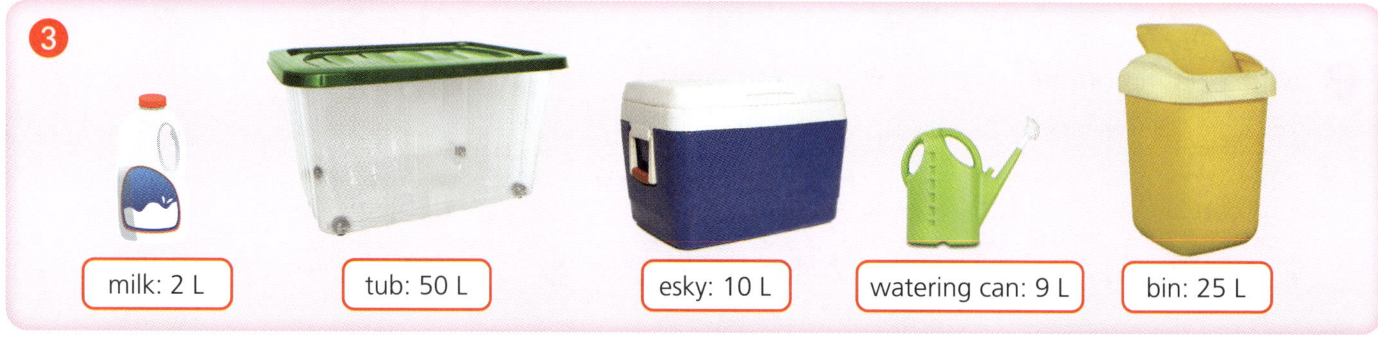

a How many full milk containers would I need to fill the esky? [ ] milk containers

b How many full eskys would I need to fill the tub? [ ] eskys

c How many full bins would I need to fill the tub? [ ] bins

d How many full watering cans would I need to fill the bin? [ ] watering cans

e What is the total capacity of the containers? [ ]

4

Container	Measure
bucket	10 L
storage bin	
esky	50 L
tub	30 L

a The total capacity of these containers is 150 L. What is the capacity of the storage bin? [ ]

b Which of these containers would I need for a total capacity of 110 L? [ ]

[ ]

The square metre

My garden has an area of about 8 square metres.

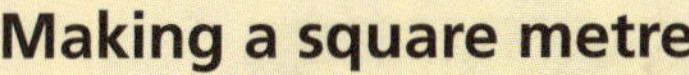

Making a square metre

- Tape large sheets of newspaper together.
- Use a metre ruler to draw a square with side lengths of 1 m on the paper.
- Cut out your square.

Because this square has side lengths of one metre, it is a square metre.

1. List things in your classroom that are bigger than a square metre.

2. List things in your classroom that are smaller than a square metre.

3. Estimate and then check to find how many:
   - a children can stand on one square metre.
   - b children can sit on one square metre.
   - c children can lie on one square metre.

4. Estimate and then check to find how many:
   - a books are needed to cover one square metre.
   - b school bags are needed to cover one square metre.
   - c boxes are needed to cover one square metre.

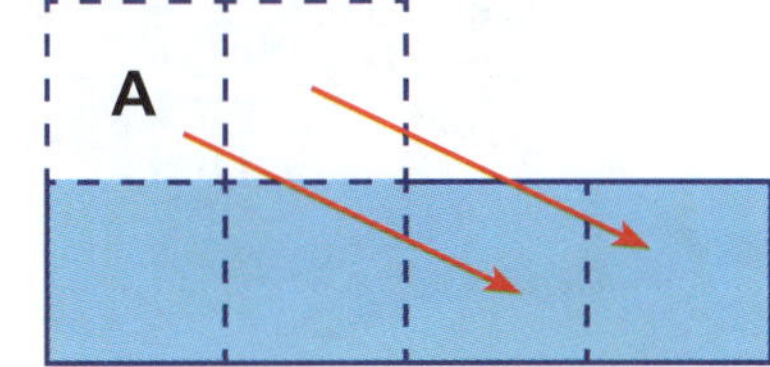

5. Estimate and then check to find how many:
   - a square metres are needed to cover a teacher's desk.
   - b square metres are needed to cover a door.
   - c square metres are needed to cover the floor.

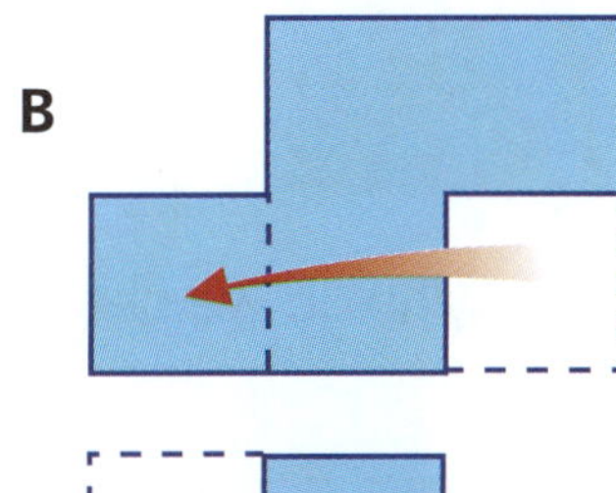

6. Cut, then join your square metre to make shapes **A**, **B** and **C**.
   - a Does each still cover one square metre?
   - b Discuss how this could help us measure different surfaces.

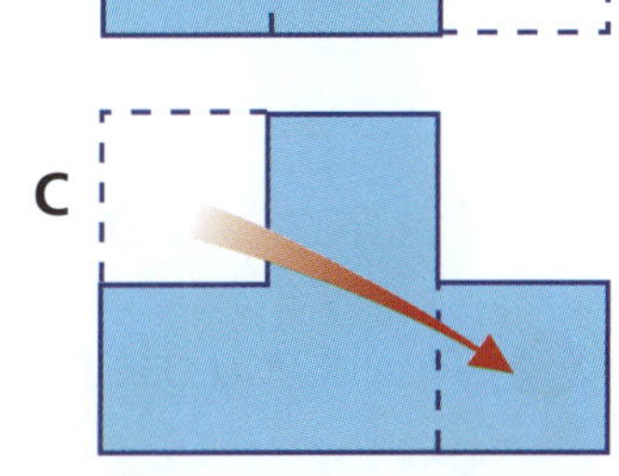

- Estimate then measure the size of a:
  - a table top ☐ square metres
  - b window ☐ square metres
  - c handball court ☐ square metres

3:28 The square metre

Leave no gaps or overlaps when measuring area.

ACTIVITY

- Make a square metre template from newspaper, plastic or cloth.
- Find surfaces that have an area:
  - less than 1 square metre
  - about 1 square metre
  - more than 1 square metre.
- Complete the table.

Size	Surface	
Less than 1 square metre		
About 1 square metre		
More than 1 square metre		

- Use your square metre template to measure larger areas.

Area or surface to be measured	Number of square metres	
	Estimate	Measure
Table cloth	square metres	square metres
Whiteboard	square metres	square metres
Section of a path	square metres	square metres
Tarpaulin	square metres	square metres

1. Why do we need a unit larger than square centimetres?

2. Would you use square centimetres or square metres to measure the top surface of:

   a a ruler?
   b a handball court?
   c a garden bed?
   d a birthday card?
   e a certificate?
   f a blanket?

3:29 The millimetre

Millimetres can be used to measure small lengths more accurately.
1 cm = 10 mm

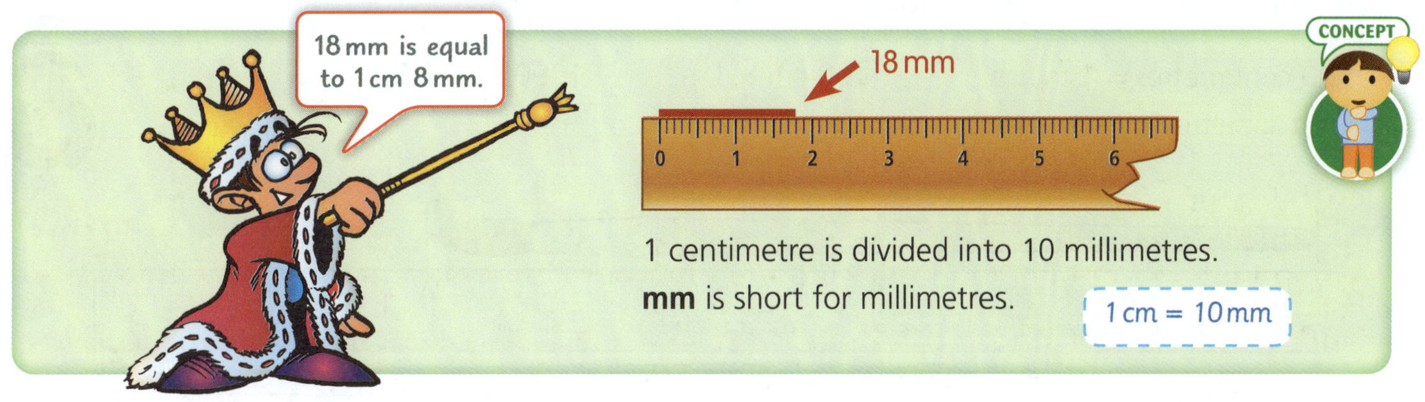

1 centimetre is divided into 10 millimetres.

mm is short for millimetres.

1 cm = 10 mm

1 Write the length of each red line.

a ☐ mm

b ☐ mm

c ☐ mm

d ☐ mm

e ☐ mm

2 Estimate and then measure the length of each line. Write the measurement.

a ☐ mm

b ☐ mm

c ☐ mm

d ☐ mm

e ☐ mm

f ☐ mm

FUN SPOT

- Play this game with a partner.
  - Take turns to choose an object.
  - Each player estimates the length and width of the object to the nearest millimetre.
  - Measure the object. The closest estimate gets 1 point.
  - The first player to 10 points wins.

Remember this.

1 cm = 10 mm

- Choose a suitable unit to measure each item. Record the measurements.
  - width of this book ☐
  - length of a pen ☐
  - length of a ruler ☐
  - length of a fingernail ☐
  - width of your hand ☐
  - width of a ruler ☐

Compare your measurements with others. Discuss the results.

  ISBN 9780655709046

3:30 Using a ruler

Some rulers have two different sides: cm and mm.

CONCEPT

100 centimetres = 1 metre   100 cm = 1 m   1000 mm = 1 m
10 millimetres = 1 centimetre   10 mm = 1 cm

0 cm   22 cm   30 cm

300 mm   220 mm   0 mm

1 Use a ruler to measure these lengths.

a Place-value ones block

Length in centimetres = ☐ cm

Length in millimetres = ☐ mm

b Place-value long block

Length in centimetres = ☐ cm

Length in millimetres = ☐ mm

Measure to the closest unit used.

2 When measuring length, why would centimetres be better than handspans?

3 When would it be better to use millimetres rather than centimetres?

INVESTIGATION

- Use a ruler to measure the lengths of 4 items in millimetres, or to the closest centimetre.

Name of item				
Length				

- Measure the height of a ball in millimetres. How did you do this?

3:31 Length problem solving

1 m = 100 cm
10 mm = 1 cm

1 **a** Use a ruler to measure the length of each animal.

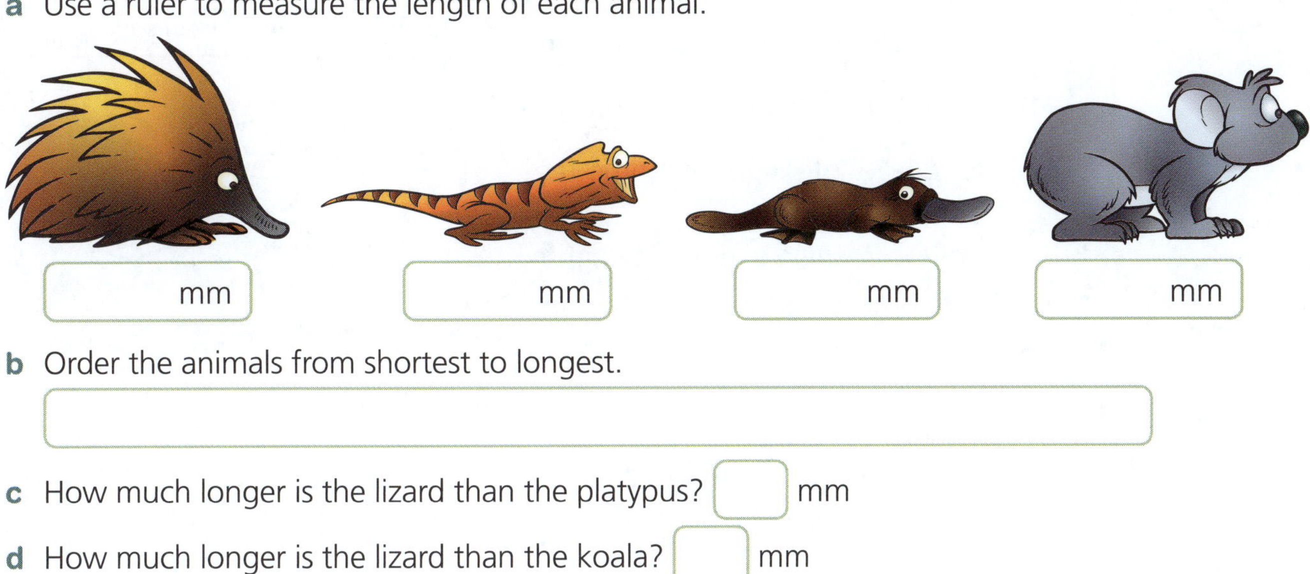

mm mm mm mm

b Order the animals from shortest to longest.

c How much longer is the lizard than the platypus? mm

d How much longer is the lizard than the koala? mm

2 On Riley's 9th birthday, he was 133 cm tall. The previous year he grew 5 cm. How tall was he on his 8th birthday?

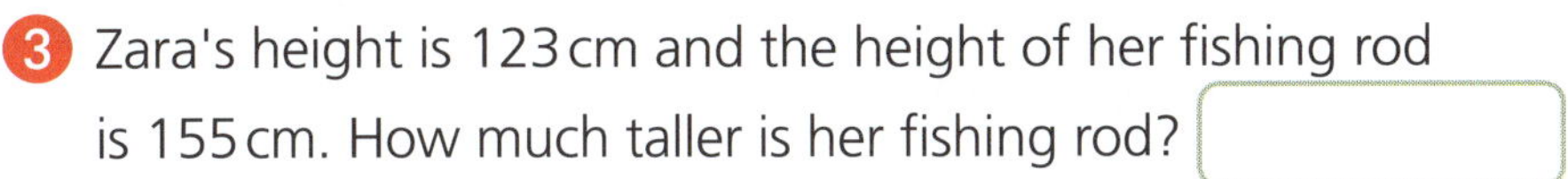

3 Zara's height is 123 cm and the height of her fishing rod is 155 cm. How much taller is her fishing rod?

4 Kasey has 50 cm of elastic. She needs 24 cm to make a bracelet. How many bracelets could she make?

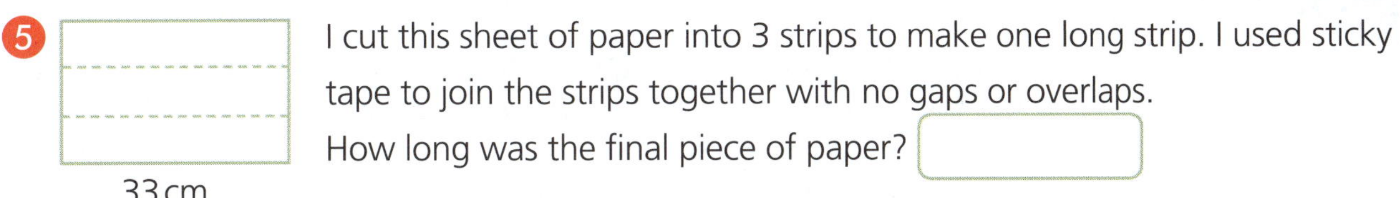

5 I cut this sheet of paper into 3 strips to make one long strip. I used sticky tape to join the strips together with no gaps or overlaps. How long was the final piece of paper?

33 cm

6 On Monday, I walked 300 metres to school and 300 metres back again in the afternoon. On Tuesday, I walked an extra 400 metres to visit the shops on my way home. How far did I walk to and from school altogether on Monday and Tuesday?

7 I ran around an 800 m track two and a half times. How far did I run altogether?

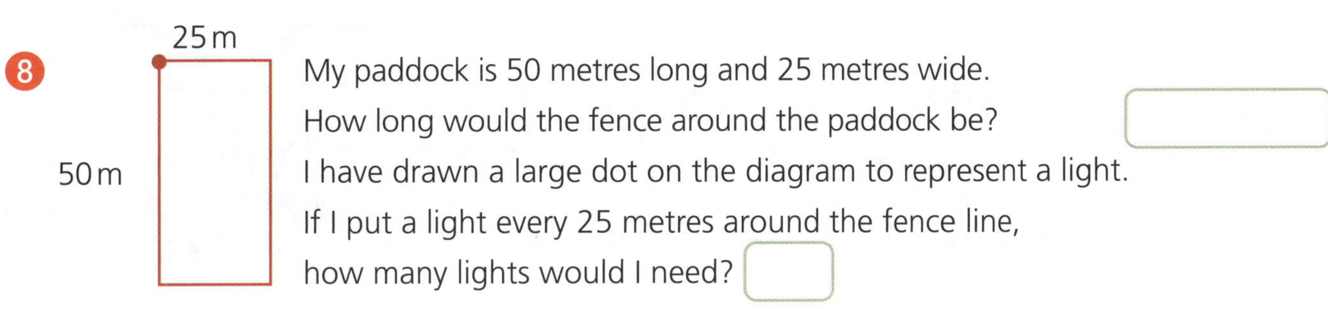

8 My paddock is 50 metres long and 25 metres wide. How long would the fence around the paddock be?
I have drawn a large dot on the diagram to represent a light. If I put a light every 25 metres around the fence line, how many lights would I need?

25 m
50 m

 • *AUSTRALIAN SIGNPOST MATHS NSW 3* • ISBN 9780655709046

3:32 The cubic centimetre

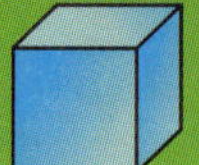

A ones block is 1 cubic centimetre.
Each side is one centimetre in length.
Each face is one square centimetre.

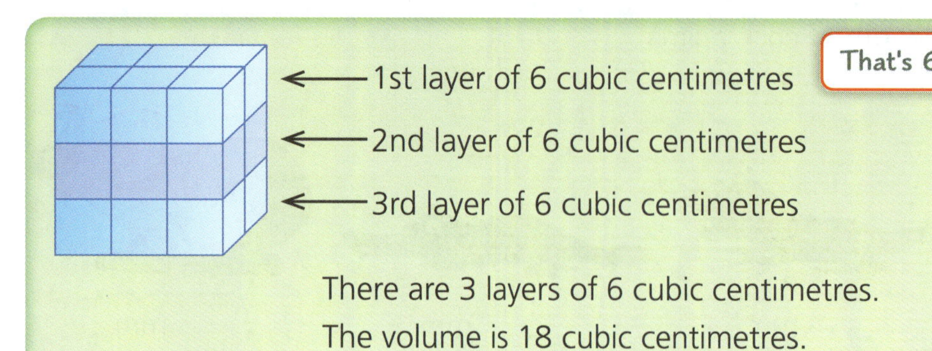

There are 3 layers of 6 cubic centimetres.
The volume is 18 cubic centimetres.

1 These models have been made using cubic centimetre blocks.

A 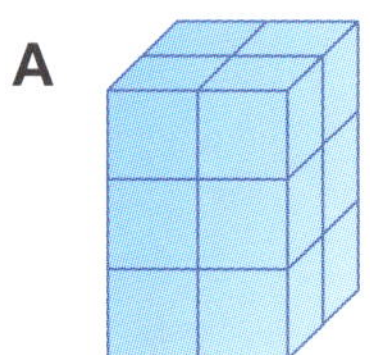

B 

C 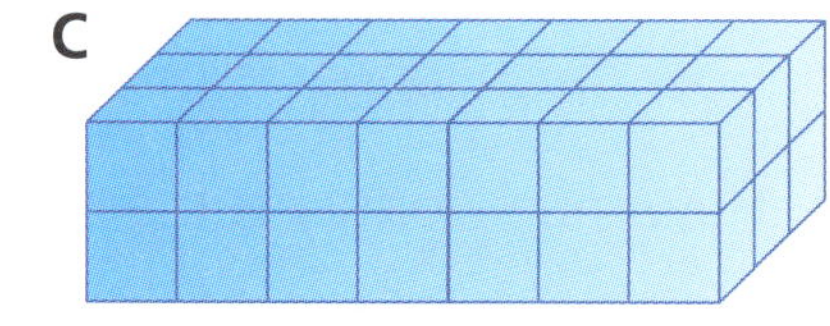

a Estimate the volume of each model in cubic centimetres.

A ______ B ______ C ______

b Describe each model in terms of layers, for example, 3 layers of 6.

A ______ B ______ C ______

c Write the volume of each model in cubic centimetres.

A ___ + ___ + ___ B ___ + ___ + ___ C ___ + ___

= ___ cubic centimetres = ___ cubic centimetres = ___ cubic centimetres

d Write the models, **A**, **B** and **C** in ascending order (smallest volume to largest). ______

2 Construct 2 rectangular prisms using cubic centimetre blocks.
Draw them below and describe the volumes.

a

layers of
+
= cubic centimetres

b

layers of
+
= cubic centimetres

The cubic centimetre

Add the volume of the layers to find the total volume: 15 + 15 + 15 = 45 cubic centimetres.

1. Use cubic centimetre blocks to build these models.

A 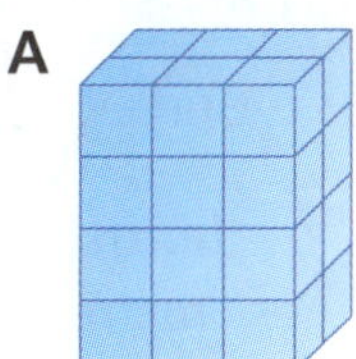 B  C 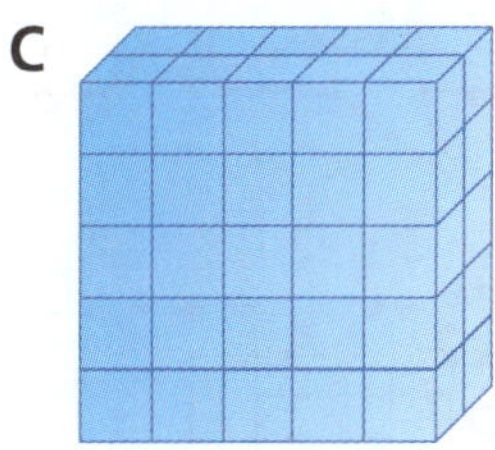

a Estimate the volume of each model in cubic centimetres.

A ______ B ______ C ______

b Describe each model in terms of layers, for example, 3 layers of 6.

A ______ B ______ C ______

c Write the volume of each model in cubic centimetres by adding the total of each layer.

A ___ + ___ + ___ + ___ = ___ cubic centimetres

B ___ + ___ + ___ + ___ = ___ cubic centimetres

C ___ + ___ + ___ + ___ + ___ = ___ cubic centimetres

d Write the models, **A**, **B** and **C** in ascending order (smallest volume to largest). ______

2. A rectangular prism was built 10 ones-blocks long, 5 ones-blocks wide and 4 ones-blocks high.

a Calculate the volume of the top layer. ___ cubic centimetres

b Calculate the volume of the prism. ___ + ___ + ___ + ___ = ___ cubic centimetres

3. Challenge: Build a model that has a volume of 36 cubic centimetres. Describe it in terms of layers.

______ ___ + ___ = 36 cubic centimetres

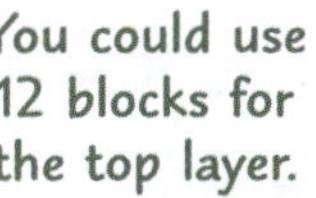

4. Construct 2 different rectangular prisms of 3 layers that have the same volume. Draw both models below and complete the labels.

a

___ layers of ___
= ___ + ___ + ___
= ___ cubic centimetres

b

___ layers of ___
= ___ + ___ + ___
= ___ cubic centimetres

 • *AUSTRALIAN SIGNPOST MATHS NSW 3* • ISBN 9780655709046

3:34 Standard metric units

Using metric units is easier.

CONCEPT

We use **standard metric units** so everybody can use the same units.

mass	capacity	length
kilograms grams	litre millilitre	metre centimetre millimetre

1 Match the unit to the type of measurement.

kilogram | metre | litre | centimetre | millimetre

capacity — How much does it hold? | mass — How heavy is it? | length — How long is it?

L | kg | cm | mm | m

2 Which quantity does each tool measure: capacity, mass or length?

a 1 litre container ________

b balance scales ________

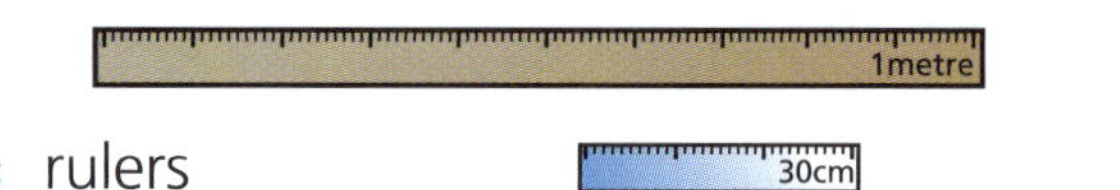

c rulers ________

3 m
3 L
3 kg

3 What is one advantage of using standard units to describe and compare objects?

____

FUN SPOT

4 Choose a container.

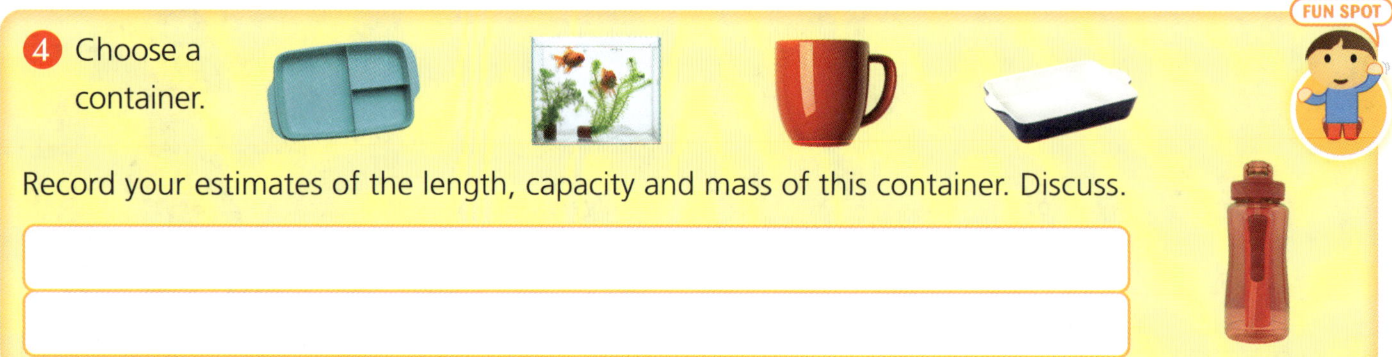

Record your estimates of the length, capacity and mass of this container. Discuss.

____

____

3:35 Personal benchmarks

1 **a** Draw a 1 metre line on the ground. Practise taking two steps that would cover one metre.

- From a starting point, use the steps you have practised to estimate a length of 5 metres. Use a tape measure to see how good your estimate was. Was your estimate close? ______
- Use this method to estimate other distances.

b Use your practised steps to estimate the length of a building. ______

c Place a 1 metre ruler vertically beside you. Remember how high it reaches on your body. Record this personal measurement for one metre. The metre ruler reached my ______.

2 1 L of water has a mass of 1 kg. Pour one litre of water into a plastic jug.

a Use hefting to find objects that have a mass of about 1 kg.

______

b Use hefting to estimate the mass of a box of toys.

TOYS

c Try to remember the mass and volume of a litre of water. These will be your personal benchmarks for one kilogram and one litre.

3 **a** Use a 1 L container to measure the capacity of a bucket. ______ litres
Use this as your benchmark for larger volumes.

- Half fill a bucket with water. Use your benchmark for a full bucket to estimate how much water is now in the bucket. ______ litres
Use a 1 litre container to check your estimate. Was your estimate close? ______
- If two buckets of water are needed to fill a fish tank, estimate its capacity. ______

4 Write your personal benchmarks for length, area, mass and capacity.

______

______

______

 • *AUSTRALIAN SIGNPOST MATHS NSW 3* • ISBN 9780655709046

The calendar

There are 7 days in a week and 365 days in a year.

November 2024						
Sun	**Mon**	**Tues**	**Wed**	**Thurs**	**Fri**	**Sat**
					1	2
3	4	5	6	7	8	9
10	11	12	13	14	15	16
17	18	19	20	21	22	23
24	25	26	27	28	29	30

How to know the number of days in each month.

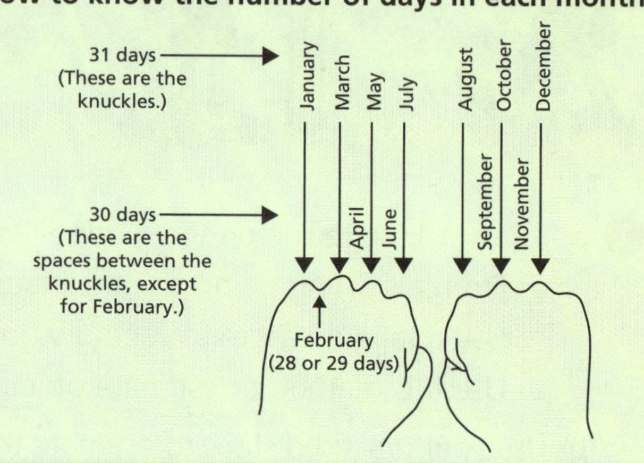

1 Study the calendar of November above and answer the questions.

a What day of the week is 1 November?

b What day of the week is 17 November?

c What is the date of the first Friday?

d What is the date of the first Monday?

e What is the date of the last Saturday?

f Write the dates of all the Mondays in November.

g How many Thursdays are in November?

h How many weekend days are there in November?

2 How many days are in the following?

a one week
b one fortnight
c January
d June
e March
f May
g April
h July
i October
j September
k November
l August

3 Write these dates in short form.

a first Sunday in November

b last Friday in November

c last Wednesday in November

13/11/24

When we write dates in short form we use numbers.

3:37 The calendar

25 December 2024
December 25th, 2024
25.12.24

A calendar shows how a year is divided into months, weeks and days.

Study the calendar for November 2024 to January 2025.

1. If the date is November 11, how many weeks and days will it be until my birthday on January 17?

2. If today is 2/11/24, how many weeks and days is it until Christmas Day?

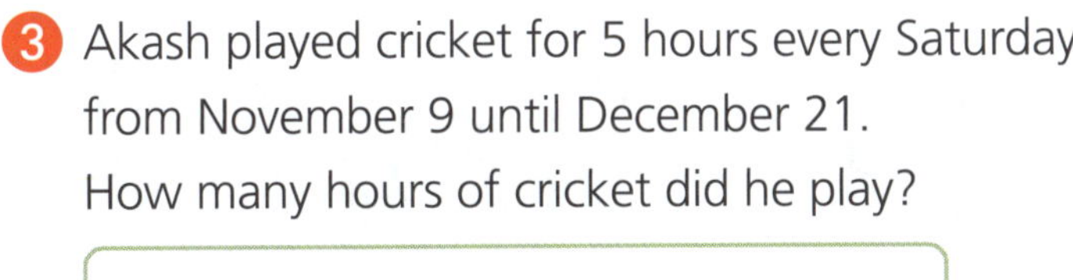

3. Akash played cricket for 5 hours every Saturday from November 9 until December 21. How many hours of cricket did he play?

4. I earn $3 pocket money every Friday. I need to save $12 so I can buy a new book. What is the earliest date that I could save the money if today's date is November 5?

5. Priya did gymnastics for 2 hours every Monday and Thursday during November. How many hours of gymnastics did she do during that time?

November 2024						
Sun	Mon	Tues	Wed	Thurs	Fri	Sat
					1	2
3	4	5	6	7	8	9
10	11	12	13	14	15	16
17	18	19	20	21	22	23
24	25	26	27	28	29	30

December 2024						
Sun	Mon	Tues	Wed	Thurs	Fri	Sat
1	2	3	4	5	6	7
8	9	10	11	12	13	14
15	16	17	18	19	20	21
22	23	24	25	26	27	28
29	30	31				

January 2025						
Sun	Mon	Tues	Wed	Thurs	Fri	Sat
			1	2	3	4
5	6	7	8	9	10	11
12	13	14	15	16	17	18
19	20	21	22	23	24	25
26	27	28	29	30	31	

Make up your own question about this calendar. See if your classmates can solve it.

6. On November 18, Mia has 7 weeks and 5 days to wait until it is her birthday. What is the date of Mia's birthday?

7. Circle these dates on the calendar: 14/11/24, 18/12/24, 29/1/25, 30/11/24, 1/1/25

 • *AUSTRALIAN SIGNPOST MATHS NSW 3* • ISBN 9780655709046

4:01 Symmetry

Draw the lines of symmetry.

The broken lines are lines of symmetry.

1. Use a ruler to draw a line of symmetry on each picture.

2. Draw lines of symmetry on these letters.

Draw the other half of each picture below.

3. Use a ruler and pencil to draw all of the lines of symmetry on each shape.

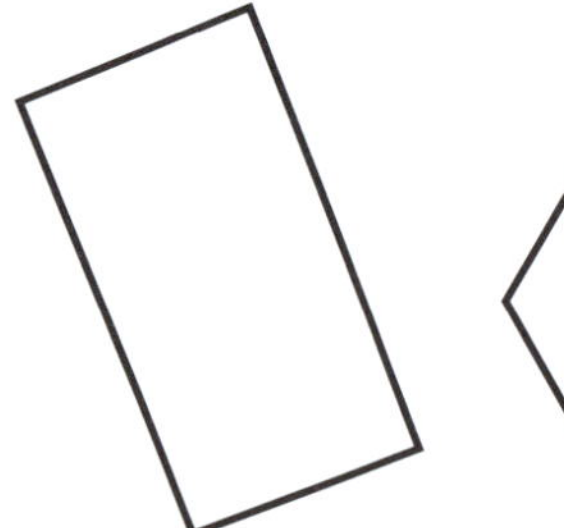
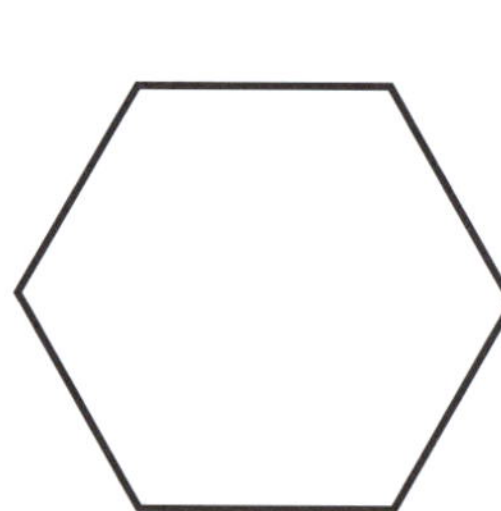

Making a symmetrical picture

1. Fold a piece of paper.
2. Draw half of a picture on one side of the fold.
3. Fold the paper under, with the drawing on top.
4. Use a marker (that shows through) at the corners.
5. Unfold the paper and join the dots.

4:02 Properties of 2D shapes

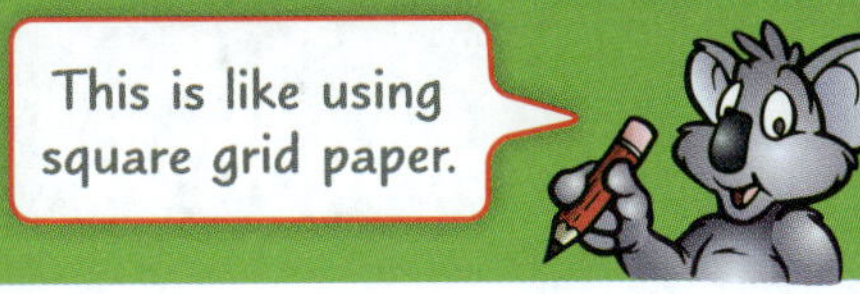

Antonio's teacher made a **geoboard** like this by hammering nails into wood. Antonio used the geoboard to make shapes by stretching a rubber band over the nails.

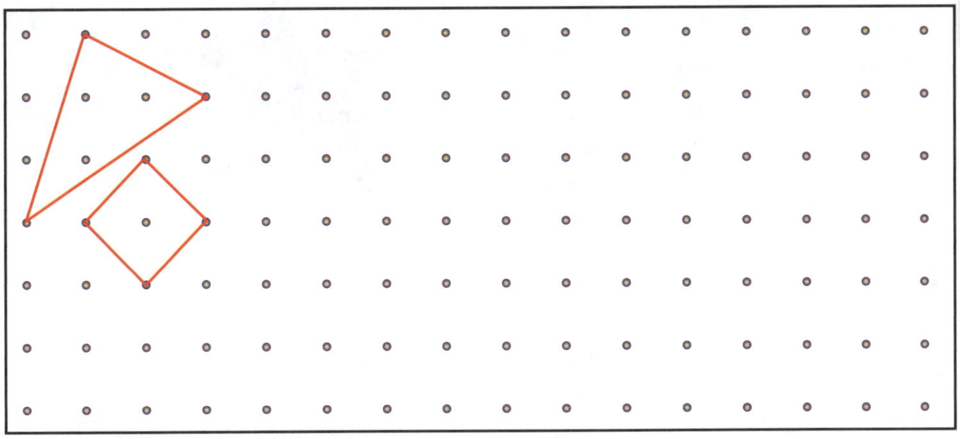

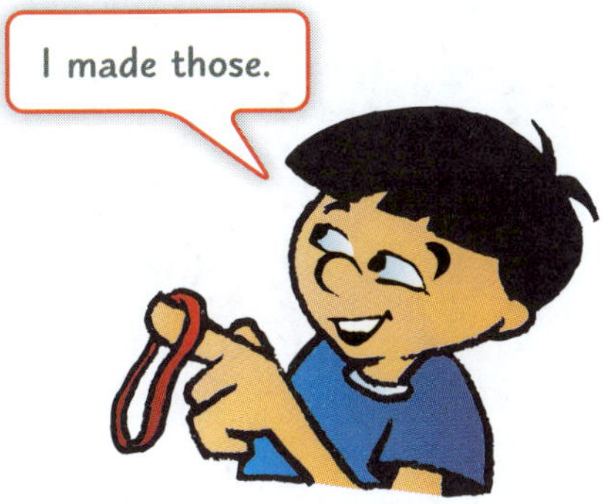

I made those.

- You can use an online geoboard.

1 a How many nails were used to make the triangle? ☐ Number of corners = ☐

b How many nails were used to make the square? ☐ Number of corners = ☐

c How many sides on a triangle? ☐ d How many sides on a square? ☐

2 Every corner of each shape on the geoboard must be at a nail.

a On the geoboard above, draw 3 triangles of different shapes and sizes.
How many sides does each triangle have? ☐

b What shapes can you draw using 4 nails as corners? ☐
Draw 3 of them on the geoboard above. ☐

c A pentagon has 5 sides. How many corners would you need to draw a pentagon? ☐
Draw a pentagon on the geoboard.

d Draw a shape on the geoboard that has 6 corners.
What is this shape called? ☐

Olena cut a square of paper into 5 pieces. She asked her friend to put the square back together again. Then she asked her friend to make a picture using the pieces.

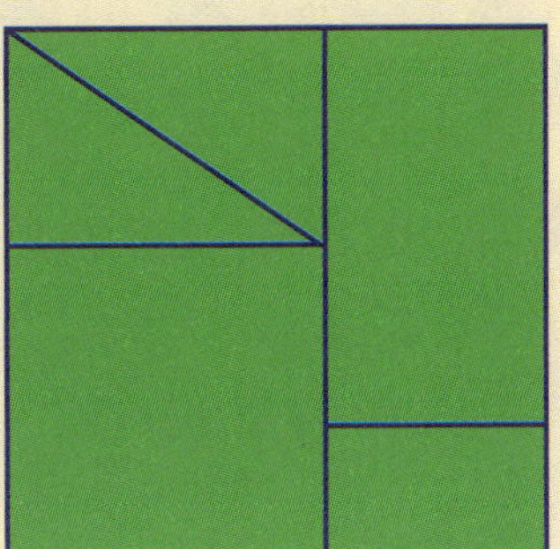

- Cut your own square of paper into 5 pieces. Colour one side.
- Discuss the shapes you cut out.
- Mix up your 5 pieces and ask a partner to put the square back together again.
- Use your pieces of paper to make pictures.

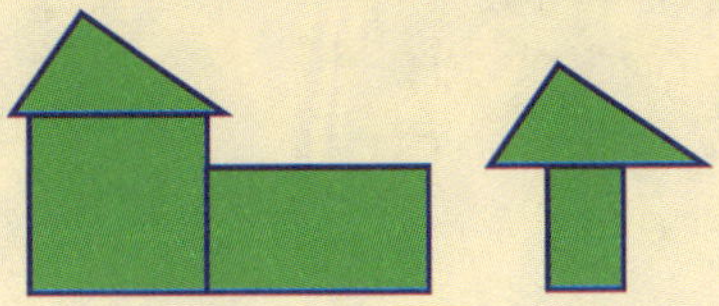

Symmetry around us

Each side is a reflection of the other.

It is hard to find perfect symmetry, but there are many examples of symmetry that are close to perfect.

We use the term symmetrical in these cases.

Discuss the symmetry.

1 Order the heads from 'most symmetrical' (1), to 'least symmetrical' (6).

2 Draw the other half to make each picture symmetrical.

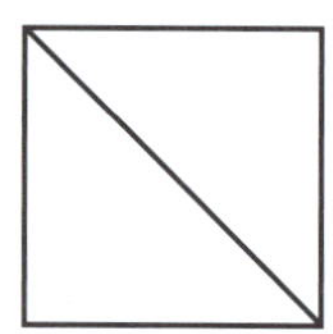

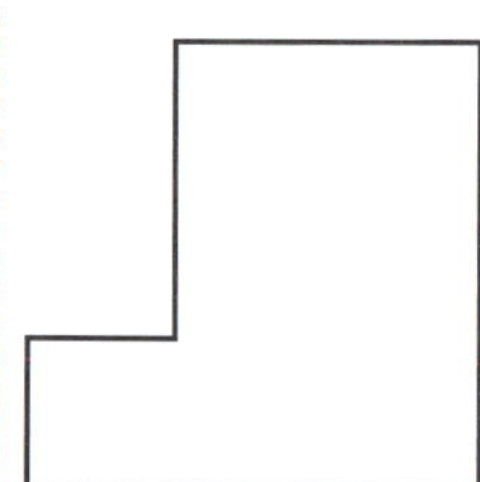

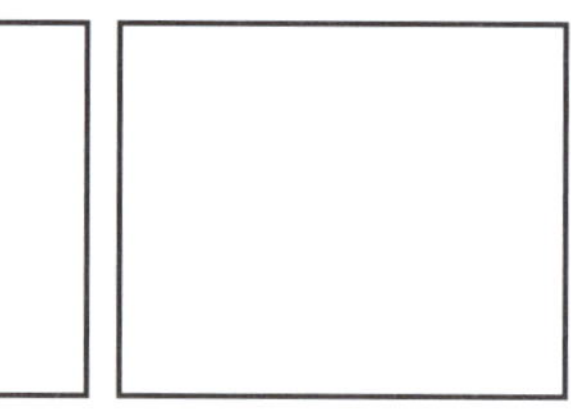

Slide back the edge of this page so that it matches the pictures on page 116 underneath. What do you see?

- Colour 8 of these shapes to make a symmetrical design.

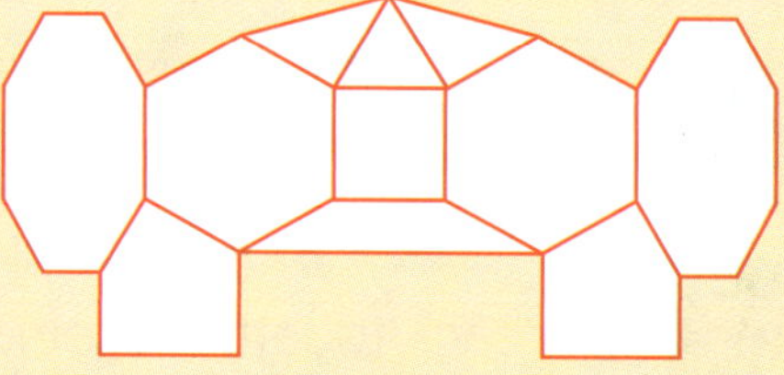

- Use pattern blocks to make your own symmetrical design and describe how the pattern was made.

 • *AUSTRALIAN SIGNPOST MATHS NSW 3* • ISBN 9780655709046

Properties of 3D objects

Which 3D objects can we see here?

A 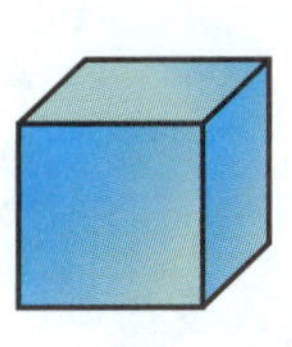

B 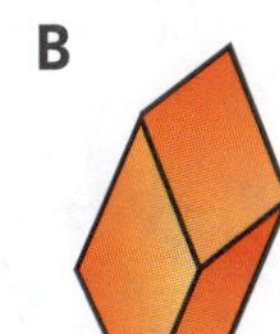

C 

D 

Some objects are really useful.

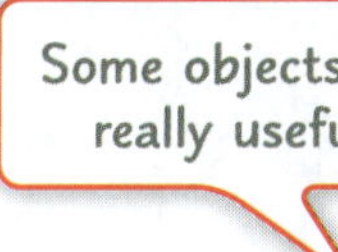

E 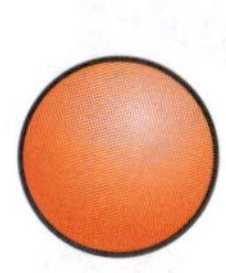

F 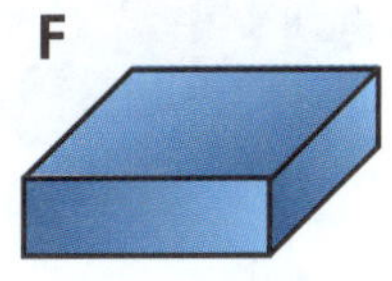

G 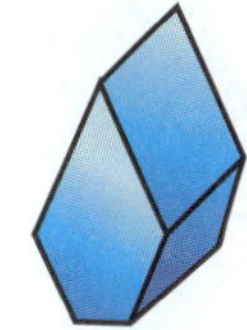

H 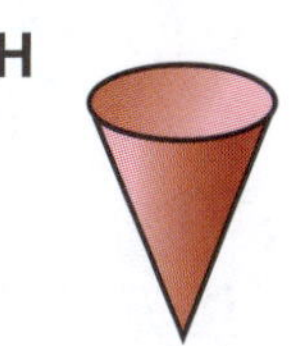

1 This picture shows holes cut in a block of wood.
Which of the objects **A** to **H** would fit through the holes?

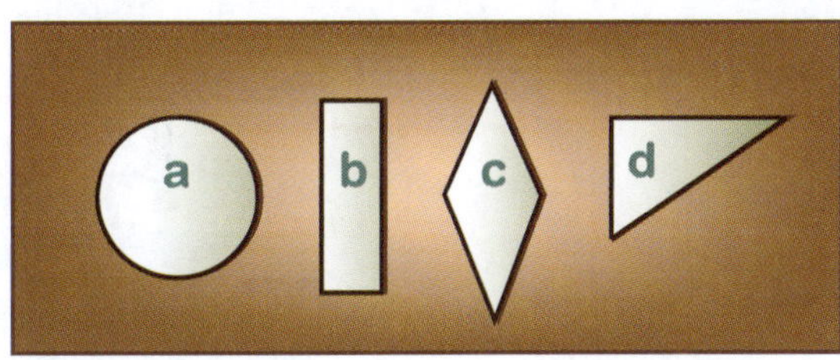

a circle hole

b rectangle hole

c rhombus hole

d triangle hole

2 Which of the objects **A** to **H** can't be easily stacked?

3 Which of the objects **A** to **H** are the same shape as these?

a 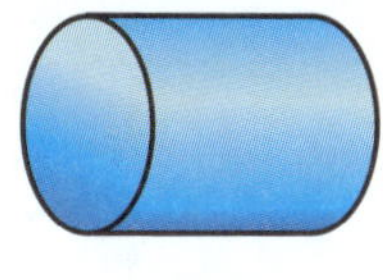

b 

c 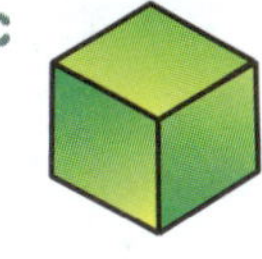

d 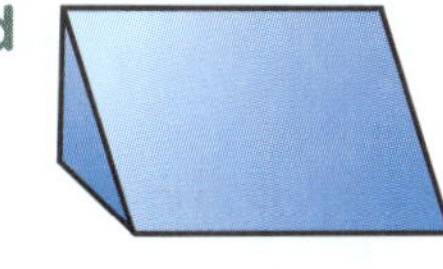

4 Which of the objects **A** to **H** could fit together like this?

a 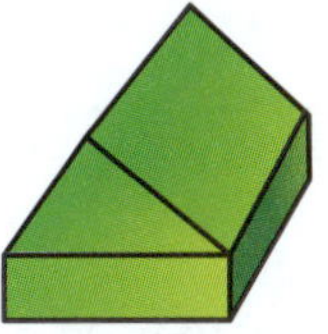

and

b 

and

c 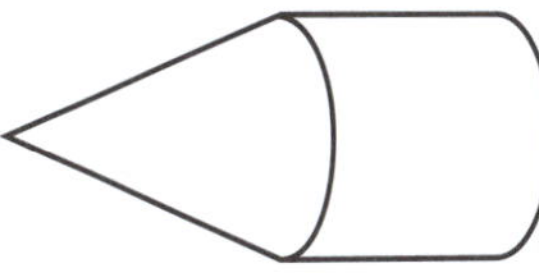

and

d Draw the hidden lines to make the diagram for part **c** look 3D.

5 Draw the missing object in each pattern.

a 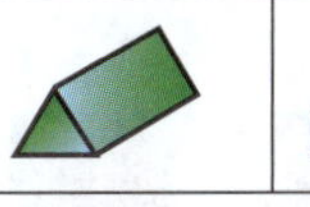 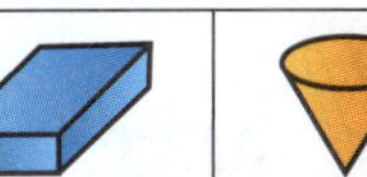 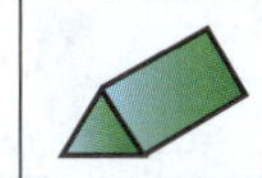 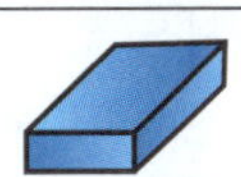   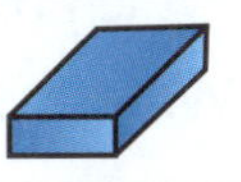

b    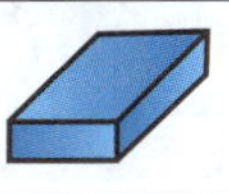 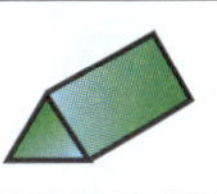 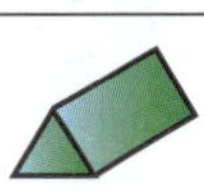  

4:05 Properties of 3D objects

We usually cut cross-sections parallel to the end.

- How would you describe the shape of this tent?

1. How many flat surfaces does each object have? Name each object.

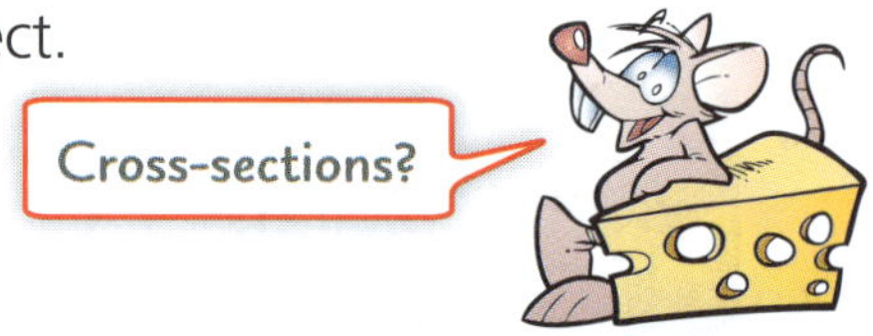

Cross-sections?

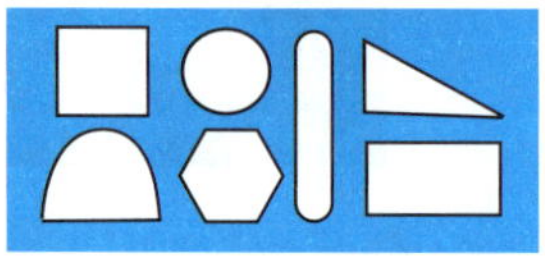

a

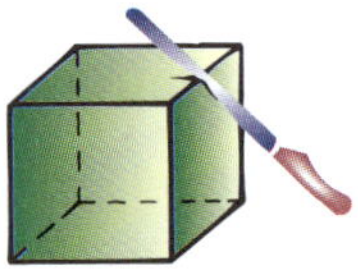

b

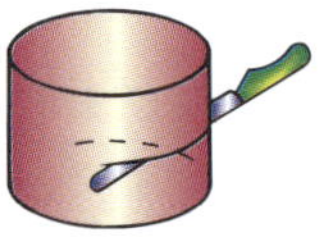

c

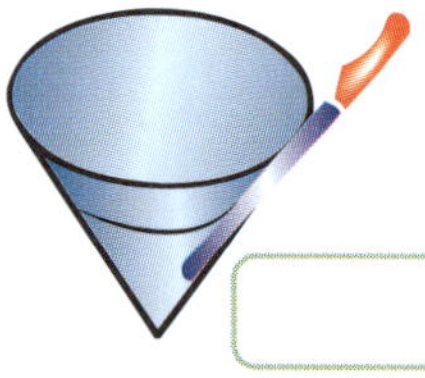

d

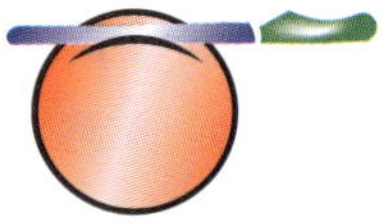

e

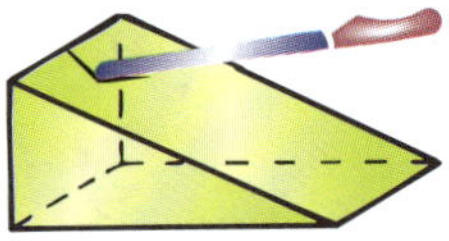

2. What is the shape of each object's cross-section?

a

b

c

d

e

3. a Which of the objects in Question 1 has six corners?
   b Which has 8 corners?
   c Which has 12 edges?
   d Which has 1 corner?
   e Which has 5 faces?
   f Which has 9 edges?
   g Which has only curved surfaces?
   h Which has only 2 flat surfaces?
   i Which have a circular cross-section?

4. Which block would fit into which hole? Write the number.

   a Hole A
   b Hole B
   c Hole C
   d Hole D

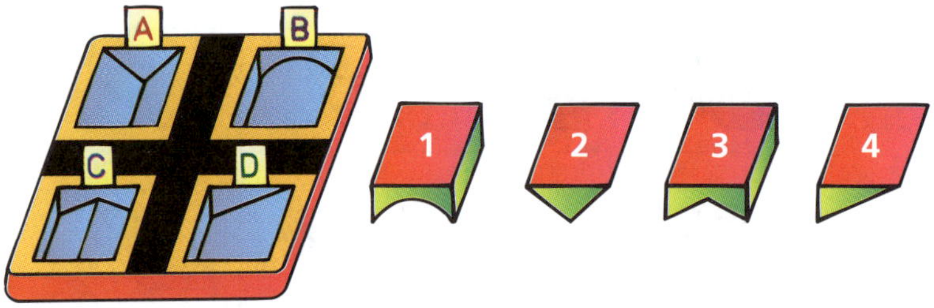

A B C D

1 2 3 4

Position and giving directions

CONCEPT

A map gives us a view from above.

- Circle the camping area.
- Draw a straight line from the roundabout to the traffic light.

1 Write directions to get from place to place.

a **A** to **C** ____________

b **A** to **D** ____________

c **A** to **E** ____________

d **A** to **F** ____________

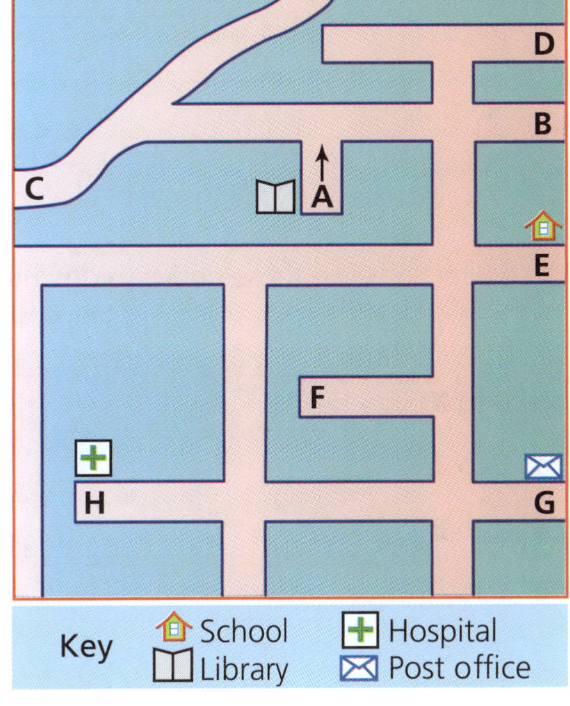

- Circle the school and the library.

2 Follow these directions. Where do they lead? Draw each path on the map.

a Start at **A**. Turn right, then the first right, then the second left.

____

b Start at **A**. Turn right, then the first right, then the first right, then the first left, then the first right.

____

3 a Jenna is sitting in seat **J**. She moves two seats to the right, then one seat forwards. Where is she now? ____

b Patrick is sitting in seat **P**. He moves three seats to the left, then two seats forwards. Where is he now? ____

c Dmitri is sitting in seat **D**. He moves three seats backwards, then two seats to the left. Where is he now? ____

d Erin is sitting in seat **E**. She moves one seat to the right, then two seats backwards, then one seat left, then two seats forwards. Where is she now? ____

Classroom

T   Forwards ↑

A	B	C	D
E	F	G	H
I	J	K	L
M	N	O	P

4:07 Giving directions

1. Follow the spider's path and write the letter for the point where it stops.

   a 4 spaces up, 2 right, 3 up

   b 3 spaces up, 1 left, 4 up

   c 2 up, 4 right, 3 up, 5 left, 2 up

   d 6 up, 2 right, 4 down, 1 left, 5 up

   e 1 right, 7 up

   f 2 up, 1 left, 2 up, 5 right, 3 up

   g Write directions to take the spider to **E**.

A B C D E F

Spider

Start

Go 2 left

Back

Right

This way

That way

2. Use directions like those above to describe these paths.

   a **A** to **Y**

   b **B** to **X**

   c **C** to **Z**

   d **X** to **B**

   e **Y** to **A**

X Y Z

A B C

3. You are in a car at **A**. To get to **E** you would follow these directions: 1 forwards, turn right, 6 forwards, turn left, 4 forwards.
   Write directions for these paths:

   a **A** to **B**

   b **A** to **C**

   c **A** to **D**

   d **F** to **D**

   e **F** to **E**

D A F B E C

4:08 Regular and irregular shapes

Irregular shapes do not have all sides and angles equal.

1. Join the dots to complete these regular shapes. Under each shape, write its name.

a b c d

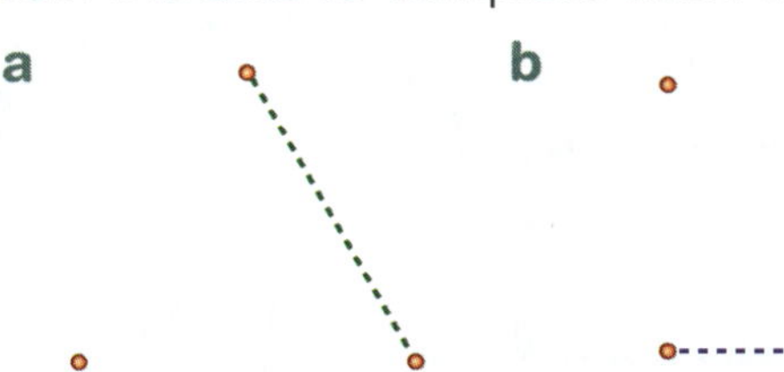

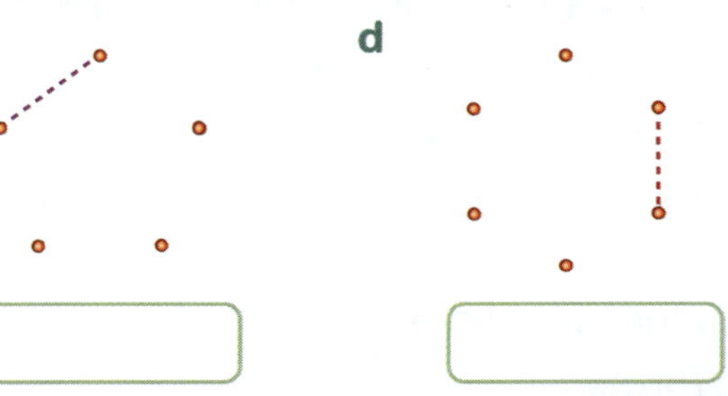

For regular shapes:
- Are all sides equal?
- Are all angles equal?

2. Which shapes in Question 1 have opposite sides parallel?

3. Join the dots to complete these irregular shapes. Under each shape, write its name.

a b c d

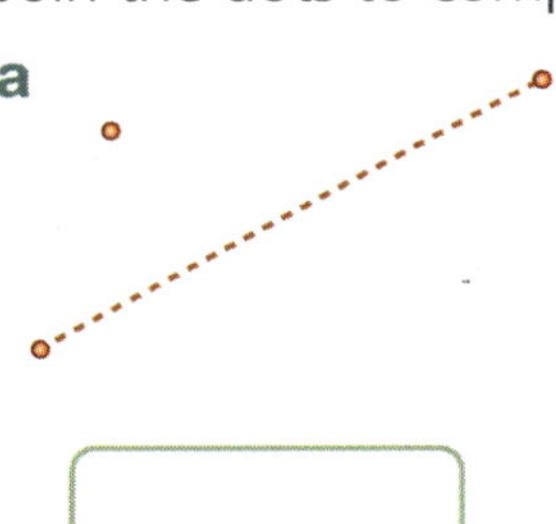

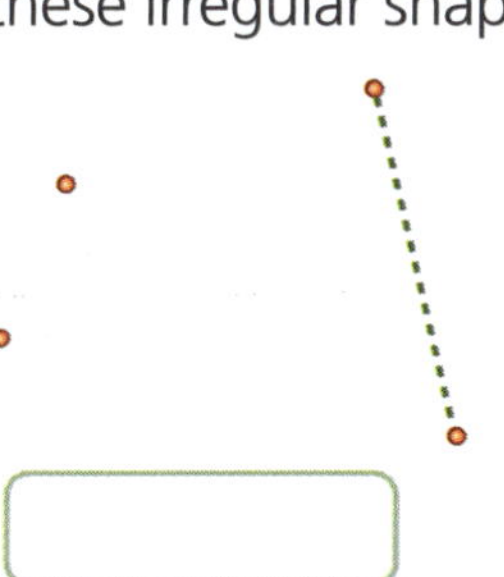

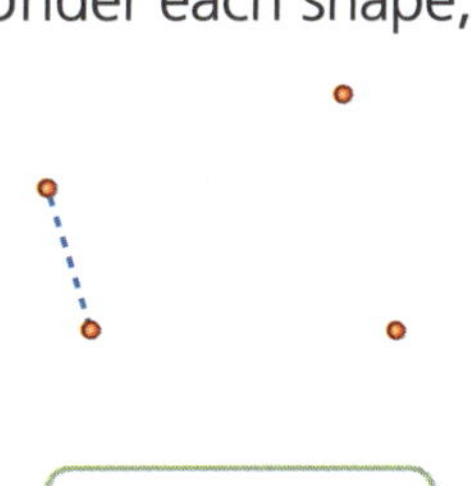

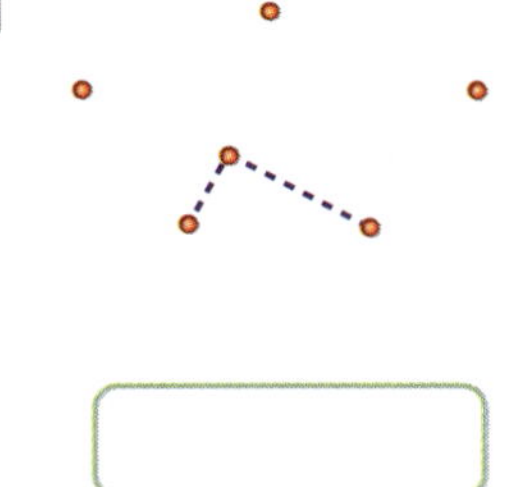

For irregular shapes:
- Are all sides equal?
- Are all angles equal?

4. Trapeze artists swing on trapeziums. A trapezium has at least one pair of parallel lines. Join the dots to complete each trapezium.

a b c

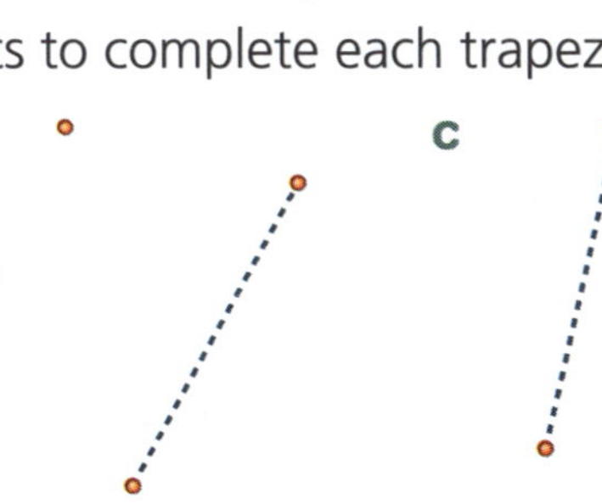

Are trapeziums regular or irregular shapes?

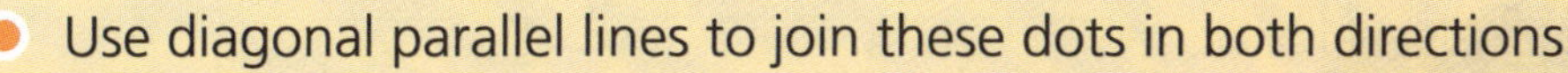

ACTIVITY

- Use diagonal parallel lines to join these dots in both directions.
- In this lattice pattern, what shape is repeated?
- Use grid paper to draw your own lattice pattern.
- Are rhombuses regular or irregular?

4:09 Parallel and perpendicular lines

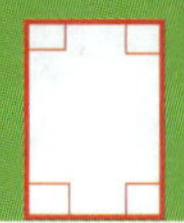

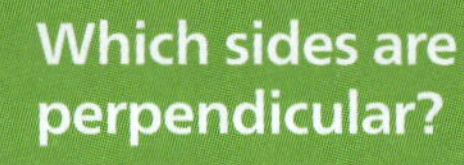

CONCEPT

Parallel lines are always the same distance apart.
- They are straight lines.
- They are in the same direction.
- They never touch.

Perpendicular lines meet at right angles.
- They are straight lines.
- They cross over at right angles.

1 At how many points does each group of lines cross?

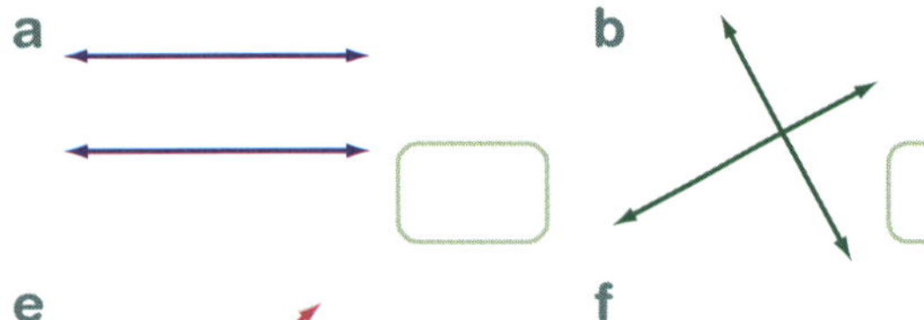

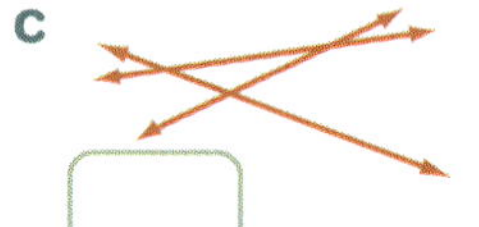

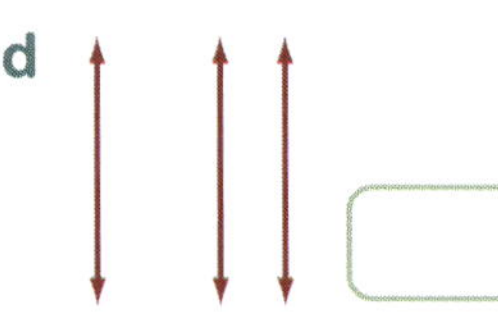

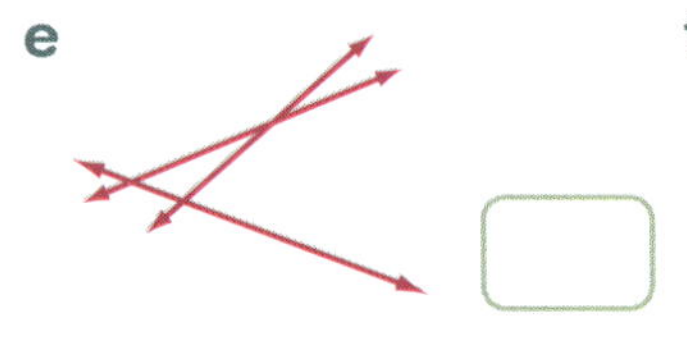

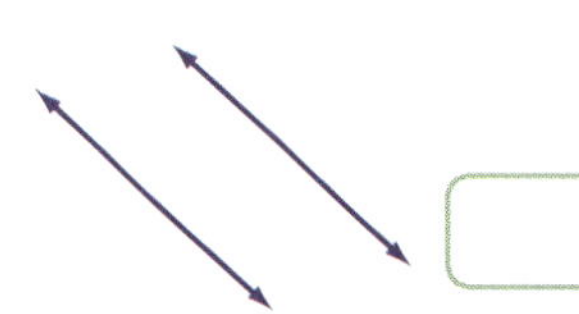

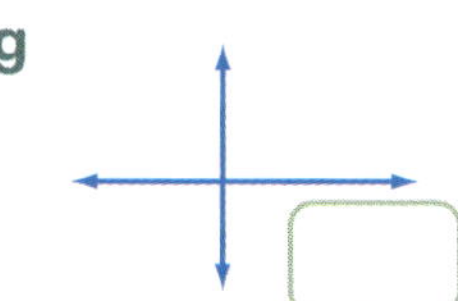

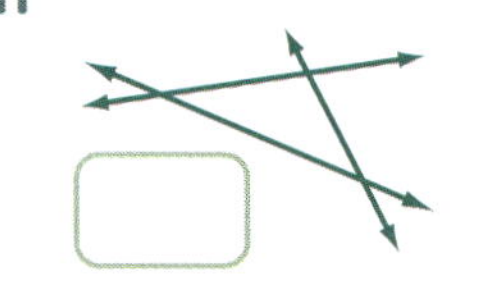

2 Which sets of lines in Question 1 are parallel?

Why are they parallel?

3 Why are the lines in 1**b** perpendicular?

4 Name two shapes that have perpendicular sides.

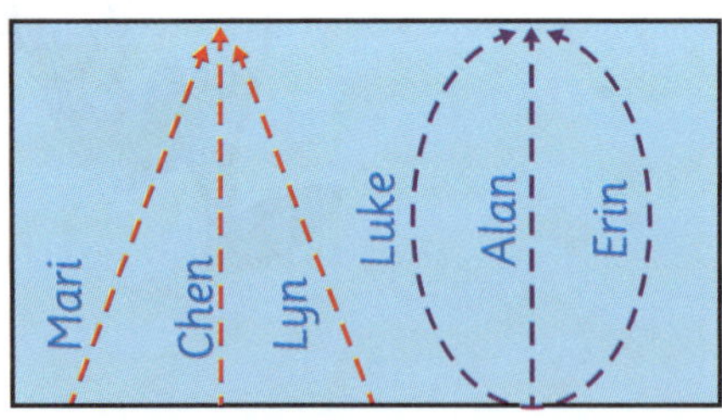

5 Six people swam across a swimming pool.

a Who swam the shortest path?

b Who swam perpendicular to the sides?

c Who swam parallel paths?

6 

a List things in this picture that are parallel.

b When parallel lines continue further away from us, do they look like they are coming together?

Are they really coming together? Discuss.

 • *AUSTRALIAN SIGNPOST MATHS NSW 3* • ISBN 9780655709046

4:10 The rhombus and the kite

The rhombus and the kite are quadrilaterals.

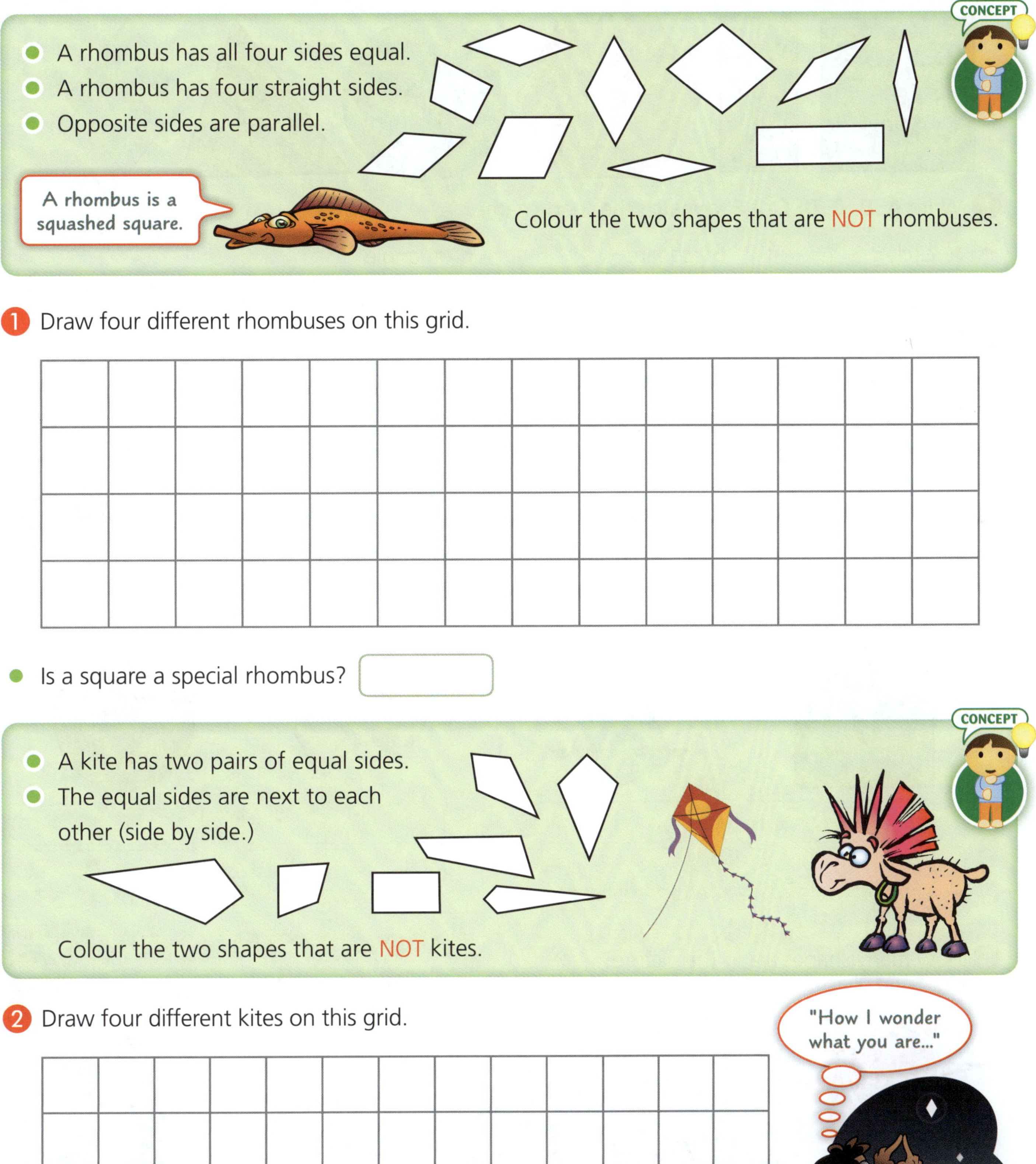

CONCEPT

- A rhombus has all four sides equal.
- A rhombus has four straight sides.
- Opposite sides are parallel.

A rhombus is a squashed square.

Colour the two shapes that are NOT rhombuses.

1. Draw four different rhombuses on this grid.

- Is a square a special rhombus?

CONCEPT

- A kite has two pairs of equal sides.
- The equal sides are next to each other (side by side.)

Colour the two shapes that are NOT kites.

2. Draw four different kites on this grid.

"How I wonder what you are..."

- Is a square a special kite?

 • *AUSTRALIAN SIGNPOST MATHS NSW 3* • ISBN 9780655709046

4:11 Shapes revision

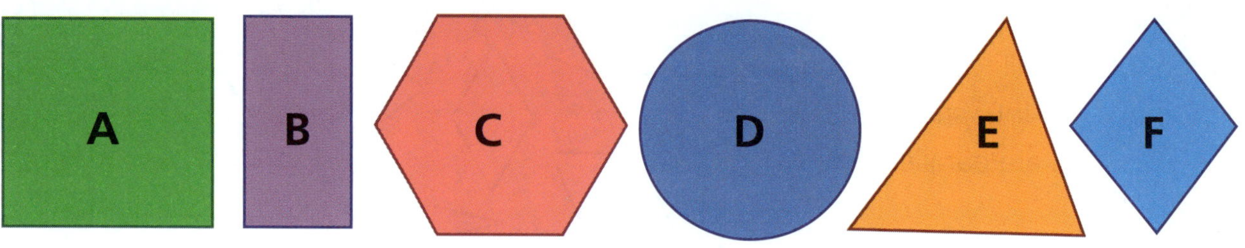

1 Write **A**, **B**, **C**, **D**, **E** or **F** to match the shape name.

a circle ☐ **b** square ☐ **c** triangle ☐

d hexagon ☐ **e** rhombus ☐ **f** rectangle ☐

Why is **B** a rectangle?

2 Write **A**, **B**, **C**, **D**, **E** or **F** to match the description.

a three sides ☐ **b** four sides ☐, ☐ and ☐

c six sides ☐ **d** no straight sides ☐

3 **a** Which of the shapes above have all sides equal? ☐

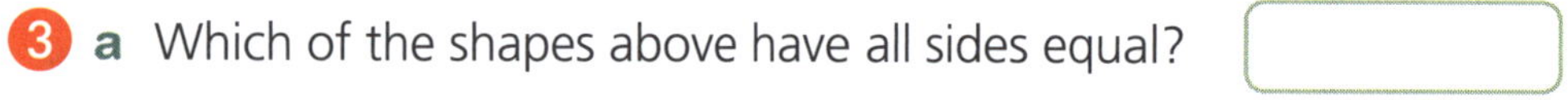

b Which of the shapes above have opposite sides equal? ☐

4 Write the names of the two shapes used in each picture.

a

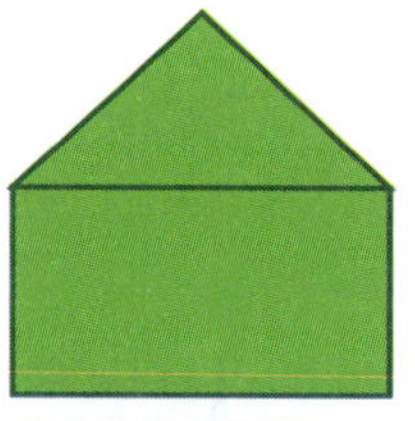

b

c

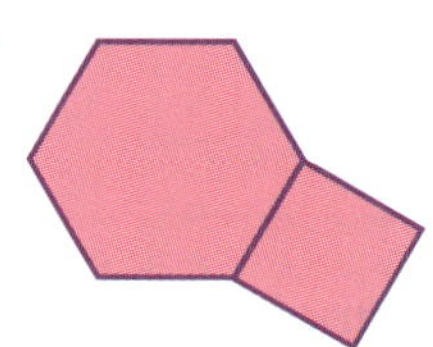

d

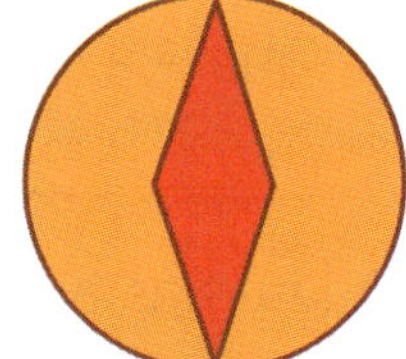

5 How many shapes are in the picture?

a squares ☐

b triangles ☐

c rectangles ☐

d circles ☐

● Draw your own picture using shapes.

This is not as easy as it looks.

4:12 Prisms and cylinders

A face is a flat surface with straight sides.

CONCEPT

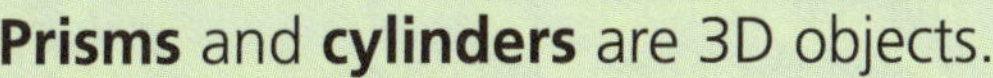

Prisms and **cylinders** are 3D objects.

- Their two ends are the same shape and size.
- Their **cross-section** is the same shape and size as their ends.
- The prism's other **faces** are rectangles.
- The cylinder's other **surface** is curved.

Prism

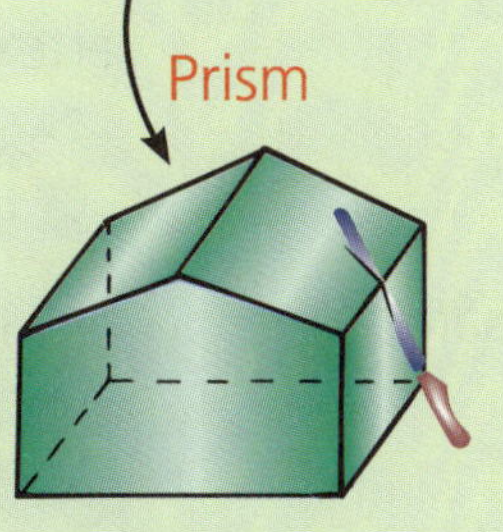

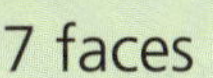

7 faces

Cylinder

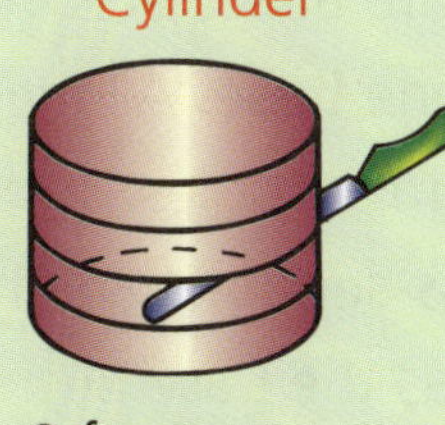

0 faces
2 flat surfaces
1 curved surface

1 Write **prism**, **cylinder** or **neither** under each picture.

a 

b 

c 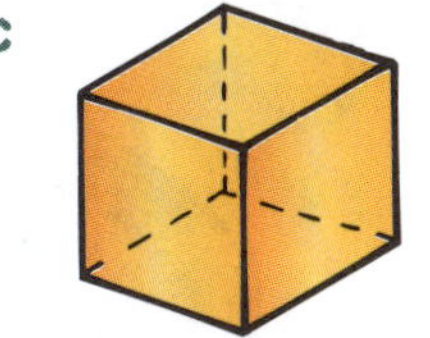

d 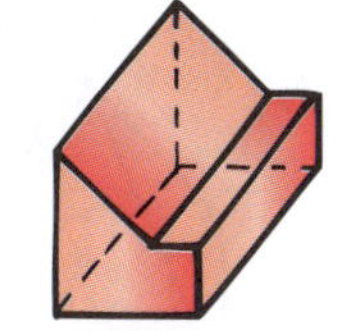

e 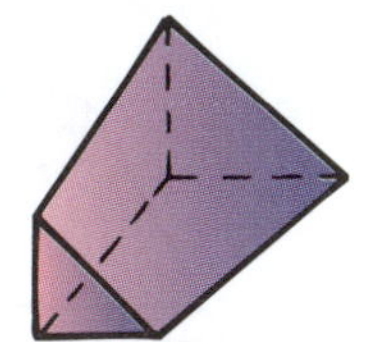

f 

g 

h 

i 

The echidna's bed

2 Match the object label **X**, **Y** or **Z** with the description.

a I have a curved surface.

b All my faces are rectangles.

c My cross-section is a hexagon.

d My base is a circle.

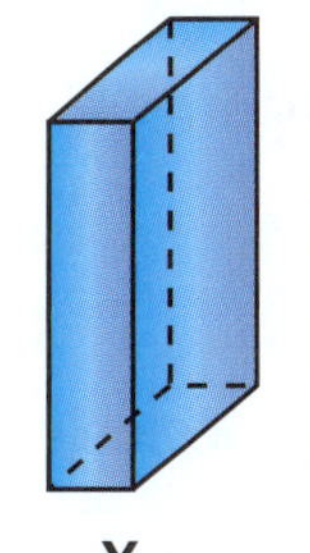

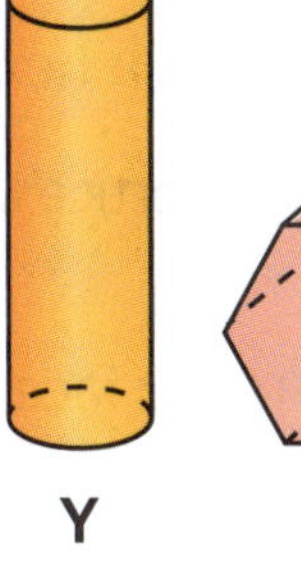

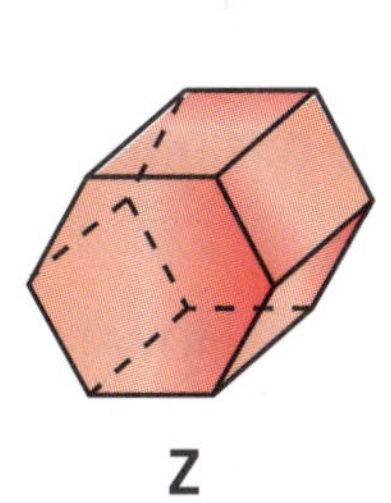

X Y Z

3 a How many faces does object **Z** have?

b How many edges does object **Z** have?

c How many vertices does object **Z** have?

Corners are also called vertices.

4 Draw each face.

The faces are:

Prism	Shape of each face				
	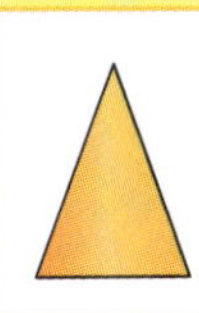				

Pyramids

Cross-sections are usually made parallel to the base.

Pyramids are 3D objects.

- It has one **base**. All the other faces are triangles.
- Its **cross-sections** are the same shape as the base but not the same size.
- One end tapers to a point.

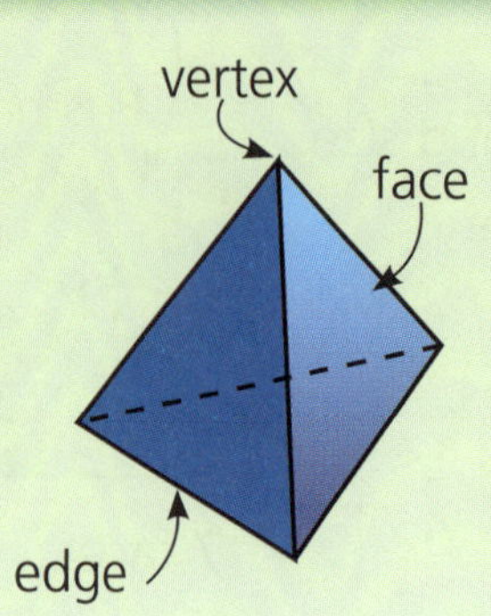

1. Which of these pictures are pyramids?

a 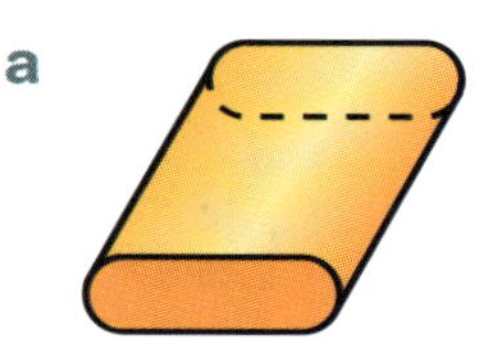 b 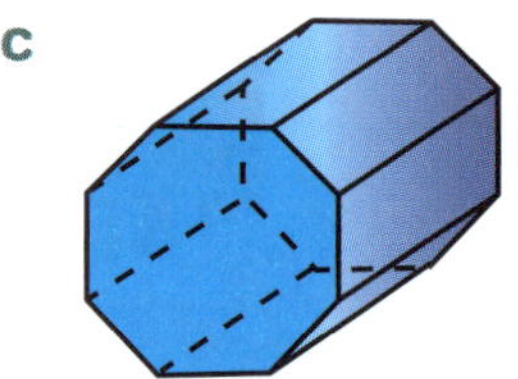 c 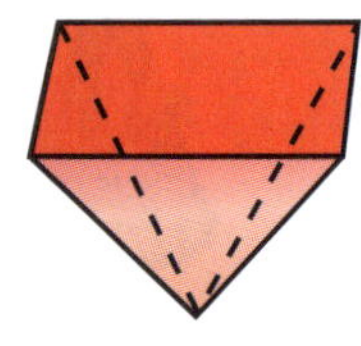 d 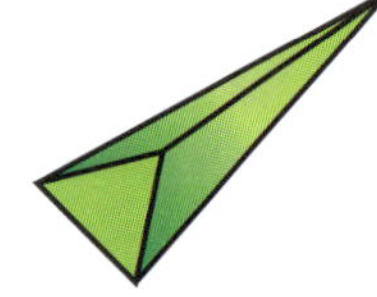 e

f g  h 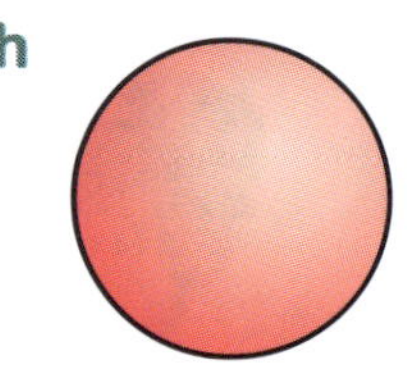 i 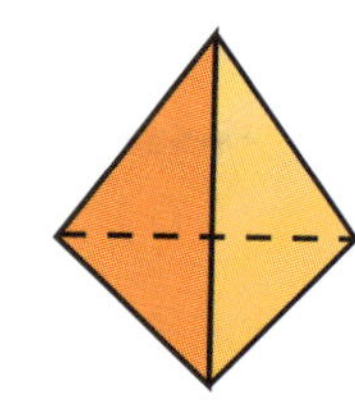 j 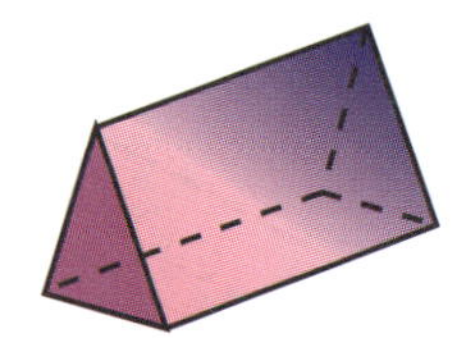

2. Match the object label **A**, **B** or **C** with the description.

   a All my faces are triangles.
   b My base is a hexagon.
   c I have 4 vertices.

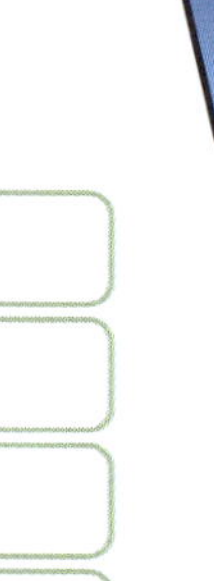

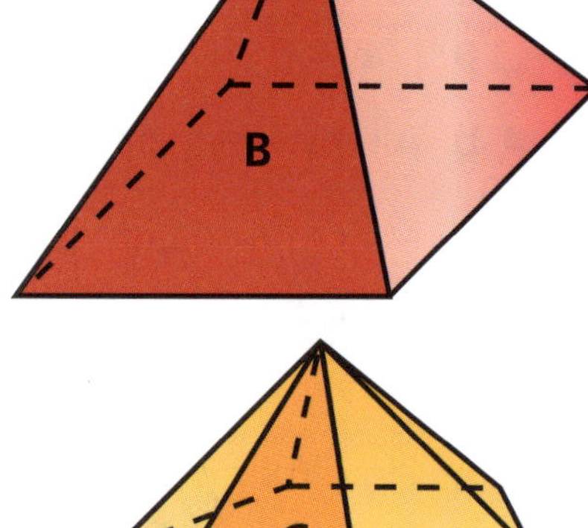

3. a How many faces does object **B** have?
   b How many edges does object **B** have?
   c How many vertices does object **B** have?
   d How many faces does object **A** have?

4. Draw each face of the pyramid. A square pyramid has a square base.

Pyramid	Shape of each face				

The faces are:

 • *AUSTRALIAN SIGNPOST MATHS NSW 3* • ISBN 9780655709046

4:14 Investigating angles

These 3 angles have been super imposed and are easier to compare.

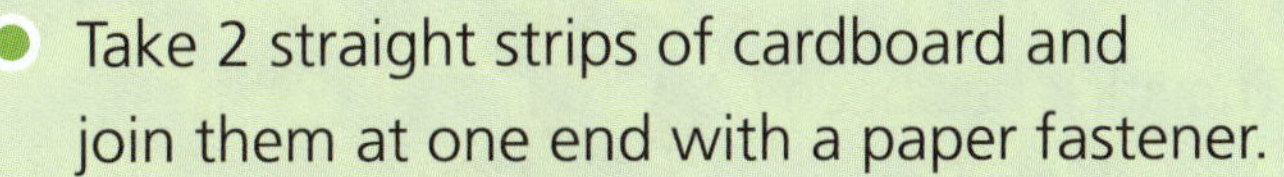

CONCEPT

- Take 2 straight strips of cardboard and join them at one end with a paper fastener.
- By turning the arms, you can make the movable angle small or large.

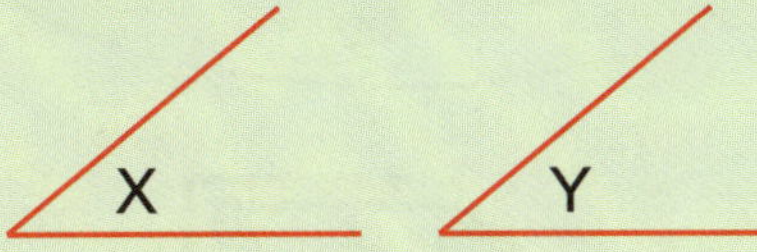

- The size of an angle is the amount of turning between the two arms.

1. Which angle is the largest? ☐
2. Which angle is the smallest? ☐

3. Use a movable angle to answer these questions.
   - **a** Which of these angles are the same size as angle **A**? ☐
   - **b** Which angles are the same size as angle **B**? ☐
   - **c** Which angle is smaller (less turn) than angle **B**? ☐
   - **d** Which angles is bigger (more turn) than angle **A**? ☐
   - **e** Is **F** the same size angle as the corner of a square? ☐

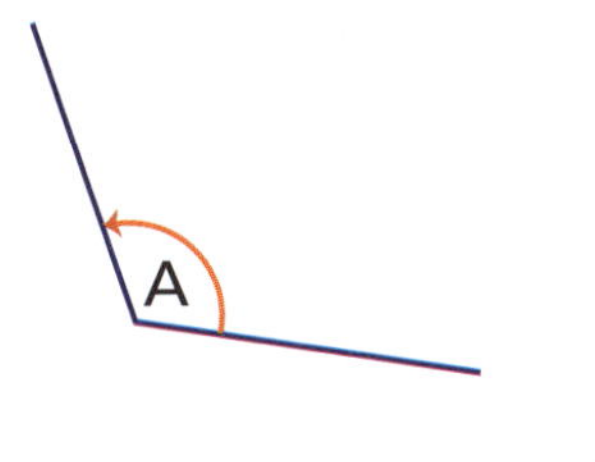

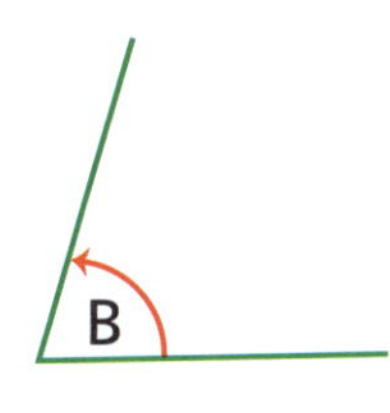

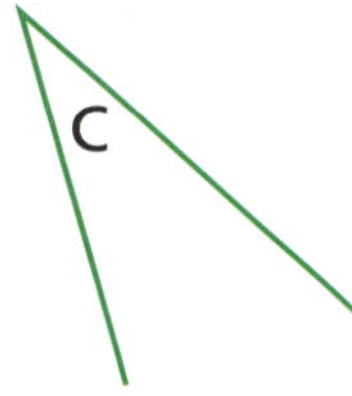

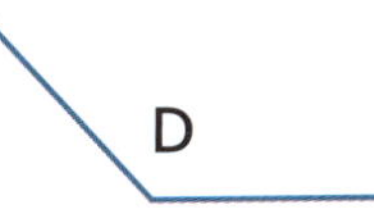

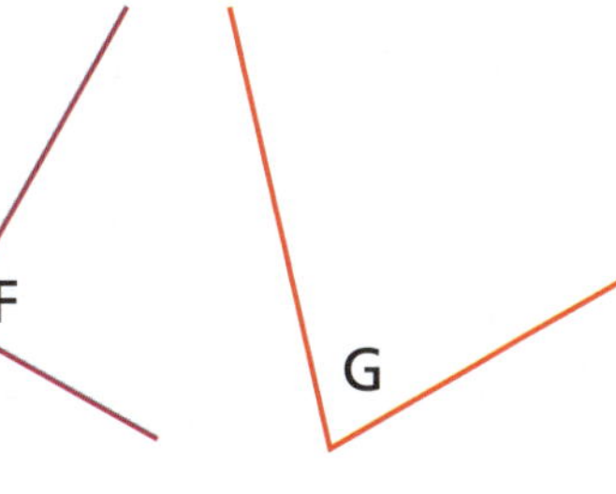

INVESTIGATION

On your own paper, superimpose one angle on another using different types of angles.

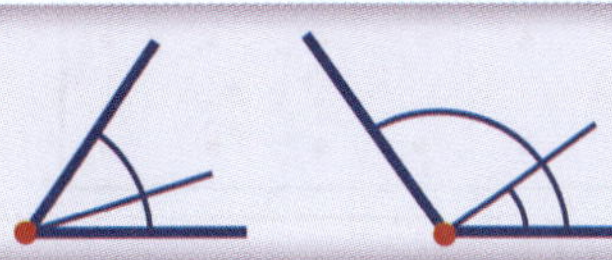

The angles will have the same vertex.

4:15 Angles

How many angles in each?

- The size of an angle is the amount of turn between the arms.

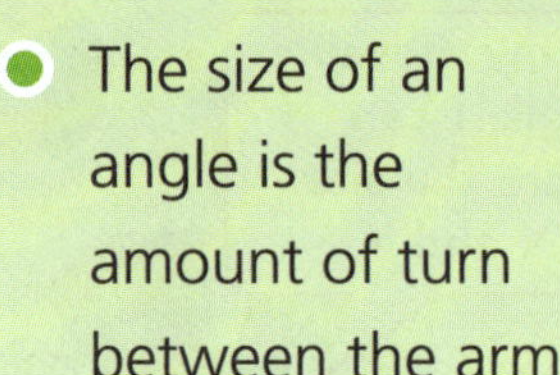
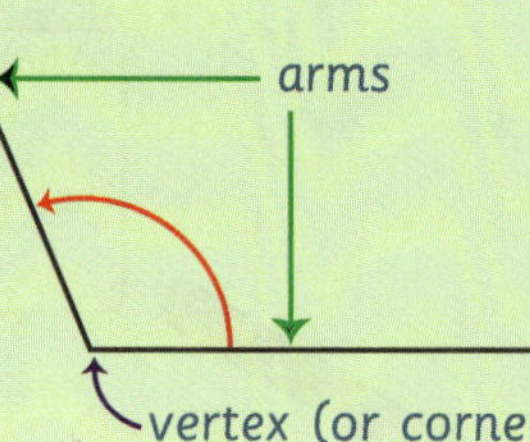

- The stick has been moved through an angle.

- These angles are the same size even though the arms are different lengths.

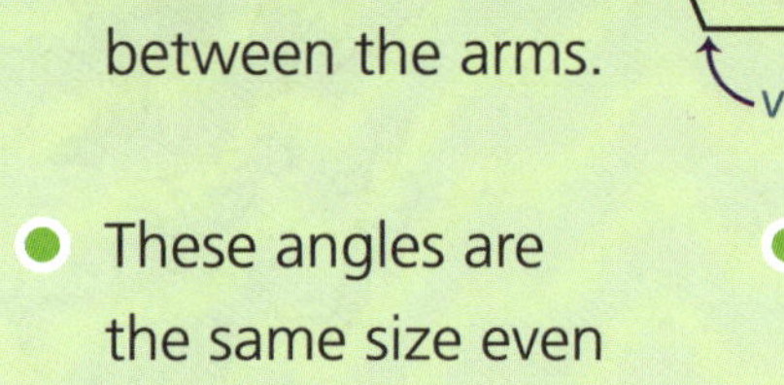
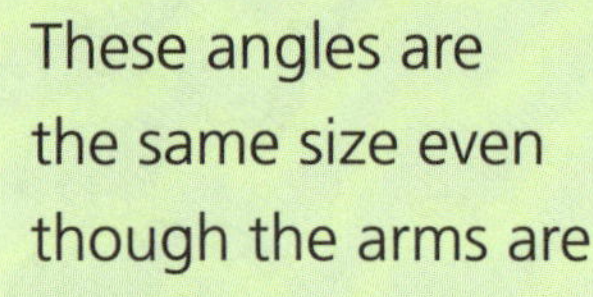
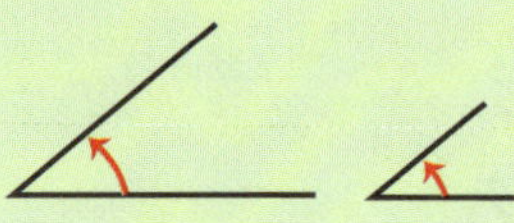

- Sometimes we have to imagine where one of the arms should be.
- The top of the door shows both arms of the angle. The bottom shows one arm, but we can imagine the other.

1 In each part, number the angles from the smallest turn (1) to the largest turn (4).

a

b

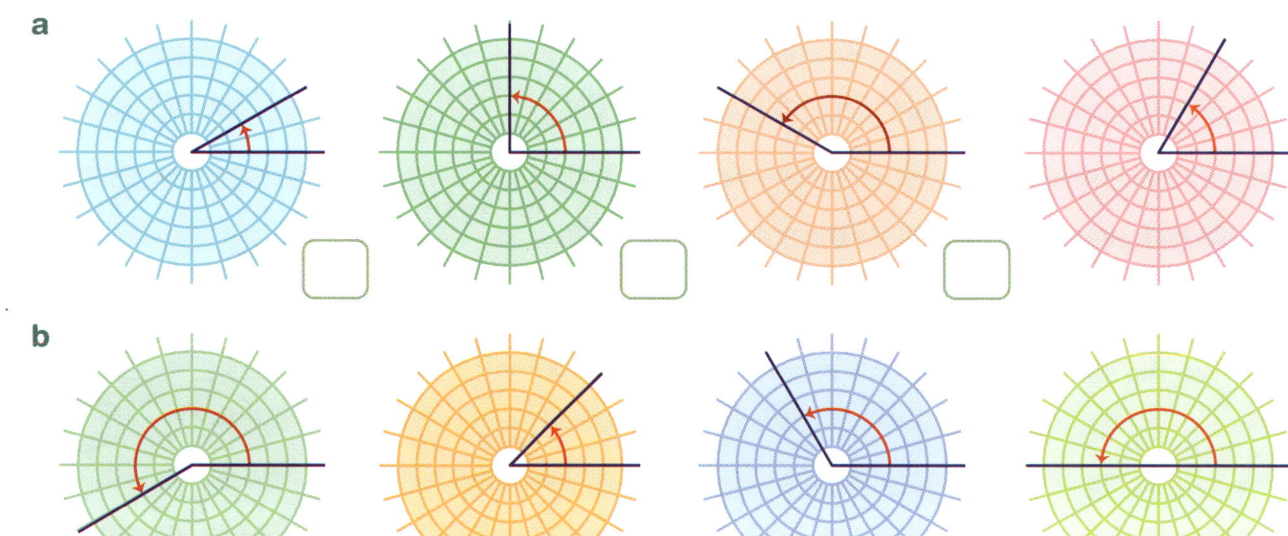

2 Use a ruler to draw angles on the dot grids.

a Draw an angle the same size as **A**.

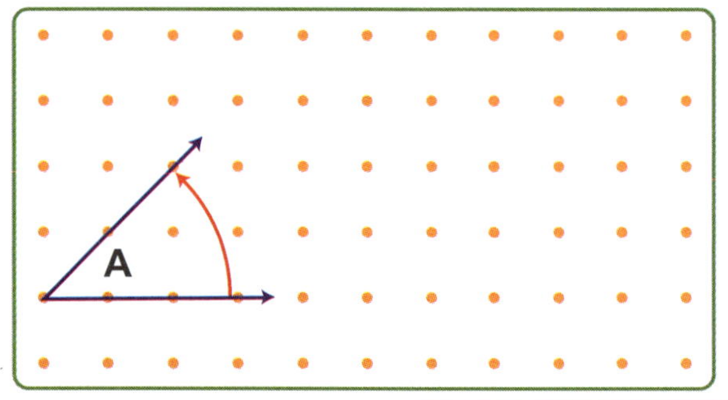

b Draw an angle the same size as **B**.

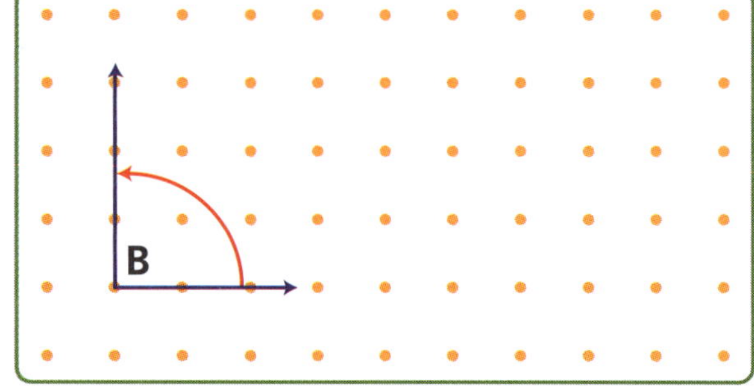

c Why is **B** a right angle? ______

 • *AUSTRALIAN SIGNPOST MATHS NSW 3* • ISBN 9780655709046

4:16 Right angles

The angles at the corners of a square are called right angles.

CONCEPT

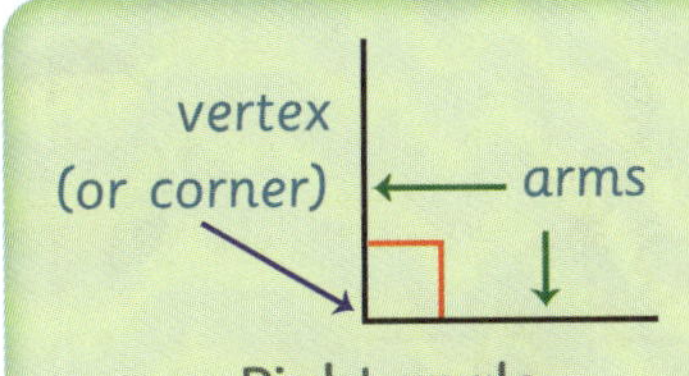

The angle at the corner of a square is called a **right angle**.
Two right angles make a half turn.

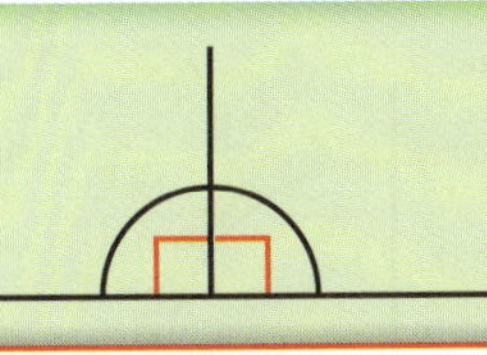

A small square drawn in the corner shows that it is a right angle.

To make a square corner, follow these steps:

1. Fold a piece of paper once to form a half turn.

2. Fold the paper again so that the second fold lies exactly on top of the first.

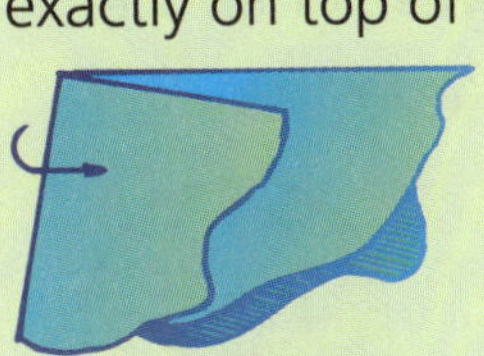

Just like magic!

3. Press all the folds down firmly. Where the folds meet, you have a square corner.

Square corner

Practise making your own square corners.

1. Use a square corner to test these angles. Which are right angles?

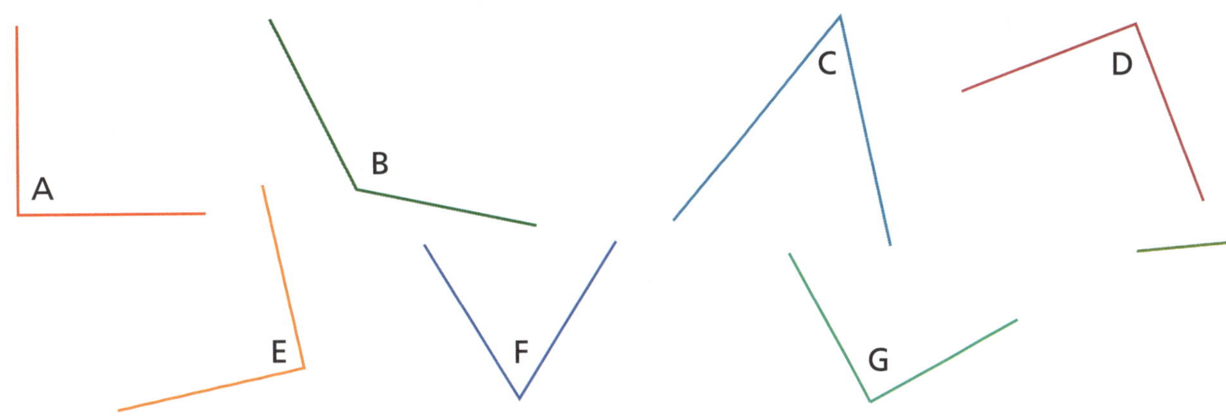

2. Which angle is larger than a right angle?

3. Use a square corner to test the corners of this page. Are they right angles?

INVESTIGATION

- Use your square corner to find shapes on page 136 that have obtuse angles (angles that are larger than right angles).
  List the letters here.
- Write the names of two shapes that always have right angles.

 • *AUSTRALIAN SIGNPOST MATHS NSW 3* • ISBN 9780655709046

4:17 Angles

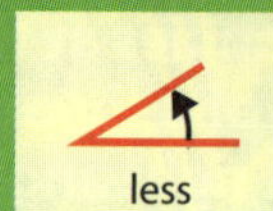

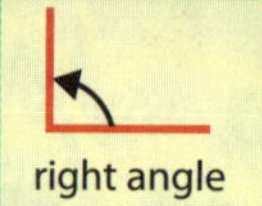

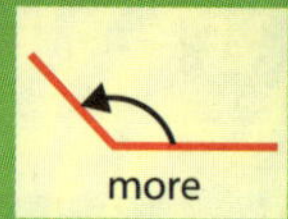

A quarter turn is a right angle.

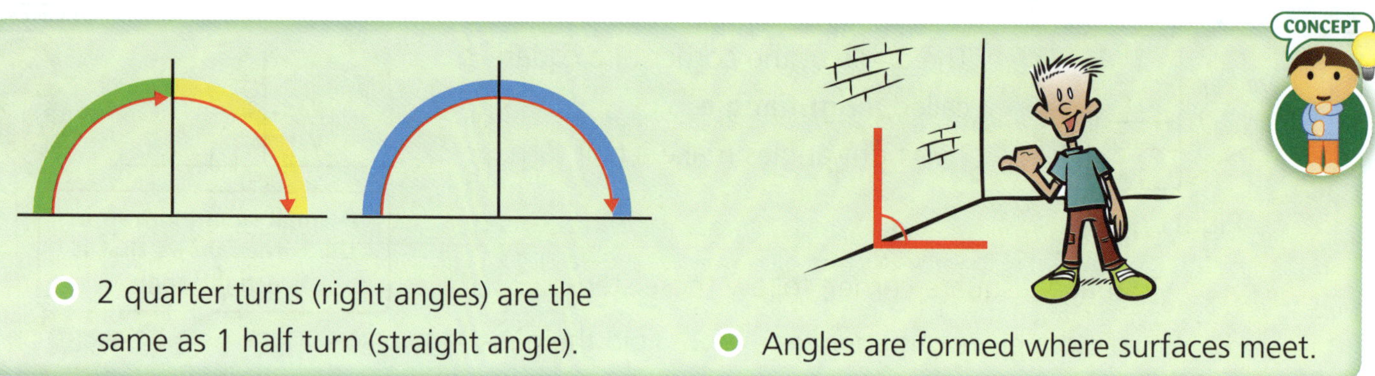

- 2 quarter turns (right angles) are the same as 1 half turn (straight angle).
- Angles are formed where surfaces meet.

1 Describe each turn as **clockwise** or **anticlockwise**, and as a **quarter**, **half** or **three-quarter turn**.

a 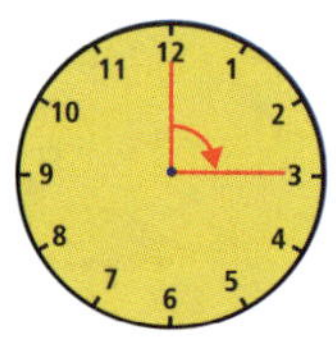

b 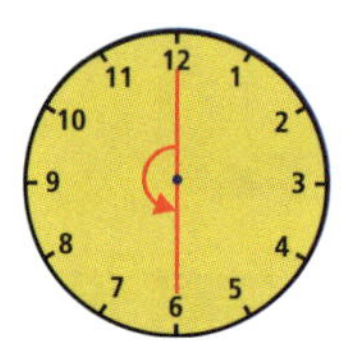

c 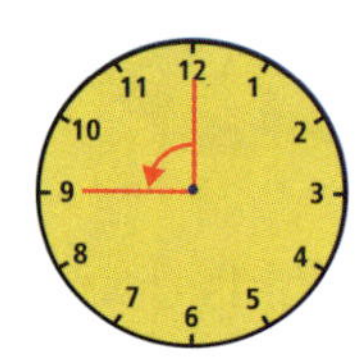

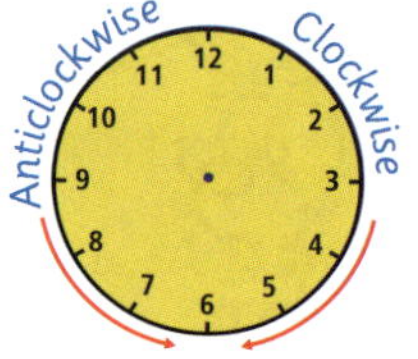

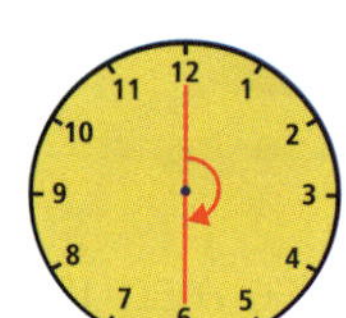

The minute hand turns a half turn in half an hour.

d 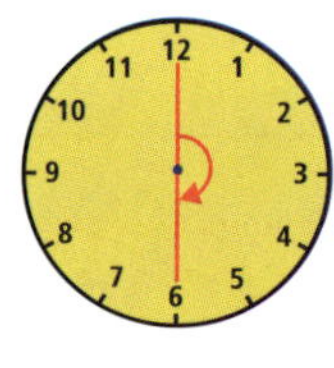

e 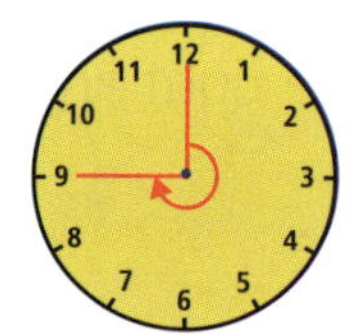

f 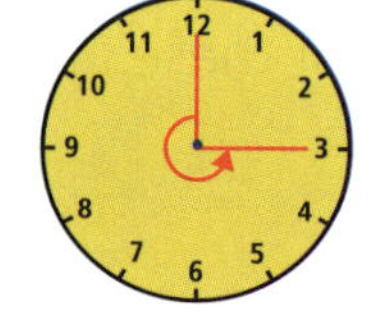

2 **a** Draw a quarter turn anticlockwise.

b Draw a three-quarter turn clockwise.

c Is a quarter turn clockwise the same as a three-quarter turn anticlockwise?

INVESTIGATION

List examples of angles made where surfaces meet.

4:18 Describing position

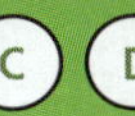
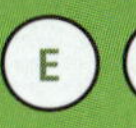

A B C D E F

4th from the left ☐ 3rd from the right ☐

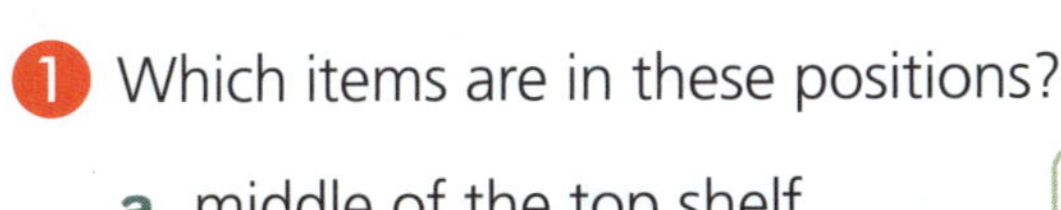

1 Which items are in these positions?

a middle of the top shelf ______

b right side of the top shelf ______

c left side of the middle shelf ______

d right side of the bottom shelf ______

In which positions are these items?

e duck ______ **f** book ______ **g** bottle ______

2 Which items are kept in these cupboards?

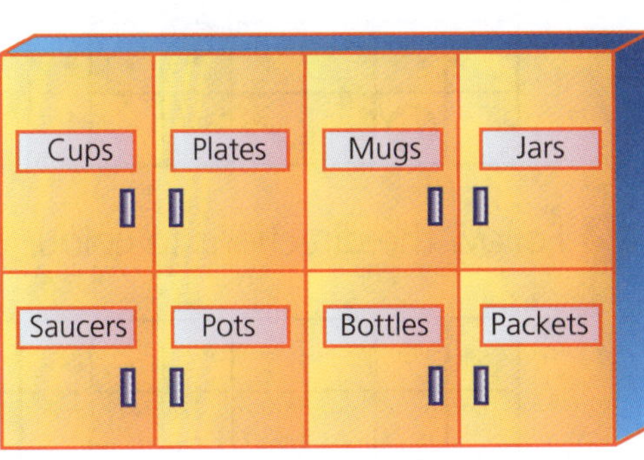

a left cupboard on the bottom row ______

b second from the left on the top row ______

c third from the left on the top row ______

d second from the left on the bottom row ______

In which cupboards are these items?

e cups ______

f bottles ______

g packets ______

h jars ______

3 Each student has their own shelf. Whose shelves are in these positions?

a fourth from the left on the top ______

b at the far right on the bottom ______

c fifth from the left on the top ______

d first on the left on the bottom ______

e What is the position of Ben's shelf? ______

f What is the position of Emma's shelf? ______

4:19 Pathways between places

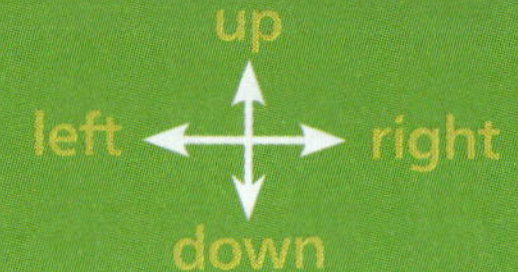

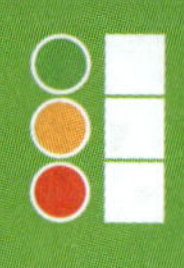

1 Move the counter along the path. Write each move in the table.

a

Moves
3 right
4 up
1
2

b

Moves

2 Follow the directions to colour the path of the counter.

a

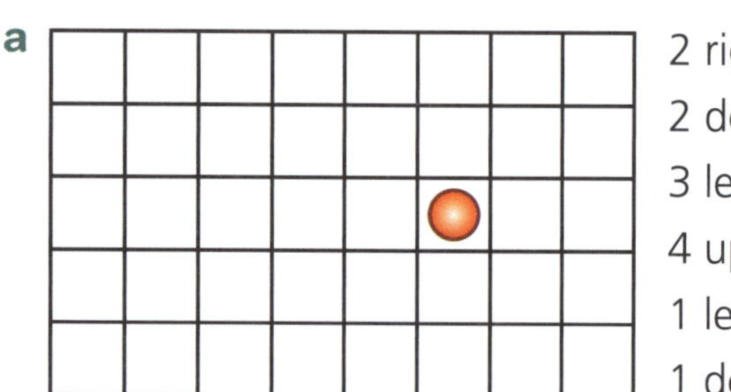

2 right,
2 down,
3 left,
4 up,
1 left,
1 down.

b

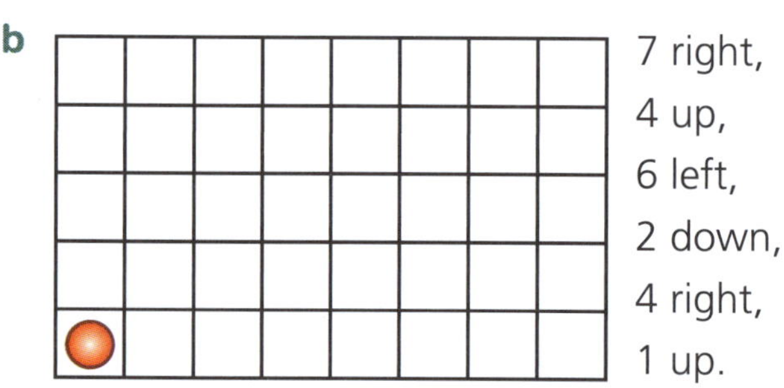

7 right,
4 up,
6 left,
2 down,
4 right,
1 up.

3 Carla has to go to every classroom and then to the office. Starting with room **H**, show the quickest route by writing the letters of the rooms in order.

Carla's shortest route is:

H C [ ] **G O**

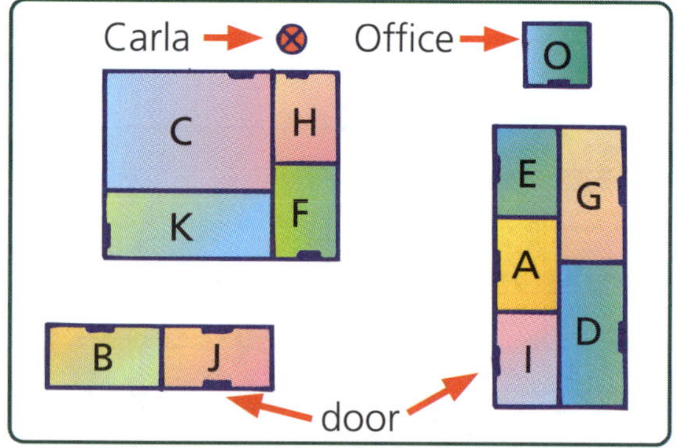

- In your school playground, mark a starting point.
- Students work in pairs to follow directions from the starting point to a secret destination. Everyone should measure distances using metre rulers or paces.
- Example directions: Move 3 m forwards, then 5 m to the right, then 7 m forwards, then 10 m to the left.

 • *AUSTRALIAN SIGNPOST MATHS NSW 3* • ISBN 9780655709046

4:20 Trapezium and parallelogram

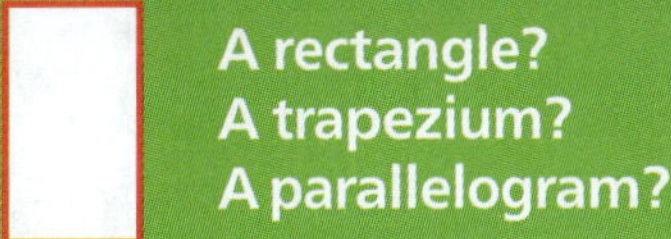

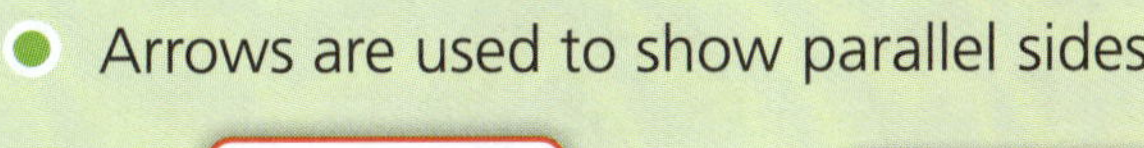

- Arrows are used to show parallel sides.

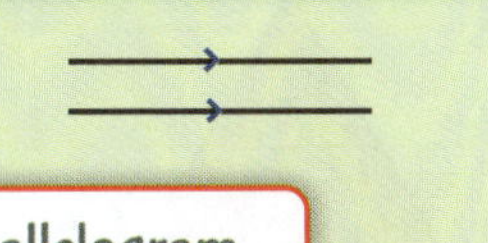

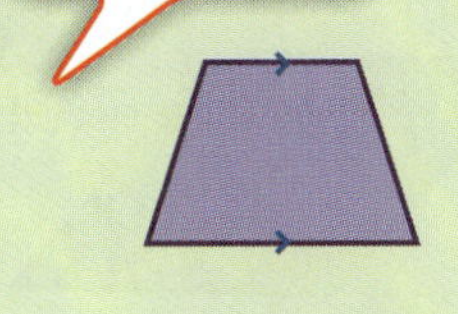

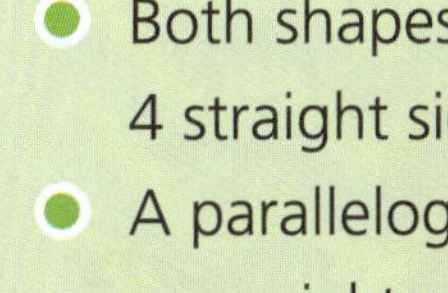

- A **trapezium** has one pair of parallel sides.
- A **parallelogram** has two pairs of parallel sides.
- Both shapes have 4 straight sides.
- A parallelogram is a special trapezium.
- Trapeziums and parallelograms are both quadrilaterals.

1

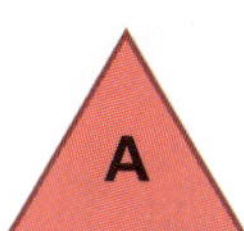

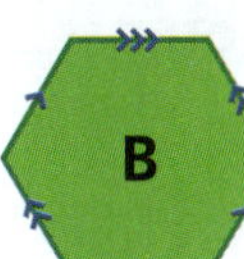

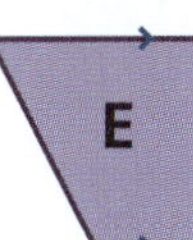

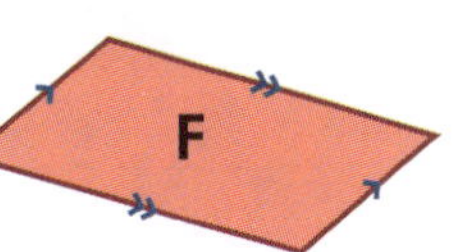

a Which of these shapes are trapeziums?

b Which shape is a parallelogram?

2 Match each shape name with one shape picture.

oval

square

triangle

rhombus (diamond)

octagon

rectangle

parallelogram

pentagon

trapezium

hexagon

3 **a** On this dot grid, draw three trapeziums.

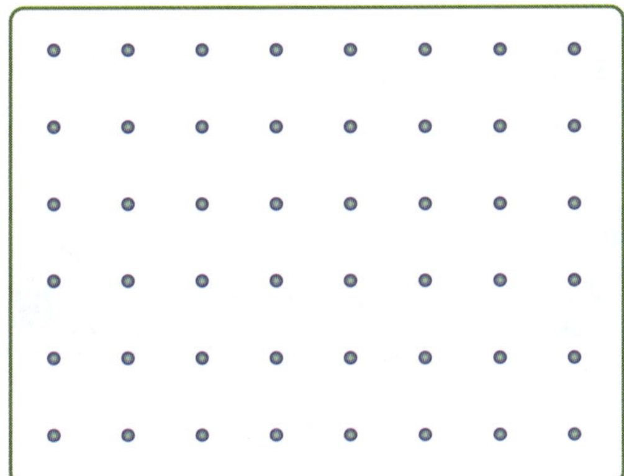

b On this dot grid, draw three parallelograms.

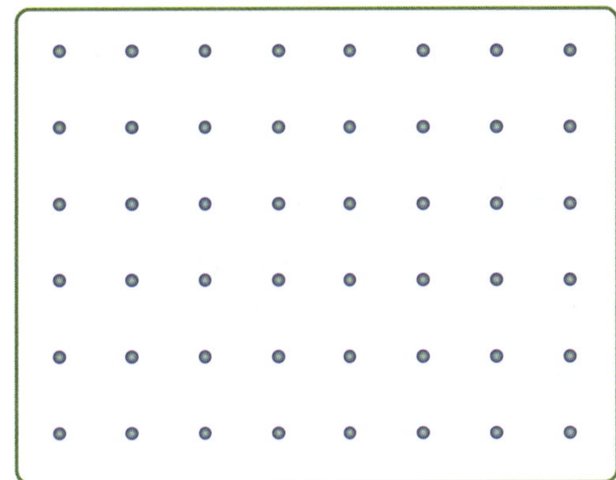

 • *AUSTRALIAN SIGNPOST MATHS NSW 3* • ISBN 9780655709046

Features of 2D shapes

Is the number of sides the same as the number of vertices?

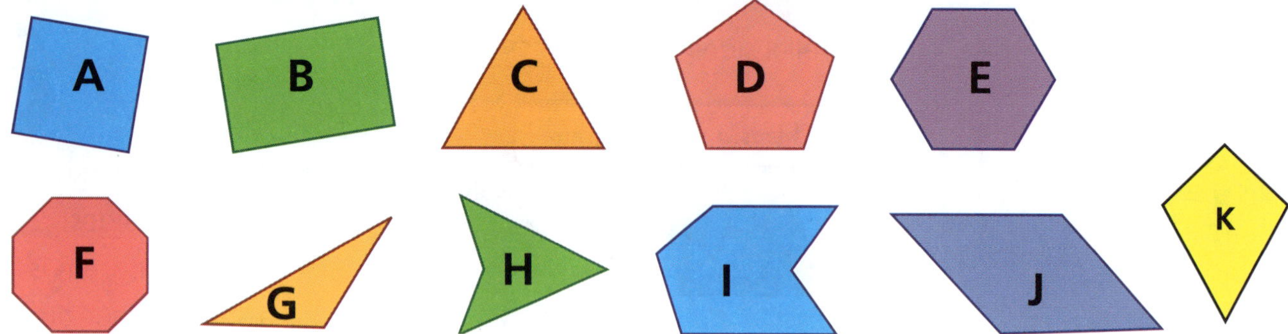

1 Write which of the shapes above have:

a 3 sides

b 4 sides

c 6 sides

d all sides equal

e sides that jut in

CONCEPT

- A **quadrilateral** has 4 sides.
- A **pentagon** has 5 sides.
- A **hexagon** has 6 sides.
- An **octagon** has 8 sides.
- A **rhombus** is a diamond.
- A **kite** has symmetry.

2 a Which of the quadrilaterals above have all sides equal?

b Which of the shapes above is an octagon?

3 What shape is a closed shape with the least possible number of straight sides and no curved sides?

4 a On this dot grid, draw 5 different quadrilaterals.

b How many dots would be inside the largest square you could draw?

c How many dots would be inside the largest hexagon you could draw on this dot grid?

d Use the dots to draw 6 squares of different size on this grid.

5 How are these shapes different from the shapes at the top of the page?

K L M

4:22 Spheres

A **sphere** is a 3D object.

- It is like a ball.
- It has one **curved surface**.
- All of the points on the surface are the same distance from the centre.
- Its **cross-section** is always a circle. The circles can be different sizes.

Which countries can you see?

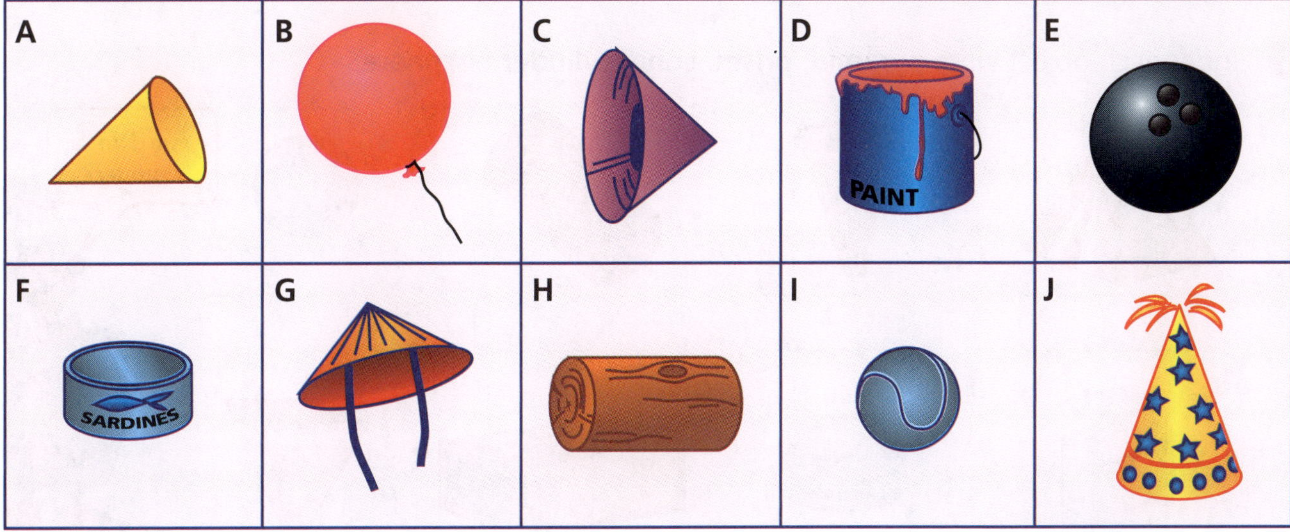

1. a Which pictures show a sphere?
   b Which have 2 flat surfaces?
   c Which have no vertices (corner points)?

2. Write **true** or **false**. A sphere:
   a can stack
   b can roll
   c can slide
   d has a flat surface
   e looks like a marble
   f looks like a can

Draw objects that have the shape of a sphere or part of a sphere.

4:23 3D objects

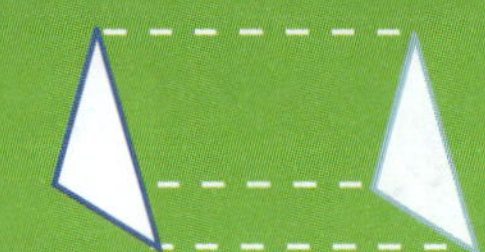

To draw a prism:
- draw two identical shapes
- Join the matching vertices.

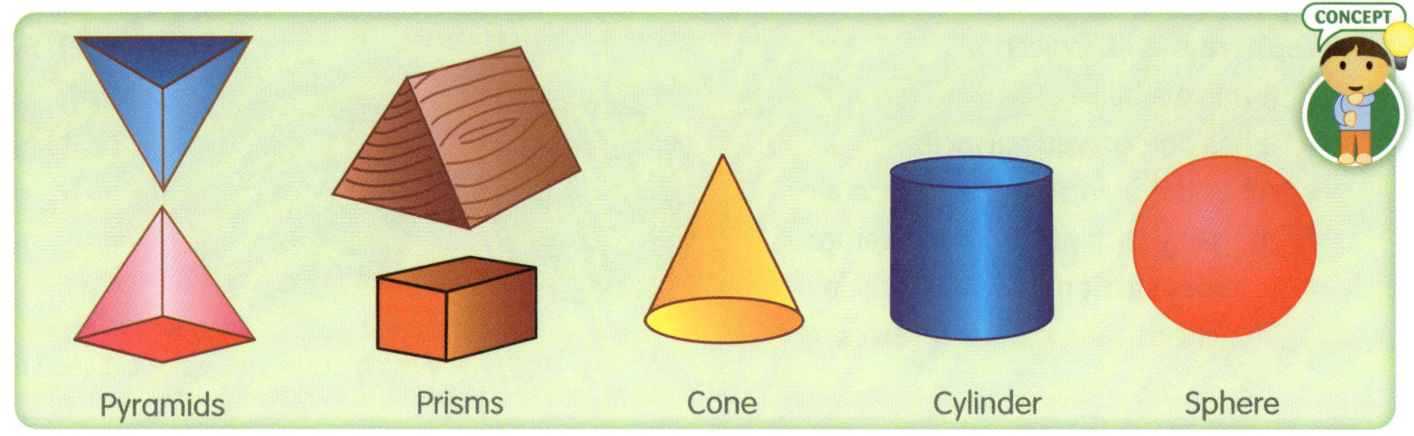

1 Under each object write **pyramid**, **prism**, **cone**, **cylinder** or **sphere**.

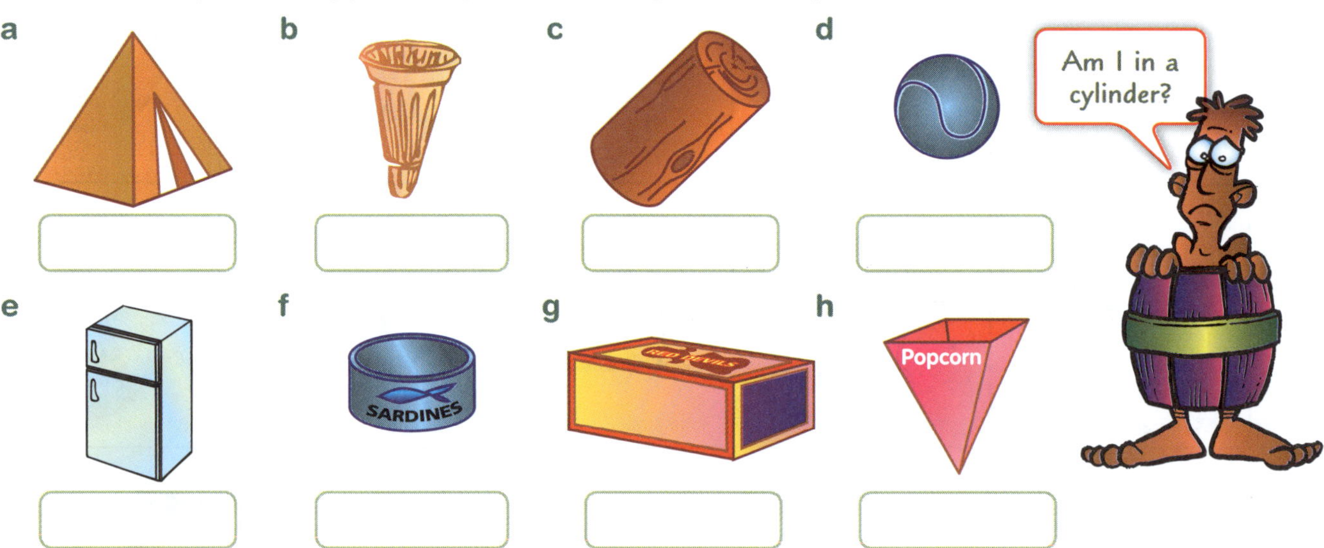

2 Complete the drawings.

a prism

b cone

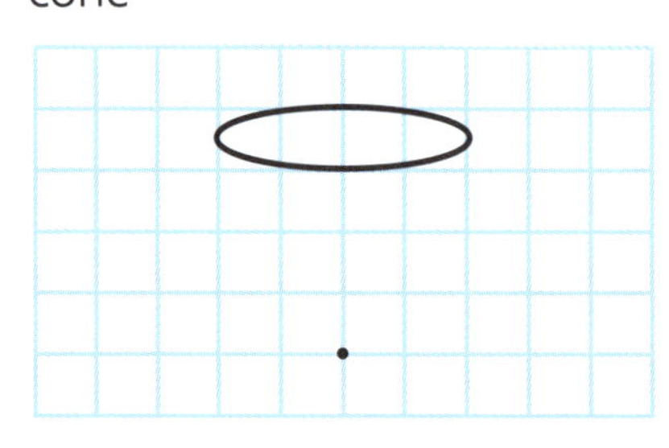

c pyramid

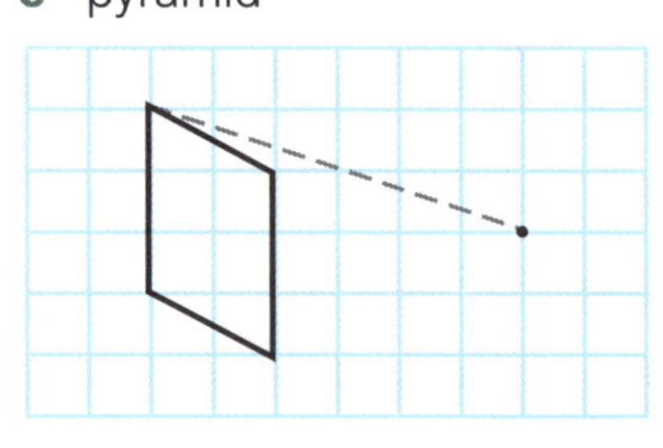

d cylinder

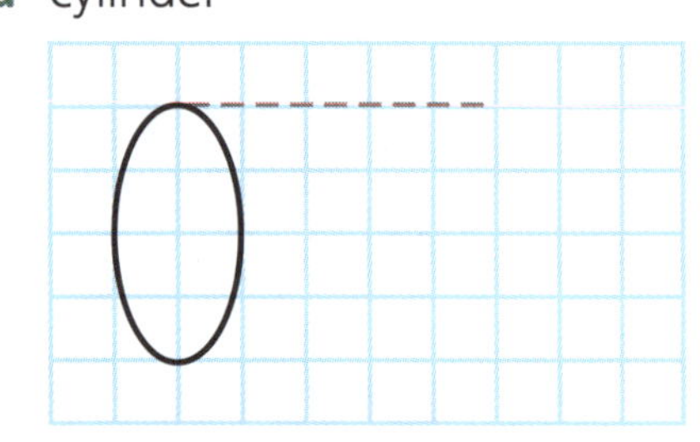

e sphere

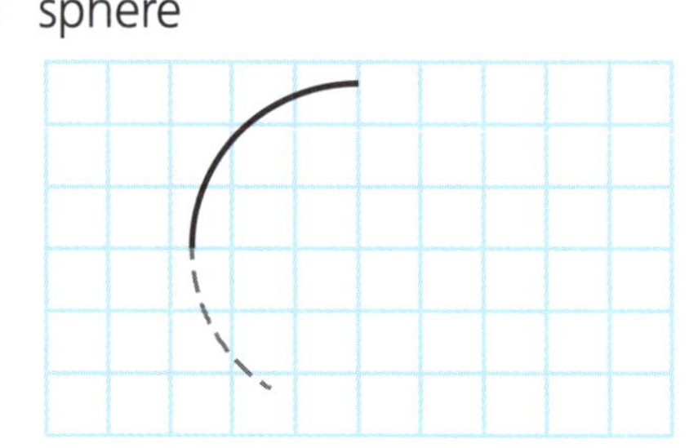

f cube

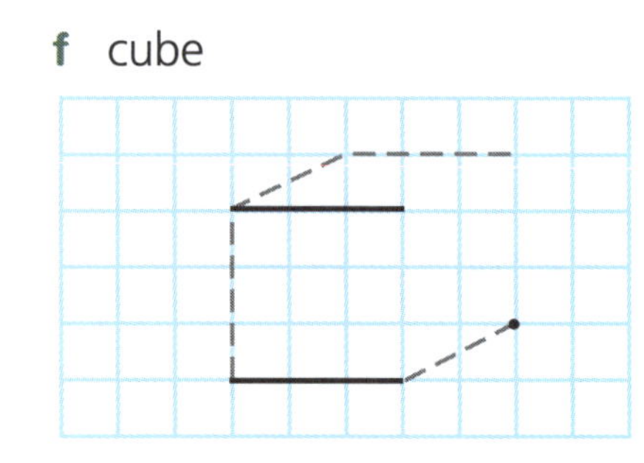

 • *AUSTRALIAN SIGNPOST MATHS NSW 3* • ISBN 9780655709046

4:24 Using coordinates

Write the letter then the number.

- To locate a position on a grid we name the column first, then the row. The yellow square is E7. Here, letters name the column and numbers name the row. The red square is A4.

8								
7								
6								
5								
4								
3								
2								
1								
	A	**B**	**C**	**D**	**E**	**F**	**G**	**H**

1 What is in square:

- **a** G4? ______
- **b** B7? ______
- **c** F3? ______
- **d** C6? ______
- **e** H8? ______
- **f** A1? ______
- **g** H4? ______
- **h** D5? ______
- **i** G6? ______
- **j** A8? ______
- **k** D8? ______

2 What are the coordinates of:

- **a** the bird? ______
- **b** the teapot? ______
- **c** the triangle? ______
- **d** the milk? ______
- **e** the glass? ______
- **f** the domino? ______
- **g** the dog? ______
- **h** the bee? ______
- **i** the flower? ______
- **j** the pear? ______
- **k** the coin? ______
- **l** the hexagon? ______

didgeridoo

boomerang

3

2			
1			
	A	**B**	**C**

shield

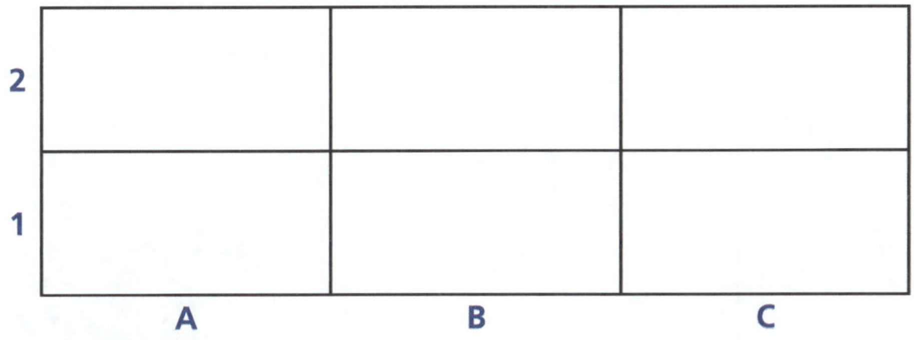

Draw: **a** a boomerang in A2 **b** a shield in B1 **c** a lizard in E3 **d** a didgeridoo in C2.

  • ISBN 9780655709046

Creating maps

What is found is C5?
What is found in G4?

CONCEPT

- **Maps** show where things are, as if you were looking down on them from above.
- This is a map of a classroom.
- The key describes the parts of the map.
- **Coordinates** are used to tell where things are found. **The door is at A5**.

Key: B = board C = cupboard
D = desk E = entry
N = noticeboard S = sinks
W = window

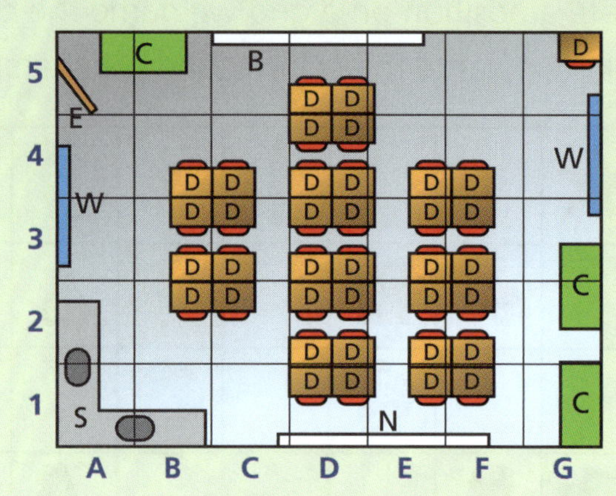

1 Use the classroom map above to answer the questions.

a How many desks are in the classroom?

b How many cupboards are there?

c What is to the left of the board?

d Where is the noticeboard?

What are the coordinates of the teacher's desk?

2 Draw a map of your own classroom or a room at home.

	A	B	C	D	E	F	G	H
8								
7								
6								
5								
4								
3								
2								
1								

Key:

Give coordinates of places on your map.

door	

INVESTIGATION

Copy a map of your local area. Make a key and use it to show places of interest on the map.

 • *AUSTRALIAN SIGNPOST MATHS NSW 3* • ISBN 9780655709046

4:26 3D models

This is a skeletal model.
How many vertices (joining points)?
How many edges (toothpicks)?

1 These models have the same height and depth but different lengths.

a Write the number of blocks used for each model.

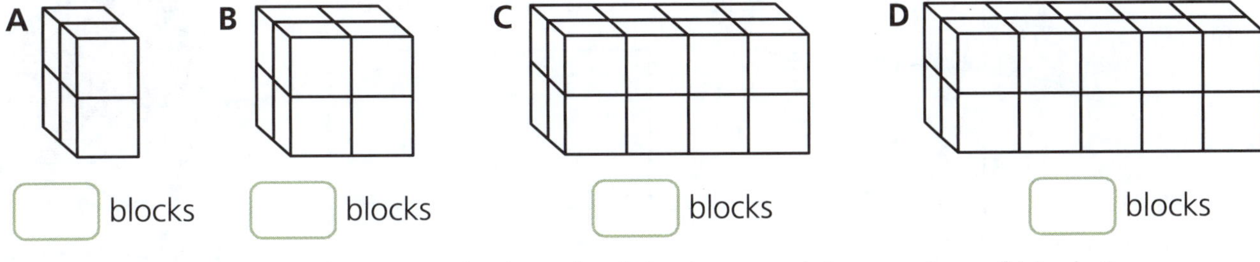

b What is the connection between the length of the base and the number of blocks?

ACTIVITY

2 Use straws or toothpicks and plasticine, Blu Tack or modelling clay to make models of:

a a rectangular prism b a triangular prism c a square pyramid

Draw the models you made here.

rectangular prism

triangular prism

square pyramid

4:27 The net of a cube

Circle the cubes.

CONCEPT

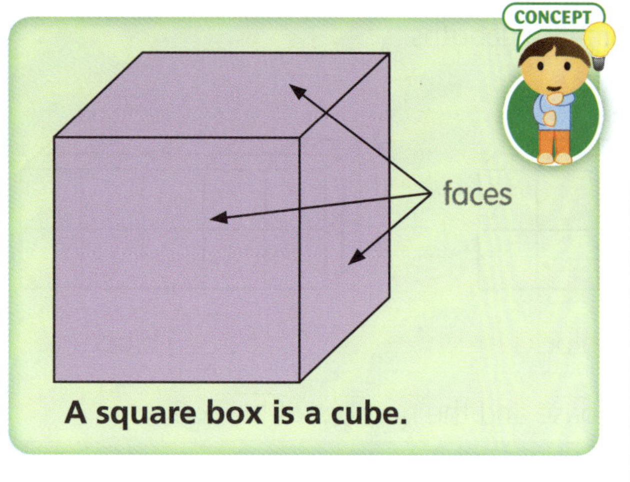

A square box is a cube.

The net of a cube

1 How many faces does a cube have? ☐

2 Which of these nets would **not** fold to make a cube? ☐

A

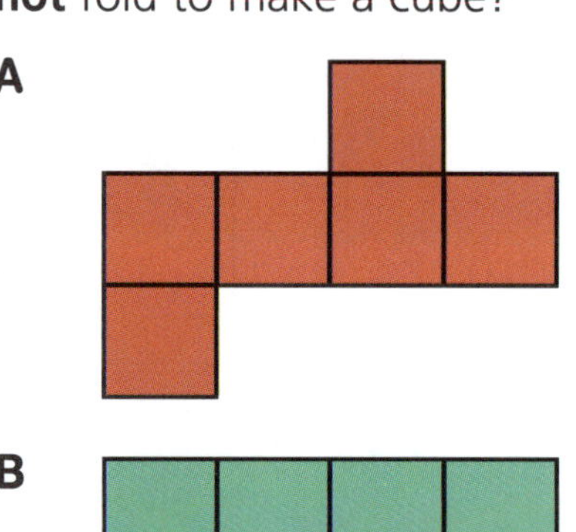

B

C

ACTIVITY

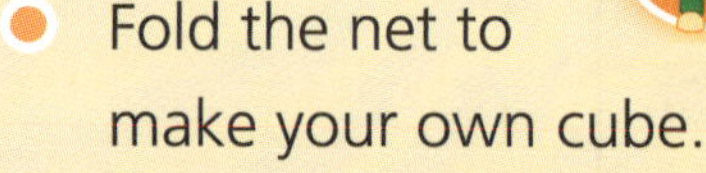

- Trace this net.
- Cut out the net.
- Fold the net to make your own cube.
- Investigate other nets that could make a cube.

ACTIVITY

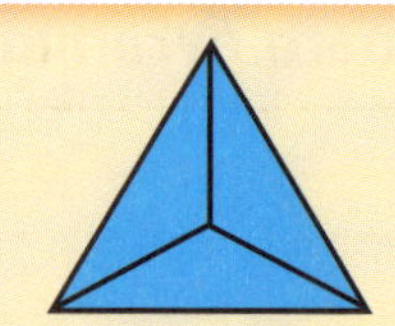

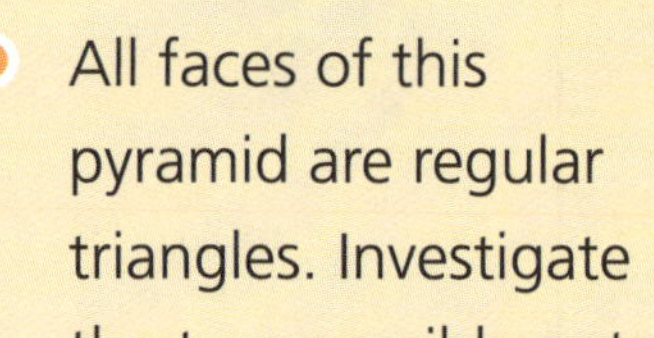

- All faces of this pyramid are regular triangles. Investigate the two possible nets.

4:28 Flip, slide, turn

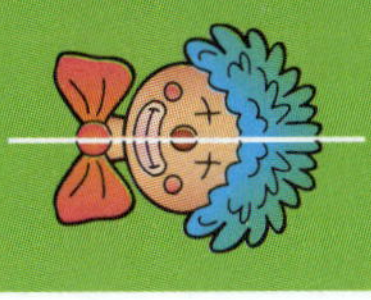

If you fold along a line of symmetry, the two halves will match.

CONCEPT

There are 3 ways to repeat a shape:

A flip the shape (reflection)
B slide the shape (translation)
C turn the shape (rotation).

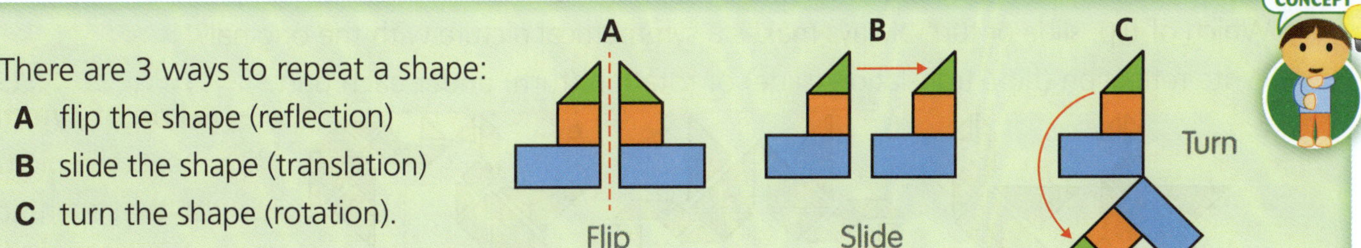

1 Is the coloured shape made by a **flip** (reflection), **slide** (translation) or **turn** (rotation)?

a ________ **b** 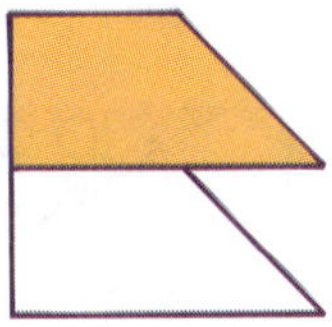 ________ **c** 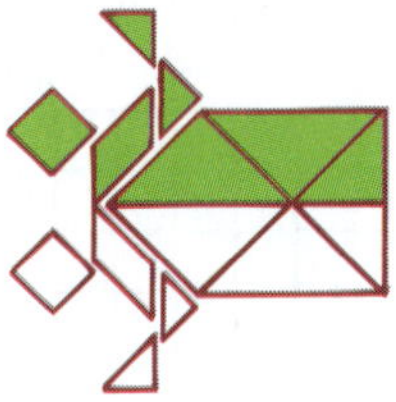 ________ **d** ________

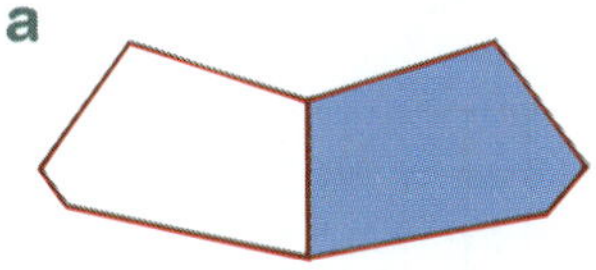

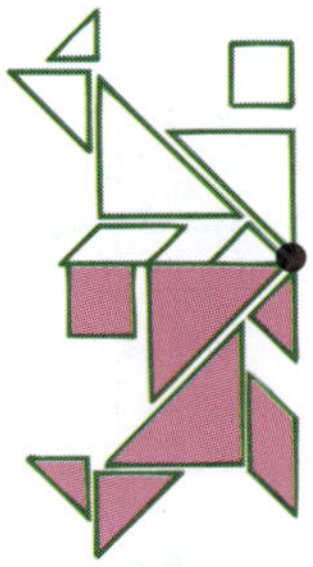

e 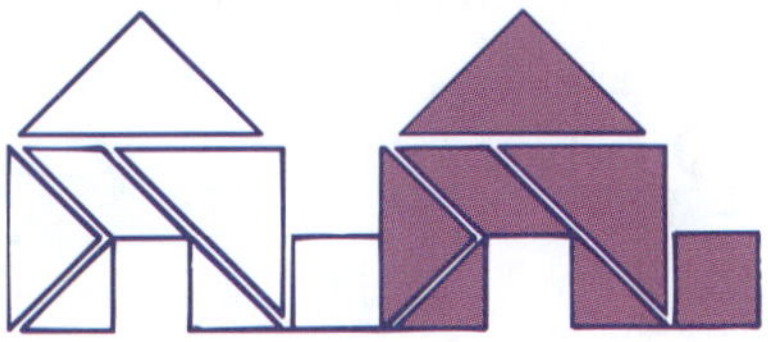 ________ **f** ________

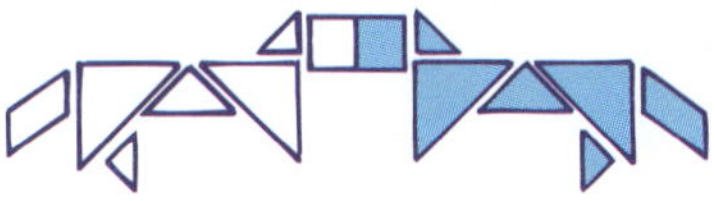

g 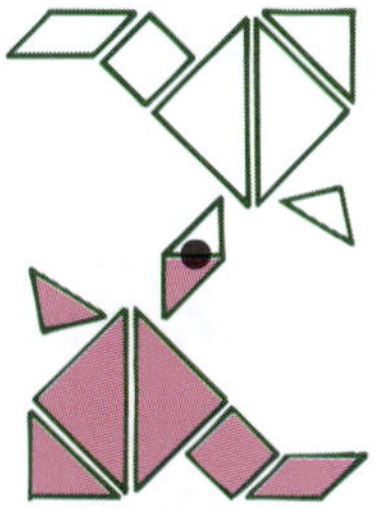 ________ **h** 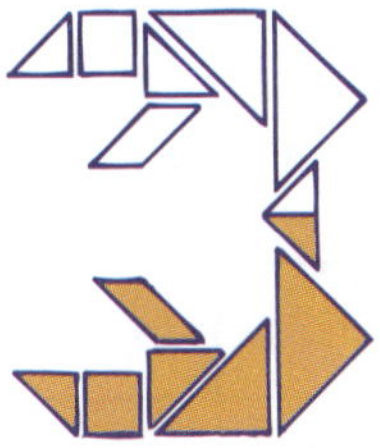 ________ **i** 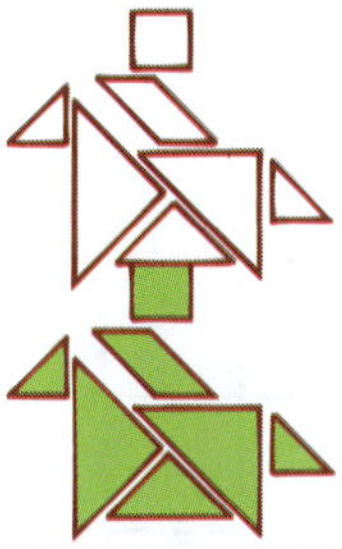 ________ **j** ________

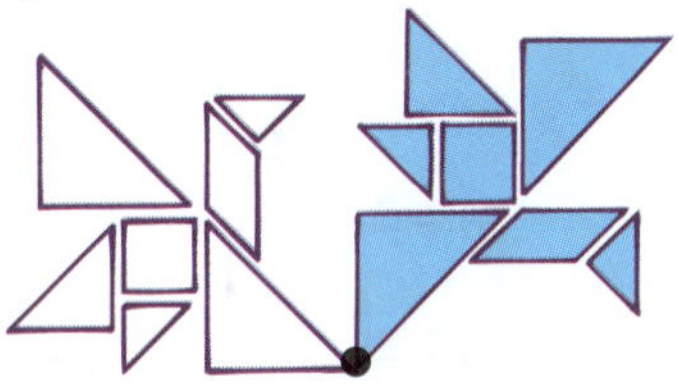

k Discuss which of these shapes are symmetrical. ________

FUN SPOT

A Chinese puzzle: tangrams

- Trace or draw this square onto a piece of paper.
- Cut out the square and cut along all the lines.
- Use the seven pieces to make these pictures.
- Try to make the pictures shown in Question 1.
- Use the pieces to make some pictures of your own.

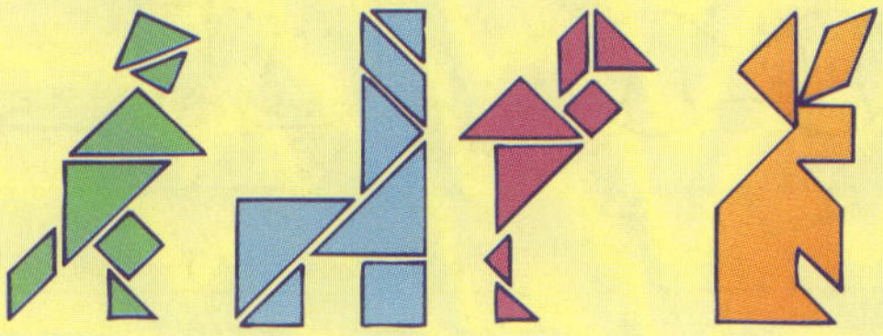

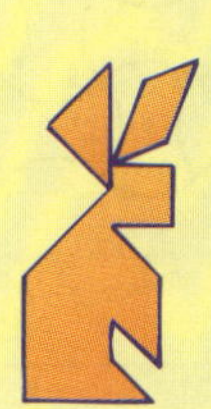

Using flip, slide and turn

Is a jigsaw puzzle a tessellation?

1 Which of flip, slide or turn always makes a symmetrical picture with the original?

Write reflection (flip), translation (slide) or rotation (turn) under each part.

a 

b 

c 

A line of symmetry cuts the picture so that each side is the mirror image of the other.

2 Use translation or reflection to complete these patterns. Which is symmetrical?

A 

B 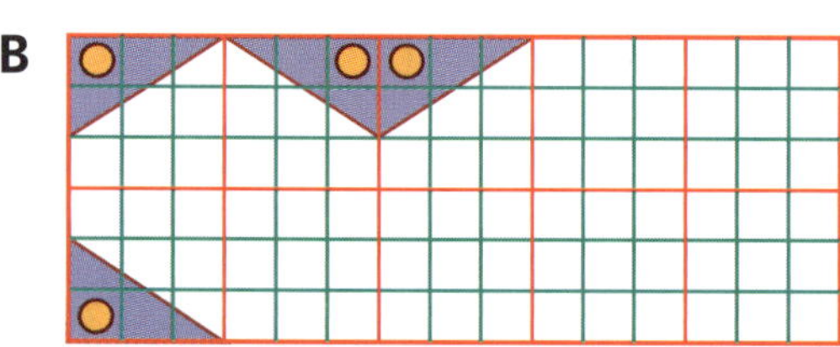

3 Use rotation to complete these patterns. Will the patterns have a line of symmetry?

A 

B 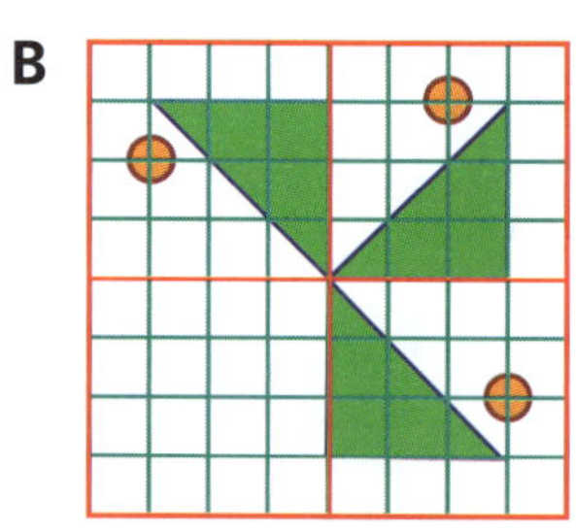

4 Make tessellating designs by flipping, sliding or turning these triangles.

A tessellation is made by repeating a shape so it fits together without gaps or overlaps.

5 Do these shapes make tessellations?

a 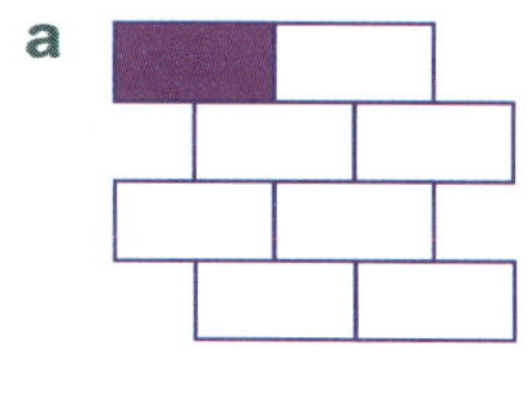

b 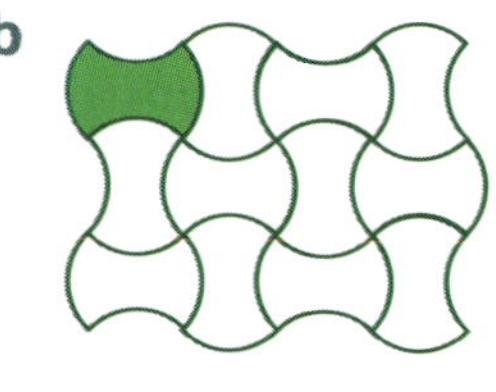

c 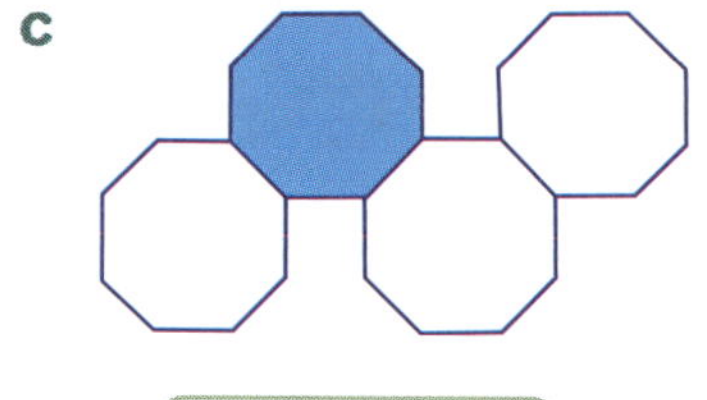

d 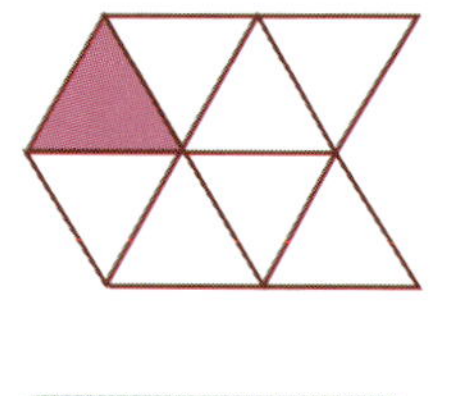

ISBN 9780655709046

4:30 Tessellations

Bricks on a wall usually tessellate.

CONCEPT

- Identical shapes tessellate if they fit together without leaving gaps or overlapping.
- To make the tessellation we may slide, flip or rotate the shape.
- Here we rotate and slide the shape. Finish this pattern.

1 Peter wanted to tile his parents' bathroom.
He used dot paper to draw the two tile patterns below.

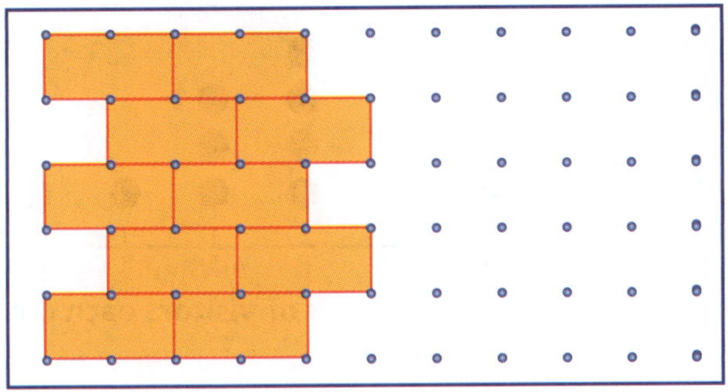

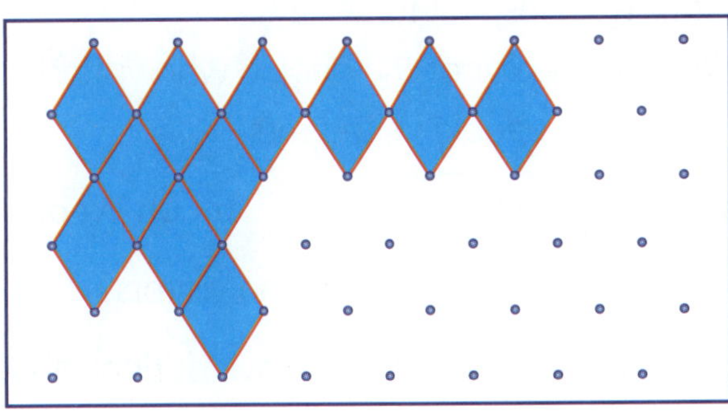

a Draw ten more tiles on each pattern.

b Do the tiles tessellate? 

2 **a** Colour the patterns made by tessellating a shape.

A 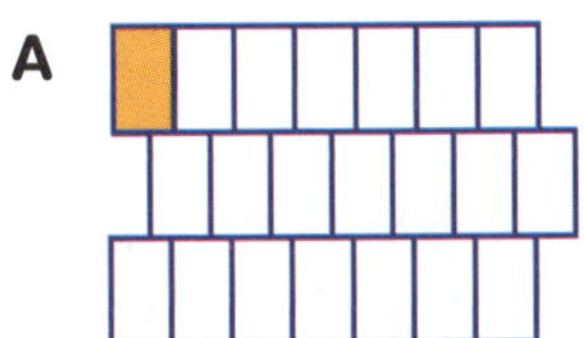

B 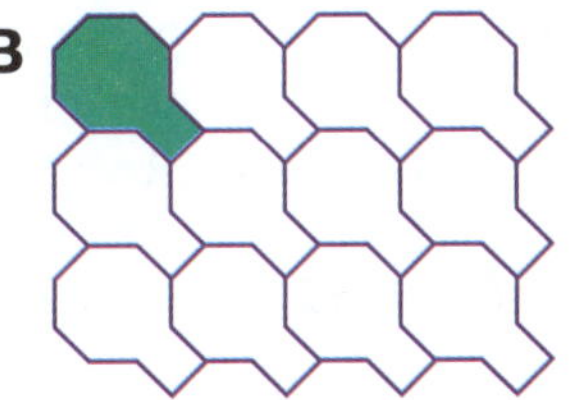

C 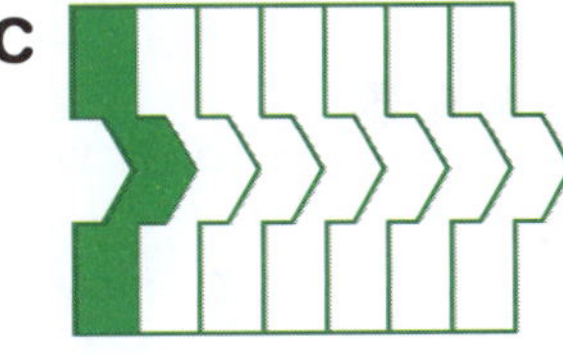

D 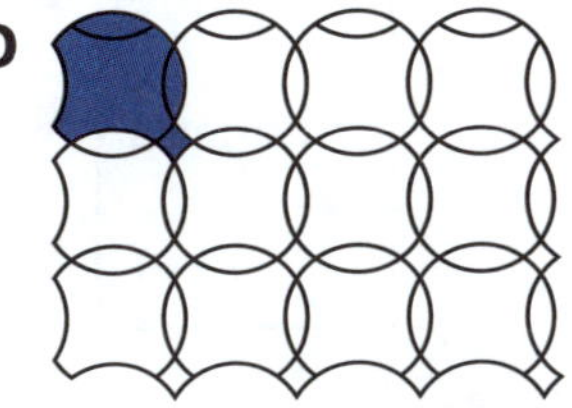

b Use your own paper to draw a tessellating shape of your own.

ICT

- Alan used this pattern to draw a tessellating bird. He used tessellation B from Question 2.
- Complete the tessellation by drawing more birds. Dots have been drawn to help you.
- Use computer drawing tools to create a tessellating design by copying, pasting and rotating regular shapes.

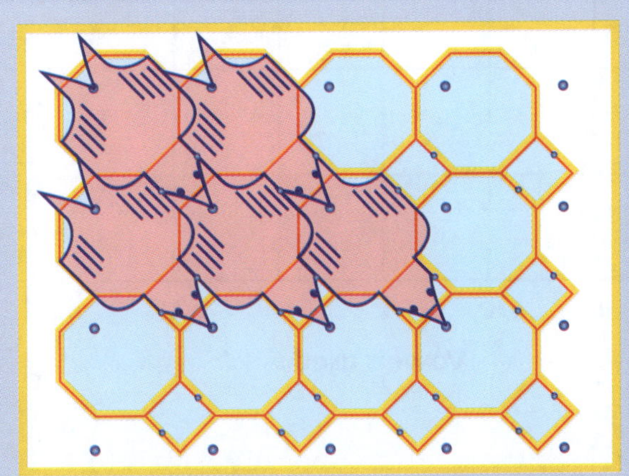

5:01 Dot plots

A dot plot is like a tally.
We use dots instead of lines.

Drawing a dot plot

- The members of our class were asked how many pets they had at home.
- The student with the most pets had 5. We wrote the numbers 0 to 6 under the line.
- As each student told us the number of pets, we put a dot above that number.

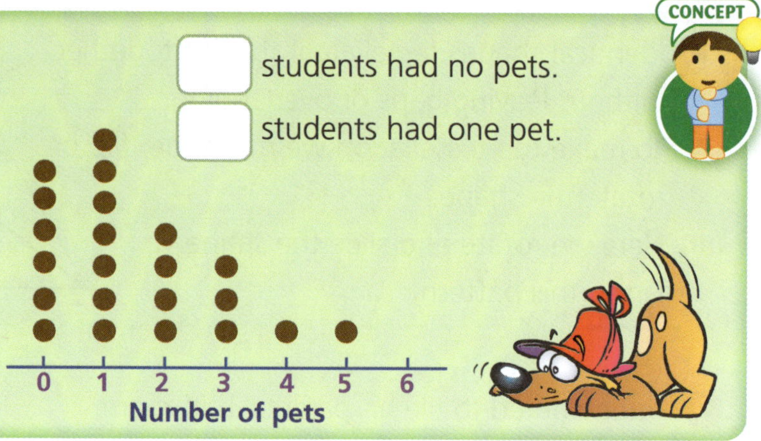

1 I stayed in hospital for 7 days.
I kept a dot plot of the people who visited me.
How many people visited me:

a on Sunday? ☐ **b** on Wednesday? ☐

c On which day did I have no visitors? ☐

d How many visitors did I have during this time? ☐

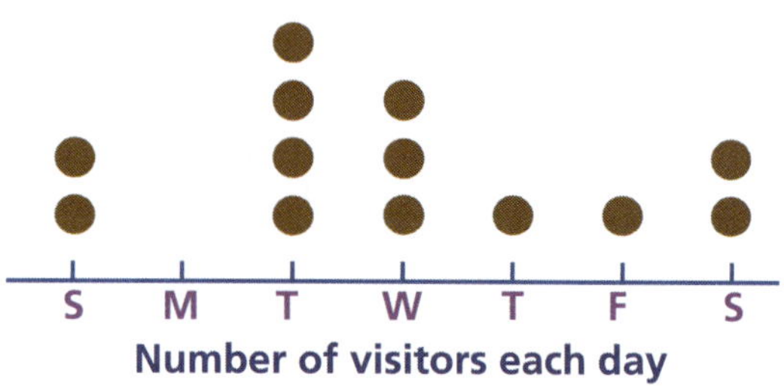

2

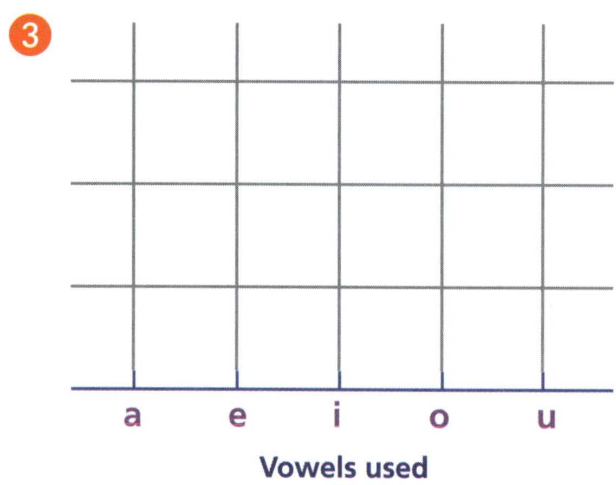

At camp, each of us took one piece of fruit. We could have an apple, orange, banana or pear. We made a dot plot of the fruit chosen.

a How many of us chose a banana? ☐

b How many pieces of fruit were taken? ☐

c How many more apples than pears were chosen? ☐

3

a e i o u

Vowels used

The letters **a**, **e**, **i**, **o** and **u** are called vowels. Make a dot plot of the vowels used in the graph of Question 2.

a Which vowel was used the most? ☐

b Which vowel was used two times? ☐

c Which two vowels were used the same number of times? ☐

d How many vowels were used altogether? ☐

e What is the difference in number, of the most used and least used vowel? ☐

5:02 Tables

Tables are used to show the data collected.

1 Each student in the class chose a colour. The results are in the **Colours chosen** table.

Colours chosen			
Blue	Green	Orange	Red
12	8	4	6

a The most popular colour was ______.

b The least popular colour was ______.

c How many students chose green? ______

d How many students are in the class? ______

2 Use the **Collections** table to answer these questions.

Collections		
Person	Number of cards	Number of stickers
Darcy	825	173
Nasha	72	201
Rachel	300	88
Rajiv	166	193
Rhonda	46	405

How many cards were collected by each person?

a Darcy ______ b Rhonda ______

c Rajiv ______ d Nasha ______

How many stickers were collected by each person?

e Rachel ______ f Nasha ______

g Rhonda ______ h Rajiv ______

i How many cards and stickers altogether were collected by Rachel? ______

3 How old is each person?

Name	Age	Name	Age
Alana	27	Alan	57
Ally	38	Luke	20
Deklyn	0	Rachel	23
Greg	10	Tom	87
Heather	17	Naomi	22

a Tom ______

b Alana ______

c Rachel ______

d Deklyn ______

e Make up your own question that could be answered using this table.

______

______

INVESTIGATION

- Do you think there are more left-handed or right-handed students in your class?
- Investigate the question by completing this tally.
- By how many is one group bigger than the other? ______

Right-handed		
Left-handed		

5:03 Tables and graphs

How is data displayed on this page?

1 a How many turtles are kept?

b How many birds are kept?

c Which rows are longest?

d Three of which pet are kept?

e How many pets altogether?

Pets kept in the classroom

Birds	🐦 🐦 🐦
Fish	🐟 🐟 🐟 🐟 🐟 🐟
Mice	🐭 🐭 🐭 🐭 🐭 🐭
Turtles	🐢

2 Use the graph above to complete these tables.

A

Pets kept in the classroom			
Birds	Fish	Mice	Turtles

B

Pets kept in the classroom	
Birds	
Fish	
Mice	
Turtles	

Pets kept in the classroom

Birds								
Fish								
Mice								
Turtles								
	0	1	2	3	4	5	6	7	8

a How many classroom pets can fly?

b How many classroom pets are there altogether?

c Which table do you think looks better, **A** or **B**?

d Complete the graph.

When the parts of a graph are aligned, it is quicker to compare the categories.

3 a Use this table to complete the graph.

Youth group attendance				
Carmen	Erika	Holly	Paul	Yong
4	5	3	7	6

Youth group attendance

Carmen	● ● ● ●
Erika	● ● ● ● ●
Holly	
Paul	
Yong	

b Who has attended the least?

c Did Yong attend more often than Erika?

d Erika has been away three times. How many times has the group met?

INVESTIGATION

4 Collecting and displaying data

Step 1: Decide on a class topic of interest.

Step 2: Collect your data. (Discuss the best way to do this.)

Step 3: Record your data in a table or spreadsheet.

Step 4: Create a graph to display your data.

Step 5: Reflect on and share what you discovered.

5:04 Picture graphs

In Question 1, each picture stands for 2 trains.

1 a How many trains were sold on Monday?

b On which day were the most trains sold?

c How many trains were sold altogether?

d If there were 30 trains for sale, how many trains were not sold?

Discuss what else this graph tells us.

Toy trains sold

Monday	
Tuesday	
Wednesday	
Thursday	
Friday	

Key: stands for 2 toy trains

2 Students cut out shapes to show some of the languages spoken at home. They made this graph using one shape for each student.

Mandarin	
French	
Greek	

a How many students speak Greek?

b How many students speak French?

c How many students speak Mandarin?

d Which row is the longest?

3 Liz made this graph using stones, blocks and counters. She used a stone for each car she saw, a block for each truck and a counter for each van.

Cars	
Trucks	
Vans	

a How many cars did Liz see?

b How many vans did she see?

c How many more cars than trucks did she see?

d How many vehicles were seen altogether?

Car colour tallies

- Work in groups. Each group records the colours of cars that drive by in 10 minutes.
- Use tally marks to record the colours of cars.
- Groups discuss and compare their results.
- Create a graph showing the popular colours.

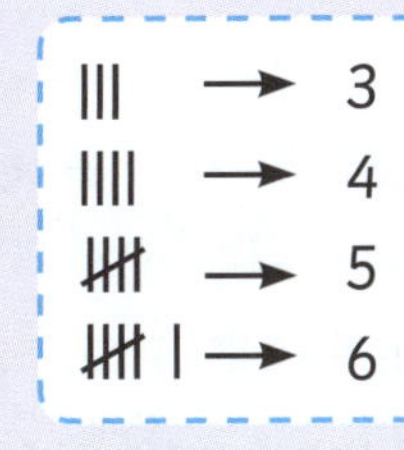

Chance

1 Is it certain, likely, unlikely or impossible that a red ball would be chosen?

a

6 red, 4 blue

b

3 red, 7 blue

c

all red

d

all blue

2 Colour these apples red or green so that green is more likely to be chosen if you are not looking.

3 A dice is rolled once. What are the possible outcomes?

Each outcome is equally likely to happen.

4 Roll a dice six times. Write each number rolled.

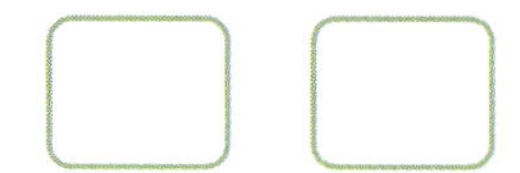

a Which number (or numbers) was rolled most?

b Which numbers were not rolled?

c Is it possible to throw six ones in a row?

Why is this almost impossible?

Once you have finished this question, roll the dice again and compare the results.

- Choose a number on the dice.
- Count how many rolls it takes until you have rolled your number twice. ☐ rolls

Prediction: ☐ rolls

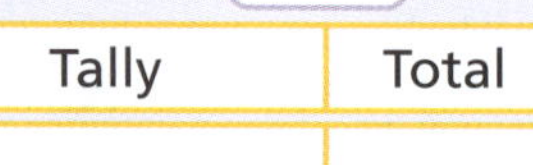

Tally	Total

 • *AUSTRALIAN SIGNPOST MATHS NSW 3* • ISBN 9780655709046

5:06 Possible outcomes

Will my plant die?
What should I do?

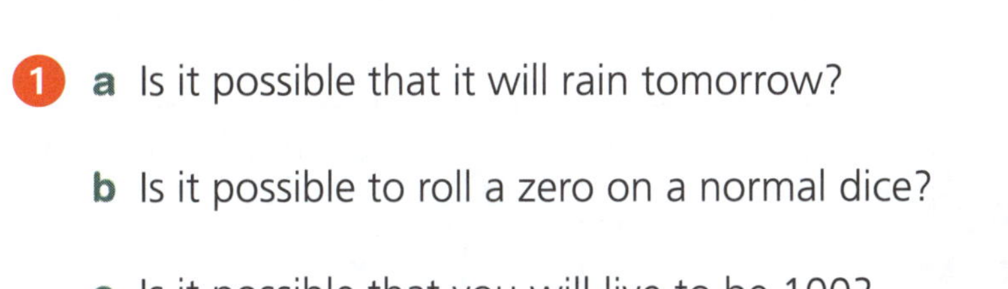

1 a Is it possible that it will rain tomorrow? ☐

b Is it possible to roll a zero on a normal dice? ☐

c Is it possible that you will live to be 100? ☐

2 a What are the possible outcomes if I play a board game?

☐

b What kinds of weather are possible for tomorrow?

☐

☐

3

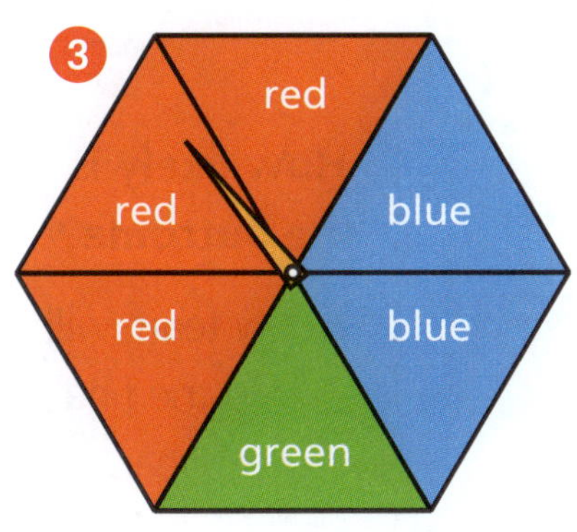

a List all possible outcomes for this spinner.

☐

b Which colour is most likely to be spun? ☐

c Which colour is least likely to be spun? ☐

d Is it possible to spin yellow? ☐

e Is there an even chance of spinning red? ☐

4 How likely is it that a three will be rolled on a dice and the three of diamonds will also be selected from the boy's hand?

☐

Possible answers: Impossible, highly unlikely, highly likely, certain

INVESTIGATION

- Toss a coin until you have tossed 3 heads.
  Have a friend count the number of tosses needed.
- Guess how many times it will take you to toss three heads next time.
- Repeat the experiment. It took ☐ tosses.

Chance outcomes

Choosing at random: Each outcome has the same chance of occurring.

1. List all possible outcomes when:

 **a** a coin is tossed.	 **b** a dice is rolled.	 **c** this spinner is spun.

2. List all possible outcomes if two counters are taken from the bag at random.

blue and blue	B B

3. List all possible outcomes if two counters are taken from the bag at random.

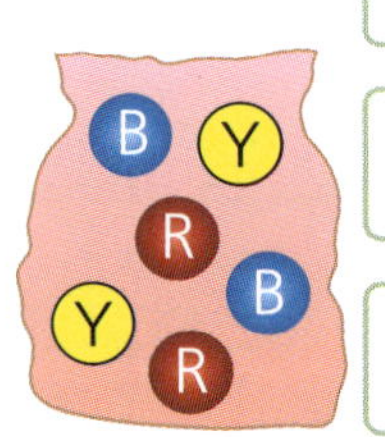

Y Y	

(Order doesn't matter.)

4. **a** Predict how many heads will be tossed in 12 tosses of a coin.

   Toss a coin 12 times. How many heads did you toss?

   b Predict how many sixes will be rolled in 12 rolls of a dice.

   Roll a dice 12 times. How many sixes did you roll?

   c One counter is taken at random from the bag in Question 2. This is done 12 times. How many blue counters would you predict?

   Place 3 blue and 3 red counters into a bag and take one at random, then return the counter.

   Do this 12 times. How many blue counters did you choose?

   d One counter is taken at random from the bag in Question 3. This is done 12 times. How many yellow counters would you predict?

   Place 2 blue, 2 red and 2 yellow counters into a bag and take one at random, then return the counter.

   Do this 12 times. How many yellow counters did you choose?

How likely is the outcome?

A My team will win the final next year.

B It will rain tomorrow.

C I will find an elephant in my hat.

5. How many different outfits can I wear if I have three different tops and two different pairs of shorts?

   a How many of these outfits have a blue item?

   b What is the chance of wearing blue or red?

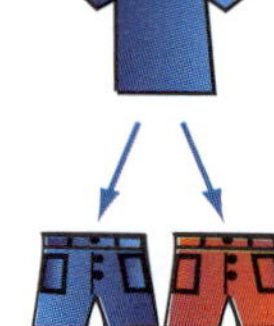

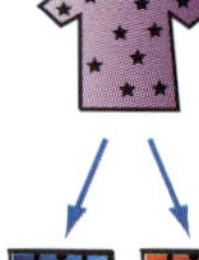

 • *AUSTRALIAN SIGNPOST MATHS NSW 3* • ISBN 9780655709046

Making graphs

A tally is used to record the data collected.

1. Tina rolled these dice. Finish the graph to show how many of each number she rolled.

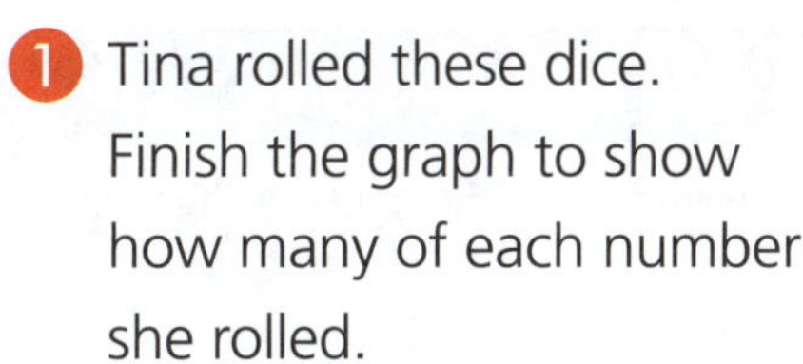

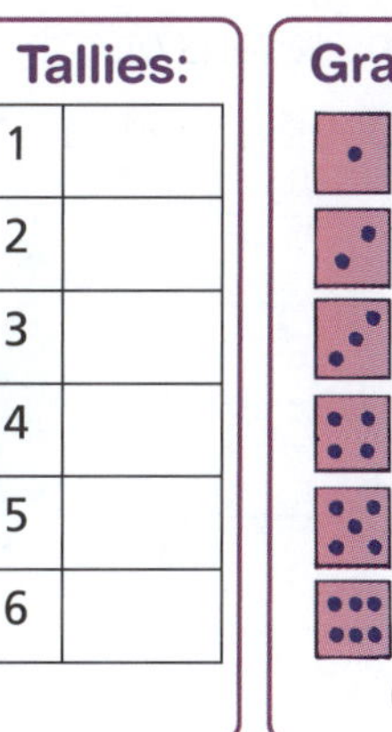

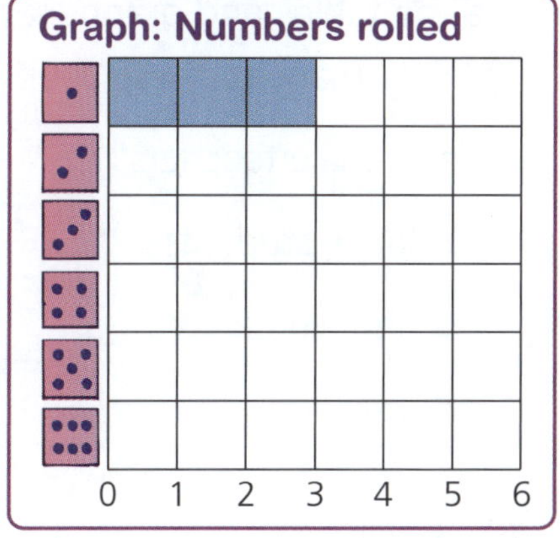

2. Gino made this table using tally marks. It shows the favourite game of each of his friends. Use this information to complete both graphs.

Game	Tally	Number
Handball	𝍸 III	8
Hopscotch	𝍸 II	7
Marbles	𝍸 𝍸	10
Skipping	IIII	4

Columns in a graph can go up or across.

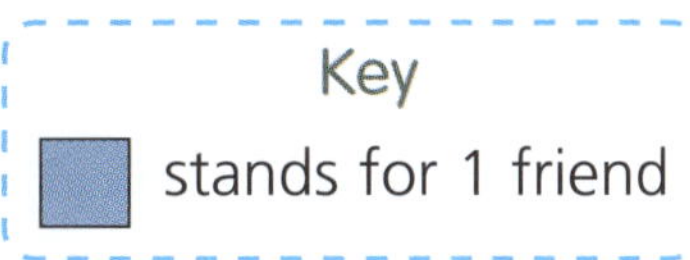

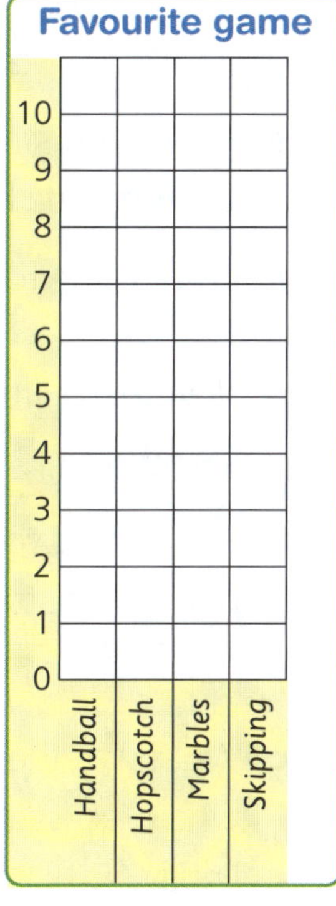

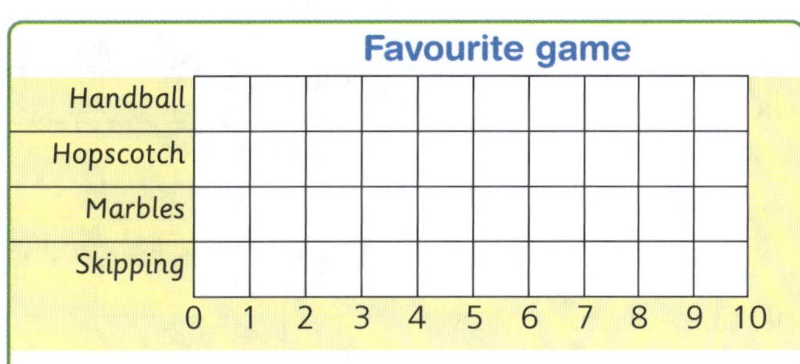

3.
- After talking to your friends, choose four popular games they like.
- Write them in the table and graph below.
- Ask people in your class to choose the game they like best out of the four games. Keep a tally of the answers in the table.
- Draw a graph to display the data.

Game	Tally	Total

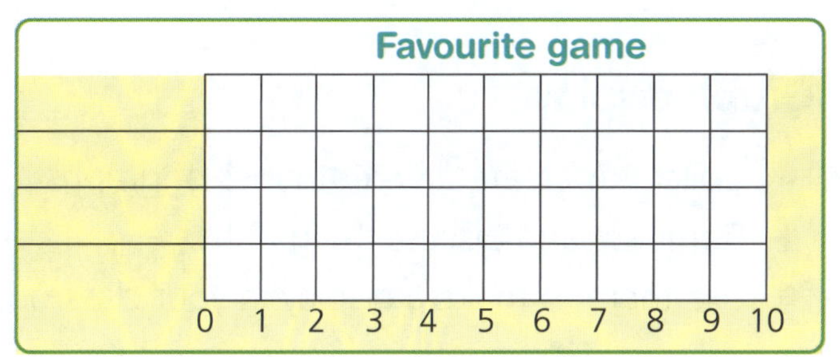

 • *AUSTRALIAN SIGNPOST MATHS NSW 3* • ISBN 9780655709046

5:09 Reading tables and graphs

Tables can be read across or down.

Use the tables and graphs to answer the questions.

1 How many of these people were at the play?

a female teachers ☐

b male students ☐

c female parents ☐

d teachers ☐

e males ☐

f altogether ☐

This is called a **two-way** table.

People at the school play

	Parents	Students	Teachers
Female	70	120	6
Male	80	100	4

2 **a** Who has the most merit stamps? ☐

b Who has the least stamps? ☐

c How many stamps does Adiva have? ☐

d How many stamps does Juan have? ☐

e How many stamps do Benjamin and Amanda have altogether? ☐

f What is the total number of stamps that Adiva and Brittany have? ☐

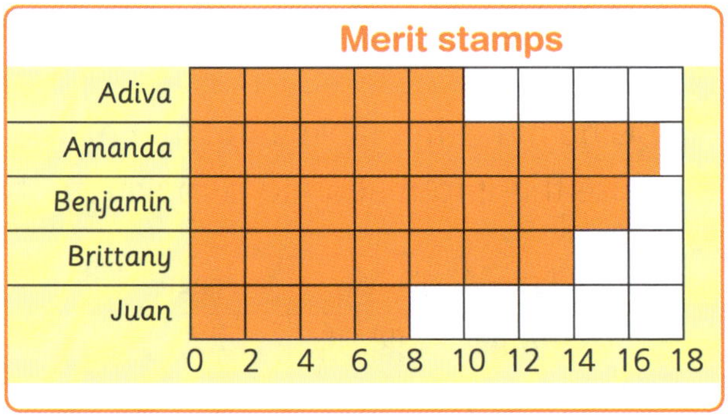

3 **a** How many students practised on:

Monday? ☐ Friday? ☐

b On which two days did the same number of students practise?

☐

c What was the total number of students who practised on Wednesday and Friday? ☐

d How many more students practised on Thursday than on Wednesday? ☐

e Can we tell how many different students practised during the week? ☐

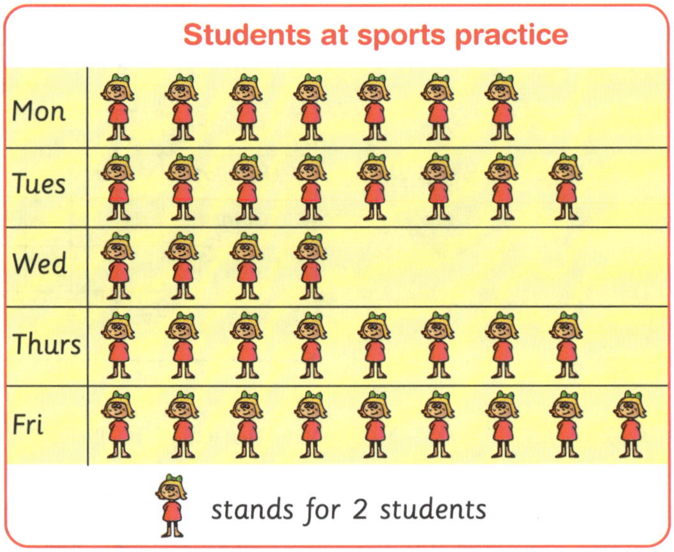

Graph display

- Collect or create different types of graphs.
- Compare and discuss the graphs.
- Use them to make a display in your classroom.

5:10 Dicey graphs

If I tossed a dice 10 times would I throw every number?

INVESTIGATION

Class investigation

Let's see what happens.

There is an equal chance of throwing each number on a dice but the results do not always show this.

Question: If we throw a dice many times would the number of 1s, 2s, 3s, 4s, 5s and 6s be very close? How close do you think?

Step 1: Form small groups in your class.

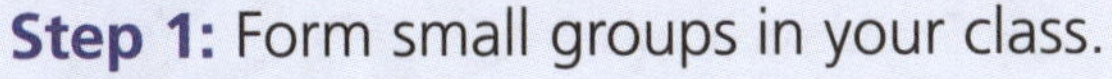

Step 2: In your group, toss a dice 100 times.

Step 3: Record the numbers thrown in the table.

My results for 100 throws

Number on dice	Tally	Total
1		
2		
3		
4		
5		
6		

1. How close are the totals?

Step 4: Use the table below to combine your results with the results of other groups.

2. How close are these totals?

Combined results

Number on dice	Results for our group	Results for group 1	Results for group 2	Results for group 3	Total
1					
2					
3					
4					
5					
6					

What did you find out?

Step 5: Graph the combined total and discuss the results.

The results for ____ throws

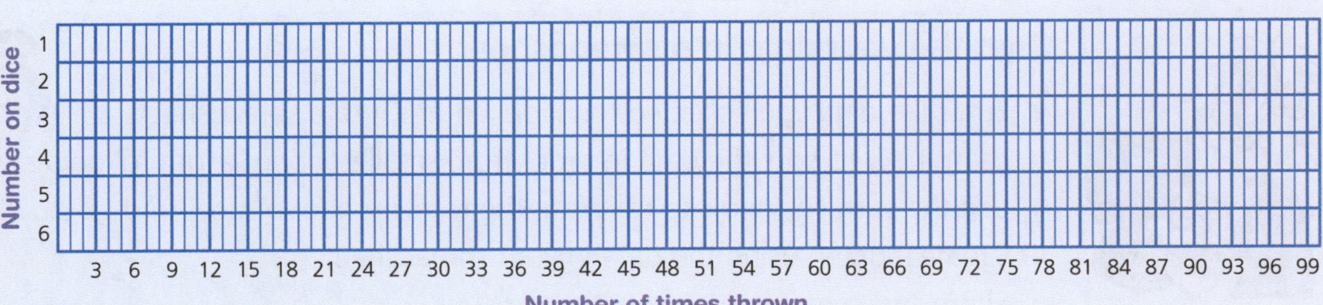

5:11 Class investigation

We need to decide on a question of interest first.

INVESTIGATION

Question of interest: Who has the longest and the shortest shoe, a boy or a girl?

Step 1: Ask for volunteers to take part (8 girls and 8 boys).

Each student taking part measures one of their shoes.

Step 2: Decide how you will measure the shoe lengths.

I will

Stand on a ruler? Trace your shoe?

Step 3: Predict who will have the longest shoe length, a boy or a girl?

Predict who will have the shortest shoe length, a boy or a girl?

Step 4: Each student measures and records their shoe length (to the nearest cm).

Shoe lengths of boys and girls

Measurement (cm)	Boys' tally	Total	Girls' tally	Total

This is an example of a spreadsheet.

Shoe lengths

cm	Boys	Girls
21		1
22	1	1
23	1	2
24	3	1
25	2	2
26		1
27	1	
Total	8	8

Step 5: Discuss your results.

The longest shoe length belonged to a ______.

The shortest shoe length belonged to a ______.

The steps are like a flowchart.

Organise your data in a spreadsheet.

ICT

- Enter the data you collected for shoe lengths into a spreadsheet.
- Learn how to **sort** the data in order from smallest shoe length to longest.
- Use the **sum function** to calculate the total number of boys and girls.
- Create a graph using the data in your spreadsheet.
- Share and compare graphs with your class.

 ISBN 9780655709046

Predicting outcomes

I predict that all of my guests will like gum leaves.

1 Without looking, Meg took a coloured ball from the beaker and did not replace it.

a Which colour is least likely to be taken?

b Which colour is most likely to be taken?

c Is there an even chance of taking a yellow ball?

d Could Meg take the red ball first?

e If Meg took the red ball first, what colours could she take next?

f If Meg took a blue ball first, what colours could she take next?

2 Put 1 yellow, 3 blue and 5 red counters into a bag. Pick one counter at random.

a Which colour is most likely to be picked?

b Which colour is least likely to be picked?

3 This spinner is spun 10 times.

a Would you be surprised if blue was spun every time?

Why or why not?

b If 3 blues are spun in a row, would this affect the chance of spinning a blue on the next spin? Why or why not?

4 a Are all three colours equally likely to be spun?

b How many red spins would you expect out of 6 spins?

- There would be 1 chance out of 243 of spinning 5 reds in a row. This is not impossible but it is highly unlikely.

INVESTIGATION

- Put 1 yellow, 3 blue and 5 red counters into a bag.
- Randomly pick one counter from the bag.
- Record a tally mark for that colour.
- Put the counter back in the bag.
- Repeat this experiment 50 times.
- What do the tallies show? Discuss your results.

Taking counters from a bag		
Blue		
Red		
Yellow		

 • *AUSTRALIAN SIGNPOST MATHS NSW 3* • ISBN 9780655709046

Statistics and probability

5:13 Ordering events

I'm more likely to see the next bird than he is.

1 Choose a label to match each statement.

impossible | unlikely | even chance | very likely | certain

a I bought a ticket in a raffle and I will win. ________

b Our next teacher will be six years old. ________

c The next school captain will be a student. ________

d If I drop an egg on the road, it will break. ________

e We will do maths on our next day at school. ________

f It will be warmer in December than in May. ________

g I will see a lion on the way home from school. ________

h This year, half the students in my class will grow tails. ________

i The next student I see will have been born after 1900. ________

j If I toss a coin, it will come up heads. ________

2 Write the letter of each part of Question 1 in the table below to show each statement's chance.

Will always happen	It can happen (but not always)	Will never happen

3 Put the following events in order from least likely to most likely.

Least likely → Most likely

A We will have an earthquake today.
B I will go to school in November.
C I will stay up late tonight.
D We will be given homework on our next school day.
E A dinosaur will walk into our classroom tomorrow.

FUN SPOT

- Use this picture to make up four events that could happen. For example, the man could drop the spinning plate.
- Write your four events in order from least likely to most likely.

 • *AUSTRALIAN SIGNPOST MATHS NSW 3* • ISBN 9780655709046

5:14 Drawing graphs

What is your favourite way to display data?

1 Kai-Lin kept a tally of the hair colour of students in her class. Use the table to finish the graph.

Hair colour	Tally	Number
Black	卌 卌 ||	12
Blonde	卌 卌	10
Brown	||||	4
Red	||	2

a Which colour was the most common?

b How many students had grey hair?

c How many more students had blonde hair than brown hair?

d How many students were there altogether?

e What is the key on the graph used for?

f Why do you think people use picture graphs?

Hair colour in Kai-Lin's class

Black	● ● ● ● ● ●
Blonde	
Brown	
Red	

Key: ● stands for 2 students

2 What are the advantages of showing information as a:

a tally?

b column graph?

c sector graph?

Cars washed		
Monday	Tuesday	Friday
6	8	4

Cars washed	
Monday	卌 |
Tuesday	卌 |||
Friday	||||

Cars washed (column graph)

Monday, Tuesday, Friday; scale 0 2 4 6 8 10

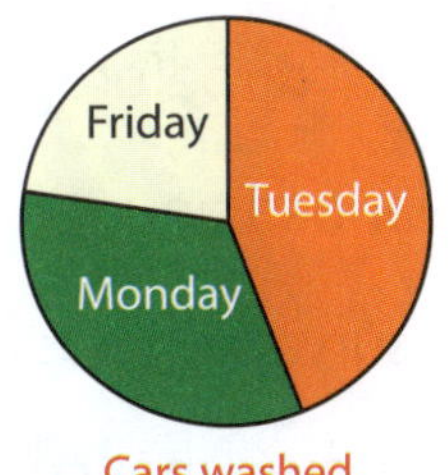

Cars washed

Cars washed

Monday	🚗 🚗 🚗
Tuesday	🚗 🚗 🚗 🚗
Friday	🚗 🚗

🚗 stands for 2 cars

Using computers

- Using a computer spreadsheet program, create a table to organise collected data for a question of interest.
- Use the spreadsheet program to make a variety of graphs from your data.
- Share and compare the graphs you made with your class.

5:15 Surveys

Do you like cats?
Yes ☐ No ☐

CONCEPT

- **Surveys** are used to discover information, to give us a general view of a situation or to check predictions.
- If everyone is surveyed from the group we wish to study, we have carried out a **census**.
- Surveys can be written or digital.

1 Jared chose as his survey topic: *The time my classmates go to bed.* He asked everyone in his class.

Jared's survey *When my classmates go to bed.*

Tick the box next to the time you went to bed last night.

- ☐ before 8 pm
- ☐ between 8 pm and 9 pm
- ☐ between 9 pm and 10 pm
- ☐ between 10 pm and 11 pm
- ☐ after 11 pm

Jared's results	*When my classmates go to bed.*
before 8 pm	卌 卌 |||
between 8 pm and 9 pm	卌 卌
between 9 pm and 10 pm	||||
between 10 pm and 11 pm	||
after 11 pm	|

How many students went to bed:

a before 8 pm? ☐ **b** between 9 pm and 10 pm? ☐

c after 11 pm? ☐ **d** before 9 pm? ☐ **e** before 11 pm? ☐

f What was the most popular bed time? ☐

g How many students were surveyed altogether? ☐ Was this a census? ☐

h Make up a question of your own that could be answered using these results.

☐

2 Write down a topic that you would like to use in a survey of your class.

☐

Write two questions you would like to ask about this topic.

a ☐

b ☐

5:16 Carry out your own survey

Do you like dogs?
Yes ☐ No ☐

INVESTIGATION

Step 1: Choose a topic you are interested in for your survey.

Topic:

Step 2: Write a question to ask people about your topic.

Question:

Step 3: Decide how you will collect and record the answers (data).

Step 4: Predict what the data will show.

I think

Step 5: Represent your results using tables and graphs. (You could use technology to do this.)

Step 6: Reflect and write what you have learnt from your data.

I found

Step 7: Share your results.

Reflection: Was using a survey useful? What did you do well and what could you do better next time? What other topics could you research using a survey?

ICT

- Research written and online surveys.
- Learn about the Australian census and research some data that has been collected.
- Use a digital tool such as Google Forms, Microsoft Forms, Kahoot or Survey Monkey.

 • • ISBN 9780655709046

5:17 Researching data

Each graph needs a title.
There are many
data displays online.

1

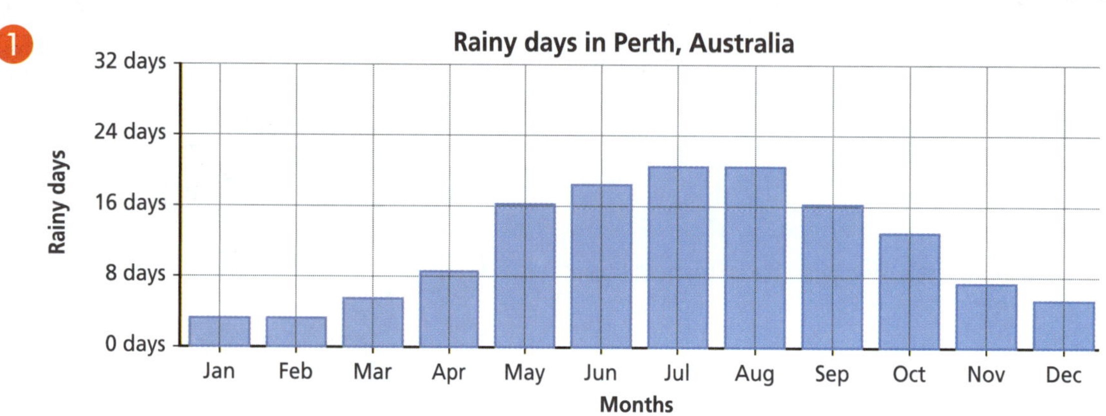

a Which months had the least rainy days in Perth?

b How many days did it rain in May?

c Which season had the most rainy days?

d Which two months had closest to 8 days of rain?

e Is it possible that June had more rain than August?

2

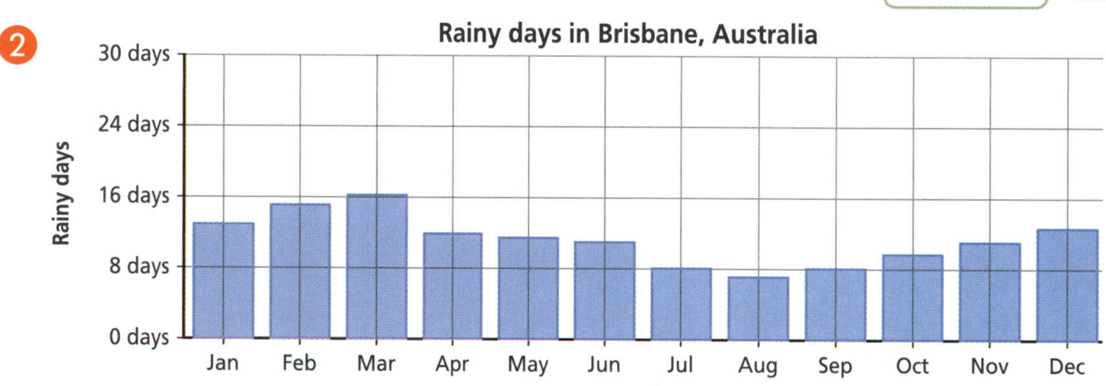

a Which month had:

i) the most rainy days?

ii) the least rainy days?

b Which season had the most rainy days in Brisbane?

c How is the rainfall for Brisbane different from the rainfall for Perth, shown in Question 1.

Let's research data!

Step 1: Select a topic of interest.

Step 2: Search online for data displays of your topic.

Step 3: Discuss and share what you found.

You could research weather records, data collected in the census or Google trends.

5:18 Repeating an experiment

In Question 2, you are asked to repeat the experiment.

CONCEPT

If we toss 4 coins, we are most likely to get **2 heads** and **2 tails** but this might not happen often.

The other possibilities are on the right.

1. Coin experiment:
   - Toss 4 coins at once.
   - Count the number of heads.
   - Write the result in the tally table.
   - Do this 16 times.

Tally		
0 heads		
1 head		
2 heads		

Tally		
3 heads		
4 heads		

What did you discover?

2. The letter most used in books is a vowel.
   Discover which one it is.
   Method: Select 3 lines of text (or use 3 lines from the *Investigation* below.
   Use this dot plot to show how many times each vowel is used.
   Results: The vowel that occurred the most is ______.
   - Do this again using 10 different lines of text. This time use a tally to record data.

a e i o u

Vowels used

INVESTIGATION

Paper experiment

- Procedure:
  - Choose 3 sheets of different coloured paper.
  - From each sheet cut 7 squares.
  - Put the 21 paper squares into a box or bag.
  - Without looking, take out 10 squares, one at a time.
  - Put the 10 squares in three columns, one for each colour. This is a column graph.
  - Compare your graph with Joe's graph.
  - Compare your graph with others in the class.
- Glue your graph into your book.
- Take another 10 squares from your box or bag. Make another graph and compare it with your first graph.

Joe's graph

Extra Support 1

Addition and subtraction facts

Learn the addition facts first.

Memorise your addition facts up to 10 + 10.

CONCEPT

- If 6 + 7 = 13, then 13 – 6 = 7 and 13 – 7 = 6.
- If 8 + 9 = 17, then 17 – 8 = 9 and 17 – 9 = 8.

1 Join each question to the correct answer using a pencil. You could practise your tables facts by rubbing out your answers and doing them again.

a +

2 + 6	1
4 + 6	7
0 + 1	8
5 + 7	9
5 + 6	10
0 + 7	11
4 + 5	12
7 + 10	15
8 + 7	17
10 + 10	18
9 + 9	20
Scores:	

b +

2 + 3	4
4 + 3	5
2 + 2	7
5 + 4	9
8 + 5	8
8 + 0	10
7 + 5	11
1 + 9	12
10 + 5	13
6 + 5	15
10 + 9	19
Scores:	

c +

3 + 6	6
2 + 8	7
4 + 2	8
5 + 2	9
4 + 7	10
3 + 5	11
9 + 6	12
6 + 6	13
8 + 8	14
7 + 6	15
10 + 4	16
Scores:	

d +

3 + 4	5
6 + 2	6
4 + 5	7
3 + 2	8
2 + 4	9
8 + 4	10
4 + 9	11
5 + 5	12
4 + 7	13
7 + 8	14
5 + 9	15
Scores:	

e –

8 – 6	1
10 – 4	0
1 – 0	2
12 – 5	4
11 – 6	6
7 – 7	5
9 – 5	7
17 – 7	8
15 – 7	10
11 – 8	9
18 – 9	3
Scores:	

f –

5 – 2	2
7 – 3	3
4 – 2	4
9 – 4	5
13 – 5	0
8 – 8	1
12 – 5	6
10 – 9	7
15 – 5	8
11 – 5	10
19 – 10	9
Scores:	

g –

6 – 4	0
5 – 2	1
10 – 9	2
7 – 7	3
9 – 3	4
7 – 3	5
10 – 3	6
14 – 5	7
9 – 4	8
18 – 8	9
10 – 2	10
Scores:	

h –

6 – 5	0
9 – 9	1
6 – 3	2
8 – 6	3
8 – 4	4
16 – 9	5
9 – 4	6
16 – 7	7
17 – 7	8
10 – 4	9
17 – 9	10
Scores:	

See 2:03 (Addition and subtraction).

Addition facts to 20

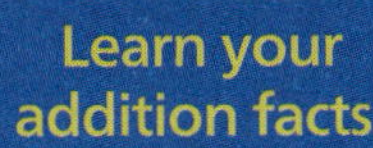

1										
A	1 + 1		2 + 4		5 + 1		2 + 3		4 + 5	
B	3 + 4		0 + 4		3 + 1		1 + 6		2 + 5	
C	0 + 7		7 + 1		1 + 3		2 + 6		3 + 6	
D	7 + 0		9 + 3		2 + 7		3 + 5		6 + 5	
E	4 + 1		8 + 3		0 + 5		9 + 0		9 + 4	
F	2 + 2		3 + 7		6 + 3		6 + 0		5 + 2	
G	5 + 3		3 + 2		2 + 8		4 + 2		1 + 7	
H	5 + 5		8 + 2		6 + 4		4 + 4		7 + 2	
I	4 + 3		5 + 4		7 + 3		6 + 2		6 + 6	
J	1 + 8		2 + 1		6 + 1		3 + 3		4 + 6	
K	7 + 7		9 + 1		5 + 6		1 + 4		9 + 9	
L	8 + 1		1 + 2		4 + 8		6 + 7		9 + 8	
M	1 + 5		0 + 9		8 + 8		8 + 0		1 + 9	
N	9 + 2		8 + 4		4 + 7		7 + 9		9 + 6	
O	7 + 6		2 + 9		7 + 4		3 + 8		5 + 7	
P	3 + 9		4 + 0		9 + 7		6 + 8		5 + 9	
Q	8 + 6		4 + 9		8 + 7		5 + 8		7 + 5	
R	7 + 8		8 + 9		8 + 5		6 + 9		9 + 5	

See 2:03 (Addition and subtraction).

 • *AUSTRALIAN SIGNPOST MATHS NSW 3* • ISBN 9780655709046

Subtraction facts to 20

Use your addition facts to do subtraction.

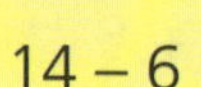

14 – 6 ☐

Ask:
6 plus what makes 14?

6 + ☐ = 14

9	?
16	

16 – 9 ☐

Ask:
9 plus what makes 16?

9 + ☐ = 16

You could also use the number line.

0 1 2 3 4 5 6 7 8 9 10 11 12 13 14 15 16 17 18 19 20

1

A	14 – 7 ☐	12 – 3 ☐	11 – 6 ☐	18 – 9 ☐
B	12 – 8 ☐	13 – 7 ☐	17 – 8 ☐	16 – 8 ☐
C	10 – 9 ☐	10 – 3 ☐	12 – 3 ☐	11 – 5 ☐
D	11 – 3 ☐	13 – 4 ☐	10 – 5 ☐	10 – 8 ☐
E	11 – 2 ☐	12 – 4 ☐	11 – 7 ☐	16 – 9 ☐
F	13 – 6 ☐	11 – 9 ☐	11 – 4 ☐	11 – 8 ☐
G	14 – 6 ☐	13 – 9 ☐	15 – 7 ☐	13 – 8 ☐
H	10 – 7 ☐	16 – 7 ☐	14 – 8 ☐	15 – 9 ☐
I	15 – 6 ☐	10 – 4 ☐	12 – 7 ☐	14 – 9 ☐
J	12 – 9 ☐	14 – 5 ☐	12 – 5 ☐	12 – 6 ☐
K	13 – 5 ☐	10 – 6 ☐	15 – 8 ☐	17 – 9 ☐

See 2:03 (Addition and subtraction).

 • *AUSTRALIAN SIGNPOST MATHS NSW 3* • ISBN 9780655709046

Know your addition facts

+	1	2	3	4	5	6	7	8	9	10
1	2	3	4	5	6	7	8	9	10	11
2	3	4	5	6	7	8	9	10	11	12
3	4	5	6	7	8	9	10	11	12	13
4	5	6	7	8	9	10	11	12	13	14
5	6	7	8	9	10	11	12	13	14	15
6	7	8	9	10	11	12	13	14	15	16
7	8	9	10	11	12	13	14	15	16	17
8	9	10	11	12	13	14	15	16	17	18
9	10	11	12	13	14	15	16	17	18	19
10	11	12	13	14	15	16	17	18	19	20

- Learn the addition tables with answers up to 10. (**2 + 5 = 5 + 2 = 7**)
- Learn the addition tables with answers up to 20. (**7 + 6 = 6 + 7 = 13**)
- Learn your doubles and halves.

7	6
6	7

Numbers	1	2	3	4	5	6	7	8	9	10
Doubles	2	4	6	8	10	12	14	16	18	20

4 + 4 = 8 **double 4 = 8** **2 × 4 = 8**

Numbers	2	4	6	8	10	12	14	16	18	20
Halves	1	2	3	4	5	6	7	8	9	10

half of 10 = 5 **10 ÷ 2 = 5**

See 2:03 (Addition and subtraction).

 • *AUSTRALIAN SIGNPOST MATHS NSW 3* • ISBN 9780655709046

Extra Support 5

Addition problems to 99

Round off to the nearest 10 when checking answers.

Problem solving

How many pencils does Maddy have if she has 24 in her bag and 47 in her desk?

Find: How many pencils?

Number sentence: 24 + 47 = ☐

Answer: Maddy has 71 pencils.

Working

tens	ones
1	
2	4
+ 4	7
7	1

1 Answer these questions, setting them out as shown above.

Use these blanks for working. Work in pencil so they can be reused.

- **a** Luke's test had 27 mistakes. Naomi's had 22 mistakes. How many mistakes do they have altogether? ☐ mistakes
- **b** Brianna had 56 pet ants. Jordan caught 8 more and gave them to her. How many did she have then? ☐ ants
- **c** Wen, an ancient Chinese king, began the first zoo 3000 years ago. He received 56 animals from the north and 27 from the south. How many animals did he receive altogether? ☐ animals
- **d** At night, an owl can see about 100 times better than a human. In one week an owl caught 53 mice. In the next week it caught 38. How many mice did it catch altogether? ☐ mice
- **e** At a waterhole, Michelle photographed 31 magpie geese, 12 Burdekin ducks and 8 pied herons. How many birds did she photograph altogether? ☐ birds
- **f** A family of 18 bandicoots lived near 13 possums and 6 native rats. How many animals were there altogether? ☐ animals

2
- **a** Alan saw three varieties of finch in one paddock. There were 35 zebra finches, 15 double-bar finches and 27 spice finches. How many were there altogether? ☐ finches
- **b** On Phillip Island, 37 penguins came ashore before 6 pm. In the next hour 18 more arrived. How many had arrived by 7 pm? ☐ penguins
- **c** Consecutive numbers follow one after the other. Find the sum of the consecutive numbers 28, 29 and 30. ☐ is the sum
- **d** In a Test cricket series, Eric batted three times. His scores were 44, 28 and 19. What was his total score? ☐ runs

tens	ones

tens	ones

tens	ones

See 2:40 (Addition to 99 with trading), 2:41 (Addition with trading), 2:42 (Addition with 2-digit numbers).

Addition to 999

H stands for hundreds.
T stands for tens.
U stands for units (or ones)

CONCEPT

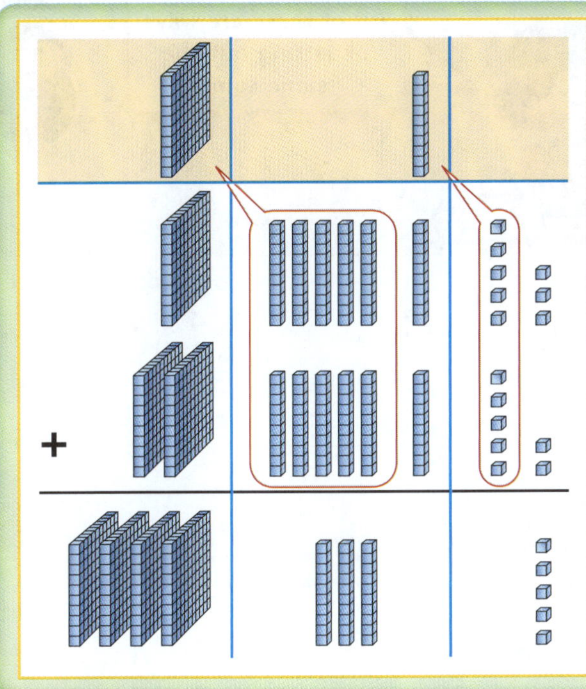

168 sheep and 267 cattle are on sale.
How many animals are there altogether?

H	T	U
1	1	
1	6	8
+ 2	6	7
4	3	5

There are 435 animals altogether.
We can check the answer by rounding to the nearest 100 (or 10).
200 + 300 = 500
435 is reasonably close to 500.

1

a

H	T	U
	6	1
+	9	3

b

H	T	U
	7	2
+	4	5

c

H	T	U
	3	0
+	7	8

d

H	T	U
2	5	8
+	2	5

e

H	T	U
	7	6
+ 7	1	4

f

H	T	U
3	6	9
+	1	9

g

H	T	U
4	3	6
+	8	0

h

H	T	U
4	2	5
+	8	5

i

H	T	U
	8	7
+ 3	4	1

j

H	T	U
1	8	8
+ 1	4	3

k

H	T	U
3	6	5
+ 1	4	9

l

H	T	U
4	5	9
+ 2	7	4

2 Check your answers by rounding each number to the nearest 100 (or 10) then adding.

See 2:43–2:45 (Addition to 999 with trading).

 • *AUSTRALIAN SIGNPOST MATHS NSW 3* • ISBN 9780655709046

Writing the addition algorithm

Be careful to keep your columns aligned.

583 apples and 179 oranges were sold. How many pieces of fruit were sold altogether?

All of these are ways of setting out the same sum.

CONCEPT

Hund	Tens	Ones
1	1	
5	8	3
+ 1	7	9
7	6	2

H	T	U
1	1	
5	8	3
+ 1	7	9
7	6	2

1	1	
5	8	3
+ 1	7	9
7	6	2

762 pieces of fruit were sold altogether.

1

a 250 + 84	**b** 534 + 128	**c** 154 + 207	**d** 92 + 340	**e** 245 + 370
f 365 + 166	**g** 209 + 583	**h** 345 + 312	**i** 507 + 220	**j** 365 + 397
k 188 + 133	**l** 365 + 366	**m** 509 + 296	**n** 381 + 259	**o** 777 + 185

2 Estimate each answer and use the estimate to check your answers.

a Luke watched 287 minutes of television on Saturday and 145 minutes on Sunday. How much did he watch altogether? Give your answer in minutes. ☐ minutes

b The attendances at two concerts on Sunday were 156 and 218. How many people attended altogether? ☐ people

c This year farmer McDonald sold 180 bags of corn. Last year he sold 17 bags more than this. How many bags were sold in the two years? ☐ bags

d Rex and Lyn bought the house next door and added 346 square metres to their original block of 575 square metres. How large is the block now? ☐ square metres

3 Use estimation to check your answers to Question 1.

See 2:43–2:45 (Addition to 999 with trading).

Addition of money

A decimal point (or full stop) separates the dollars and cents.
10 lots of 10 cents make 1 dollar.

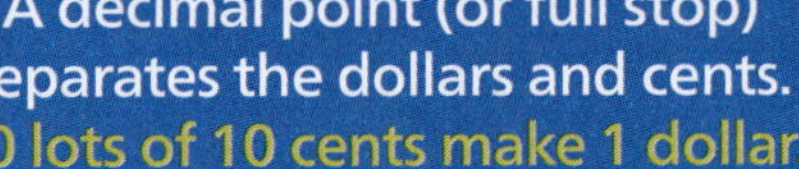

1

a $0.41 + $0.37	**b** $0.64 + $0.88	**c** $1.26 + $3.47	**d** $2.24 + $3.07	**e** $3.75 + $2.94
f $4.69 + $3.56	**g** $2.63 + $2.07	**h** $5.83 + $2.68	**i** $4.96 + $1.47	**j** $2.79 + $4.32
k $2.41 + $3.67	**l** $4.06 + $2.91	**m** $3.77 + $1.63	**n** $1.92 + $4.37	**o** $5.16 + $1.98

2 Write each as an algorithm or use a mental strategy to find your answer.

a $1.56 + $2.23 ______ **b** $4.01 + $1.76 ______

c $3.51 + $2.17 ______ **d** $5.03 + $3.65 ______

e $2.37 + $4.12 ______ **f** $6.45 + $2.03 ______

3 Find the total cost if I bought:

a a cake for $5.50 and a drink for $4.05. ______

b a dessert for $4.95 and a drink for $3.25. ______

c a sandwich for $7.30 and a drink for $1.55. ______

d a biscuit for $3.75 and a drink for $4.95. ______

4

a $2.21 + $0.85 + $1.82	**b** $1.61 + $3.17 + $4.05	**c** $4.68 + $1.83 + $2.86	**d** $5.91 + $1.45 + $1.65

See 2:43–2:45 (Addition to 999 with trading).

 • *AUSTRALIAN SIGNPOST MATHS NSW 3* • ISBN 9780655709046

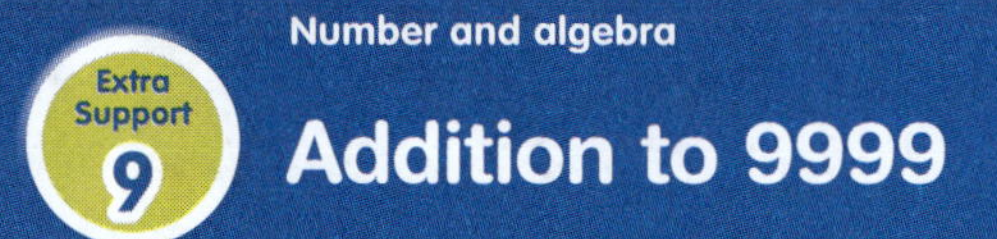

Addition to 9999

Th means thousands.
H means hundreds.
T means tens.
U means ones.

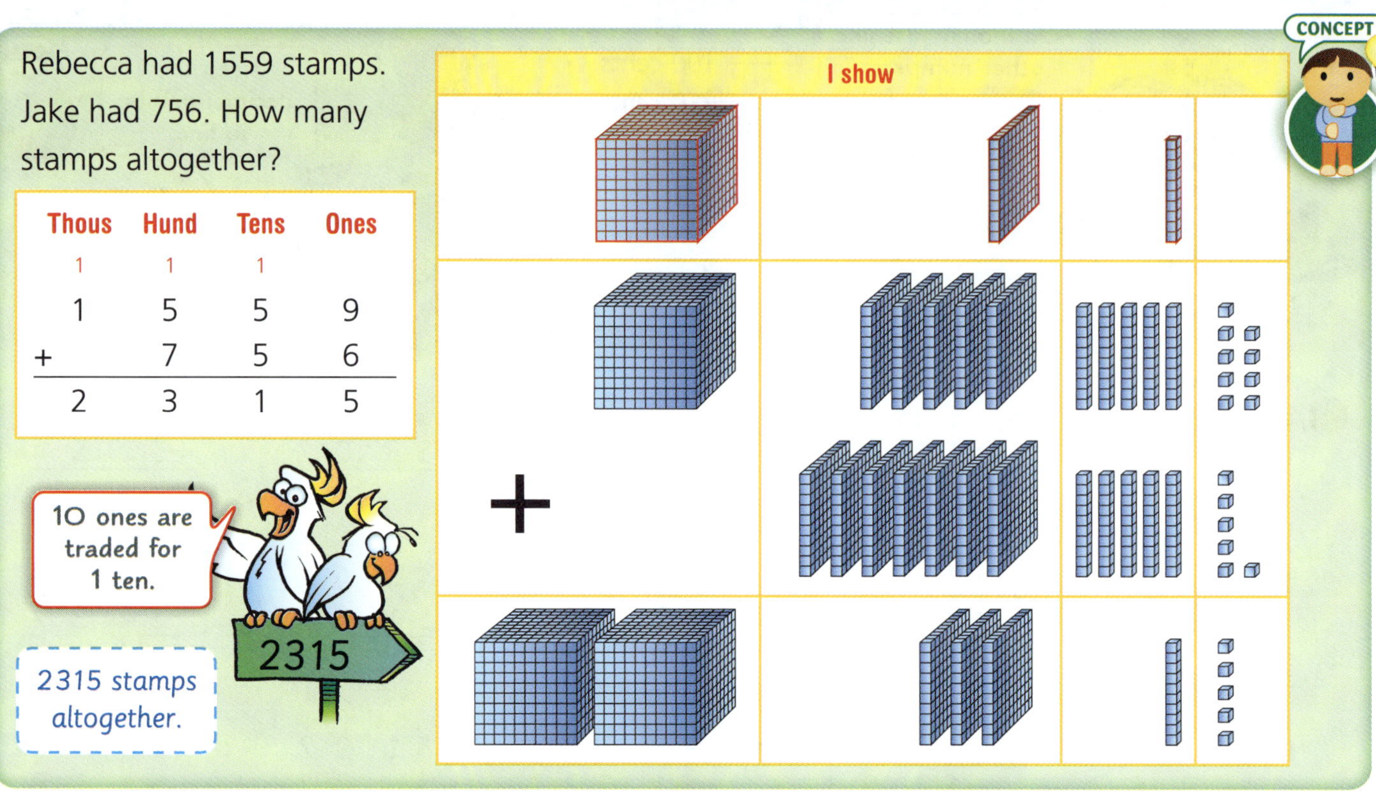

Rebecca had 1559 stamps. Jake had 756. How many stamps altogether?

	Thous	Hund	Tens	Ones
	1	1	1	
	1	5	5	9
+		7	5	6
	2	3	1	5

2315 stamps altogether.

1

	Th H T U		Th H T U		Th H T U		Th H T U		Th H T U
a	3416 + 2052	b	8104 + 871	c	6318 + 1270	d	392 + 3406	e	35 + 7932
f	3418 + 2906	g	7950 + 650	h	6087 + 1164	i	946 + 2627	j	6492 + 1748

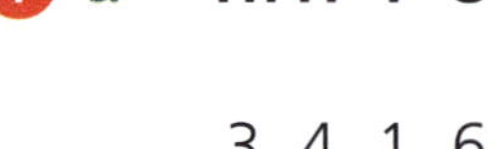

2

a	5071 + 2124	b	3831 + 1054	c	2516 + 1827	d	3195 + 5730	e	7041 + 978
f	4692 + 2813	g	7472 + 1809	h	479 + 3860	i	1793 + 5824	j	6097 + 1835

3

a	$7542 + $1607	b	$6549 + $1742	c	$3581 + $4328	d	$2591 + $3706	e	$7059 + $2371

See 2:43–2:45 (Addition to 999 with trading).

 • *AUSTRALIAN SIGNPOST MATHS NSW 3* • ISBN 9780655709046

Addition to 9999

13 hundreds
= 1 thousand + 3 hundreds

CONCEPT

I have three stamp albums. In the first is 3087 stamps, in the second 1872 stamps and in the third 4378. How many stamps do I have altogether?

How many stamps?

3087 + 1872 + 4378 =

Answer

I have 9337 stamps.

	Thous	Hund	Tens	Ones
	1	2	1	
	3	0	8	7
	1	8	7	2
+	4	3	7	8
	9	3	3	7

1 a

	Th	H	T	U
	1	8	3	5
		4	0	8
+	5	3	1	8

b

	Th	H	T	U
		9	9	9
	4	2	5	6
+	1	6	8	0

c

	Th	H	T	U
	8	4	1	8
		6	4	7
+		7	5	3

d

	Th	H	T	U
	3	8	4	2
		7	0	6
+	2	9	3	4

2 a

```
   386
  2514
   977
+   27
```

b

```
   183
   964
  1863
+ 2098
```

c

```
  5142
   863
   744
+ 1088
```

d

```
  2099
  1847
  1935
+ 1207
```

3 a

```
 $61.29
 $13.91
+$10.94
```

b

```
 $28.18
 $14.63
+$ 9.72
```

c

```
 $ 8.47
 $60.08
+$21.55
```

d

```
 $28.47
 $29.66
+$28.67
```

4 Estimate then calculate. (E = estimate, A = answer)

a Residents were phoned at 3187 homes in Bendigo, 1394 in Ballarat and 914 in Geelong. How many residents were phoned? E = ______ A = ______

b A bookshop kept 3096 books in room A, 2515 in room B and 2845 in room C. How many books were in the three rooms? E = ______ A = ______

c Sandy spent $3245 renovating her laundry, $2188 on landscaping and $2840 on furniture. How much did she spend? E = ______ A = ______

See 2:43–2:45 (Addition to 999 with trading).

 • *AUSTRALIAN SIGNPOST MATHS NSW 3* • ISBN 9780655709046

Subtraction, no trading to 999

'hund' means hundreds.

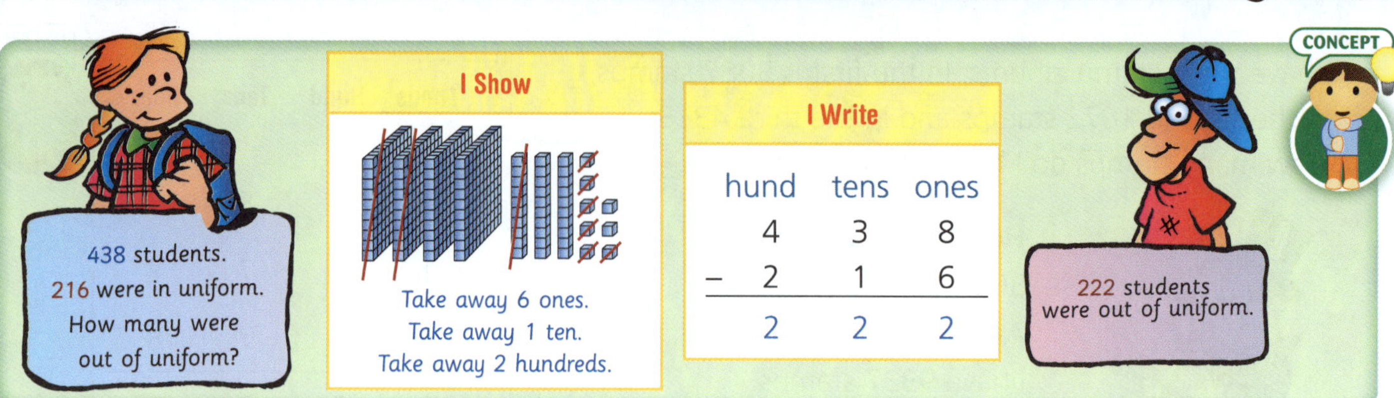

1 **a**

4 hundreds	7 tens	6 ones
– 2 hundreds	3 tens	1 one

b

8 hundreds	9 tens	7 ones
– 2 hundreds	5 tens	2 ones

2 **a**

	hund	tens	ones
	8	5	2
–	7	2	1

b

	hund	tens	ones
	9	6	7
–	2	3	4

c

	hund	tens	ones
	9	9	8
–	4	6	5

d

	hund	tens	ones
	3	4	2
–		1	1

e

	hund	tens	ones
	6	9	8
–		2	4

f

	hund	tens	ones
	9	4	5
–		4	3

g

	hund	tens	ones
	6	8	6
–			4

h

	hund	tens	ones
	7	4	7
–		3	4

i

	hund	tens	ones
	3	6	9
–			7

j

	hund	tens	ones
	5	5	9
–	4	3	0

k

	hund	tens	ones
	1	7	3
–		5	0

l

	hund	tens	ones
	6	4	6
–	2	0	3

m

	hund	tens	ones
	7	7	8
–	6	0	0

n

	hund	tens	ones
	5	2	9
–	1	2	9

o

	hund	tens	ones
	5	8	7
–	3	8	2

Estimate to check each answer.

- Make up a problem to match each of parts **e** to **h**, in Question 2 above.

See 2:46–2:48 (Subtraction no trading).

Subtraction, one trade to 999

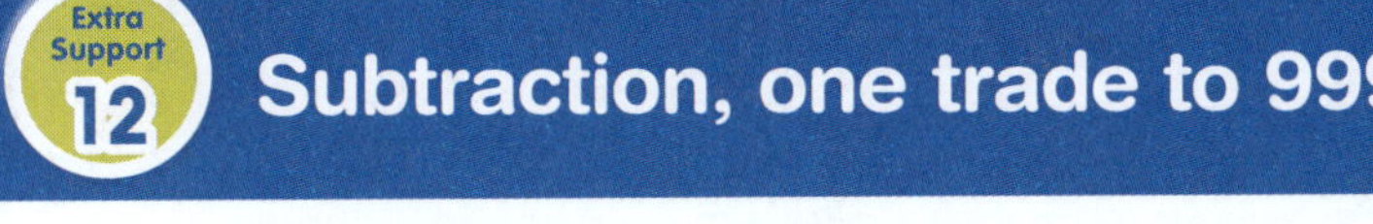

8 tens is the same as 7 tens and 10 ones.

CONCEPT

28 of my 384 stamps are Chinese. How many are not Chinese?

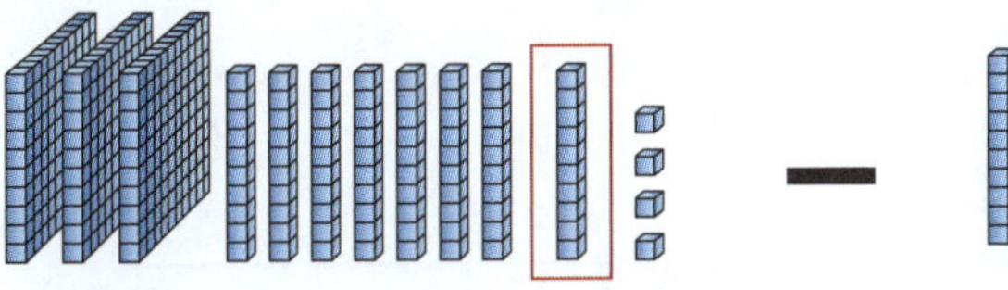

We can't take 8 ones from 4 ones, so trade 1 ten for 10 ones.

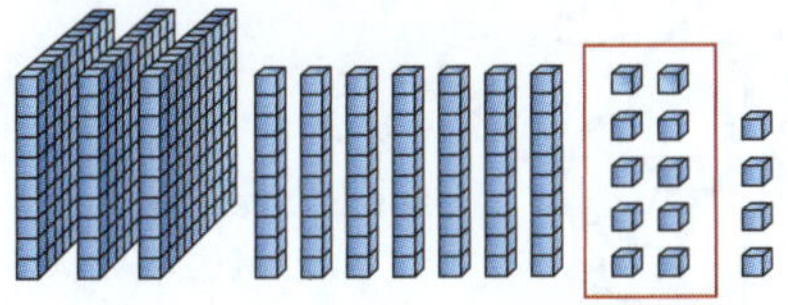

356 stamps are not Chinese.

From this we take 2 tens and 8 ones.

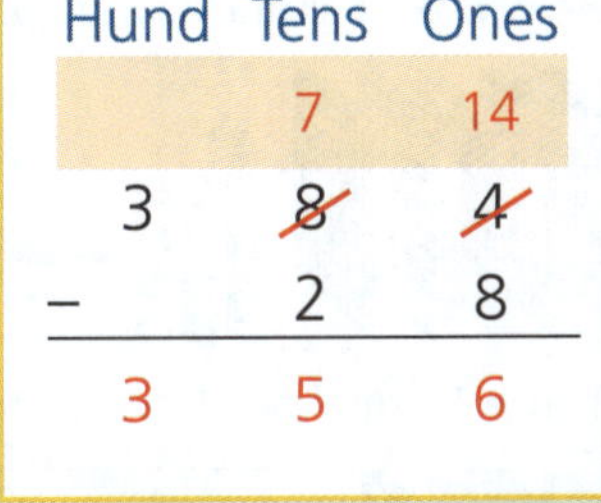

	Hund	Tens	Ones
		7	14
	3	~~8~~	~~4~~
−		2	8
	3	5	6

1

a
	H	T	U
	5	8	1
−		5	3

b
	H	T	U
	3	4	3
−		2	8

c
	H	T	U
	2	9	6
−		6	7

d
	H	T	U
	4	6	0
−		3	9

e
	H	T	U
	2	7	3
−			9

f
	H	T	U
	1	6	6
−		5	8

g
	H	T	U
	8	4	4
−			8

h
	H	T	U
	9	7	3
−		6	5

i
	H	T	U
	7	5	0
−		3	9

j
	H	T	U
	3	4	1
−		2	6

k
	H	T	U
	2	8	0
−		3	2

l
	H	T	U
	6	4	7
−		1	9

m
	8	3	5
−	1	0	8

n
	8	9	1
−	8	3	6

o
	5	2	0
−	4	1	5

p
	6	8	4
−		7	6

q
	2	1	4
−	2	0	8

r
	7	8	4
−		5	0

s
	3	9	1
−	3	7	5

t
	6	6	4
−	5	5	7

2 Check your answers to Question 1 by rounding the numbers to the nearest 100 (or 10).

See 2:46–2:48 (Subtraction with trading).

 • *AUSTRALIAN SIGNPOST MATHS NSW 3* • ISBN 9780655709046

Subtraction, one trade to 999

Trade 1 hundred for 10 tens.

CONCEPT

354 of the 718 birds in the zoo are parrots. How many are not parrots?

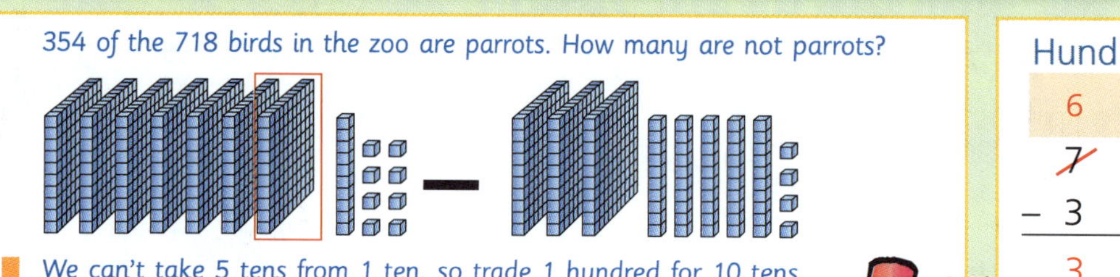

We can't take 5 tens from 1 ten, so trade 1 hundred for 10 tens.

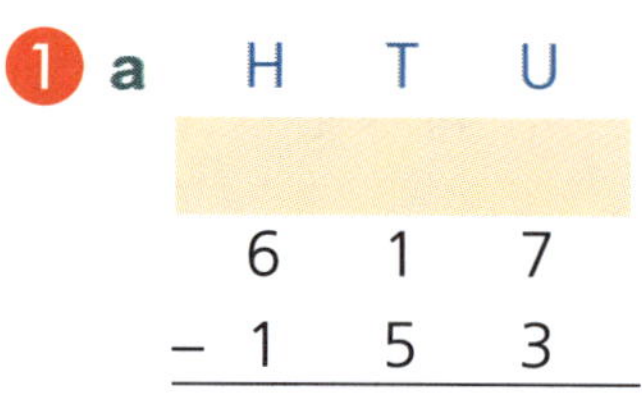

From this we take 3 hundreds, 5 tens and 4 ones.

	Hund	Tens	Ones
	6	11	
	~~7~~	~~1~~	8
−	3	5	4
	3	6	4

364 of the birds are not parrots.

1

a)

	H	T	U
	6	1	7
−	1	5	3

b)

	H	T	U
	8	2	6
−	5	7	1

c)

	H	T	U
	4	3	4
−	2	4	0

d)

	H	T	U
	7	2	9
−		3	8

e)

	H	T	U
	5	2	8
−	1	5	2

f)

	H	T	U
	6	0	7
−	3	5	2

g)

	H	T	U
	6	8	5
−		9	1

h)

	H	T	U
	2	1	5
−	1	7	5

i)

	H	T	U
	4	3	9
−	1	5	0

j)

	H	T	U
	6	1	7
−	3	2	6

k)

	H	T	U
	5	0	4
−	1	9	2

l)

	H	T	U
	9	0	9
−	3	4	7

m)
```
   7 0 8
 − 1 3 3
```

n)
```
   9 1 6
 − 8 3 6
```

o)
```
   6 0 8
 − 4 1 5
```

p)
```
   7 2 9
 − 2 7 6
```

q)
```
   4 0 7
 − 2 1 7
```

r)
```
   9 2 4
 − 5 6 0
```

s)
```
   8 6 6
 − 3 7 5
```

Use rounding to check your answers.

See 2:46–2:48 (Subtraction with trading).

Subtraction, two trades to 999

Trade 1 ten for 10 ones.
Trade 1 hundred for 10 tens.

CONCEPT

I had $524 and spent $245. How much do I have left?

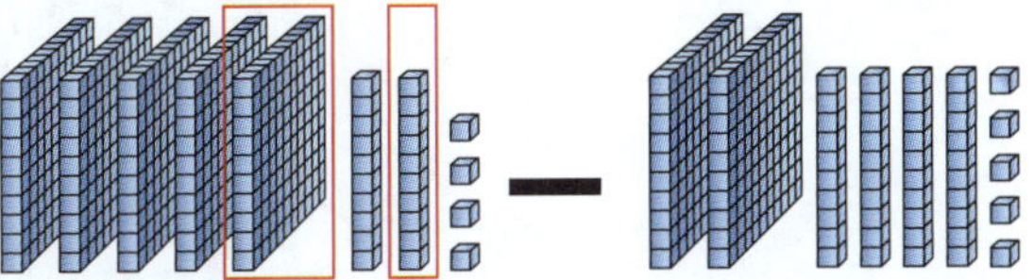

I trade 1 ten for 10 ones, and 1 hundred for 10 tens.

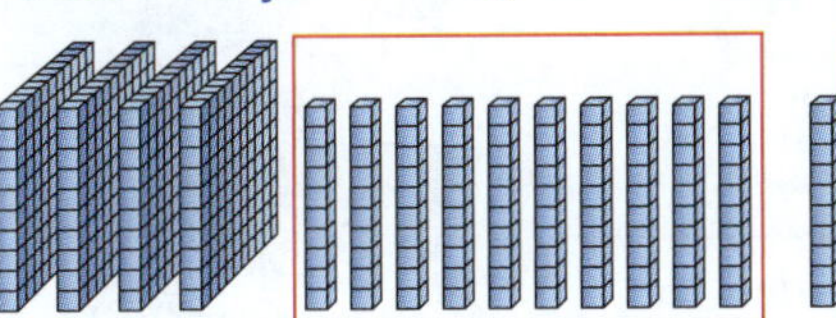

From this we take 2 hundreds, 4 tens and 5 ones.

Hund	Tens	Ones
	11	
4	~~1~~	14
~~5~~	~~2~~	~~4~~
− 2	4	5
2	7	9

I had $279 left.

Use rounding to check your answers.

1

	H	T	U
a	3	1	4
−		5	6

	H	T	U
b	2	4	6
−		6	7

	H	T	U
c	1	3	2
−		9	8

	H	T	U
d	7	3	5
−		8	9

	H	T	U
e	4	3	0
−	1	5	6

	H	T	U
f	3	4	1
−	2	7	8

	H	T	U
g	6	2	4
−	1	3	5

	H	T	U
h	9	2	2
−	3	3	3

	H	T	U
i	7	1	5
−	5	7	7

	H	T	U
j	4	7	0
−	2	9	3

	H	T	U
k	8	4	2
−	1	8	3

	H	T	U
l	9	1	1
−	3	4	4

m
$$\begin{array}{r} 614 \\ -\,585 \\ \hline \end{array}$$

n
$$\begin{array}{r} 528 \\ -\,429 \\ \hline \end{array}$$

o
$$\begin{array}{r} 755 \\ -\,668 \\ \hline \end{array}$$

p
$$\begin{array}{r} 415 \\ -\,387 \\ \hline \end{array}$$

q
$$\begin{array}{r} 706 \\ -\,249 \\ \hline \end{array}$$

r
$$\begin{array}{r} 601 \\ -\,184 \\ \hline \end{array}$$

s
$$\begin{array}{r} 506 \\ -\,278 \\ \hline \end{array}$$

In Questions 1q–1s, start by trading 1 hundred for 10 tens.

See 2:46–2:48 (Subtraction with trading).

Subtraction from hundreds

Trade 1 hundred for 10 tens.
Trade 1 of the tens for 10 ones.

CONCEPT

Of $600 Kim earned, he donated $155 to charity. How much money did he have left?

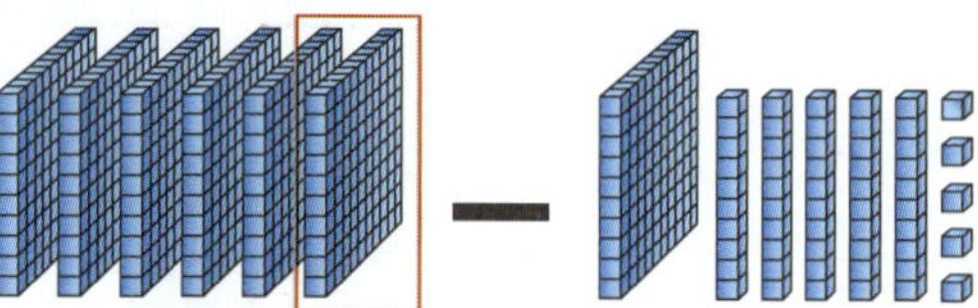

We can't take 5 ones from 0 ones, so we need to trade 1 ten for 10 ones. Since there are no tens we must first trade 1 hundred for 10 tens. Then trade 1 of the tens for 10 ones.

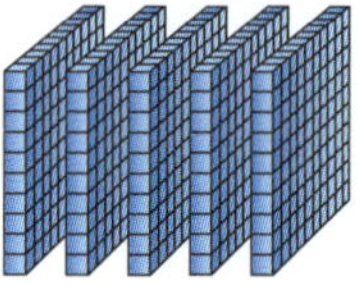

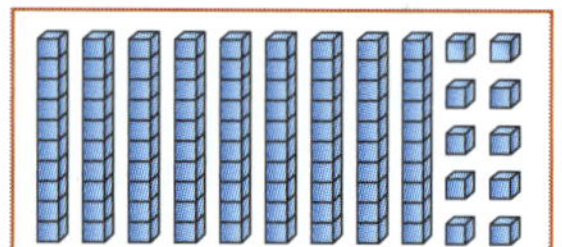

From this we take 1 hundred, 5 tens and 5 ones.

hund	tens	ones
	9	
5	~~10~~	10
~~6~~	~~0~~	~~0~~
− 1	5	5
4	4	5

1

	H	T	U
a	1	0	0
	−	2	7

	H	T	U
b	2	0	0
	−	3	8

	H	T	U
c	9	0	0
	−	6	1

	H	T	U
d	6	0	0
	−	5	5

e
  7 0 0
− 3 0 2

f
  9 0 0
− 7 9 3

g
  4 0 0
− 1 0 6

h
  3 0 0
− 2 5 3

2

a
  6 0 0
− 5 3 4

b
  5 0 0
− 3 9 9

c
  8 0 0
− 6 7 4

d
  7 0 0
− 6 6 8

3 Estimate each answer and use the estimates to check your answers.

a Chloe needed 600 points to qualify for a state team. She earned only 487. How far short of her target was she? ☐ points

b Blackburn Post Office was sent 900 stamp albums to sell. If 481 were sold in the first month, how many were left? ☐ albums

c In our class library we have 400 books. I have read 147. How many have I not read? ☐ books

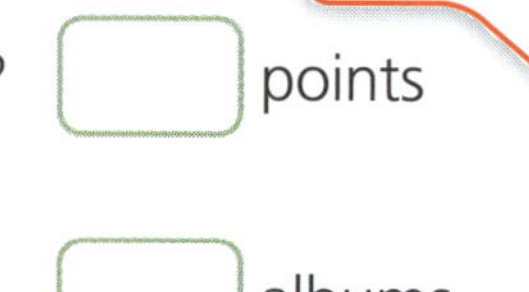

See 2:46–2:48 (Subtraction with trading).

 • *AUSTRALIAN SIGNPOST MATHS NSW 3* • ISBN 9780655709046

Subtraction from 100s strategy

400
= 399 + 1

CONCEPT

$$\begin{aligned} & 700 - 372 \\ = \; & 699 + 1 - 372 \\ = \; & 699 - 372 + 1 \\ = \; & 327 + 1 \\ = \; & 328 \end{aligned}$$

OR

$$\begin{array}{r} 700 \\ -\;372 \\ \hline \\ \hline \end{array} \;\rightarrow\; \begin{array}{r} 699 + 1 \\ -\;372 \\ \hline 327 + 1 \\ \hline = 328 \end{array}$$

1

a H T U
$$\begin{array}{r} 99 + 1 \\ \not{1}\not{0}\not{0} \\ -\;37 \\ \hline +\;1 \\ \hline = \square \end{array}$$

b H T U
$$\begin{array}{r} 299 + 1 \\ \not{3}\not{0}\not{0} \\ -\;48 \\ \hline +\;1 \\ \hline = \square \end{array}$$

c H T U
$$\begin{array}{r} 899 + 1 \\ \not{9}\not{0}\not{0} \\ -\;71 \\ \hline +\;1 \\ \hline = \square \end{array}$$

d
$$\begin{array}{r} +\;1 \\ \not{7}\not{0}\not{0} \\ -\;469 \\ \hline +\;1 \\ \hline = \square \end{array}$$

e
$$\begin{array}{r} +\;1 \\ \not{5}\not{0}\not{0} \\ -\;285 \\ \hline +\;1 \\ \hline = \square \end{array}$$

f
$$\begin{array}{r} +\;1 \\ \not{2}\not{0}\not{0} \\ -\;137 \\ \hline +\;1 \\ \hline = \square \end{array}$$

g
$$\begin{array}{r} +\;1 \\ 400 \\ -\;321 \\ \hline +\;1 \\ \hline = \square \end{array}$$

h
$$\begin{array}{r} +\;1 \\ 600 \\ -\;293 \\ \hline +\;1 \\ \hline = \square \end{array}$$

i
$$\begin{array}{r} +\;1 \\ 800 \\ -\;546 \\ \hline +\;1 \\ \hline = \square \end{array}$$

j
$$\begin{array}{r} 600 \\ -\;271 \\ \hline + \\ \hline = \square \end{array}$$

k
$$\begin{array}{r} 900 \\ -\;349 \\ \hline + \\ \hline = \square \end{array}$$

l
$$\begin{array}{r} 500 \\ -\;156 \\ \hline + \\ \hline = \square \end{array}$$

See 2:46–2:48 (Subtraction with trading).

Subtraction of money

Trade $1 for 10 ten-cent coins.
Trade a ten-cent coin for 10 cents.

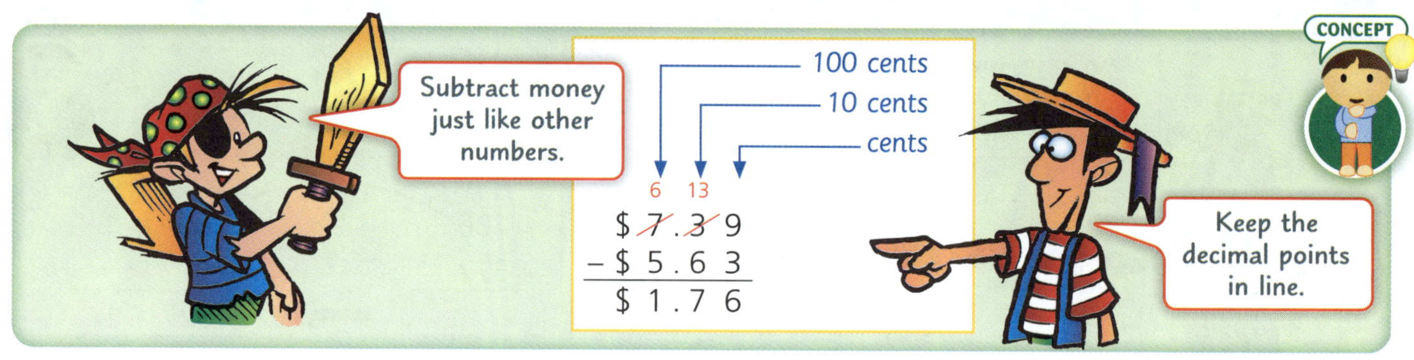

1

a	$6.52 − $1.30	**b**	$8.79 − $3.62	**c**	$9.85 − $3.51	**d**	$7.82 − $5.43	**e**	$6.24 − $2.07
f	$4.47 − $2.63	**g**	$5.38 − $2.61	**h**	$7.50 − $1.42	**i**	$3.54 − $0.20	**j**	$7.55 − $3.47
k	$8.57 − $6.87	**l**	$9.57 − $6.99	**m**	$6.50 − $2.61	**n**	$7.90 − $2.45	**o**	$3.52 − $1.48

2 Write each as an algorithm or use a mental strategy to find your answer.

a $3.35 – $1.24

b $8.98 – $4.00

c $8.56 – $3.21

d $4.54 – $4.49

e $7.00 – $1.50

f $3.50 – $1.99

3 I started with $8.50. What do I have left if I buy:

a a book for $7.45?

b an icy pole for $2.30?

c a drink for $3.05?

d a keyring for $7.30?

e a pen for $4.95

f marbles for $3.55?

First to $5

FUN SPOT

- Each player begins the game with $10 and takes turns to roll a dice.
- The number shown on each dice is multiplied by 10 and that number of cents is subtracted from the player's total.
- The game continues until one player reaches $5.

See 2:46–2:48 (Subtraction with trading).

Answers

1:01

1 a–d

1	2	3	4	5	6	7	8	9	10
11	12	13	14	15	16	17	18	19	20
21	22	23	24	25	26	27	28	29	30
31	32	33	34	35	36	37	38	39	40
41	42	43	44	45	46	47	48	49	50
51	52	53	54	55	56	57	58	59	60
61	62	63	64	65	66	67	68	69	70
71	72	73	74	75	76	77	78	79	80
81	82	83	84	85	86	87	88	89	90
91	92	93	94	95	96	97	98	99	100

c (Answers may vary): Every second even number is the pattern for counting by 4s.
d 8, 18, 28, 38, 48, 58, 68, 78, 88, 98

2 2, 4, 6, 8 or 0

3 5 or 0

4 0

5 a 20, 25, 30, 35, 40 b 12, 10, 8, 6, 4
c 177, 187, 197, 207, 217 d 144, 134, 124, 114, 104
e 400, 500, 600, 700, 800

6 a The rule is start at 147 and add 10 each time.

147 157 167 177 187 197 207 217

b The rule is start at 174 and subtract 10 each time.

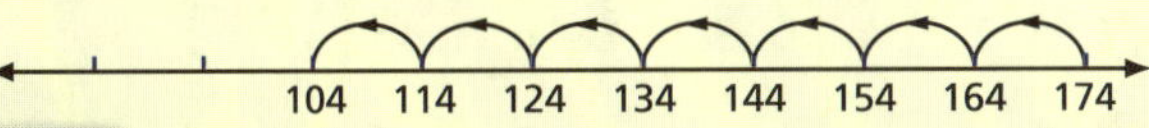

1:02

1 a 76, 78, 80, 82, 84, 86, 88, 90, 92, 94
b 1000, 900, 800, 700, 600, 500, 400, 300, 200, 100, 0
c 645, 650, 655, 660, 665, 670, 675, 680, 685, 690
d 500, 490, 480, 470, 460, 450, 440, 430, 420, 410, 400

2 a 845, 835, 825, 805, 795
b 615, 610, 600, 595, 590
c 408, 406, 402, 400, 398

3 2, (4), 6, (8), 10, (12), 14, (16), 18, (20), 22, (24), 26, (28), 30, (32), 34, (36), 38, (40)
The pattern is counting by 4, or add 4.

4 5, (10), 15, (20), 25, (30), 35, (40), 45, (50), 55, (60), 65, (70), 75, (80), 85, (90), 95, (100)
The pattern is counting by 10, or add 10.

5 Group the coins into stacks of ten. Group stacks into ten groups of ten to make one hundred. Make sure that you have three groups of ten stacks of ten.

6 a The rule is start at 76 and add 2 each time.

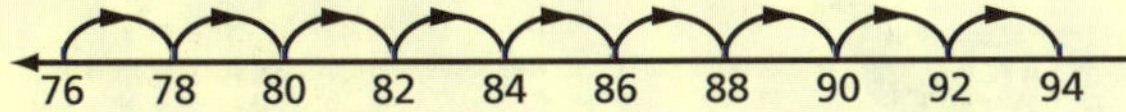

b The rule is start at 1000 and subtract 100 each time.

c The rule is start at 645 and add 5 each time.

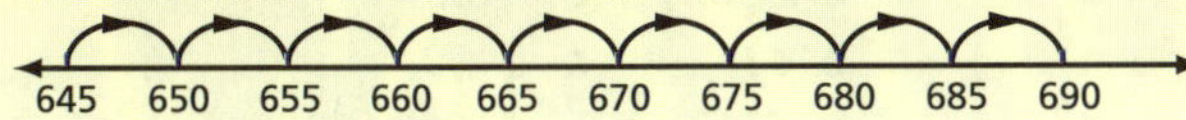

1:03

Header: 2 hundreds, 3 tens, 8 ones

1 a 316 b 512 c 145 d 224
e 232 f 129 g 221 h 324
i 268 j 519 k 674 l 953

2 a 346 b 723 c 962 d 634
e 572 f 914

3 a 137, 446, 653 b 237, 491, 974
c 106, 567, 819 d 250, 683, 749

1:04

Header: 380 (4), 38 (1), 308 (3), 803 (5), 83 (2)

1 a 413 4 hundreds 1 tens 3 ones
four hundred and thirteen

b 324 3 hundreds 2 tens 4 ones
three hundred and twenty-four

2 a 2 b 3 c 3 d 2 e 3
f 2 g 1 h 3 i 4 j 3

3 a 260 b 152 c 940 d 718
e 679 f 534 g 868 h 306

4 a 998, 1000 b 862, 864 c 658, 660
d 305, 307 e 498, 500 f 708, 710

1:05

1 a

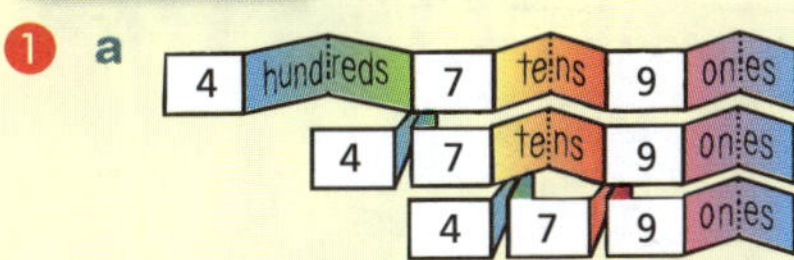

b

c

d

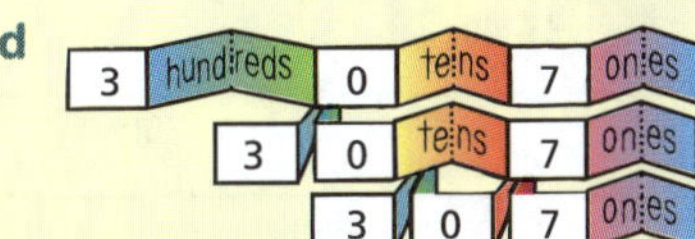

2 a 632 b 817 c 429 d 763
e 238 f 562 g 940 h 351

3 a one hundred and six b six hundred and seven
c three hundred and ten
d eight hundred and forty-one

1:06

1 a 10 b 80 c 20 d 90 e 30 f 110

2 a 20 b 40 c 60 d 50 e 90 f 70
g 60 h 80 i 100 j 120 k 120 l 130

3 a 57, 58, 64, 61, 62, 56 will be circled.
b 187, 186, 194, 193, 185, 189, 188, 191 will be circled.

4 a 60 + 20 = 80 b 40 − 20 = 20 c 130 − 30 = 100
d 70 + 70 = 140 e 120 − 30 = 90 f 240 − 60 = 180
g 50 + 80 = 130 h 670 − 50 = 620 i 450 − 120 = 330

1:07

1 a 200 b 400 c 500 d 600
e 400 f 300 g 800 h 300

2 a 100 b 400 c 500 d 500
e 200 f 800 g 900 h 600
i 200 j 500 k 400 l 900
m 400 n 200 o 700 p 600

3 a 163, 220, 186, 217, 237, 205 will be circled.
b 467, 456, 483, 532, 521 will be circled.

4 a false b false c true d true
e true f false g true h true

5 a 200 + 100 = 300 b 200 + 400 = 600
c 300 + 200 = 500 d 200 + 300 = 500

1:08

Header: 421 (3), 42 tens (2), 4 hundreds (1)

1 a 746 b 183 c 575 d 397

2 a 513 | 5 | hundreds | 1 | tens | 3 | ones |
five hundred and thirteen
b 342 | 3 | hundreds | 4 | tens | 2 | ones |
three hundred and forty-two

3 a
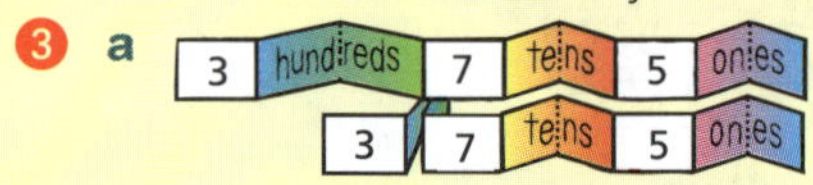

b
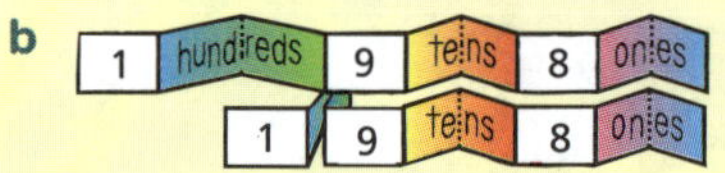

4 a 400 b 800 c 300 d 400 e 700
f 300 g 900 h 500 i 800

1:09

1 a 5 10 20 40
b 5 10 30 60
c 5 10 25 50
d 5 10 35 70

2 a 360, 370, 380, 390, 400 Add 10.
b 750, 740, 730, 720, 710 Subtract 10.
c 577, 677, 777, 877, 977 Add 100.
d 656, 556, 456, 356, 256 Subtract 100.
e 298, 308, 318, 328, 338 Add 10.

3 a 47 tens and 2 ones b 52 tens and 9 ones
c 83 tens and 6 ones d 54 tens and 7 ones

4 a 5 hundreds and 61 ones
56 tens and 1 one
561 ones
b 9 hundreds and 37 ones
93 tens and 7 ones
937 ones

1:10

1

Group	Number coloured	Total in group	Fraction coloured
	4	5	$\frac{4}{5}$
	3	4	$\frac{3}{4}$
	5	8	$\frac{5}{8}$
	2	4	$\frac{2}{4}$

2 a $\frac{5}{8}$, $\frac{3}{8}$ b $\frac{3}{4}$, $\frac{1}{4}$ c $\frac{3}{4}$, $\frac{1}{4}$
d $\frac{5}{8}$, $\frac{3}{8}$ e $\frac{3}{5}$, $\frac{2}{5}$ f $\frac{5}{6}$, $\frac{1}{6}$

3 a 3 fish are coloured. b 7 beetles are coloured.
c 5 pencils are coloured. d 2 mushrooms are coloured.
e 3 bats are coloured.

4 a $\frac{1}{4}$ b $\frac{1}{8}$ c $\frac{1}{6}$ d $\frac{3}{5}$

1:11

1 a 2, 3, $\frac{2}{3}$ b 3, 5, $\frac{3}{5}$ c 3, 4, $\frac{3}{4}$

2 a $\frac{3}{11}$ b $\frac{3}{5}$ c $\frac{8}{11}$ d $\frac{3}{4}$

3 a 4 of the 10 parts will be coloured.
b 8 of the 10 parts will be coloured.
c 2 of the 4 parts will be coloured.
d 4 of the 5 parts will be coloured.
e 2 of the 3 parts will be coloured.

1:12

Header: 100 (1), 10 000 (3), 1000 (2)

1 a 1518
| 1 | thousands | 5 | hundreds | 1 | tens | 8 | ones |
one thousand, five hundred and eighteen
b 1332
| 1 | thousands | 3 | hundreds | 3 | tens | 2 | ones |
one thousand, three hundred and thirty-two

2 a 2 b 4 c 1 d 2
e 4 f 2 g 4 h 4

1:13

Header: The letter 'O' can be mistaken for the number '0'.

1 a 1519 b 1354 c 1395 d 8405 e 4092

2 a 5837 b 6902 c 4189

3 a 2547 b 4263 c 5409
d 2157 e 4312 f 10 000

Investigation: 100 is ten tens. 1000 is ten hundreds.

 • *AUSTRALIAN SIGNPOST MATHS NSW 3* • ISBN 9780655709046

1:14

Header: 3 hamburgers

1. a 2 of the 4 parts will be coloured.
   b 3 of the 8 parts will be coloured.
   c 3 of the 4 parts will be coloured.
   d 7 of the 8 parts will be coloured.
   e 1 of the 4 parts will be coloured.
   f 4 of the 8 parts will be coloured.
   g 2 of the 3 parts will be coloured.
   h 5 of the 8 parts will be coloured.
2. a $\frac{2}{4}$ b $\frac{5}{8}$ c $\frac{1}{4}$ d $\frac{1}{8}$
   e $\frac{3}{4}$ f $\frac{4}{8}$ g $\frac{1}{3}$ h $\frac{3}{8}$
3. a 2 of the 5 parts will be coloured.
   b 8 of the 10 parts will be coloured.
   c 2 of the 6 parts will be coloured.
   d 5 of the 10 parts will be coloured.
4. a $\frac{1}{3}, \frac{2}{3}, \frac{3}{3}$ b $\frac{1}{4}, \frac{2}{4}, \frac{3}{4}, \frac{4}{4}$

1:15

Header: 4 balls

1. a 3 of the 3 parts will be coloured.
   b 3 of the 8 parts will be coloured.
   c 3 of the 4 parts will be coloured.
   d 6 of the 8 parts will be coloured.
2. a 0 b $\frac{5}{8}$ c $\frac{1}{4}$ d $\frac{2}{8}$
3. a $\frac{1}{5}, \frac{2}{5}, \frac{3}{5}, \frac{4}{5}, \frac{5}{5}$ or 1 b $\frac{1}{8}, \frac{2}{8}, \frac{3}{8}, \frac{4}{8}, \frac{5}{8}, \frac{6}{8}, \frac{7}{8}, \frac{8}{8}$ or 1
4. a $\frac{1}{2}$ b $\frac{1}{8}$ c $\frac{1}{3}$ d $\frac{1}{4}$
5. a 0 $\frac{1}{2}$
   b 0 $\frac{1}{3}$
   c 0 $\frac{1}{4}$
   d 0 $\frac{1}{8}$
6. a $\frac{2}{8}$ (or $\frac{1}{4}$), $\frac{6}{8}$ (or $\frac{3}{4}$) b $\frac{4}{8}$ (or $\frac{1}{2}$), $\frac{4}{8}$ (or $\frac{1}{2}$)

1:16

1. a 7 b 16 c 40 d 8
   e 30 f 11 g 22 h 60 i 62
2. a Add 2. b Add 3. c Add 10.
   d Subtract 4. e Subtract 1. f Subtract 11.
   g Add 4. h Subtract 5. i Add 8.
3. a 27, 33, 39 b 40, 39, 38 c 72, 70, 68
   d 42, 50, 58 e 43, 63, 83 f 36, 32, 28
   g 6, 12, 24 h 20, 35, 50 i 53, 43, 33 j 2, 4, 8
4. a 6, 9, 12 Add 3 each time.
   b 15, 20, 25 Add 5 each time.

1:17

1. a 8, 10, 12, 14, 16, 18, 20 b 16, 20, 24, 28, 32, 36, 40
   c 20, 25, 30, 35, 40, 45, 50
2. a 423, 433, 443, 453, 463 b 423, 523, 623, 723, 823
   c 1220, 1230, 1240, 1250, 1260
   d 1220, 1320, 1420, 1520, 1620
3.

1	2	3	4	5	6	7	8	9	10
11	12	13	14	15	16	17	18	19	20
21	22	23	24	25	26	27	28	29	30
31	32	33	34	35	36	37	38	39	40
41	42	43	44	45	46	47	48	49	50
51	52	53	54	55	56	57	58	59	60

Answers will vary.

4. a Start at 125 and add 5 each time.
   b Start at 790 and subtract 100 each time.

1:18

3210

1. a 1594 b 1625 c 1465 d 1613 e 1079 f 1802
2. 1514
   1 thousands 5 hundreds 1 tens 4 ones
   one thousand, five hundred and fourteen
3. a 3 b 2 c 4 d 3
4. a 1010, 1020, 1030, 1040, 1050, 1060
   b 4370, 4400, 4420, 4430
   c 7905, 8005, 8405, 8505
   d 1123, 1023, 923, 823, 723, 623
5. a 347 b 680 c 1000 d 1317
   e 4877 f 3208 g 2650 h 3641
   i 2200 j 5011 k 10 000 l 1002

1:19

1. a
   b
   c

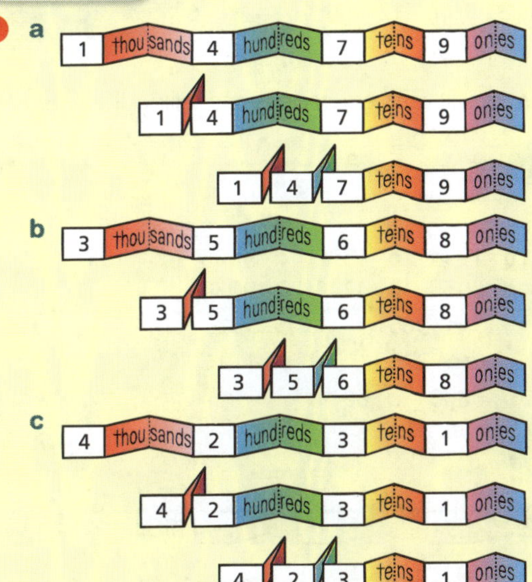

d

2. a 5763 b 8956 c 6275 d 4649 e 9582
3. a six thousand, eight hundred and twenty-four
   b two thousand, three hundred and nineteen
4. a 5000 b 3000 c 10 000

1:20

1. a $\frac{1}{4}$ b $\frac{2}{4}$ c $\frac{3}{4}$ **a** will be circled.
   d $\frac{3}{8}$ e $\frac{5}{8}$ f $\frac{7}{8}$ **d** will be circled.
2. a $\frac{1}{4}$ b $\frac{2}{4}$ or $\frac{1}{2}$ c $\frac{3}{4}$

Investigation

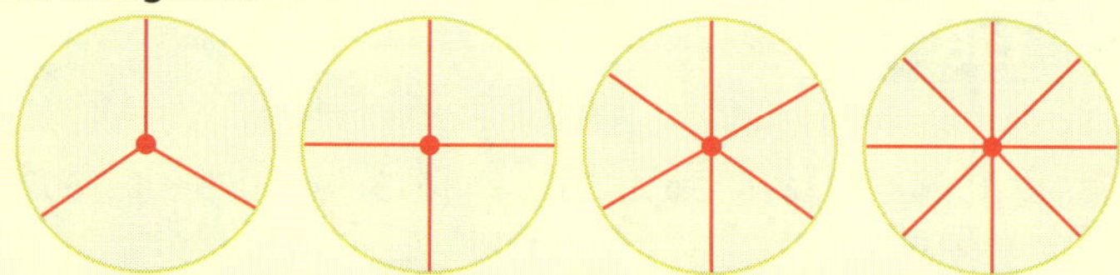

'smaller' will be circled.

1:21

1. a b c
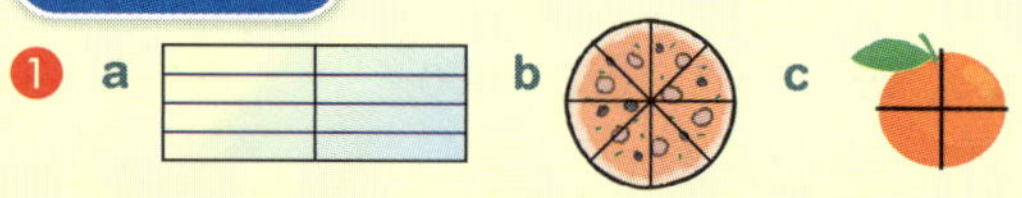

   d
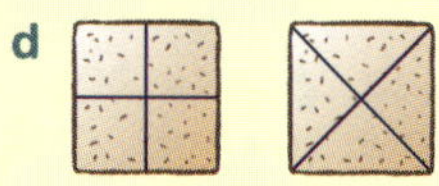

2. a b c d
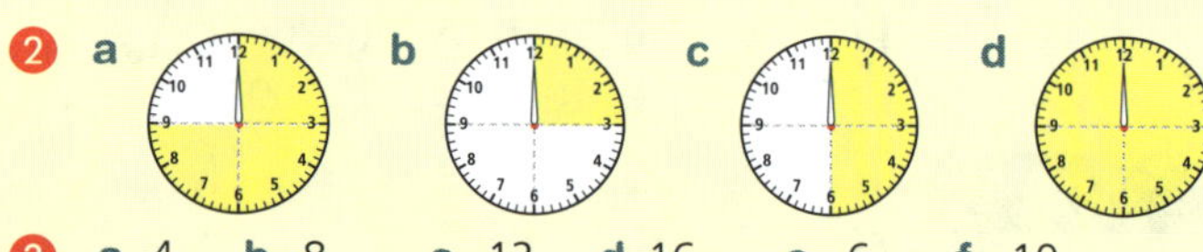

3. a 4 b 8 c 12 d 16 e 6 f 10

Box: 6

Activity: Answers will vary, e.g. recipes and telling the time.

1:22

Header: 3019

1. a 1352 b 1234 c 1392 d 9646 e 1255
   f 9708 g 2055 h 4249 i 9030
2. a 723 b 965 c 631
   d 1264 e 2753 f 4194
3. a 600 b 6000 c 60

1:23

1. a
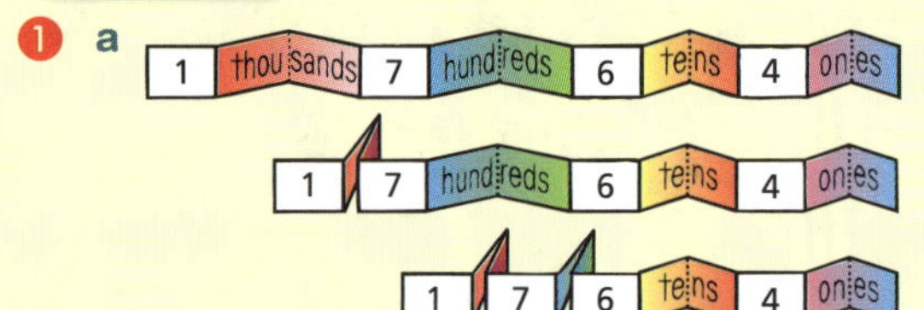

b c d
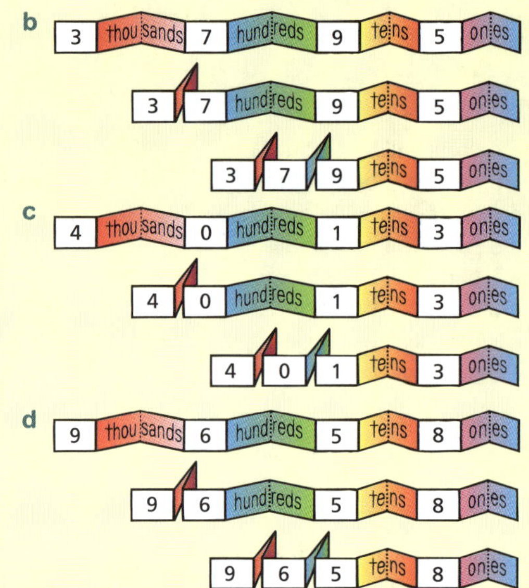

2. a 15 b 12 c 23 d 61 e 74 f 93
3. a 174 b 162 c 490 d 726
4. a 1210 b 5641 c 6301 d 2516
5. a 300 tens, 30 hundreds
   b 70 tens, 7 hundreds

1:24

1. a 3769 b 4637 c 2581
   d 5476 e 3958 f 6843
2. a 4000 + 200 + 40 + 7 b 3000 + 100 + 60 + 9
   c 2000 + 600 + 70 + 5 d 5000 + 100 + 90 + 2
3.

	Thousands	Hundreds	Tens	Units
a	4	3	7	8
b	6	2	4	9
c	3	8	2	1
d	5	8	7	3

4. a 900 b 4000 c 9 d 80
   e 3000 f 5 g 600 h 30
5. a 966 b 1235 c 2190 d 4629
   e 5728 f 6309 g 3399 h 7019

1:25

Concept box: 12

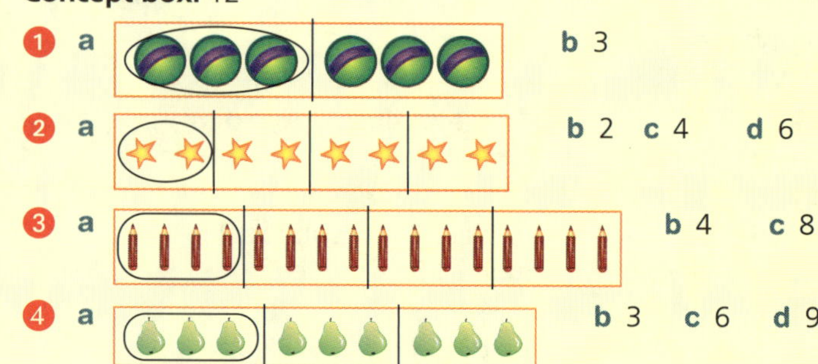

1. a b 3
2. a b 2 c 4 d 6
3. a b 4 c 8
4. a b 3 c 6 d 9
5. a 5 out of 8 or $\frac{5}{8}$
   b 4 out of 8 or $\frac{4}{8}$ or $\frac{1}{2}$

1:26

1 a $\frac{3}{6}$ b $\frac{4}{6}$ c $\frac{5}{6}$ d $\frac{2}{6}$ e $\frac{1}{4}$ f $\frac{2}{2}$
g $\frac{3}{8}$ h $\frac{4}{4}$ i $\frac{5}{8}$ j $\frac{8}{8}$ k $\frac{3}{4}$ l $\frac{7}{8}$

2 a b c d

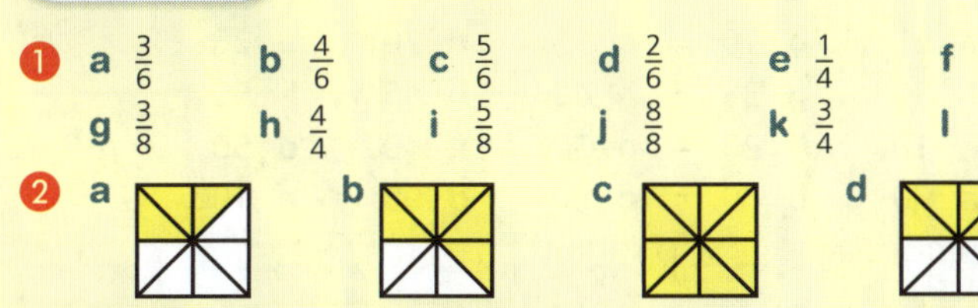

e f g h

3 a b
c d

1:27

1 a

b

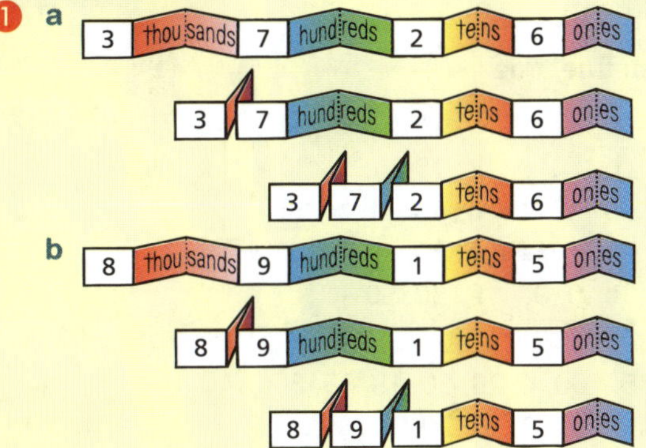

2 Answers may vary.
a 6 thousands and 218 ones
62 hundreds and 18 ones
621 tens and 8 ones
6218 ones
b 3 thousands and 274 ones
32 hundreds and 74 ones
327 tens and 4 ones
3274 ones

3 a 71 hundreds and 23 ones
b 93 hundreds and 62 ones
c 62 hundreds and 17 ones
d 85 hundreds and 92 ones
e 19 hundreds and 75 ones
f 25 hundreds and 46 ones

4 a 780, 790, 800, 810, 820, Add 10.
b 1110, 1100, 1090, 1080, 1070 Subtract 10.
c 1530, 1630, 1730, 1830, 1930 Add 100.
d 4429, 4329, 4229, 4129, 4029 Subtract 100.
e 5267, 5257, 5247, 5237, 5227 Subtract 10.

1:28

1 a 49 734 b 68 392 c 56 438

2

	T Thous	Thousands	Hundreds	Tens	Units
a	2	6	3	2	4
b	3	5	1	6	2
✓c	8	2	9	7	0
d	5	2	8	1	4
e	7	4	2	6	0

3 a 34 528 b 67 934 c 58 462
d 92 748 e 82 359 f 48 673

4

	Thousands	Hundreds, Tens, Ones
a	47	500
b	263	280
c	984	0

1:29

1 a 58 437 b 50 437 c 81 526
d 14 201 e 35 832 f 72 600 g 462 937

2 These numbers will be circled.
a 34 728 b 15 906 c 79 207
d 69 999 e 60 913 f 49 502

3 a 9752, 50 712, 50 752, 51 270
b 69 999, 70 789, 75 098, 508 970

4 a 5 b 4 c 5 d 6

5

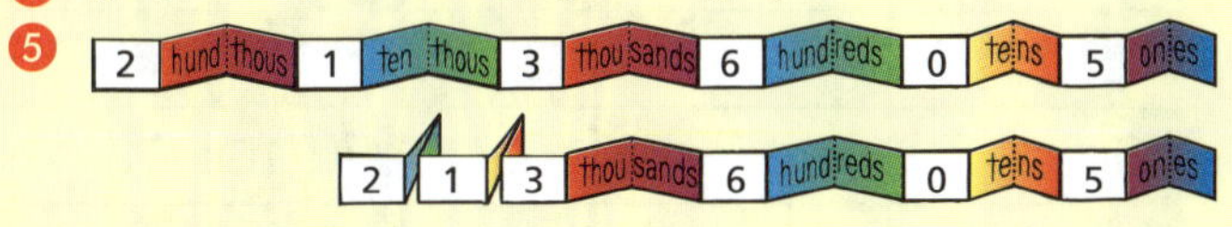

6 a 10 b 10 c 10 d 10

2:01

1 a 2 rows of 3, 3 columns of 2, (6)
b 2 rows of 5, 5 columns of 2, (10)
c 2 rows of 10, 10 columns of 2, (20)
d 4 rows of 3, 3 columns of 4, (12)
e 4 rows of 5, 5 columns of 4, (20)
f 4 rows of 10, 10 columns of 4, (40)
- If you double the number of rows, you double the answer.

2 a 4 rows of 4, 4 columns of 4, 16
b 3 rows of 5, 5 columns of 3, 15
c 6 rows of 3, 3 columns of 6, 18
d 6 rows of 6, 6 columns of 6, 36

2:02

1 a 5 rows of 5 = 25, 5 × 5 = 25 b 49
c 6 rows of 6 = 36, 6 × 6 = 36 d 16
e 3 rows of 3 = 9, 3 × 3 = 9 f 64

2 a 9 b a square
c

3 1, 4, 9, 16, 25, 36, 49, 64, 81, 100

4 Answers can vary. (Some are 121, 144, 169, 196, 225, 256 and 289.)

5 Counters representing square numbers can be arranged in the shape of a square.

2:03

1 **a** 5, 5, 1, 4 **b** 6, 6, 2, 4 **c** 10, 10, 9, 1
d 10, 10, 8, 2 **e** 15, 15, 9, 6

2

+	0	1	2	3	4	5	6	7	8	9	10
0	0										
1		2									
2			4			7					
3				6							
4					8				12		
5			7			10	11	12		14	
6						11	12	13			
7						12	13	14	15	16	
8					12			15	16	17	
9						14		16	17	18	
10											20

Matching pairs of numbers will be coloured.

3 **a** 10, 10, 10, 10, 10, 10, 10, 10, 10
b 1, 2, 3, 4, 5, 6, 7, 8, 9

2:04

1 **a** 2 **b** 4 **c** 6 **d** 8 **e** 10
f 12 **g** 14 **h** 16 **i** 18 **j** 20
k 4 **l** 8 **m** 12 **n** 16 **o** 20

2 **a** 16, 6, 22 **b** 14, 10, 24 **c** 8, 18, 26 **d** 20, 12, 8

3 **a** 14 **b** 16 **c** 22 **d** 24

4 **a**

	3	10	2	1	5	4	7	9	8	6
× 2	6	20	4	2	10	8	14	18	16	12

b

	6	4	8	2	5	10	1	7	9	3
× 2	12	8	16	4	10	20	2	14	18	6

c

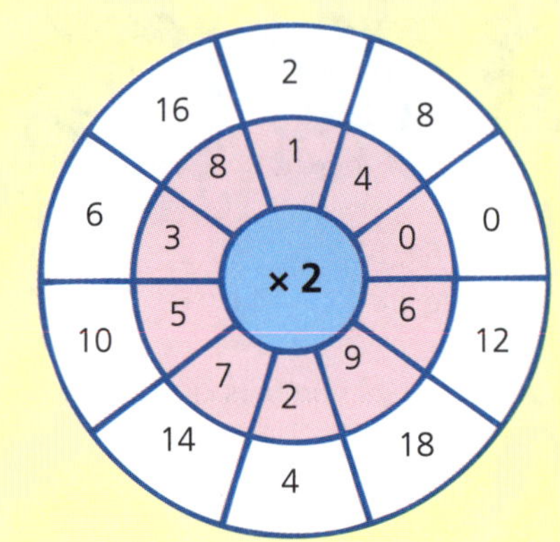

2:05

1 **a** 5 **b** 10 **c** 15 **d** 20 **e** 25
f 30 **g** 35 **h** 40 **i** 45 **j** 50
k 10 **l** 20 **m** 30 **n** 40 **o** 50

2 **a** 60 **b** 70 **c** 80 **d** 90 **e** 100

3 **a**

	3	10	2	1	5	4	7	9	8	6
× 10	30	100	20	10	50	40	70	90	80	60

b

	3	10	2	1	5	4	7	9	8	6
× 5	15	50	10	5	25	20	35	45	40	30

c yes **d** yes **e** yes

2:06

Investigation: true, true

1 **a** 12 **b** 35 **c** 14 **d** 80 **e** 70 **f** 16
g 25 **h** 50 **i** 18 **j** 30 **k** 60 **l** 90
m 40 **n** 22 **o** 45 **p** 55

2 **a** 2, 2 **b** 10, 10 **c** 20, 20
d 5, 5 **e** 0, 0 **f** 50, 50

3 **a** 0, 7, 30, 50, 6, 25, 40, 12, 40, 70
b 0, 6, 45, 100, 4, 20, 50, 18, 35, 80
c 0, 9, 40, 20, 10, 15, 20, 14, 45, 60
d 0, 8, 35, 10, 8, 10, 30, 16, 30, 90

2:07

1 **a**

	=
2 × 2	0
4 × 2	2
0 × 2	4
1 × 2	6
3 × 2	8
7 × 2	10
5 × 2	12
10 × 2	14
9 × 2	16
6 × 2	18
8 × 2	20

b

	=
3 × 2	0
0 × 2	2
5 × 2	4
1 × 2	6
7 × 2	8
2 × 2	10
8 × 2	12
4 × 2	14
6 × 2	16
10 × 2	18
9 × 2	20

c

	=
1 × 10	0
3 × 10	10
0 × 10	20
5 × 10	30
2 × 10	40
7 × 10	50
4 × 10	60
6 × 10	70
10 × 10	80
9 × 10	90
8 × 10	100

d

	=
4 × 10	70
2 × 10	20
7 × 10	40
3 × 10	90
9 × 10	30
1 × 10	60
6 × 10	10
10 × 10	50
5 × 10	80
8 × 10	100
0 × 10	0

e

	=
1 × 5	50
6 × 5	25
10 × 5	5
5 × 5	30
8 × 5	0
0 × 5	40
2 × 5	15
9 × 5	35
3 × 5	20
7 × 5	10
4 × 5	45

f

	=
0 × 5	0
6 × 5	15
3 × 5	30
8 × 5	20
4 × 5	25
10 × 5	40
5 × 5	10
2 × 5	50
1 × 5	35
7 × 5	45
9 × 5	5

20 is 1 × 20, 2 × 10, 4 × 5, 5 × 4, 10 × 2 or 20 × 1.

 • *AUSTRALIAN SIGNPOST MATHS NSW 3* • ISBN 9780655709046

2:08

1. The tens digit: increases by one
   The ones digit: decreases by one
   So, to add 9 we can add 10 and subtract 1.
2. The tens digit: decreases by one
   The ones digit: increases by one
   So, to subtract 9 we can subtract 10 and add 1.
3. **a** 16 **b** 25 **c** 37 **d** 51 **e** 8
   f 25 **g** 72, 63, 54, 45
4. **a** 14 **b** 27 **c** 61 **d** 83 **e** 15
   f 59 **g** 56, 64, 72, 80
5. **a** 9 **b** 15 **c** 9
6. **a** 27, 37, 47 **b** 26, 36, 46 **c** 29, 39, 49

2:09

1. **a** 8, 8, 8 (cm) **b** 7, 7, 7 (cm)
   c 9, 9, 9 (cm) **d** 6, 6, 6 (cm)
2. **a** 63, 27, 36 **b** 38, 38, 38 **c** 24, 24, 73 − <u>24</u> = <u>49</u>

2:10

1. **a** \$25 **b** \$60 **c** \$20 **d** \$50
2. **a** The amount on the left will be circled.
   b The amount on the right will be circled.
   c The amount on the right will be circled.
3. <u>2</u> \$50 notes, <u>5</u> \$20 notes, <u>10</u> \$10 notes, <u>20</u> \$5 notes
4. \$5, \$10, \$20, \$50, \$100

2:11

1. Coloured coins:
   a 50c, 20c, 20c **b** \$1, 50c, 20, 10c, 5c
   c \$2, 50c, 20c, or \$2, 50c, 10c, 10c
   d \$2, \$1, 20c, 10c, 10c, 10c, 10c
   e \$2, 50c, 20c, 20c, 5c
   f \$2, \$1, 20c
   g \$5, \$2, 50c, 20c, or \$5, \$2, 50c, 10c, 10c
   h \$5, 20c, 10c
2. Answers will vary. Examples:
   a \$2, \$1, 50c, 20c, 10c **b** \$2, 50c, 20c, 20c, 5c
   c \$2, \$2, 20c, 10c, 5c **d** \$5, \$2, \$2, 10c
   e \$10, \$2, 50c, 20c **f** \$10, \$5, 50c

2:12

Header: 2, 10, 4, 20

1. **A** 65c **B** \$2.35 **C** \$1.15 **D** 65c
   E \$1.30 **F** \$2.35 **G** 35c **H** \$2.60
2. **a** 200 cents **b** 500 cents **c** 800 cents
3. **a** \$1.30 **b** \$3.65 **c** \$1.50
4. **a** O **b** Q **c** M **d** S

2:13

1. **a** 5 + 12 = 17 **b** 13 + 32 = 45
2. **a** 27 **b** 43 **c** 37 **d** 53
   e 48 **f** 39 **g** 48 **h** 29
3. **a** 4 tens and 7 ones **b** 4 tens and 9 ones
   c 3 tens and 9 ones
4. **a** 98 **b** 88 **c** 68

2:14

Header: 25

1. **a** 35 **b** 33 **c** 51 **d** 93 **e** 64 **f** 72
2. **a** 14 **b** 8 **c** 14 **d** 19 **e** 37
   f 31 **g** 6 **h** 19 **i** 29

2:15

Header: 95

1. **a** 91 **b** 82 **c** 63 **d** 72
   e 78 **f** 92 **g** 101 **h** 103
2. **a** 73 **b** 38 **c** 28 **d** 27
   e 31 **f** 7 **g** 17 **h** 59
3. **a** 83 **b** 36 **c** 124

2:16

Header: true

1.

Add 3 to each part:	Subtract 2 from each part:	Subtract 10 from each part:
25 − 7 = (28) − (10) 18	21 − 12 = (19) − (10) 9	20 − 12 = (10) − (2) 8
27 − 17 = (30) − (20) 10	32 − 22 = (30) − (20) 10	30 − 17 = (20) − (7) 13
36 − 27 = (39) − (30) 9	51 − 32 = (49) − (30) 19	20 − 19 = (10) − (9) 1
64 − 47 = (67) − (50) 17	64 − 42 = (62) − (40) 22	40 − 18 = (30) − (8) 22

2. The answer has been written beside each number sentence in Question 1.
3. **a** 24 − 20 (= 4) **b** 28 − 20 (= 8)
   c 37 − 30 (= 7) **d** 38 − 30 or 28 − 20 (= 8)
   e 41−30 (= 11) **f** 41 − 20 (= 21)
   g 43−30 (= 13) **h** 52 − 30 (= 22)
4. **a** 9 − 2 (= 7) **b** 17 − 5 (= 12)
   c 18 − 1 (= 17) **d** 26 − 8 (= 18)
   e 17 − 8 (= 9) **f** 21 − 4 (= 17)

2:17

1. **a** 700 **b** 900 **c** 700 **d** 600
2. **a** 27 **b** 34 **c** 78 **d** 34
3. **a** 46 **b** 33 **c** 43 **d** 61
4. **a** 56 **b** 92 **c** 67 **d** 64
5. **a** 73 **b** 89 **c** 39 **d** 48 **e** 57 **f** 80

6 a 89

b 78

c 61

d 62

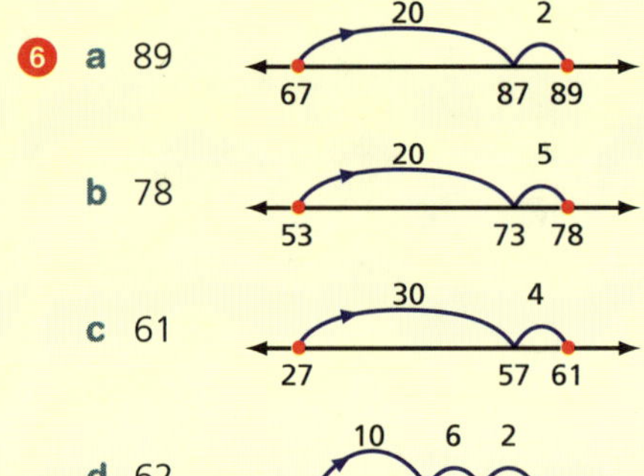

7 Strategies used may vary.

a 88, E b 43, B c 53, C or D
d 45, C or D e 800, A f 66, D or F

2:18

1 a 3 b 6 c 9 d 12 e 15
f 18 g 21 h 24 i 27 j 30

2 a 0 b 0 c 30 d 30
e 6 f 6 g 3 h 3
i 15 j 15 k 24 l 12
m 27 n 18 o 9 p 21

3 a 5 b 5 c 10 d 10
e 0 f 0 g 50 h 50
i 20 j 20 k 25 l 100

4 a 3 × 8 = 24 b 3 × 9 = 27

5 a

	4	7	9	5	8	6
× 3	12	21	27	15	24	18

b

	4	7	9	5	8	6
× 5	20	35	45	25	40	30

c

	4	7	9	5	8	6
× 2	8	14	18	10	16	12

d

	4	7	9	5	8	6
× 10	40	70	90	50	80	60

2:19

1 a

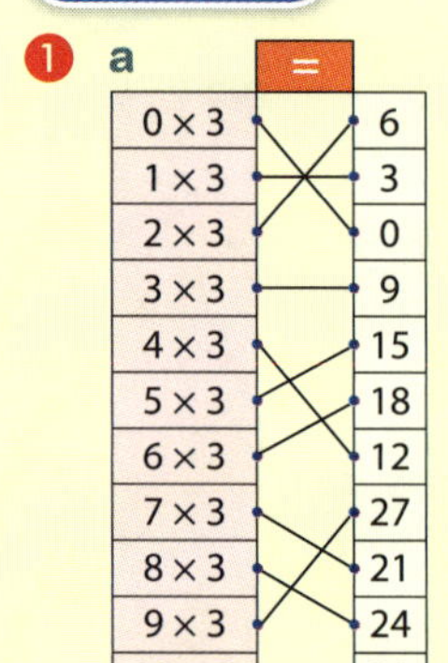

b

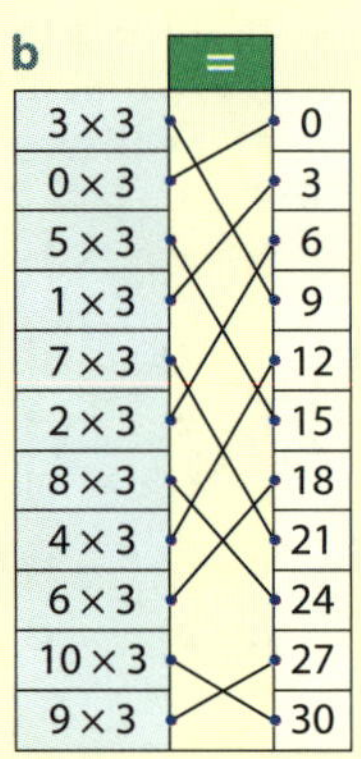

c

=	
1 × 3	9
3 × 3	3
0 × 3	0
5 × 3	21
2 × 3	12
7 × 3	15
4 × 3	6
6 × 3	27
10 × 3	24
9 × 3	18
8 × 3	30

d

=	
4 × 2	35
2 × 3	6
7 × 5	8
3 × 10	9
9 × 1	30
4 × 0	40
8 × 5	0
10 × 2	50
5 × 10	20
8 × 0	21
7 × 3	0

e

=	
1 × 5	18
6 × 3	50
10 × 5	5
5 × 5	24
8 × 3	0
0 × 5	25
2 × 5	27
9 × 3	10
3 × 5	21
7 × 3	12
4 × 3	15

f

=	
7 × 1	18
6 × 3	7
3 × 5	24
8 × 3	15
4 × 3	10
8 × 5	40
5 × 2	12
6 × 5	21
1 × 0	30
7 × 3	27
9 × 3	0

30 is 3 × 10, 10 × 3, 6 × 5.

2:20

Header: 3

1 a 50, 50 b 10, 10 c 20, 20
d 5, 5 e 0, 0 f 12, 12

2 a 0, 7, 12, 50, 6, 25, 40, 8, 16, 70
b 0, 6, 6, 100, 4, 20, 50, 18, 14, 80
c 0, 9, 16, 12, 10, 6, 20, 14, 18, 60
d 0, 3, 14, 10, 8, 10, 30, 16, 12, 90

3 a 4 b 14 c 2 d 8 e 15 f 16
g 25 h 20 i 18 j 30 k 6 l 12
m 40 n 10 o 45 p 22

2:21

1 a 4 b 8 c 12 d 16 e 20 f 24
g 28 h 32 i 36 j 40

2 a 20 b 4 c 24 d 8 e 28 f 36
g 32 h 12 i 36 j 24 k 40 l 16

3 a

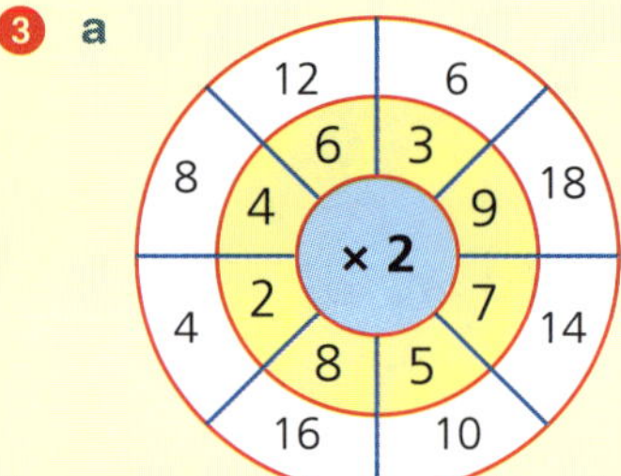

b

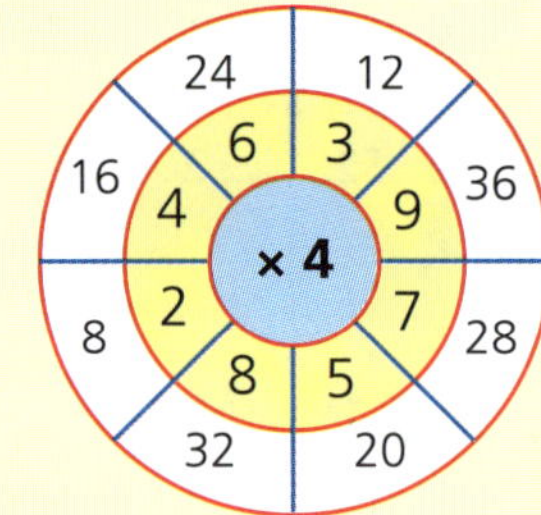

c

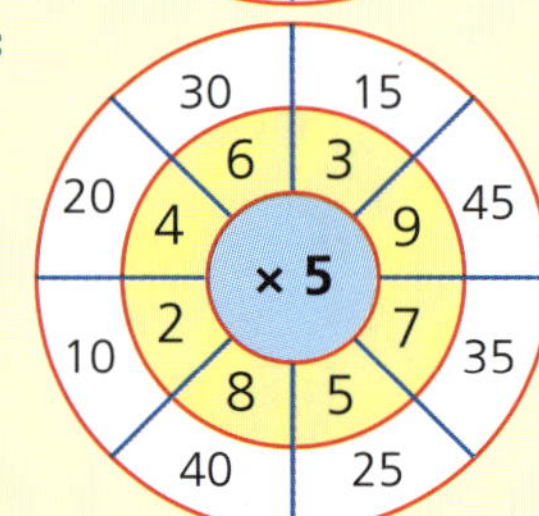

4 a 20, 4, 24 b 24, 4, 28

5 a

	2	1	5	10	3	4	8
× 4	8	4	20	40	12	16	32

b

	4	6	8	5	9	7	3
× 4	16	24	32	20	36	28	12

  • ISBN 9780655709046

2:22

1 **a**

	=
3 × 2	0
2 × 2	2
4 × 2	4
0 × 2	6
1 × 2	8
7 × 2	10
5 × 2	12
6 × 2	14
10 × 2	16
8 × 2	18
9 × 2	20

b

	=
3 × 4	0
2 × 4	4
0 × 4	8
6 × 4	12
1 × 4	16
4 × 4	20
5 × 4	24
9 × 4	28
10 × 4	32
7 × 4	36
8 × 4	40

c

	=
2 × 10	10
4 × 10	0
1 × 10	60
0 × 10	20
6 × 10	40
3 × 10	50
5 × 10	30
8 × 10	90
7 × 10	100
9 × 10	80
10 × 10	70

d

	=
2 × 2	0
4 × 2	2
1 × 2	4
0 × 2	6
6 × 2	8
3 × 2	10
5 × 2	12
8 × 2	14
7 × 2	16
9 × 2	18
10 × 2	20

e

	=
0 × 5	45
9 × 5	40
8 × 5	0
6 × 5	15
3 × 5	30
5 × 5	10
4 × 5	5
7 × 5	25
2 × 5	20
1 × 5	50
10 × 5	35

f

	=
0 × 4	4
6 × 4	12
1 × 4	0
3 × 4	20
10 × 4	24
4 × 4	40
8 × 4	16
5 × 4	36
9 × 4	32
2 × 4	28
7 × 4	8

g

	=
1 × 5	0
3 × 5	25
0 × 5	5
5 × 5	15
2 × 5	30
6 × 5	10
4 × 5	45
9 × 5	35
7 × 5	20
10 × 5	40
8 × 5	50

h

	=
6 × 5	20
4 × 5	28
7 × 4	30
8 × 4	36
5 × 5	45
9 × 4	32
9 × 5	25
5 × 4	35
7 × 5	20
4 × 4	40
8 × 5	16

2 **a**

	5	3	4	8	6	9	7
× 3	15	9	12	24	18	27	21

b

	5	3	4	8	6	9	7
× 4	20	12	16	32	24	36	28

2:23

1 **a** 7 × 5 = 35 **b** 4 × 10 = 40 **c** 5 × 5 = 25

d 5 × 8 = 40 **e** 5 × 6 = 30

2 **a** 18 **b** 20 **c** 80 **d** 14 **e** 4 **f** 12
g 30 **h** 10 **i** 15 **j** 3 **k** 70 **l** 0

3 The numbers 2, 4, 6, 8, 10, 12, 14, 16, 18, 20, 22, 24, 26, 28, 30, 32, 34, 36, 38, 40, 42, 44, 46, 48, 50 will be coloured yellow. The numbers 5, 10, 15, 20, 25, 30, 35, 40, 45 and 50 will be coloured green. The numbers 4, 8, 12, 16, 20, 24, 28, 32, 36, 40, 44, 48 will be circled.

4

×	0	1	2	3	4	5	6	7	8	9	10
0			0		0	0					0
1			2		4	5					10
2	0	2	4	6	8	10	12	14	16	18	20
3			6		12	15					30
4	0	4	8	12	16	20	24	28	32	36	40
5	0	5	10	15	20	25	30	35	40	45	50
6			12		24	30					60
7			14		28	35					70
8			16		32	40					80
9			18		36	45					90
10	0	10	20	30	40	50	60	70	80	90	100

5 A square number array should be drawn. e.g. a 5 × 5 array.

2:24

Header: 16 **Box:** 79

1 How many cards?
43 + 25 = 68
68 cards

2 How many bottles altogether?
3 × 5 = 15
15 bottles

3 How many sheep left?
96 – 28 = 68
68 sheep left

4 How many cans?
54 + 37 = 91
91 cans

5 How many seeds?
(6 × 5) + 4 = 34
34 seeds

6 **a** 10 **b** 5 **c** 3

2:25

1 **a** 20 **b** 10 **c** 3 **d** 30 **e** 8 **f** 60

2 **a** 7, 14, 14 **b** 3, 15, 15 **c** 40, 4, 4
d 20, 4, 4 **e** 10, 5, 5 **f** 10, 20, 20

3 **a** 6 **b** 10 **c** 30 **d** 4 **e** 8
f 50 **g** 9 **h** 7 **i** 45 **j** 6

Fun spot: Answers will vary.

2:26

Header: 6

1 **a** 3 rows of 5 = 15, 5 columns of 3 = 15, 15 divided by 3 = 5, 15 divided by 5 = 3
15, 15, 5, 3
b 8, 8, 4, 2 **c** 20, 20, 5, 4
d 10, 10, 5, 2 **e** 18, 18, 6, 3

2 **a** 16, 16, 8, 2 **b** 8, 8, 2, 4
c 12, 12, 2, 6 **d** 20, 20, 10, 2

2:27

1. **a** 12, 12, 6, 2 **b** 12, 12, 3, 4 **c** 15, 15, 3, 5
   d 20, 20, 4, 5 **e** 10, 10, 2, 5 **f** 30, 30, 10, 3
   g 18, 18, 2, 9 **h** 50, 50, 10, 5
2. **a** 4 × 10 = 40, 10 × 4 = 40, 40 ÷ 10 = 4, 40 ÷ 4 = 10
   b 7 × 2 = 14, 2 × 7 = 14, 14 ÷ 7 = 2, 14 ÷ 2 = 7
   c 6 × 5 = 30, 5 × 6 = 30, 30 ÷ 6 = 5, 30 ÷ 5 = 6
3. Answers will vary. You could ask, 'What times 3 gives 18?'

2:28

Concept: 20, 5.

1. **a** 10, 5, 10, 5 **b** 30, 6, 30, 6 **c** 25, 5, 5
   d 40, 4, 4 **e** 35, 7, 7, 7 **f** 16, 8, 8
2. **a** 9 **b** 6 **c** 4 **d** 7 **e** 5 **f** 8 **g** 10
3. **a** 6 **b** 7 **c** 9 **d** 7 **e** 7 **f** 10 **g** 8
4. **a** 10 **b** 3

2:29

1. **a** 20, 20 **b** 4, 4 **c** 5, 5
2. **a** 24, 24 **b** 3, 3 **c** 8, 8
3. **a** 20, 20, 10, 2
   b 6 × 5 = 30, 5 × 6 = 30, 30 ÷ 6 = 5, 30 ÷ 5 = 6
   c 9 × 2 = 18, 2 × 9 = 18, 18 ÷ 2 = 9, 18 ÷ 9 = 2
4. **a** 5, 2 **b** 10, 3 **c** 7, 2 **d** 9, 4
5. **a** 4 × 3 = 12, 3 × 4 = 12 **b** 7 × 5 = 35, 5 × 7 = 35
   c 5 × 10 = 50, 10 × 5 = 50 **d** 8 × 10 = 80, 10 × 8 = 80

2:30

Header: 5

1. **a** 4, 4 **b** 10, 10 **c** 5, 5 **d** 4, 4
   e 9, 9 **f** 6, 6 **g** 7, 7 **h** 8, 8
2. **a** 2, 10 **b** 6, 2 **c** 5, 3 **d** 8, 5
3. **a** 1 **b** 10 **c** 6 **d** 9
   e 1 **f** 10 **g** 2 **h** 8
4. **a** 5 **b** 4 **c** 7 **d** 6 **e** 5 **f** 6
   g 8 **h** 9 **i** 2 **j** 8 **k** 9 **l** 7
5. **a** 5, 5 **b** no **c** no

Activity: Answers will vary.

2:31

1. **a**

=	
2 × 5	0
4 × 5	5
0 × 5	20
1 × 5	10
3 × 5	35
7 × 5	25
5 × 5	15
10 × 5	45
9 × 5	50
6 × 5	40
8 × 5	30

b

=	
3 × 4	4
0 × 4	20
5 × 4	0
1 × 4	8
7 × 4	32
2 × 4	16
8 × 4	12
4 × 4	28
6 × 4	36
10 × 4	24
9 × 4	40

c

=	
6 × 10	25
9 × 2	3
5 × 5	40
3 × 1	18
8 × 5	60
9 × 10	14
7 × 2	35
7 × 5	20
8 × 1	90
4 × 5	40
8 × 5	8

d

=	
4 ÷ 2	8
60 ÷ 10	3
16 ÷ 2	9
30 ÷ 10	2
18 ÷ 2	6
70 ÷ 10	1
6 ÷ 6	7
50 ÷ 10	4
20 ÷ 2	0
8 ÷ 2	5
0 ÷ 10	10

e

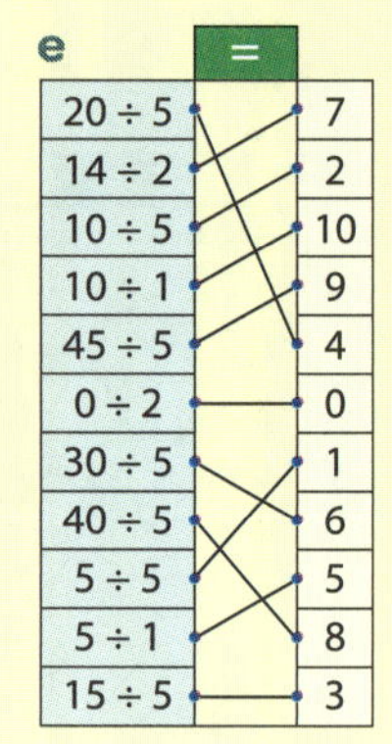

=	
20 ÷ 5	7
14 ÷ 2	2
10 ÷ 5	10
10 ÷ 1	9
45 ÷ 5	4
0 ÷ 2	0
30 ÷ 5	1
40 ÷ 5	6
5 ÷ 5	5
5 ÷ 1	8
15 ÷ 5	3

f

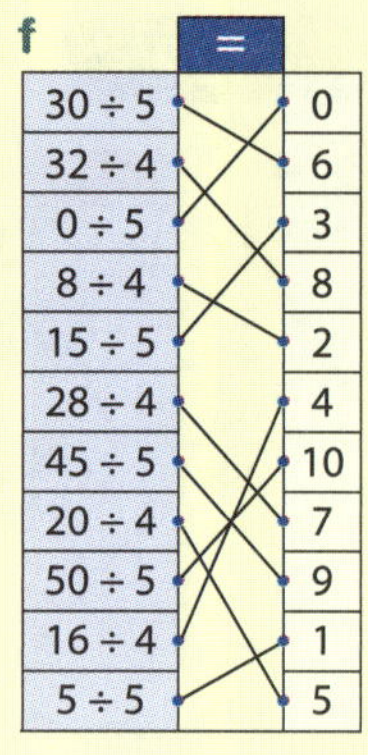

=	
30 ÷ 5	0
32 ÷ 4	6
0 ÷ 5	3
8 ÷ 4	8
15 ÷ 5	2
28 ÷ 4	4
45 ÷ 5	10
20 ÷ 4	7
50 ÷ 5	9
16 ÷ 4	1
5 ÷ 5	5

Answers will vary. 20 is 1 × 20, 2 × 10, 4 × 5, 5 × 4, 10 × 2 or 20 × 1.

2:32

1. How many bones were left?
   100 – 40 = 60
   There were 60 bones left.
2. How many pies?
   3 × 10 = 30
   There were 30 pies.
3. How many friends?
   24 ÷ 2 = 12
   There were 12 friends.
4. How many books?
   24 + 55 = 79
   There were 79 books.
5. How many people got off?
   15 + 10 + 8 = 33
   33 people got off altogether.
6. How many each?
   45 ÷ 5 = 9
   9 books each.
7. How many rows of bottles?
   45 ÷ 5 = 9
   You could make 9 rows.
8. **a** 899 **b** 890 **c** 590 **d** 490
   e 698 **f** 198 **g** yes

2:33

1. **a** 160 **b** 680 **c** 269 **d** 187
   e 35 **f** 87 **g** 69 **h** 282
   i 155 **j** 793
2. **a** 61 **b** 885 **c** 33 **d** 72
   e 96 **f** 44 **g** 24 **h** 73
   i 33 **j** 95 **k** 293 **l** 525
   m 881 **n** 365 **o** 74 **p** 884
   q 565

2:34

1. **a** 15 **b** 44 **c** 35 **d** 559 **e** 884
2. **a** 55 **b** 18 **c** 25 **d** 219 **e** 413
3. **a** 46 **b** 68 **c** 748 **d** 637 **e** 357
   f 519 **g** 25 **h** 44 **i** 173 **j** 486
   k 73 **l** 49 **m** 28 **n** 35 **o** 19
   p 57 **q** 46 **r** 48

2:35

1. **a** 107 **b** 140 **c** 120 **d** 180 **e** 220
   f 360 **g** 780 **h** 505 **i** 930 **j** 920
   k 808 **l** 947

2 a 60 b 58 c 46 d 160 e 736
f 573 g 306 h 320 i 120 j 162
k 670 l 290

3 a 798 b 941

2:36

1 Coloured coins:
a 50c, $1, 20c, 5c = $1.75 b $1, 20c, 10c, 5c = $1.35
c 50c, 20c, 10c, 5c = 85c

2 b 5c, 10c = 15c c 5c, 20c, 20c = 45c
d 5c, 20c = 25c

3 a $1.30 b 60c c $1.55 d 95c

2:37

1 1, 2, 4, 5 and 6

2 a $6 b $1 c $8 d $5

3 5-point stars = 3, 6-point stars = 1

4 a 10, 8, 6 or 10, 10, 4 or 8, 8, 8
b No. Answers will vary. Three even numbers can't add to an odd number.

5 2 × 10, 10 × 2, 1 × 20, 20 × 1, 4 × 5, 5 × 4

6 1 × 30, 30 × 1, 2 × 15, 15 × 2, 3 × 10, 10 × 3, 5 × 6, 6 × 5

2:38

1 a 58 b 78 c 77 d 89 e 96 f 77
g 89 h 98 i $89 j $97 k $79 l $89

2 a 8 tens and 8 ones b 8 tens and 7 ones
c 7 tens and 9 ones d 8 tens and 9 ones
e 8 tens and 9 ones f 7 tens and 8 ones

3 a $96 b 29 c 57 d $77

2:39

1 a 36 – 4 = 32 b 55 – 23 = 32 c 47 – 5 = 42
d 68 – 34 = 34 e 76 – 42 = 34 f 59 – 46 = 13

2 a 36 b 31 c 23 d 27 e 35 f 34
g 42 h 34 i $63 j $40 k $4 l $52

2:40

1 a 31 b 33 c 41 d 65 e 71
f 74 g 90 h 82 i 72 j 58
k 94 l 76 m $94 n $83 o $60
p $97

2 a 4 + 29 = 33 (animals) b 16 + 27 = 43 (birds)
c 65 + 28 = 93 (insects) d 57 + 26 = 83 (coins)

2:41

1 a 40 b 72 c 61 d 61 e 93 f 70
g 93 h 52 i 94 j 95 k 82 l 82
m $54 n $96 o $90 p $80

2 a 53 students b 80 cans
c 72 stamps d 93 cards

2:42

1 a 73 b 45 c 83 d 65 e 73
f 80 g 71 h 93

2 odd

3 a 83 b 70 c 91
d 60 e 80 f 94

2:43

1 a 62 + 144 = 206, 206 b 173 + 251 = 424, 424

2 a 105 b 507 c 336 d 227 e 719
f 688 g 325 h 419 i 828 j 718
k 547 l 937 m 509 n 537 o 928
p 827

2:44

1 a 159 b 842 c 618 d 173 e 459
f 557 g 674 h 485 i 978 j 585
k 780 l 870 m 612 n 893 o 490
p 619

2 a $470 b $825 c $907 d $754

2:45

1 a 128 b 820 c 504 d 200 e 532
f 810 g 602 h 920 i 821 j 650
k 620 l 744 m 806 n 751 o 900
p 932

2 a 224 birds b 312 sheets
c 197 meals d 374 cows

2:46

1 a

tens	ones
4	10
~~5~~	~~0~~

b

tens	ones
6	10
~~7~~	~~0~~

c

tens	ones
3	10
~~4~~	~~0~~

d

tens	ones
8	10
~~9~~	~~0~~

2 a 56 b 73 c 44 d 82 e $14
f $13 g $45 h $48

3 a 16 b 53 c 14 d 12

4 a $53 b $34 c $22

2:47

1 a

tens	ones
2	14
~~3~~	~~4~~

b

tens	ones
4	17
~~5~~	~~7~~

c

tens	ones
3	16
~~4~~	~~6~~

d

tens	ones
6	12
~~7~~	~~2~~

e

tens	ones
5	13
~~6~~	~~3~~

f

tens	ones
7	15
~~8~~	~~5~~

2 a 18 b 16 c 29 d 49
e 68 f 57 g 28 h 37

2:48

1 a

tens	ones
3	15
~~4~~	~~5~~

b

tens	ones
1	17
~~2~~	~~7~~

c

tens	ones
2	11
~~3~~	~~1~~

d

tens	ones
6	12
~~7~~	~~2~~

2 a 38 b 54 c 28 d 19
e 14 f 29 g 25 h 57

2:49

1 a 22 b $45 c 38 d 16
2 a 19 km b 34 km c 28 km
3 a 12 km b 74 km c 62 km
d 35 km e 39 km f 27 km

3:01

1 a A, B, C b B, A, C c C, B, A
2 Answers will vary.
3 Answers will vary.
4 It should make it easier to estimate. If not, another personal benchmark could be used.

3:02

1 a L: 6 cm, W: 3 cm b L: 3 cm, W: 3 cm
c L: 3 cm, W: 2 cm
2 a b

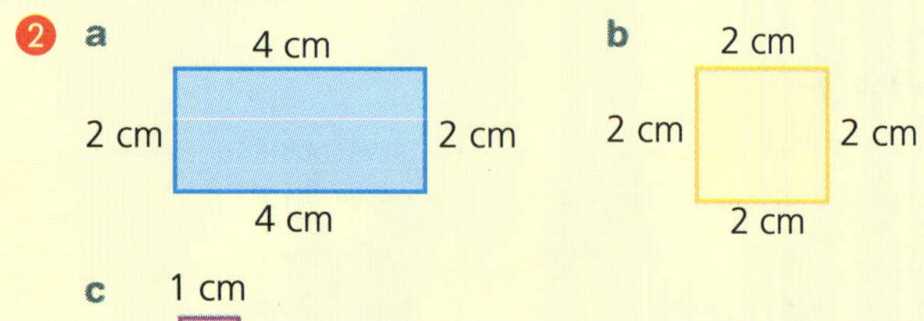

c

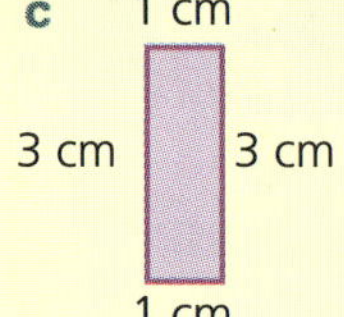

3 a length = 28 cm, width = 21 cm
b length = 18 cm, width = 3 cm

Activity: Answers will vary.

3:03

1 a L: 6 cm, W: 2 cm b L: 4 cm, W: 3 cm
c L: 3 cm, W: 1 cm
2 Estimates will vary.
a b

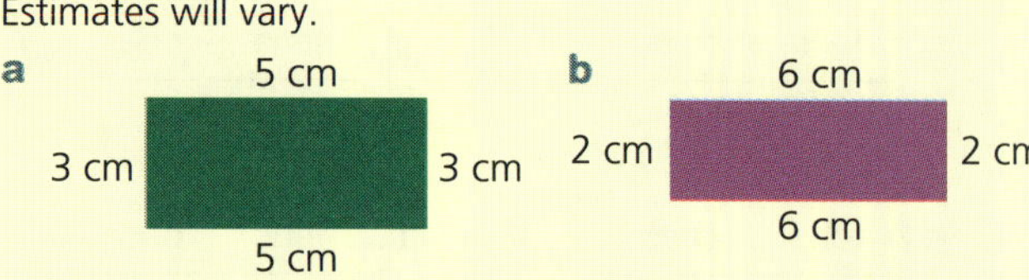

Activity: Answers will vary.

3:04

1 a quarter past 6 b half past 9
c 1 o'clock d quarter to 2
e quarter past 2 f half past 5
g six o'clock h quarter to 9
2 a b c d
3 Answers will vary.

3:05

1 a 5 minutes past 4 b 20 minutes past 1
c 10 minutes past 11 d 25 minutes past 7
e 20 past 5 f 5 past 9
g 10 past 6 h 25 past 9
2 a 50 past 7, 10 minutes to 8
b 40 past 3, 20 minutes to 4
c 55 past 1, 5 to 2 d 35 past 4 or 25 to 5

3:06

Header: 25 to the hour

1 a 5 to 2 b 25 to 6 c 10 past 10
d 20 to 5 e 20 past 12
f a quarter past 11 (or 15 past 11)
g a quarter to 7 (or 15 to 7)
h 25 past 2 i 10 to 8 j 5 past 3
2 a b c

d e

3 a 10 past 8 b a quarter past 7 (or 15 past 7)
c 5 to 12 d 20 past 6
e a quarter to 8 (or 15 to 8)
f 10 to 3 g 25 past 3
h 20 to 3 i 9 o'clock
4 a 20 past 1 b 5 past 4 c 20 to 4
d a quarter to 5 (or 15 to 5)
e a quarter past 6 (or 15 past 6)
f half past 7 (or 30 past 7)
g 10 past 10 h 25 to 11 i 2 o'clock

3:07

1 a 4 cups b 4 cups c 8 cups d 2 cups
e 6 cups f 2 cans g 4 cans
2 a Answers will vary. b Answers will vary.

 • *AUSTRALIAN SIGNPOST MATHS NSW 3* • ISBN 9780655709046

3:08

1

2 a 11 L b 75 L c 60 L d 34 L
e **B, E, C, D, A**

3 Answers will vary.

3:09

1 yes
2 Answers will vary.
3 Answers will vary.
4 A discussion will occur
5 Answers will vary.

3:10

1 **a** 1 m 25 cm **b** 2 m 34 cm **c** 5 m 9 cm
d 7 m 96 cm **e** 8 m 42 cm **f** 4 m 22 cm
2 **a** 1 m 19 cm **b** 3 m 45 cm **c** 4 m 81 cm
d 7 m 38 cm **e** 4 m 5 cm **f** 8 m 1 cm
3 **a** 128 cm **b** 314 cm **c** 642 cm **d** 573 cm
e 530 cm **f** 680 cm Order = a, b, e, d, c, f
4 Answers will vary.

3:11

1 **a** 1 m 70 cm **b** 3 m 36 cm **c** 4 m 26 cm
d 7 m 13 cm **e** 6 m 83 cm **f** 5 m 42 cm
2 **a** d **b** a
3 **a** m **b** cm **c** cm **d** m **e** cm **f** cm **g** m **h** cm
4 **a** 484 cm **b** 953 cm **c** 172 cm
d 392 cm **e** 730 cm **f** 205 cm
Order = c, f, d, a, e, b
5 **a** 1 m 87 cm **b** 4 m 26 cm **c** 2 m 86 cm
d 8 m 36 cm **e** 8 m 6 cm **f** 5 m 72 cm
Order = a, c, b, f, e, d

3:12

Header: a ruler **b** tape measure **c** trundle wheel
1 Answers will vary. You may find it is close to your arm span in length. You could use this as a personal benchmark for 1 m.
2 Answers may vary.
3 Answers will vary.

3:13

1 Answers will vary.
2 Answers will vary.
3 Answers will vary.

3:14

1 **a** 10:26, 26 past 10 **b** 11:17, 17 past 11
c 3:39, 39 past 3 **d** 2:21, 21 past 2
e 4:07, 7 past 4 **f** 5:48, 48 past 5
g 2:37, 37 past 2 **h** 4:41, 41 past 4
i 7:54, 54 past 7 **j** 2:58, 58 past 2
k 34 past 9 **l** 28 past 2 **m** 41 past 5
n 47 past 8 **o** 59 past 6

2 **a**
11:36 — eleven thirty-six
6:12 — 12 minutes past 6
9:57 — 57 minutes past 9

b
1:43 — 43 minutes past 1
8:26 — 26 minutes past 8
5:07 — five-oh-seven

3:15

1 **a** 7 to 2 **b** 16 to 1 **c** 18 to 10 **d** 3 to 9
e 18 to 12 **f** 27 to 5 **g** 5 to 2 **h** 12 to 6
2 **a** **b** **c** **d**
3 **a** 16 to 6 **b** 11 to 9 **c** 21 to 3
d 16 to 10 **e** 21 to 11 **f** 6 to 7
4 Answers will vary.

3:16

1 **a** 22 past 7 **b** 3 to 7 **c** 18 past 12 **d** 6 past 10
e 12 to 1 **f** 8 past 12 **g** 22 to 4 **h** 7 to 8
2 **a** 27 past 6 **b** 18 past 7 **c** 10 past 8 **d** 6 to 5
e 1 to 7
3 Answers will vary.
4 **a** 60 minutes **b** 30 minutes **c** 15 minutes

3:17

1 Answers will vary.
2 Answers will vary.
3 1 L of water has the same mass as 1 kg. The mass of the container itself will increase the mass. If a container is added to both sides then 1 L will balance with 1 kg.

3:18

1 Answers will vary.
2 Answers will vary.
3 Answers will vary.
4 Answers with yes will be circled.
a yes **b** no **c** no **d** yes **e** no **f** no
g yes **h** no **i** no **j** no **k** yes **l** yes
5 Answers with yes will be circled.
a no **b** yes **c** yes **d** no **e** no
f yes **g** no **h** no **i** yes

3:19

1 **a** 3 kg **b** 10 kg **c** 8 kg **d** 5 kg **e** 7 kg
f 11 kg
2 Answers with yes will be circled.
a yes **b** yes **c** no **d** yes **e** yes **f** no
g yes **h** yes **i** no **j** yes **k** yes **l** no

3 a 4 kg b 10 kg c 29 kg d 27 kg
e 23kg f 8 kg g 45 kg h 21 kg

4 Answers with yes will be circled.
a yes b no c yes d no e no
f yes g yes h yes i no j yes

3:20

1 a the duck and the pelican
b 34 kg
c about 3 (pelicans could vary in mass)
d 12 kg

2 a 5 kg b 9 kg c 46 kg d 51 kg

3 a 28 kg b 10 c yes d 30 kg

4

Fruit	My fruit's mass	World record mass	Difference between the World record and my fruit
pineapple	18 kg	28 kg	28 kg – 18 kg = 10 kg
cabbage	1 kg	62 kg	62 kg – 1 kg = 61 kg
watermelon	9 kg	118 kg	118 kg – 9 kg = 109 kg
squash	3 kg	981 kg	981 kg – 3 kg = 978 kg

3:21

1 a no b 1 book c 8
d Books are a good unit because they fit together without leaving gaps or overlaps, however they would not be suitable to measure a small area.

2 a 4 rows of 4 b 5 rows of 2 or 2 columns of 5
c A rectangle with 3 rows of 4 will be drawn and labelled with a **D**.
d A rectangle with 2 columns of 2 will be drawn and labelled with an **E**.
e **B** f **E**

3 Estimates will vary.
a 16 b 15 c 12 d 12

Activity: Answers will vary.

3:22

1 **A** 20 square centimetres **B** 6 square centimetres
C 15 square centimetres **D** 16 square centimetres
E 1 square centimetre **F** 24 square centimetres

2 a **F** b **E** c **B** or **E** d **F** e **D**

3:23

1 **L** 15 square centimetres **M** 8 square centimetres
N 12 square centimetres Order = **M**, **N**, **L**

2 a Estimates will vary. b **X** 12 square centimetres
Y 8 square metres **Z** 10 square centimetres
c Order = **Y**, **Z**, **X**

3 a **A** 6 × 4 squares, 24 square centimetres
B 2 × 7 squares, 14 square centimetres
C 4 × 7 squares, 28 square centimetres
b **B**, **A**, **C**

Fun spot: Answers will vary.

3:24

1 a 2 rows of 8, Area = 16 square centimetres
2 rows of 6, Area = 12 square centimetres
The first area will be ticked.
b 4 rows of 3, Area = 12 square centimetres
2 rows of 4, Area = 8 square centimetres
The first area will be ticked.
c 1 rows of 8, Area = 8 square centimetres
2 rows of 5, Area = 10 square centimetres
The second area will be ticked.
d 3 rows of 3, Area = 9 square centimetres
3 rows of 4, Area = 12 square centimetres
The second area will be ticked.

2 Answers will vary.

Activity: Answers will vary.

3:25

Activity: Answers will vary.

1 a 2 L b 4 L c 1 L d 10 L e 7 L
f 5 L g 19 L h 20 L i 14 L

2 a C b D c C d D e 23 L f 16 L

3:26

1 a 12 b 30

2 a 2 b 6 c 45, 53, 8 d 10

3 a 5 b 5 c 2 d 3 e 96 L

4 a 60 L b the storage bin and the esky

3:27

1–5 Answers will vary.

6 a yes
b When you cut the square metre it makes it easier to measure shapes that are not square shaped.

Investigation: Answers will vary.

3:28

Activity: Answers will vary.

1 Answers will vary. We need a larger unit because it makes measuring larger areas quicker and more accurate as not as many units are needed to cover the area.

2 a square centimetres b square metres
c square metres d square centimetres
e square centimetres f square metres

3:29

1 a 24 mm b 16 mm c 31 mm d 62 mm e 47 mm

2 a 27 mm b 57 mm c 65 mm d 36 mm e 17 mm
f 72 mm

Fun spot: Answers will vary.

3:30

1 a 1 cm, 10 mm b 10 cm, 100 mm (or 99 mm)

2 Answers will vary. Example: Centimetres are a better unit because they are always the same length while handspans vary in length for each person.

3. We use millimetres when we need exact measurements (e.g. when building, or making clothing).
Also, if we are measuring small objects (less than 5 cm), millimetres would usually be preferred over centimetres.

Investigation: Answers will vary. You could place a ruler on the left and right side of the ball, mark the position of the rulers and measure the distance between them.

3:31

1. **a** Echidna: 37 mm, Lizard: 44 mm, Platypus: 41 mm, Koala: 38 mm
   b echidna, koala, platypus, lizard
   c 3 mm
   d 6 mm
2. 128 cm
3. 32 cm
4. 2
5. 99 cm
6. 1600 m (or 1 km 600 m)
7. 2000 m (or 2 km)
8. 150 m fence, 6 lights

3:32

1. **a** Estimates will vary.
   b **A:** 3 layers of 4, **B:** 3 layers of 15, **C:** 2 layers of 21
   c **A:** 4 + 4 + 4 = 12 cubic centimetres,
   B: 15 + 15 + 15 = 45 cubic centimetres,
   C: 21 + 21 = 42 cubic centimetres
   d A, C, B
2. Answers will vary.

3:33

1. **a** Estimates will vary. (**A:** 24, **B:** 40, **C:** 50)
   b **A:** 4 layers of 6, **B:** 4 layers of 10, **C:** 5 layers of 10
   c **A:** 6 + 6 + 6 + 6 = 24 cubic centimetres,
   B: 10 + 10 + 10 + 10 = 40 cubic centimetres,
   C: 10 + 10 + 10 + 10 + 10 = 50 cubic centimetres
   d A, B, C
2. **a** 50 cubic centimetres
   b 50 + 50 + 50 + 50 = 200 cubic centimetres
3. Answers will vary. The model could be 3 cm wide, 4 cm long and 3 cm high. This is 3 layers of 12 so 12 + 12 + 12 = 36 cubic centimetres.
4. Answers will vary.

3:34

1. 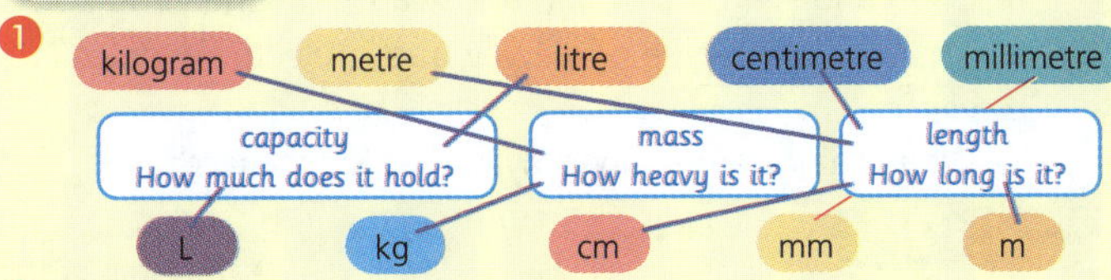

2. **a** capacity **b** mass **c** length
3. Answers will vary.
4. Answers will vary.

3:35

Answers will vary.

3:36

1. **a** Friday **b** Sunday
   c 1st November or November 1, 2024
   d 4th November or November 4, 2024
   e 30th November or November 30, 2024
   f 4th November, 11th November, 18th November, 25th November, 2024
   g 4 **h** 9
2. **a** 7 **b** 14 **c** 31 **d** 30
   e 31 **f** 31 **g** 30 **h** 31
   i 31 **j** 30 **k** 30 **l** 31
3. **a** 3/11/24 **b** 29/11/24
   c 27/11/24

3:37

1. 9 weeks and 4 days
2. 7 weeks and 4 days
3. 35 hours (Note: Akash played in 7 matches, not 6.)
4. 29th November
5. 16 hours
6. January 11th
7.

November 2024

Sun	Mon	Tues	Wed	Thurs	Fri	Sat
					1	2
3	4	5	6	7	8	9
10	11	12	13	(14)	15	16
17	18	19	20	21	22	23
24	25	26	27	28	29	(30)

December 2024

Sun	Mon	Tues	Wed	Thurs	Fri	Sat
1	2	3	4	5	6	7
8	9	10	11	12	13	14
15	16	17	(18)	19	20	21
22	23	24	25	26	27	28
29	30	31				

January 2025

Sun	Mon	Tues	Wed	Thurs	Fri	Sat
			(1)	2	3	4
5	6	7	8	9	10	11
12	13	14	15	16	17	18
19	20	21	22	23	24	25
26	27	28	(29)	30	31	

4:01

1. 

2. 

3. 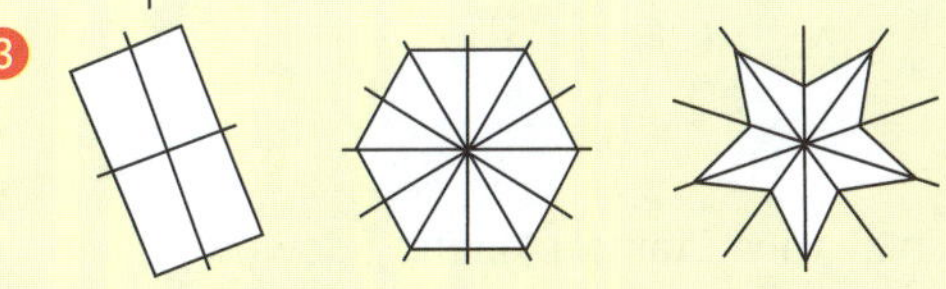

The second half of each koala will be drawn.

 • *AUSTRALIAN SIGNPOST MATHS NSW 3* • ISBN 9780655709046

4:02

1. **a** 3, 3 **b** 4, 4 **c** 3 **d** 4
2. **a** 3
   b any quadrilateral: square, rectangle, rhombus, trapezium, parallelogram, kite, irregular quadrilateral
   c 5 **d** hexagon

4:03

1. Answers will vary.
2. 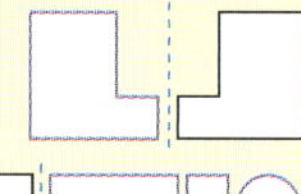

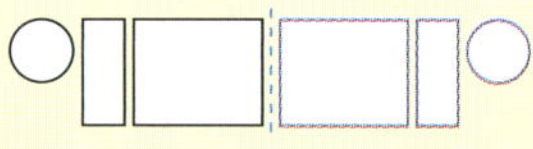

Fun spot: Answers will vary.

4:04

1. **a** C, E, H **b** F **c** B, G **d** D
2. E, H
3. **a** C **b** H **c** A **d** D
4. **a** D, F **b** A, F **c** C, H **d**
5. **a**  **b** 

4:05

1. **a** 6, cube **b** 2, cylinder **c** 1, cone
   d 0, sphere **e** 5, (triangular) prism
2. **a** square **b** circle **c** circle
   d circle **e** triangle
3. **a** e **b** a **c** a **d** c **e** e
   f e **g** d **h** b **i** b, c, d
4. **a** 2 **b** 1 **c** 3 **d** 4

4:06

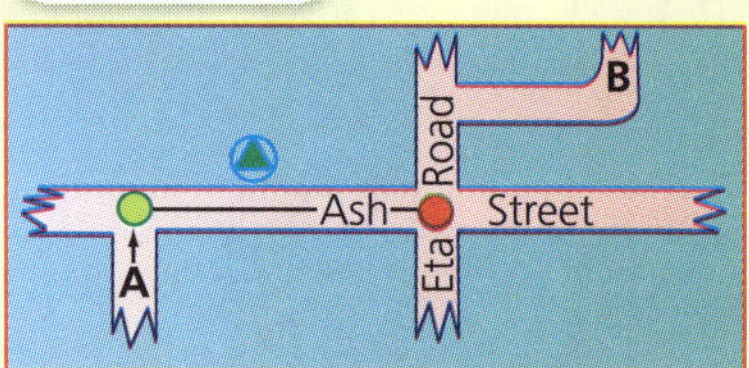

1. **a** turn left, then first left
   b turn right, then first left, then first right
   c turn right, then first right, then first left
   d turn right, then first right, then second right
2. **a** G (Post office) **b** H (Hospital)
3. **a** H **b** E **c** N **d** E

4:07

Header: Answers may vary. Example: 4 left, 7 down

1. **a** D **b** A **c** A **d** C **e** C **f** F
   g Answers will vary. Example: 3 right, 7 up.
2. **a** 3 up, 2 right, 4 up **b** 2 up, 1 left, 5 up
   c 6 up, 1 left, 3 down, 1 left, 4 up
   d 5 down, 1 right, 2 down **e** 4 down, 2 left, 3 down
3. **a** 3 forwards
   b 1 forwards, turn right, 2 forwards, turn left, 4 forwards
   c 1 forwards, turn right, 6 forwards, turn right, 2 forwards
   d 2 forwards, turn left, 2 forwards, turn right, 2 forwards
   e 2 forwards, turn left, 2 forwards, turn left, 4 forwards

4:08

1. **a** triangle  **b** square 
   c pentagon 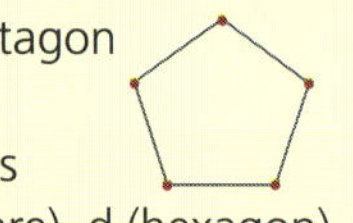 **d** hexagon 
   yes, yes
2. b (square), d (hexagon)
3. **a** triangle 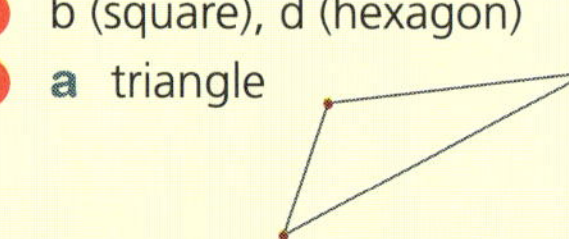 **b** quadrilateral
   c pentagon **d** hexagon
   no, no
4. **a** **b** **c**
   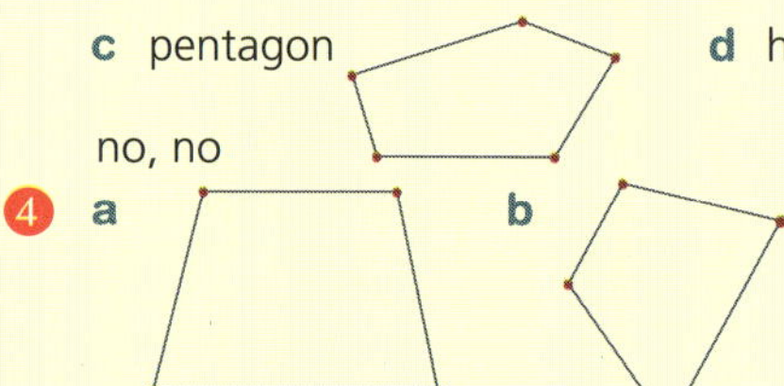
   irregular

Activity:

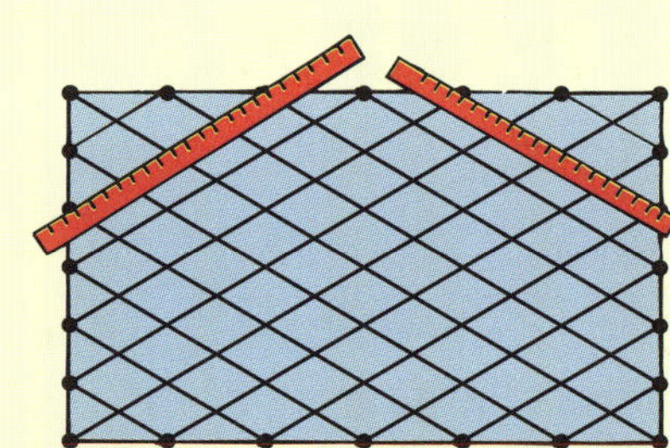

The shape repeated is a parallelogram, rhombus or diamond. Rhombuses are irregular.

4:09

Header: Each side is perpendicular to the sides next to it.

1. **a** 0 **b** 1 **c** 3 **d** 0 **e** 3 **f** 0 **g** 1 **h** 3
2. a, d, f. The lines are going in the same direction and will not meet.
3. Where the lines meet, they form a right angle (square corner).
4. square, rectangle
5. **a** Chen and Alan **b** Chen and Alan **c** Chen and Alan
6. **a** Answers will vary, e.g. railway tracks, electricity poles.
   b yes, no
   When things are further away they look smaller.

4:10

Concept: The rectangle and the second shape from the left will be coloured.

1. 4 different rhombuses will be drawn. Yes.
2. 4 different kites will be drawn. Yes.

 ISBN 9780655709046

4:11

Header: A, B, C

1. **a** D **b** A **c** E **d** C **e** F **f** B
2. **a** E **b** A, B and F **c** C **d** D
3. **a** A, C, F **b** A, B, C, F
4. **a** rectangle, triangle **b** triangle, triangle
   c hexagon, square
   d circle, rhombus (or diamond)
5. **a** 2 **b** 23 **c** 9 **d** 5

4:12

1. **a** cylinder **b** neither **c** prism **d** prism **e** neither
   f prism **g** cylinder **h** neither **i** prism
2. **a** Y **b** X **c** Z **d** Y
3. **a** 8 **b** 18 **c** 12
4. 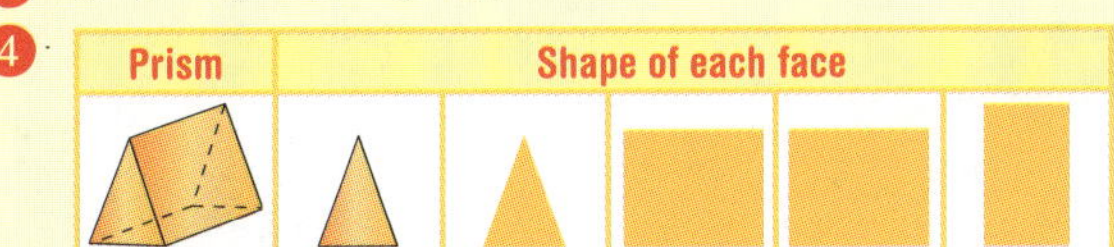

   The faces are triangles and rectangles.

4:13

1. b, d, e, f, g, i
2. **a** A **b** C **c** A
3. **a** 5 **b** 8 **c** 5 **d** 4
4. 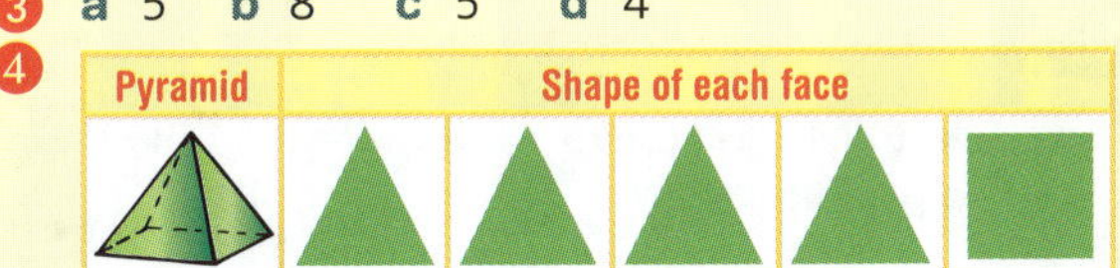

   The faces are 4 triangles and 1 square.

4:14

1. J
2. L
3. **a** H, I **b** E, G **c** C **d** D **e** yes

4:15

Header: 4, 3, 5, 8, 6

1. **a**

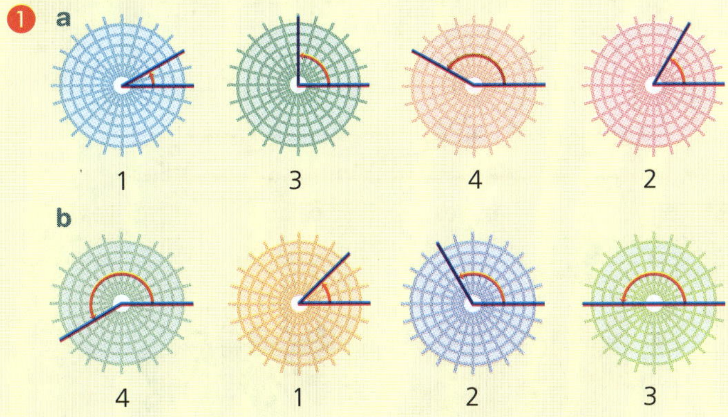

2. **a** 

   b 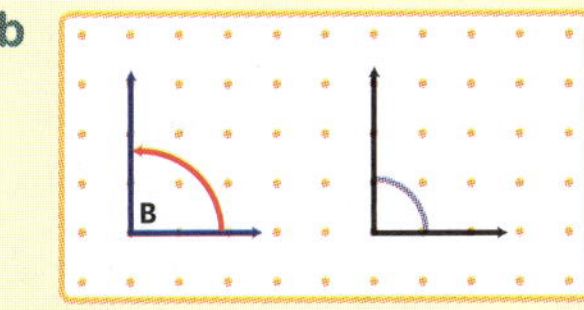

   c B is a right angle because the two arms makes a square corner.

4:16

1. A, D, E, G
2. B
3. yes

Investigation: D, E, F, G, I, J, K
A square and rectangle will always have right angles.

4:17

1. **a** clockwise, quarter turn **b** anticlockwise, half turn
   c anticlockwise, quarter turn **d** clockwise, half turn
   e clockwise, three-quarter turn
   f anticlockwise, three-quarter turn
2. **a** 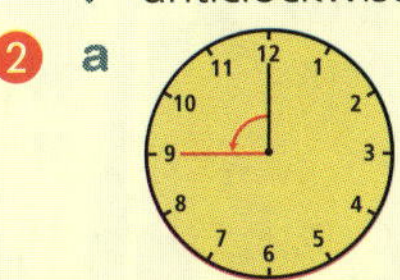
   b 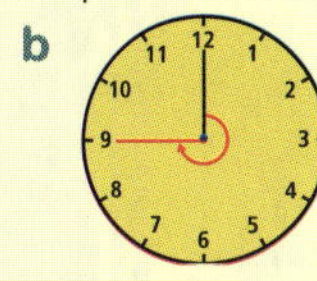
   c yes

Investigation: Answers will vary, e.g. angle made between the pages when you open a book.

4:18

1. **a** pencil **b** duck **c** doll **d** ball
   e right side of top shelf **f** left side of top shelf
   g middle of middle shelf
2. **a** saucers **b** plates **c** mugs **d** pots
   e first on the left (or fourth from the right) on the top
   f second from the right (or third from the left) on the bottom
   g first on the right (or fourth from the left) on the bottom
   h first on the right (or fourth from the left) on the top
3. **a** Tran **b** Sophie **c** Mark **d** Felicity
   e second from the left (or fourth from the right) on the top
   f fourth from the left (or second from the right) on the bottom

4:19

1. **a**

Moves
3 right
4 up
1 left
2 up
3 left
3 up
4 right
2 down

b

Moves
5 left
9 up
2 right
7 down
2 right
4 up
1 right
3 up

2 a 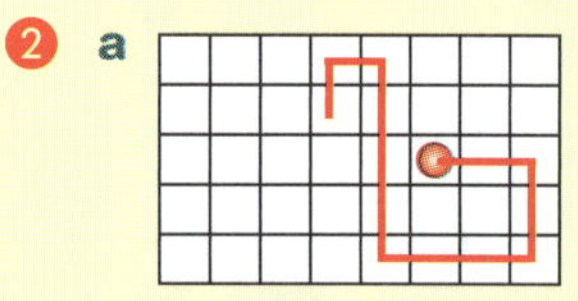 b 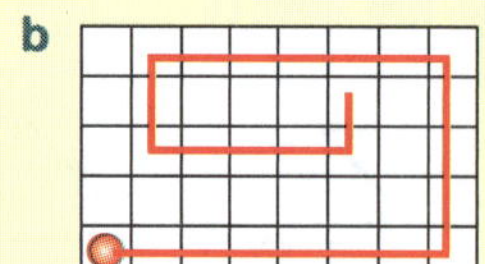

3 H C K B J F E A I D G O

Activity: Answers will vary.

4:20

1 a C, E, F (Note: F is a parallelogram, which is a kind of trapezium.)
b F

2 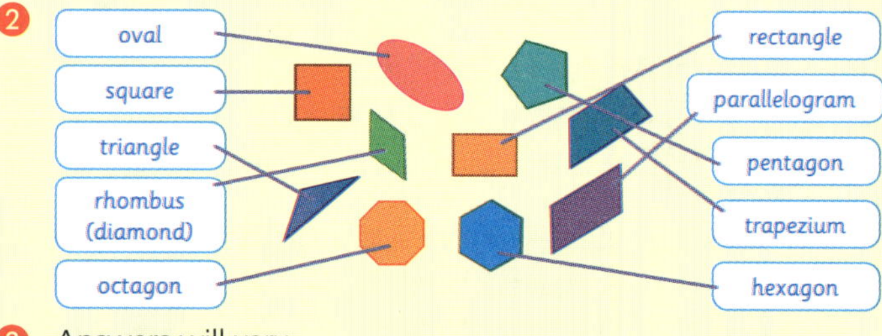

3 Answers will vary.

4:21

Header: yes

1 a C, G b A, B, H, J, K c E, I d A, C, D, E, F, J e H, I

2 a A, C, D, E, F, J
b F

3 a triangle

4 a Answers will vary.
b 8 (including 4 squares leaning at an angle)
c 9 d 12

5 Each shape has a curved side.

4:22

1 a B, E, I b D, F, H c B, D, E, F, H, I

2 a false b true c false
d false e true f false

Activity: Answers will vary, e.g. an orange.

4:23

1 a pyramid b cone c cylinder d sphere
e prism f cylinder g prism h pyramid

2 a 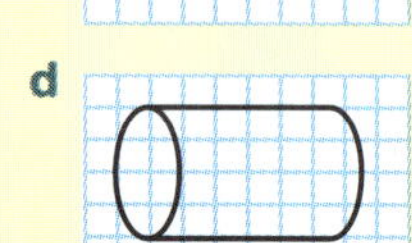 b 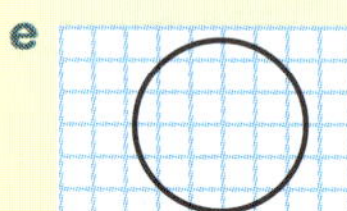 c 
d e f

4:24

1 a a glass b a shoe c a dice d a cupcake
e a chair f a ball g an ice cream h an ant
i a tea cup j a star k a pencil

2 a A5 b D2 c A3 d C4 e G4 f H5
g B2 h D3 i E1 j F7 k E6 l E4

3 a A boomerang will be drawn in A2.
b A shield will be drawn in B1.
c A lizard will be drawn in E3.
d A didgeridoo will be drawn in C2.

4:25

1 a 37 b 3 c cupboard d on the back wall

2 Answers will vary.

4:26

Header: 8 vertices, 12 edges

1 a **A** 4 blocks **B** 8 blocks **C** 16 blocks **D** 20 blocks
b The longer the base, the greater the number of blocks.

2 Answers will vary.

4:27

1 6

2 B

4:28

1 a flip b slide c flip d turn e slide
f flip g turn h flip i slide j turn
k a, c, f and h are symmetrical. They are all made by flips.

4:29

1 flip a translation (slide) b reflection (flip)
c rotation (turn)

2 no
A B 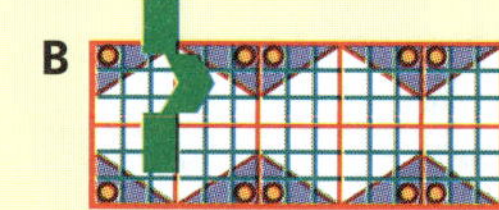

3 no
A B

4 Answers may vary.

5 a yes b yes c no d yes

4:30

1 a 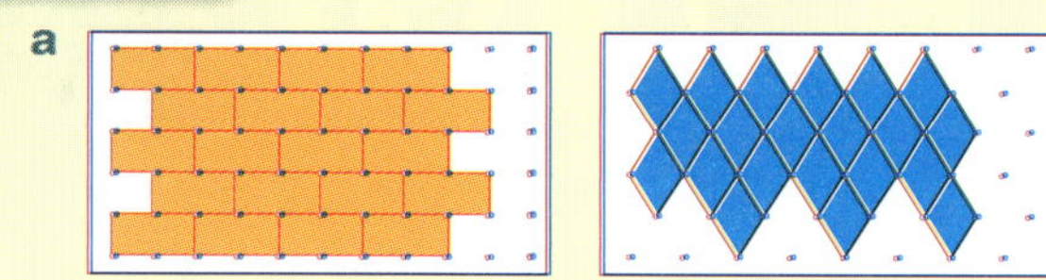
Ten more tiles will be drawn on each.
b yes

 • *AUSTRALIAN SIGNPOST MATHS NSW 3* • ISBN 9780655709046

2 a These tessellating shapes will be coloured in different colours.

A 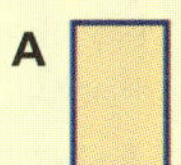

B 

C

D 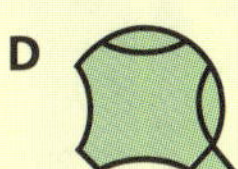

b Answers will vary.

5:01

Concept: 6 students had no pets.
7 students had one pet.

1 a 2 b 3 c Monday d 13

2 a 7 b 24 c 3

3 a a b o c i and u
d 14 e 5

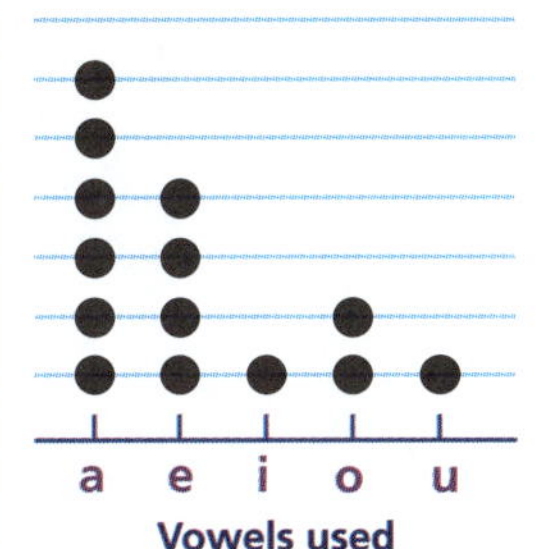

5:02

1 a blue b orange c 8 d 30

2 a 825 b 46 c 166 d 72 e 88
f 201 g 405 h 193 i 388

3 a 87 b 27 c 23 d 0
e Answers will vary.

Investigation: Answers will vary.

5:03

1 a 1 b 3 c Fish and Mice d Birds e 16

2

Pets kept in the classroom			
Birds	Fish	Mice	Turtles
3	6	6	1

Pets kept in the classroom	
Birds	3
Fish	6
Mice	6
Turtles	1

a 3 b 16 c Answers will vary.

d

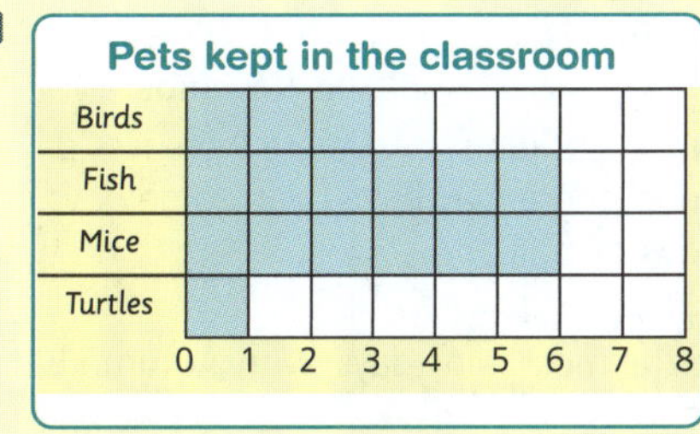

3 a

Youth group attendance	
Carmen	●●●●
Erika	●●●●●
Holly	●●●
Paul	●●●●●●●
Yong	●●●●●●

b Holly c yes d 8 times

4 Answers will vary.

5:04

1 a 6 b Tuesday c 20 d 10

2 a 7 b 6 c 8 d Mandarin

3 a 21 b 15 c 10 d 47

5:05

1 a likely b unlikely c certain d impossible

2 Answers will vary. There will be more green apples coloured than red.

3 1, 2, 3, 4, 5, 6

4 a, b Answers will vary. c Yes. There is only one way of throwing six 1s in a row (1, 1, 1, 1, 1, 1) which makes it very unlikely. If you think of another example like throwing two 1s out of six throws, there are lots of ways for this to happen (for example, 1, 1, 2, 5, 4, 4 or 3, 6, 1, 4, 1, 6). This means that throwing two 1s out of six throws is much more likely than throwing six 1s in a row.

Investigation: Answers will vary.

5:06

1 a yes b no c yes

2 Answers will vary.
a win, lose, draw
b sunny, rainy, windy, stormy

3 a red, blue, green b red c green
d no

4 highly unlikely

Investigation: Answers will vary.

5:07

1 a head, tail b 1, 2, 3, 4, 5, 6
c 1 (red), 2 (blue), 3 (yellow)

2 B B (blue blue), R R (red red), R B (red and blue)

3 Y Y (yellow yellow), R R (red red), B B (blue blue),
Y R (yellow red), Y B (yellow blue), R B (red blue)

4 a 6 is most likely. Answers will vary.
b 2 is most likely. Answers will vary.
c 6 is most likely. Answers will vary.
d 4 is most likely. Answers will vary.

5 6
a 4 b certain

5:08

1

<table>
<tr><th>Dice</th><th>Tally</th><th>Number</th></tr>
<tr><td>1</td><td>|||</td><td>3</td></tr>
<tr><td>2</td><td>|||</td><td>3</td></tr>
<tr><td>3</td><td>||</td><td>2</td></tr>
<tr><td>4</td><td>||||</td><td>4</td></tr>
<tr><td>5</td><td>𝍸</td><td>5</td></tr>
<tr><td>6</td><td>|||</td><td>3</td></tr>
</table>

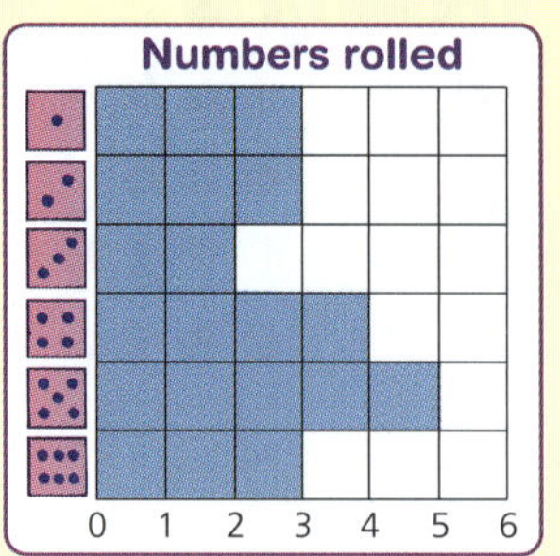

2

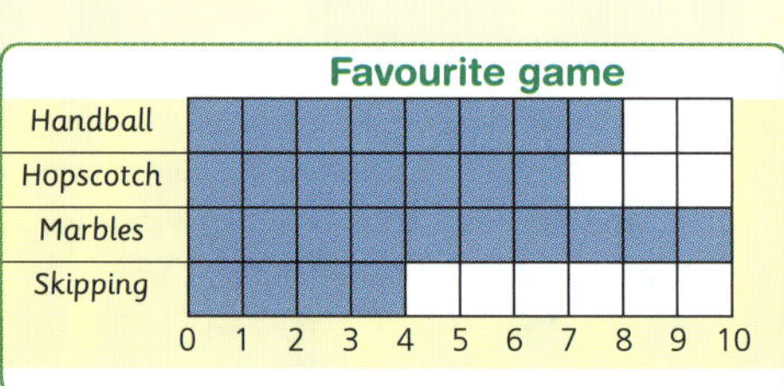

3 Answers will vary.

5:09

1 a 6 b 100 c 70 d 10 e 184 f 380

2 a Amanda b Juan c 10
d 8 e 33 f 24

3 a 14, 18 b Tuesday and Thursday
c 26 d 8
e No, because some students may have practised more than once during this week.

5:10

Investigation: Answers will vary.

5:11

Investigation: Answers will vary.
ICT: Answers will vary.

5:12

1 a red b yellow c no d yes
e blue or yellow f blue, red or yellow

2 a red b yellow

3 a Yes. There is an even chance of spinning blue or red.
b No. In each spin there is an even chance of spinning blue.

4 a yes b 2

Investigation: Answers will vary.

5:13

1 a unlikely b impossible c certain d very likely
e very likely f very likely g unlikely h impossible
i certain j even chance

2

Will always happen	It can happen (but not always)	Will never happen
c i	a d e f g j	b h

3 Answers will vary. Example: E A C D B

Fun spot: Answers will vary.

5:14

1

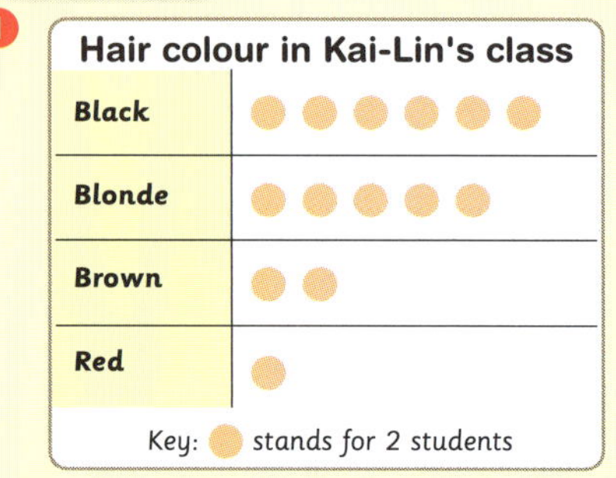

a Black b none c 6 d 28
e To tell the value of each picture on the graph.
f Answers will vary. Example: They are easy to draw and read and are attractive

2 Answers will vary. Examples:
a It is useful for recording information as it is observed.
b It looks impressive and interesting.
c You can compare categories at a glance. It is attractive.

ICT: Answers will vary.

5:15

1 a 13 b 4 c 1 d 23 e 29
f before 8 pm g 30, yes
h Answers will vary.

2 Answers will vary.

5:16

Investigation: Answers will vary.
ICT: Answers will vary.

5:17

1 a January and February b 16 days
c Winter d April and November
e Yes. Although the graph shows there were less days that had rain in June, there may have been some days in June with very heavy rainfall.

2 a i March ii August
b Summer had the most rainy days, with Autumn having almost as many.
c Brisbane has fewer rainy days on average than Perth. The wettest time of year is different in each city.

 • *AUSTRALIAN SIGNPOST MATHS NSW 3* • ISBN 9780655709046

5:18

1. Answers will vary.
2. Answers will vary. The most likely answer is **e**.

Investigation: Answers will vary.

ES 1

1.

a

+	
2 + 6	1
4 + 6	7
0 + 1	8
5 + 7	9
5 + 6	10
0 + 7	11
4 + 5	12
7 + 10	15
8 + 7	17
10 + 10	18
9 + 9	20

b

+	
2 + 3	4
4 + 3	5
2 + 2	7
5 + 4	9
8 + 5	8
8 + 0	10
7 + 5	11
1 + 9	12
10 + 5	13
6 + 5	15
10 + 9	19

c

+	
3 + 6	6
2 + 8	7
4 + 2	8
5 + 2	9
4 + 7	10
3 + 5	11
9 + 6	12
6 + 6	13
8 + 8	14
7 + 6	15
10 + 4	16

d

+	
3 + 4	5
6 + 2	6
4 + 5	7
3 + 2	8
2 + 4	9
8 + 4	10
4 + 9	11
5 + 5	12
4 + 7	13
7 + 8	14
5 + 9	15

e

–	
8 – 6	1
10 – 4	0
1 – 0	2
12 – 5	4
11 – 6	6
7 – 7	5
9 – 5	7
17 – 7	8
15 – 7	10
11 – 8	9
18 – 9	3

f

–	
5 – 2	2
7 – 3	3
4 – 2	4
9 – 4	5
13 – 5	0
8 – 8	1
12 – 5	6
10 – 9	7
15 – 5	8
11 – 5	10
19 – 10	9

g

–	
6 – 4	0
5 – 2	1
10 – 9	2
7 – 7	3
9 – 3	4
7 – 3	5
10 – 3	6
14 – 5	7
9 – 4	8
18 – 8	9
10 – 2	10

h

–	
6 – 5	0
9 – 9	1
6 – 3	2
8 – 6	3
8 – 4	4
16 – 9	5
9 – 4	6
16 – 7	7
17 – 7	8
10 – 4	9
17 – 9	10

ES 2

1. **A** 2, 6, 6, 5, 9 **B** 7, 4, 4, 7, 7
C 7, 8, 4, 8, 9 **D** 7, 12, 9, 8, 11
E 5, 11, 5, 9, 13 **F** 4, 10, 9, 6, 7
G 8, 5, 10, 6, 8 **H** 10, 10, 10, 8, 9
I 7, 9, 10, 8, 12 **J** 9, 3, 7, 6, 10
K 14, 10, 11, 5, 18 **L** 9, 3, 12, 13, 17
M 6, 9, 16, 8, 10 **N** 11, 12, 11, 16, 15
O 13, 11, 11, 11, 12 **P** 12, 4, 16, 14, 14
Q 14, 13, 15, 13, 12 **R** 15, 17, 13, 15, 14

ES 3

1. **A** 7, 9, 5, 9 **B** 4, 6, 9, 8 **C** 1, 7, 9, 6
D 8, 9, 5, 2 **E** 9, 8, 4, 7 **F** 7, 2, 7, 3
G 8, 4, 8, 5 **H** 3, 9, 6, 6 **I** 9, 6, 5, 5
J 3, 9, 7, 6 **K** 8, 4, 7, 8

ES 4

There are no answers for this page.

ES 5

1. **a** 49 **b** 64 **c** 83
d 91 **e** 51 **f** 37
2. **a** 77 **b** 55 **c** 87 **d** 91

ES 6

1. **a** 154 **b** 117 **c** 108 **d** 283 **e** 790
f 388 **g** 516 **h** 510 **i** 428 **j** 331
k 514 **l** 733
2. Answers will vary.

ES 7

1. **a** 334 **b** 662 **c** 361 **d** 432 **e** 615
f 531 **g** 792 **h** 657 **i** 727 **j** 762
k 321 **l** 731 **m** 805 **n** 640 **o** 962
2. **a** 432 **b** 374 **c** 377 **d** 921

ES 8

1. **a** \$0.78 **b** \$1.52 **c** \$4.73 **d** \$5.31 **e** \$6.69
f \$8.25 **g** \$4.70 **h** \$8.51 **i** \$6.43 **j** \$7.11
k \$6.08 **l** \$6.97 **m** \$5.40 **n** \$6.29 **o** \$7.14
2. **a** \$3.79 **b** \$5.77 **c** \$5.68
d \$8.68 **e** \$6.49 **f** \$8.48
3. **a** \$9.55 **b** \$8.20 **c** \$8.85 **d** \$8.70
4. **a** \$4.88 **b** \$8.83 **c** \$9.37 **d** \$9.01

ES 9

1. **a** 5468 **b** 8975 **c** 7588 **d** 3798 **e** 7967
f 6324 **g** 8600 **h** 7251 **i** 3573 **j** 8240
2. **a** 7195 **b** 4885 **c** 4343 **d** 8925 **e** 8019
f 7505 **g** 9281 **h** 4339 **i** 7617 **j** 7932
3. **a** \$9149 **b** \$8291 **c** \$7909 **d** \$6297 **e** \$9430

ES 10

1. **a** 7561 **b** 6935 **c** 9818 **d** 7482
2. **a** 3904 **b** 5108 **c** 7837 **d** 7088
3. **a** \$86.14 **b** \$52.53 **c** \$90.10 **d** \$86.80
4. Estimates will vary.
a A = 5495 **b** A = 8456 **c** A = \$8273

ES 11

1 a 2 hundreds, 4 tens, 5 ones
b 6 hundreds, 4 tens, 5 ones

2 a 131 b 733 c 533 d 331
e 674 f 902 g 682 h 713
i 362 j 129 k 123 l 443
m 178 n 400 o 205

Fun spot: Answers will vary.

ES 12

1 a 528 b 315 c 229 d 421
e 264 f 108 g 836 h 908
i 711 j 315 k 248 l 628
m 727 n 55 o 105 p 608
q 6 r 734 s 16 t 107

2 Answers will vary.

ES 13

1 a 464 b 255 c 194 d 691
e 376 f 255 g 594 h 40
i 289 j 291 k 312 l 562
m 575 n 80 o 193 p 453
q 190 r 364 s 491

ES 14

1 a 258 b 179 c 34 d 646
e 274 f 63 g 489 h 589
i 138 j 177 k 659 l 567
m 29 n 99 o 87 p 28
q 457 r 417 s 228

ES 15

1 a 73 b 162 c 839 d 545
e 398 f 107 g 294 h 47

2 a 66 b 101 c 126 d 32

3 a 113 b 419 c 253

ES 16

1 a 62 + 1 = 63 b 251 + 1 = 252
c 828 + 1 = 829 d 230 + 1 = 231
e 214 + 1 = 215 f 62 + 1 = 63
g 78 + 1 = 79 h 306 + 1 = 307
i 253 + 1 = 254 j 328 + 1 = 329
k 550 + 1 = 551 l 343 + 1 = 344

ES 17

1 a $5.22 b $5.17 c $6.34 d $2.39
e $4.17 f $1.84 g $2.77 h $6.08
i $3.34 j $4.08 k $1.70 l $2.58
m $3.89 n $5.45 o $2.04

2 a $2.11 b $4.98 c $5.35 d $0.05
e $5.50 f $1.51

3 a $1.05 b $6.20 c $5.45 d $1.20
e $3.55 f $4.95

 • *AUSTRALIAN SIGNPOST MATHS NSW 3* • ISBN 9780655709046